POETIC PROMPTS
TURN POEMS INTO IMAGES
RICHARD MARVIN VOIGT

TITLE: POETIC PROMPTS
Sub Title: Turn Poems Into Images

AI Cover Image Prompt: ***"Young Woman Writing In A Book Lying On The Floor Of The Forest, Epic, 3D, Hyper-Realistic, Celestial, Hyper-Detailed, Cinematic, Atmospheric Lighting"***
ISBN-13: 978-1-940961-62-0
ISBN-10: 1940961-62-9

Cover Design, Artwork & Prompts were created & compiled by artist using the latest technology provided by OpenAI, ChatGPT and AI Art Generators actually utilized by Richard Marvin Voigt -RIVO. Lynn Voigt provided proofing and editing services via RIVO Books,

First Printing 2024 LTY-MTT4EvR5-12
Printed in the United States of America

POETIC PROMPTS - Turn Poems Into Images

Embark on a transformative journey through the rich tapestry of poetic expression with these "Poetic Prompts That Turn Poems Into Images." This innovative book seamlessly merges the world of poetry with a plethora of captivating topics, inviting readers to explore nearly 2,000 unique AI poems across 40 distinct classifications.

From the depths of sonnets to the heights of haikus, each classification offers a portal into a different realm of emotion, imagery, and thought-provoking reflection. Whether you're drawn to the structured elegance of a villanelle or the free-flowing rhythm of a blank verse, there's something within these pages to spark your imagination and ignite your creativity.

Within this treasure-trove of verse, you'll find 50 intriguing topics carefully related to each of the 40 classifications, arranged in a way to inspire each of your poetic prompting. Explore the depths of nature's beauty with poems evoking the tranquility of a forest glade or the power of an approaching storm. Explore the complexities of human emotion as poems unravel the intricacies of love, loss, hope, dreams, desire and resilience in Epic Sonnet or poetic Prose. Delve into the realms of mythology, history, and fantasy, where imagination knows no bounds with words as the brushstrokes on the canvas of the mind.

Each prompt serves as a catalyst, inviting you to use as is, modify, replace and weave into your own tapestry of words and images as part of your prompt portfolio. Whether you're a seasoned poet seeking fresh inspiration or a newcomer eager to explore the magic of verse, "Poetic Prompts" offers a boundless playground for creative expression.

As you journey through the pages of this educational book, allow yourself to be swept away by the rhythm of the lines, the beauty of the imagery, and the endless possibilities that await within each classification. Let your words dance across the page like brushstrokes painting vivid pictures that linger in your mind long after you've turned the final page and the beginning of your expanding poetic prompt experience.

Discover the transformative power of poetry and unlock the secrets of your imagination with "Poetic Prompts Turn Poems Into Images."

DEDICATION

This fifth publication is again dedicated to my incredible loving wife and my ultimate friend, Lynn, who has always supported my entire career interests. She has truly been my guardian angel here on Earth for nearly 60 years, as of this publication, teaching me the true meaning of unconditional love and love of family. She has always been, and always will be, the inspiration, passion and light of my life.

With love to our three gifted and talented children, Lace, Keye & Skye, through difficult times of balancing work and spending quality time together, even with an endless parade of friends with whom they eagerly brought home. Now, we continue to watch each of them grow, prosper, and find their way through life, getting to love them even more deeply, enjoying them as friends.

I also dedicate this publication to our amazing grandson Logan who makes time to spend with his GMa & GPa, how sweet is that. I also wish to thank Lace's hard-working husband Scott for his kind patience along my lovely baby sister Barbara and her husband Dave. Last but not least, I dedicate this publication to the thousands of creative students, K-12 and the adults who allowed me to be their teacher, not only in art class, and other presentations, but throughout life which are far too many to properly credit here.

I will leave this earthly body a blessed man who will never be able to fully express my deepest love and gratitude to you all. May each of our spirits live on through endless kind thoughts and lots of great memories, as it should be for all humanity. Thank You All!

<u>I'd Like To Present You With My Quotes From My Human Perspective:</u>

"Creative Thought Is The Only Reality,
Everything Else Is Merely The By-Product Of That Thought"

"Words Come Out Of My Mouth, Before I Can Say Them"

"I Don't Subscribe To Earth Age Nor It's Magazine Subscription."

The Quality Of The Question Asked,
Predetermines The Quality Of The Answer Received"

"If It Isn't FUN – It Isn't Worth Doing – AMEN!"

"Art Is More Than Just A Noun, It's A Verb To Be Seen, Then Understood"

"Keep The Love Growing Creatively"

May You Be Blessed With Great Health, Prosperity & Love!
Richard Marvin Voigt - RIVO

About The Author

Richard Marvin Voigt, aka RIVO, has been fascinated with computers and digital art since the mid-1980s working with early Atari and Commodore personal computers. His friends call him Ricky V. Now, at the age of 82, he's had an award-winning career as a classroom educator and art specialist with Milwaukee Public Schools for nearly 30-years. He's earned recognition and awards for his innovative artwork and has co-published nearly 100 books and journals while team-teaching Life-Long Learning courses they created, working side-by-side with his beautiful wife Lynn, for the University of Wisconsin's Osher and Waukesha County Technical College LIR programs, local libraries, churches, businesses & non-profit organizations.

He's had the pleasure of working with thousands of students, many colleagues, artists, models, and local businesses while pursuing his personal passion for creating visual works of fine art as a very prolific artist who shares many interests. He created a unique doodling technique that shows even those who claim they can't draw, drawing in a matter of minutes. One of his projects is called the 'Digital Quilt Series" which currently consists of over 1,700 digital compositions. Each composition is designed to be 38" x 38" that when place end-to-end, span the length of over 17, yes, seventeen football fields, and can be arranged in endless two and three-dimensional configurations.

Over the past couple of years, Richard has ventured into the exciting and intriguing world of AI Art generation exploring existing potential. This massive publication is but a brief example of his research and experimentation as he produces and prints an amazing collection of digital fine art. When asked, he refers to his art as a Verb, not merely a Noun. While he no longer publicly exhibits his works, he continues to create and print nearly every day each as a gift to his wife. Over the past 25+ years, his massive private art collection has grown substantially. Since he doesn't create for monetary gain, he chooses not to sell or market his work other than exhibit works and animations on his websites. It is his final wish that only after his passing, will his entire collection be shown and eventually donated to a worthy organization to remain part of their permanent collection.

Richard and Lynn Voigt are also inventors who hold patent (No. 6,322,878) presented to the Mattel Toy Corporation, and other related toy companies via their agent in California. They're also UW-extension SEW Master Gardeners, teaching classes and giving private tours of their eclectic experimental gardens surrounding their home, producing nearly 1,100 videos for their Wisconsin Garden YouTube channel seen by over 6 million viewers, gaining a faithful following with tens of thousands of subscribers from over 130 countries worldwide.

As history continues to record the imaginative works of artists and the art movements they helped create, we must recognize the influence of technology and its impact upon the arts. Whether a rock, chisel, wood, paint, canvas or a holographic paint brush, every technological advancement played a direct role in what is now possible. While many artist's early works were dismissed by formality and ignorance as to what art is or should be, many of those early rejected works are now revered and eagerly sold for millions. Gifted artist creates from within completing a vision. Like Ricky V, we continually enter exciting creative portals to unlimited visions. Today is always the first day of your new reality, so claim yours TODAY!

WHAT IS ARTIFICAL INTELLIGENCE TECHNOLOGY ANYWAY?

If you're new to areas of Artificial Intelligence, there are some additional things you should know continuing your education within this industry which are already part of your daily life. In today's world we all need to continue educating ourselves, especially in the area of technological advancements. Here is a brief introduction to three areas of amazing technology that continues to grow and expand, as should each of us. Here's some terms you need to know, if you don't already.

OpenAI, ChatGPT, and AI Art Generations represent the latest cutting-edge advancements in the field of artificial intelligence (AI) technology, with applications ranging from natural language understanding and communication to creative content generation and artistic expression.

It helps when one understands the basic concepts of Open AI, ChatGPT and AI Art Generators in encouraging you to gain a greater understanding of this amazing technology as programming it expands. I'll discuss my experiences with these areas of Artificial Intelligence (AI) including what I've learned, created and published. You'll have the opportunity to see unique examples of digital art, video productions and personal publications at **www.ART262.com.**

OpenAI is a research organization dedicated to developing artificial intelligence (AI) technology in a safe and beneficial manner. It aims to advance the field of AI and make its benefits widely accessible to humanity. OpenAI conducts research in various areas of AI, including natural language processing, reinforcement learning, computer vision, and robotics. The organization also releases open-source software and publishes research papers to contribute to the advancement of AI technology globally.

ChatGPT is a conversational AI model developed by OpenAI it's now expanded to version 3.5. It uses deep learning techniques to understand and generate human-like text responses based on input provided by users. ChatGPT can engage in conversations on a wide range of topics, answer questions, provide explanations, and even offer suggestions. It powers chatbots, virtual assistants, and other applications where human-like interaction is desired, such as customer support, language translation, and educational platforms. VISIT: https://chat.openai.com/chat

AI Art Generations refer to the use of AI algorithms and neural networks to create, modify, or enhance visual artworks. These algorithms can generate new images, transform existing images into different styles, or assist artists in the creative process. AI Art Generators leverage techniques such as deep learning, generative adversarial networks (GANs), and style transfer to produce visually compelling and diverse artwork. They can be used for various purposes, including digital art creation, photo editing, image synthesis, and visual effects generation. AI Art Generators have sparked interest and experimentation among artists, designers, photographers, and enthusiasts, offering new possibilities for creative expression and exploration. We'll show you some to explore.

To Infinity & Beyond - Is Real!

Here Are Several Unique Considerations Marking A Distinctive Shift In The Way Art Is Created Which Can Make The Results From AI Art Generation Truly Amazing.

Algorithmic Creativity:
Generative Algorithms: AI art generation relies on generative algorithms that can produce new and unique pieces of art based on patterns and information learned from existing data.

Non-deterministic Output: The algorithms introduce an element of randomness, allowing for a wide range of creative outputs, making each piece of generated art unique.

Learning from Data:
Machine Learning Techniques: AI art generation often employs machine learning models, such as neural networks, which learn patterns and styles from vast datasets of existing artworks.

Adaptive Improvement: These models continuously improve their ability to generate art by learning from a diverse range of artistic styles, genres, and techniques.

Collaboration with Artists:
Human-AI Collaboration: Many AI art projects involve collaboration between artists and AI algorithms. The AI serves as a tool or a source of inspiration for artists to enhance their creative process. Amplifying

Artistic Vision: AI can amplify an artist's vision by suggesting new ideas, styles, or even completing parts of an artwork based on the artist's input.

Exploration of Unconventional Styles:
Cross-Stylistic Creativity: AI can seamlessly blend and experiment with various artistic styles, pushing the boundaries of what is traditionally possible in art creation.

Emergence of New Styles: AI art generation can lead to the emergence of entirely new and unconventional artistic styles that may not have been explored before.

Accessibility and Democratization:
Artistic Tools for All: AI art generation tools are becoming increasingly accessible, allowing individuals without traditional art training to engage in the creative process.

Democratizing Creativity: AI-driven art democratizes creativity, enabling a broader range of people to express themselves artistically and participate in the creation of unique artworks.

AI's Interpretation of Creativity:
Machine Understanding of Aesthetics: AI algorithms can be trained to understand and interpret aesthetic principles, leading to the creation of art that aligns with human perceptions of beauty.

Beyond Imitation: AI doesn't merely imitate existing styles; it can reinterpret and synthesize elements to produce novel and innovative artworks.
Dynamic and Evolving Art:

Real-Time Adaptation: AI art generation can adapt in real-time to user input, creating a dynamic and interactive artistic experience.
Continuous Evolution: AI algorithms can be updated and improved over time, ensuring a continuous evolution of artistic capabilities and styles.

Ethical Considerations:
Ownership and Authorship: The question of ownership and authorship arises as AI contributes significantly to the creation process. Discussions around the attribution of creative work in collaborations between AI and humans are ongoing.

WHY AI IMAGE GENERATORS CONTINUE GETTING SMARTER & SMARTER

The future of Artificial Intelligence (AI) image generators holds promising possibilities for creating amazing imagery even from simple word and phrase prompts. Even single words now show great promise. When I started creating AI images several years ago, I had to refine the vision I had roaming around inside my head and figure out all the keywords I could think of. Some prompts became a paragraph - YIKES! My first book, *13,000 AI Prompts Turning Words Into Visions,* shares much longer prompt sentences. My second book, *5555 FUN & FUNNY PROMPTS Turning Words Into Images*, began shortening my fun and silly prompts which led me to create my third book: *5000 SIMPLE WORD PROMPTS - Creating Images With Phrases*, simplifying prompts to short phrases with results that are equally impressive. Then came my fourth book titled: *8,400 CLICHÉ PROMPTS* and my fifth book titled: *POETIC PROMPTS.* As AI technologies continue to advance, we can expect to see more refined developments in each of these areas:

Improved Image Quality: AI image generators will continue becoming more adept at producing high-quality and realistic images based on simple prompts. With advancements in machine learning algorithms and access to vast datasets, these generators can refine their understanding of visual concepts and produce more visually appealing results.

Enhanced Creativity: AI models are increasingly capable of understanding and interpreting creative prompts, allowing them to generate imaginative and unique imagery. As AI systems become more sophisticated, they may develop the ability to incorporate artistic principles and styles into their generated images, leading to even more stunning and creative results.

Personalization and Customization: AI image generators could offer personalized and customized imagery tailored to individual preferences and needs. Users may be able to provide specific criteria or preferences, such as color schemes, styles, or themes, and the AI generator could generate images accordingly, providing a more personalized experience.

Integration with Other Technologies: AI image generators may integrate with other emerging technologies, such as augmented reality (AR) and virtual reality (VR), to create immersive and interactive visual experiences. This integration could enable users to interact with and manipulate generated imagery in real-time, opening up new possibilities for creative expression and storytelling.

Ethical and Social Considerations: As AI image generators become more powerful, ethical and social considerations surrounding their use will become increasingly important. It will be crucial to address issues related to copyright, authenticity, bias, and the potential misuse of AI-generated imagery to ensure that these technologies are used responsibly and ethically.

Remember, AI Image Generators can inspire artists by generating amazing images, novel ideas, visual concepts, and stylistic variations that artists may not have considered. They serve as creative tools for exploration and experimentation, sparking new directions and possibilities in artistic expression.

The future of AI image generators holds immense potential for transforming creative expression and visual storytelling. With ongoing advancements in AI technology and continued research and development efforts, we can expect to see even more impressive and innovative applications of AI-generated imagery in the years to come.

Despite the controversy over machine learning, art generation represents a convergence of smarter technology expanding artistic expression with unlimited possibilities and challenges in the ever-evolving landscape of creative endeavors. Its uniqueness lies in the blend of computational power, learning algorithms, and human creativity, pushing the boundaries of what 'Art' can be. Now you can make the final decision for yourself.

Creating Images Using AI Image Generator

Image generators can augment artists' creative capabilities by providing alternative perspectives, stylistic influences, and compositional suggestions. Artists can leverage AI-generated content as a source of inspiration and a catalyst for creative innovation.

AI generators can help streamline certain aspects of the artistic process, such as sketching, rendering, and composition, thereby saving artists time and effort. They can automate repetitive tasks, generate preliminary designs, and assist artists in refining their ideas more efficiently.

It's also providing accessibility and inclusivity to artistic tools and resources, making creative expression more accessible and inclusive to individuals with diverse backgrounds, skill levels, and abilities. They empower aspiring artists to explore their artistic potential and participate in the creative community.

Within the workforce, they enable collaborative and co-creative interactions between artists and AI systems, fostering interdisciplinary collaborations, and expanding the boundaries of artistic collaboration. Artists can collaborate with AI systems to co-create artworks, explore new artistic techniques, and push the boundaries of artistic innovation.

AI art generators represent a transformative paradigm shift in the creative process, offering artists new opportunities for exploration, inspiration, efficiency, and collaboration. As AI technologies continue to evolve and mature, the value of AI art generators to artists is expected to grow, shaping the future of artistic expression and creative innovation in diverse and exciting ways.

As mentioned, over the past couple of years I've been experimenting with a wide variety of word prompts. I began with prompts loaded with keywords that defined my vision and soon realized that using simple word prompts began creating unexpected and surprising results. While I'm not advocating eliminating complex loaded keyword prompts, I understand that as AI expands it's learning capabilities, sometimes less produces more than anticipated.

For the purposes of this book, I decided to share some very simple word phrases collected from a variety of animals, clichés, creatures, flowers, foods, games, movies, mythology, philosophy, places, poems, songs, along with a variety of additional universal and futuristic ideas.

Remember, the purpose of this list of simple word phrase prompts is to get your juices flowing and expand image generation possibilities. This list is merely a starting point in exploring prompt engineering and the images they create. Always feel free to add your ideas, your choice keywords, and add them to augment and expand them in a way that best serves your prompting requirements.

SO HOW DO ARTIFICIAL INTELLIGENCE (AI) ART GENERATORS WORK?

Imagine a magical machine that can make beautiful pictures or drawings all by itself using Prompts. An image generator is basically a computer program that uses artificial intelligence algorithms to create original works of art, such as paintings, drawings, or digital images. These algorithms analyze patterns, styles, and compositions from existing databases, then generates new original images. AI has now added another amazing tool in every artist's tool belt, harnessing the power of machine learning and computational creativity, to produce original artistic content autonomously.

Using your creative imagination and lots of powerful keyword Prompts, you can now create something truly incredible. It's like giving your magical machine a stronger creative idea each time, then watching it turn your ideas into colorful and beautiful images, drawings or designs, just like magic.

While most of us may have little or no coding skills, it's still a lot of fun learning and creating AI Art. For those still curious, here's a partial sampling of an AI Art generated algorithm code:

```
import tensorflow as tf
import numpy as np
import PIL.Image

# Load the pre-trained Inception model
base_model =
tf.keras.applications.InceptionV3(include_top=False,
weights='imagenet')

# Choose a layer to maximize activations
names = ['mixed3', 'mixed5']
layers = [base_model.get_layer(name).output for name in
names]

# Create the feature extraction model
dream_model = tf.keras.Model(inputs=base_model.input,
outputs=layers)

def calc_loss(img, model):
# Pass the image through the model to get feature activations
img_batch = tf.expand_dims(img, axis=0)
layer_activations = model(img_batch)

losses = []
for act in layer_activations:
loss = tf.math.reduce_mean(act)
losses.append(loss)

return tf.reduce_sum(losses)

def deepdream(model, img, steps=100, step_size=0.01):
for step in range(steps):
with tf.GradientTape() as tape:
# Set the image variable
tape.watch(img)
loss = calc_loss(img, model)
# Calculate the gradient of the loss with respect to the image
gradients = tape.gradient(loss, img)

# Normalize the gradients
gradients /= tf.math.reduce_std(gradients) + 1e-8

# Update the image with the scaled gradients
img = img + gradients * step_size
img = tf.clip_by_value(img, -1, 1)

return img.numpy()

def run_deep_dream_simple(img, steps=100, step_size=0.01):
img = tf.keras.preprocessing.image.img_to_array(img)
img = tf.keras.applications.inception_v3.preprocess_input(img)

img = tf.constant(img)
img = deepdream(dream_model, img, steps=steps,
step_size=step_size)

img = tf.keras.preprocessing.image.array_to_img(img)
return img

#
Example usage
image_path = 'path/to/your/image.jpg'
original_img = PIL.Image.open(image_path)
dream_img = run_deep_dream_simple(img=original_img,
steps=100, step_size=0.01)

# Display the original and generated images
original_img.show()
dream_img.show()
```

HERE ARE SEVERAL INTERESTING AI ART GENERATOR WEBSITES:

https://nightcafe.studio/	https://replicate.com/pixray/text2image/
https://openai.com/product/dall-e-2/	https://runwayml.com/
https://www.bing.com/create/	https://rytr.me/
https://dreamstudio.ai/	https://stablecog.com/
https://www.midjourney.com/	https://starryai.com/
https://openart.ai/create/	https://vanceai.com/image-generator/
https://app.prodia.com/	https://writesonic.com/
https://deepai.org/	https://www.artbreeder.com/
https://deepdreamgenerator.com/	https://www.canva.com/ai-image-generator/
https://dream.ai/	https://www.craiyon.com/
https://firefly.adobe.com/	https://www.creativefabrica.com/spark/
https://getimg.ai/	https://www.fotor.com/images/create/
https://land.prisma-ai.com/magic-avatars/	https://www.jasper.ai/art/
https://letsenhance.io/	https://www.tryleap.ai/
https://palette.fm/	
https://picsart.com/ai-image-generator/	

https://apps.apple.com/us/app/artout-ai-image-generator/
https://www.gettyimages.com/ai/generation/create/
https://www.myheritage.com/ai-time-machine/
https://www.shutterstock.com/ai-image-generator/

You will find many apps and websites that help beginners and advanced users create amazing ideas faster than it took me to write this sentence. But no matter which app or website you choose to use, it will be your unique use of power word prompts that will determine the image quality you create.

NightCafe isn't the only AI Art Generator you should consider testing, but it's one I have been using for several years that produces great image results. You may want to visit their website before deciding to proceed.

For demonstration purposes I'll use NightCafe for Generating AI Images

CREATE A NEW ACCOUNT AT: https://creator.nightcafe.studio/
SIGN UP IS FREE Simply Provide A User Name, Email Address & Strong Password
ALWAYS KEEP YOUR PASSWORDS SAFE & PRIVATE

At the time of this writing, New Accounts receive 50 FREE Credits in their Account
PLUS 5 FREE Credits each day – So, check your email daily
Then you can start creating a new image for generally 1 credit.

HERE'S SOME HELPFUL NIGHTCAFE STEP-BY-STEP INSTRUCTIONS:

PREPARATION – OPEN ALL FILES AS NEEDED:
Open Your NightCafe Account - resize your viewing monitor windows as needed:
Open My Computer – Select an internal or external hard drive and open said drive
Create a new AI IMAGE Folder & give it a Name you'll remember
Keep Folder Open for upcoming images and text downloads
Create and Title a new WORD doc for keeping track of all your new word PROMPTS
Find and Open your DOWNLOAD FOLDER found under your C Drive desktop listing
(Optional) Open NOTEBOOK where you can write, copy and paste items

YOU CAN USE ANY POETIC PROMPTS TO CREATE AMAZING IMAGES
It could be as simple as using just a Subject: "WHITE DAISIES" and nothing more.

Or you could expand your simple phrase prompt by adding
(Verbs & Descriptive Adjectives & Adverbs) and additional KEYWORDS

Adding These To Your Basic PROMPT Could Look Something Like This:
"WHITE DAISIES in a Blue Vase, in the style of Van Gogh

THEN ADD MY 'SECRET SAUCE' KEYWORD TOKENS AFTER EACH PROMPT
, Epic, 3D, Hyper-Realistic, Hyper-Detailed, Hyper-Colorful, Atmospheric, Cinematic Lighting"

THE FINAL PROMPT READY TO CREATE MIGHT THEN LOOK LIKE THIS
"White Daisies in a Blue Vase, in the style of Van Gogh, Epic, 3D, Hyper-Realistic, Hyper-Detailed, Hyper Colorful, Atmospheric, Cinematic Lighting"

White Daisies

Sun Flowers

Bearded Iris

These were created by my wife, Lynn at her very first attempt using an AI Image Generator.
The originals were in color, but I turned them Black & White for this publication.

SO, IF YOU'RE READY, HERE'S SOME HELPFUL STEP-BY-STEP INSTRUCTIONS:
(REMEMBER TO SAVE AFTER EVERY CHANGE)

HERE'S HOW YOU START GENERATING IMAGES?

1. **Open NightCafe – Click the red CREATE button (TOP BAR Upper Right)**

2. **Write out your NEW PROMPT IDEA – SAVE in your WORD DOC**

3. **Locate add TEXT PROMPT (Left Create Column) on NightCafe Page**

4. **Copy & Paste OR Write your own PROMPT Into TEXT PROMPT box that says 'Type Something'**

5. **Select MODEL (little side >) SDXL 1.0, Juggernaut XL, etc. Test different ones**

6. **Select STYLE (side arrow >) NightCafe, Hyperreal, Epic, Dark Fantasy, Artistic Portrait, etc.**

7. **Select Number of Images (Always select '1' when testing a new prompt)**

8. **Select SETTINGS (side arrow >) and your desired size format 1:1 Square Images, or 3:4 Vertical Rectangle or 4:3 Horizontal Rectangle etc.**

9. **WHEN ALL SETTINGS READY - Click the bottom red "CREATE" button To Start Generating Image**

10. **When Image Appears and you want to SAVE IT move your mouse over the bottom of image and look for the downward image arrow under image**

11. **Click & Select DOWNLOAD IMAGE – It begins automatically saving your Selected Image to your computer's download folder**

12. **Open your 'This PC' and locate your computer's Download Folder Highly Recommend RETITLING Image(s) Now**

13. **Transfer this image from Download Folder To Your AI IMAGE FOLDER HOLD DOWN LEFT MOUSE KEY & DRAG Image into your FOLDER**

14. **You will need photo editing software (Photoshop etc.) to edit your images**

ALWAYS KEEP IN MIND – EACH WORD ADDED TO A PROMPT HAS POWER
You may need to constantly tweak your prompts by adding more descriptive power words while eliminating fluff words that have little meaning or value to the completion of the composition you have in mind. Word prompts help one expand their vocabulary very quickly. I've prepared a list of power words to add to your prompts a little later in this publication, words charged with commanding emotion.

PROMPT SIZING: For Example - Night Cafe offers "More Settings" option
Number of images: 1, 4, 9, & 16 at a time
Output Resolution changes based on Generator Model selected
Runtime: Short costs 1 credit, medium costs 1.25 credits, or long costs 1.5 credits
1:1 Square (**DEFAULT SETTING)** ***Change This Setting Any Of These Sizes That You Want:***
3:4 Vertical Rectangle
4:3 Horizontal Rectangle
9:16 Tall Vertical, and **16:9** Wide Horizontal, etc.

I remember a woman criticizing entries in my first book that used **ar 4:3** in several prompts. She thought I was promoting a secret code that meant automatic rifle into my prompts. This is why taking time to understand how AI really works becomes educationally useful.

OTHER SYSTEMS FOR PROMPT SIZING
Image Aspect Ratio Sizing: **(ar) represents proportions - not automatic rifle**
Depending of the Image Generation you use, these may also show up as options:
ar-9:16 Often used for mobile or vertical size ratios
ar-10:16 This may be great for a portrait
ar-4:3 Commonly used as aspect ratio for 35mm celluloid film, TVs and monitors
ar-4:5 Perhaps more appropriate for creating an Instagram type portrait
ar-2:1 The Univisium ratio is a compromise between cinema screens and TV screens, now famous in video streaming.

OTHER CHOICES IN ADJUSTING YOUR WORD PROMPTS
Type in a full descriptive Prompt Word(s) sentence, as if you were writing a caption for a photo. Include as much detail as you see fit, including colors, styles, and emotions. Then click the CREATE button to generate your image

Some AI Generators allow you to use multiple prompts that varying weights.
Use weights to include or exclude specific concepts from your image.
Weight values should typically be in the range from -2.0 to +2.0.
Weights are optional, but most have a default of 1.0.

You can also animate your photos (costing 5-credits each) – Check in daily and watch for new features being added as this new technology literally changes overnight.

AI

© 2024

Generated Art by
RIVO

It's important to acknowledge AI when exhibiting or printing generated images.
This is the ethical symbol sticker I created and add to each of my AI prints

CONSIDER Adding To Your Prompts - *IN THE STYLE OF* AN ARTISTS' NAME:

Examples *"Oil Painting in the style if* or *Abstract Rendering in the style of" or:*

Realistic Rendering in the style of:* or simply: *In The Style of:

OR BY ADDING *IN THE STYLE OF* YOUR FAVORITE ARTIST

Alberto Vargas	Grandma Moses	Paul Cezanne
Alphonse Mucha	Gustav Klimt	Paul Rubens
Andy Warhol	Henri Matisse	Auguste Renoir
Anish Kapoor	JM William Turner	Pieter Bruegel-Elder
Bob Ross	Jackson Pollock	Rembrandt
Cai Guo-Qiang	James Audubon	Rene Magritte
Camille Pissarro	Jan Van Eyck	Roy Lichtenstein
Caravaggio	Jean Baptiste Monge	Salvador Dali
Chuck Close	Jeff Koons	Sandro Botticelli
Claude Monet	Johannes Vermeer	Thomas Cole
Damien Ortega	John Constable	Tim Burton
David Hockney	Joseph Mallard	Victor Hugo
Diego Velázquez	Kwame Brathwaite	Vincent Van Gogh
Edvard Munch	Leonardo Da Vinci	Walt Disney
Edward Hopper	Liu Xiaodong	William Turner
Eugene Delacroix	Mariko Mori	Yoko Ono
Frida Kahlo	Mary Cassatt	
Georgia O'Keeffe	Michelangelo	
Goerge Seurat	Pablo Picasso	

OR BY ADDING - *IN THE STYLE OF* AN ILLUSTRATORS' NAME:

Sir John Tenniel 1820-1914 English
Walter Crane 1845-1915 English
Kate Greenaway 1846-1901 English
Edwin Austin Abbey 1852-1911 American
Howard Pyle 1853-1911 American
Louis John Rhead 1858-1926 English
Jessie Willcox Smith 1863-1935 American
Edward Penfield 1866-1925 American
Beatrix Potter 1866-1943 English
Charles Dana Gibson 1867-1944 American
Arthur Rackham 1867-1939 English
Maxfield Parrish 1870-1966 American
Charles Robinson 1870-1937
Elizabeth Shippen Green 1871-1954 American
Aubrey Beardsley 1872-1898 English

J.C. Leyendecker 1874-1951 American
Violet Oakley 1874-1961 American Muralist
Ivan Bilibin 1876-1942 Russian
Harrison Fisher 1877-1934 American
James Montgomery Flagg 1877-1960 American
Frank E. Schoonover 1877-1972 American
Millicent Sowerby 1878-1967 English
C. Coles Phillips 1880-1927 American
Joseph Clement Coll 1881-1921 American
Edmund Dulac 1882-1953 French
N.C. Wyeth 1882-1945 American
Edward Julius Detmold 1883-1957 English
Kay Nielsen 1886-1957 Danish/American
OR YOUR FAVORITES

OR BY ADDING - *IN THE STYLE OF* A FASHION DESIGNERS' NAME:

Alexander McQueen
Alice + Olivia
Amsale
Anne Barge
Badgley Mischka
Balmain
BCBG Max Azria
Berta Bridal
BHLDN
Carolina Herrera
Chanel
David's Bridal
Dior
Elie by Elie Saab
Elie Saab
Enzoani
Galia Lahav

Giambattista Valli
Givenchy
Gucci
Hayley Paige
J. Mendel
Jenny Packham
Jenny Yoo
Justin Alexander
Lela Rose
Maggie Sottero
Marchesa
Michael Kors
Monique Lhuillier
Naeem Khan
Nicole Miller
Oscar de la Renta
Prada

Pronovias
Rachel Gilbert
Ralph & Russo
Reem Acra
Romona
Rosa Clará
Tadashi Shoji
Temperley London
Tom Ford
Valentino
Vera Wang
Versace
Watters
YolanCris

ALSO EXPLORE ADDING UNIQUE BACKGROUNDS TO YOUR PROMPTS

Solid White Background
Solid Black Background
Solid Color Background
White Crumpled Paper
Black Textured Paper
Gradient Paper Background
Muslin Background
Canvas Background
Textured Fabric Background
Velvet Background
Silk Fabric Background
Burlap Background
Woodgrain Background
Brick Wall Background
Stone Wall Background
Concrete Wall Background
Weathered Door Background
Distressed Wood Background
Graffiti Wall Background
Urban Street Background
Industrial Warehouse Background
Autumn Leaves Background
Spring Blossoms Background
Summer Field Background
Winter Snow Background
Tropical Beach Background
Watercolor Background
Abstract Painted Background
Oil Painting Background
Galaxy Background
Starry Night Background
Cloudscape Background

Mountain Landscape Background
Desert Dunes Background
Ocean Waves Background
Underwater Background
City Skyline Background
Sunset Gradient Background
Sunrise Gradient Background
Rainbow Background
Retro Wallpaper Background
Vintage Textile Background
Shabby Chic Background
Lace Background
Polka Dot Background
Striped Background
Chevron Background
Plaid Background
Herringbone Background
Damask Background
Moroccan Tile Background
Celtic Knot Background
Floral Print Background
Botanical Garden Background
Macro Flower Background
Fern Leaves Background
Tropical Foliage Background
Mossy Forest Floor Background
Rustic Wooden Floor Background
Victorian Wallpaper Background
Star Wars-inspired Background
Harry Potter-inspired Background

Sci-fi Futuristic Background
Cyberpunk City Background
Steampunk Gear Background
Vintage Bookshelf Background
Antique Map Background
Glitter Backgrounds
Bokeh Lights Background
Colorful Gradient Background
Water Ripple Background
Sand Dunes Background
Rusty Metal Background
Gothic Architecture Background
Sports Stadium Background
Urban Graffiti Background
Vintage Car Background
Retro Diner Background
Movie Theater Background
Casino Table Background
Christmas Tree Background
Hanukkah Celebration Background
Diwali Festival Background
Easter Egg Background
Halloween Spooky Forest Background
Thanksgiving Feast Background
Valentine's Day Hearts Background
4th of July Fireworks Background
New Year's Eve Party Background
Masquerade Ball Background

Circus Tent Background
Pirate Ship Background
Fairy Tale Castle Background
Vintage Plane Background
Police Lineup Background
Jail Cell Background
Ancient Ruins Background
Spaceship Interior Background
Underworld Cavern Background
Japanese Garden Background
Tea Ceremony Background
Samurai Dojo Background
Sushi Bar Background
Balloon Festival Background
Butterfly Garden Background
Candyland Background
Driftwood Beach Background
Enchanted Forest Background
Gingerbread House Background
Hot Air Balloon Background
Ice Cream Parlor Background
Jellyfish Aquarium Background
Koi Pond Background
Lighthouse Background
Mermaid Underwater Background
Neon Cityscape Background
Origami Paper Crane Background
Parisian Cafe Background
Rainbow Bridge Background

Sakura Blossom Background
Space Shuttle Launch Background
St. Patrick's Shamrock Background
Time Travel Portal Background
Venice Canal Background
Vintage Barber Shop Background
Victorian Ballroom Background
Waterfall Oasis Background
Wizard's Library Background
Zen Garden Background
Art Studio Background
Carnival Ferris Wheel Background
Crystal Cave Background
Dystopian Alley Background
Eiffel Tower Background
Fairy Ring Background
Fantasy Castle Background
Flower Shop Background
Futuristic City Background
Gingerbread Village Background
Grand Staircase Background
Greenhouse Background
Hobbit Hole Background
Ice Palace Background
Irish Pub Background
Library of Alexandria Background
Mad Hatter's Tea Party Background
Moroccan Bazaar Background
Observatory Background
Owl Café Background

Pastel Cloudscape Background
Pumpkin Patch Background
Quaint Village Background
Renaissance Fair Background
Riverboat Casino Background
Rock Concert Background
Roman Colosseum Background
Secret Garden Background
Sky Lantern Festival Background
Space Colony Background
Speakeasy Background
Sports Stadium Background
Steampunk Laboratory Background
Stonehenge Background
Summer Campfire Background
Sunflower Field Background
Superhero City Background
Surreal Cloudscape Background
Taj Mahal Background
Time Square Background
Tokyo Street Background
Underwater Volcano Background
Upside-Down World Background
Victorian Parlor Background
Viking Longhouse Background
Vintage Toy Store Background
Volcanic Lava Flow Background

Watercolor Galaxy Background
Winding Forest Path Background
Windmill Countryside Background

Winter Village Background
Yacht Club Background
Yellowstone National Park
Zen Bamboo Forest Background

Zen Rock Garden Background
Zootopia Cityscape Background

CONSIDER PLAYING WITH OTHER UNUSUAL SIMPLE AI PROMPT PHRASES:

Algorithmic Phantasmagoria
Algorithmic Serendipity
Algorithmic Sonnets
Algorithmic Syllogism
Binary Ballet
Binary Mirage
Binary Murmurs
Binary Odyssey
Binary Sonnets
Binary Symphony
Binary Whispers
Celestial Algorithms
Celestial Cipher
Celestial Dreamscape
Celestial Murmurs
Celestial Riddles
Celestial Whispers
Cerebral Symphony
Cosmic Byte Ballet
Cosmic Enigma
Cosmic Kaleidoscope
Cosmic Sonnets
Cryptic Byte Dance
Cybernetic Dreamscape
Cybernetic Serendipity
Cybernetic Whimsy
Digital Daydreams
Digital Labyrinth
Digital Phantasmagoria
Digital Sonnets
Esoteric Algorithms

Esoteric Byte Ballet
Esoteric Data Ballet
Esoteric Dreams
Esoteric Phantasmagoria
Esoteric Whispers
Ethereal Algorithms
Fractal Daydreams
Fractal Dreamscape
Fractal Echoes
Galactic Whispers
Holographic Algorithms
Holographic Byte Dance
Holographic Dreamscape
Holographic Enigma
Holographic Interlude
Holographic Riddles
Holographic Syllogism
Holographic Symphony
Nanoscopic Dreams
Nanoscopic Whimsy
Neural Labyrinth
Neural Paradox
Neural Serendipity
Neural Syllogism
Neural Tapestry
Pixelated Paradox
Pixelated Whispers
Quantum Byte Ballet
Quantum Byte Dance
Quantum Conundrum
Quantum Echoes

Quantum Entanglement
Quantum Labyrinth
Quantum Murmurs
Quantum Reverie
Quantum Whimsy
Quantum Whispers
Robotic Dreamscape
Robotic Kaleidoscope
Robotic Paradox
Robotic Reverie
Robotic Serendipity
Robotic Sonnets
Robotic Symphony
Synaptic Dreamscape
Synaptic Enigma
Synaptic Kaleidoscope
Synaptic Murmurs
Synaptic Phantasmagoria
Synaptic Sonnets
Synaptic Whispers
Synthetic Dreamscape
Techno-Ethereal Odyssey
Techno-Ethereal Riddles
Techno-Ethereal Sonnets
Techno-Ethereal Whispers
Virtual Enigma
Virtual Mirage
Virtual Riddles
Virtual Symphony

POETIC PROMPTS THAT TURN POEMS INTO IMAGES

This collection of AI poetry encourages you to look deeper into visionary words and lines of poetry as you create your own master list of powerful poetic prompts. Poetry is a major form of visionary literature that encompasses a variety of styles, topics and techniques. Now that I've done the initial work of presenting you with endless poetic idea, it's time for you to begin fleshing out the exact prompt ideas you want.

Your goal is to create your own prompts by using each poem, either in whole or in part, by simply extracting a line of a poetry and test it out as a prompt. I encourage you to modify these poetic ideas by replacing and adding other token keywords mentioned, in order for you to create the ultimate image prompt you wanted to create and/or animate.

We'll explore each of the following poetic types and create 50 topical poems for each type.

Here's A List Of 40 Types Of Poetry We'll Be Exploring As Prompts

Sonnet
Haiku
Free Verse
Limerick
Ode
Epic
Ballad
Vaillanelle
Sestina
Concrete
Acrostic
Elegy
Pastoral
Satire

Lyrik
Ghazal 1
Tanka
Cinquain
Terza Rima
Pantoum
Sestain
Virelay
Epigram
Villancico
Found
Pantun
Rubaiyat
Ghazal 2

Sijo
Blank Verse
Rondeau
Triolet
Haibun
Prose
Villanella
Lai
Skeltonic Verse
Haiga
Nonsense Verse
Tonque-Twister

Here's an introductory list of various styles of poetry each with a brief description:

1. Sonnet: A 14-line poem traditionally written in iambic pentameter, often focusing on themes of love or beauty.

2. Haiku: A traditional Japanese form consisting of three lines with a syllable pattern of 5-7-5, typically capturing a moment in nature.

3. Free Verse: Poetry without a fixed meter or rhyme scheme, allowing for greater freedom in expression.

4. Limerick: A humorous poem consisting of five lines with a strict AABBA rhyme scheme, often featuring witty or nonsensical subject matter.

5. Ode: A lyrical poem praising a person, event, or thing, often written in a formal and elevated style.

6. Epic: A lengthy narrative poem that tells the story of heroic deeds and adventures, often featuring grand themes.

7. Ballad: A narrative poem that tells a story, often focusing on themes of love, tragedy, or adventure, typically written in a simple, rhythmic style.

8. Villanelle: A 19-line poem consisting of five tercets followed by a quatrain, with a specific rhyme scheme and repeated lines.

9. Sestina: A highly structured poem consisting of six six-line stanzas followed by a three-line stanza, with the same six end words repeated in a specific pattern.

10. Concrete Poetry: Poetry in which the visual arrangement of words on the page enhances meaning or imagery, often taking on shapes related to the poem's subject matter.

11. Acrostic: A poem in which the first letter of each line spells out a word or message when read vertically.

12. Elegy: A mournful poem lamenting the death of a person or reflecting on loss and mortality.

13. Pastoral: A poem that idealizes rural life or the simplicity of nature, often depicting shepherds or rural settings.

14. Satire: Poetry that uses humor, irony, or exaggeration to criticize society or human behavior.

15. Lyric Poetry: Short, musical poems that express the poet's emotions or thoughts, often focusing on personal experiences and feelings.

16. Ghazal 1: A poetic form with rhyming couplets and a refrain, typically dealing with themes of love, loss, and longing.

17. Tanka: A traditional Japanese form similar to haiku but longer, consisting of five lines with a syllable pattern of 5-7-5-7-7.

18. Cinquain: A five-line poem with a specific syllable pattern (2-4-6-8-2), often focusing on a single subject or image.

19. Terza Rima: A form of poetry with interlocking tercets rhyming in the pattern ABA, BCB, CDC, etc., popularized by Dante's Divine Comedy.

20. Pantoum: A poem with a specific structure of repeating lines, where the second and fourth lines of each stanza become the first and third lines of the next stanza.

21. Sestain: A six-line poem with a specific rhyme scheme, often used to explore a single theme or idea.

22. Virelay: A medieval French form consisting of stanzas of varying lengths with a refrain, often focusing on themes of courtly love.

23. Epigram: A short, witty poem often characterized by brevity and cleverness, conveying a single idea or observation.

24. Villancico: A Spanish poetic form often used for Christmas or other festive occasions, characterized by its lively and rhythmic nature.

25. Found Poetry: Poetry created by selecting and rearranging words or phrases from existing texts, such as newspapers, magazines, or other written materials.

26. Pantun: A traditional Malay verse form consisting of interlocking quatrains, with the second and fourth lines of each stanza rhyming.

27. Rubaiyat: A Persian form of poetry consisting of quatrains with a specific rhyme scheme (AABA).

28. Ghazal 2: Apart from the previously mentioned ghazal, there are variations of this form found in different cultures, such as Urdu, Arabic, and Persian, each with its own conventions and rhyme schemes.

29. Sijo: A traditional Korean poetic form with three lines, each with a specific syllable count and a pause in the middle, often exploring themes of nature and human emotions.

30. Blank Verse: Unrhymed poetry written in iambic pentameter, often used in epic and dramatic poetry.

31. Rondeau: A French form of poetry consisting of 15 lines with a specific rhyme scheme and a repeating refrain.

32. Triolet: A short poetic form with eight lines, often humorous or light-hearted, with a specific rhyme scheme and repeated lines.

33. Haibun: A combination of prose and haiku, often used to describe a journey or experience with elements of both narrative and poetic reflection.

34. Prose Poetry: Poetry written in prose form, blurring the lines between prose and poetry with its lyrical and evocative language.

35. Villanella: Similar to a villanelle but with a different rhyme scheme and stanza structure, originating from Italian poetry.

36. Lai: A medieval French poetic form with a specific stanza structure and rhyme scheme, often used for narrative or lyrical poetry.

37. Skeltonic Verse: Named after English poet John Skelton, this verse form is characterized by short lines with irregular meter and rhyme, often used for comic effect.

38. Haiga: A combination of haiku and visual art, often featuring a painting, photograph, or drawing alongside a haiku poem.

39. Nonsense Verse: Playful and humorous poetry that often uses invented words, nonsense language, and whimsical themes.

40. Tongue-Twister Poetry: While not necessarily a distinct form with strict rules, tongue-twister poetry involves creating verses that are intentionally difficult to articulate due to their complex or repetitive phonetic patterns. These poems are often characterized by their playful and challenging nature, requiring careful pronunciation and rhythm. Tongue-twister poetry is less common compared to more traditional forms, but it can be found in children's literature, language learning materials, and occasional artistic endeavors.

Each style offers its own unique characteristics and challenges for poets to explore and master.

Here's A List Of 50 Topics We will Be Creating As AI Poetic Prompts

Love	Doubt	Discovery
Nature	Solitude	Wonder
Beauty	Joy	Journey
Time	Sorrow	Reflection
Death	Childhood	Harmony
Dreams	Wisdom	Imagination
Hope	Innocence	Silence
Despair	Passion	Laughter
Friendship	Serenity	Tears
Loneliness	Freedom	Strength
Memories	Justice	Vulnerability
Music	Change	Renewal
Art	Resilience	Acceptance
Inspiration	Gratitude	Mystery
Creativity	Forgiveness	Transformation
Courage	Longing	Eternity
Faith	Belonging	

Here Are Some Poetic Prompt Samples Extracted From Famous Poems That Help Paint, Draw, Design or Illustrate A Vision:

"The woods are lovely, dark and deep." - Robert Frost
"I wandered lonely as a cloud." - William Wordsworth
"O Captain! my Captain! our fearful trip." - Walt Whitman
"Do I dare disturb the universe?" - T.S. Eliot
"Because I could not stop for Death." - Emily Dickinson
"How do I love thee? Let me count the ways." - Elizabeth Barrett Browning
"I am the master of my fate." - William Ernest Henley
"The road not taken made all difference." - Robert Frost
"I have measured out my life with coffee spoons." - T.S. Eliot
"Out of the night that covers me." - William Ernest Henley
"To be or not to be, that is the question." - William Shakespeare

"Once upon a midnight dreary." - Edgar Allan Poe
"The fog comes on little cat feet." - Carl Sandburg
"Because I could not stop for Death." - Emily Dickinson
"Shall I compare thee to a summer's day?" - William Shakespeare
"Hope is the thing with feathers." - Emily Dickinson
"I know why the caged bird sings." - Maya Angelou
"In Flanders fields the poppies blow." - John McCrae
"The sky was dark, the moon was high." - Ernest Hemingway
"To see a world in a grain." - William Blake
"It was many and many a year ago." - Edgar Allan Poe
"The soul selects her own society." - Emily Dickinson
"Let me not to the marriage of true minds." - William Shakespeare
"I am the master of my fate." - William Ernest Henley
"The woods are lovely, dark and deep." - Robert Frost
"I wandered lonely as a cloud." - William Wordsworth
"O Captain! my Captain! our fearful trip." - Walt Whitman
"Do I dare disturb the universe?" - T.S. Eliot
"Because I could not stop for Death." - Emily Dickinson
"How do I love thee? Let me count the ways." - Elizabeth Barrett Browning
"I am the master of my fate." - William Ernest Henley
"The road not taken made all difference." - Robert Frost
"I have measured out my life with coffee spoons." - T.S. Eliot
"Out of the night that covers me." - William Ernest Henley
"To be or not to be, that is the question." - William Shakespeare
"Once upon a midnight dreary." - Edgar Allan Poe
"The fog comes on little cat feet." - Carl Sandburg
"Because I could not stop for Death." - Emily Dickinson
"Shall I compare thee to a summer's day?" - William Shakespeare
"Hope is the thing with feathers." - Emily Dickinson
"I know why the caged bird sings." - Maya Angelou
"In Flanders fields the poppies blow." - John McCrae
"The sky was dark, the moon was high." - Ernest Hemingway
"To see a world in a grain." - William Blake
"It was many and many a year ago." - Edgar Allan Poe
"The soul selects her own society." - Emily Dickinson
"Let me not to the marriage of true minds." - William Shakespeare
"I am the master of my fate." - William Ernest Henley
"The woods are lovely, dark and deep." - Robert Frost
"I wandered lonely as a cloud." - William Wordsworth
"The sun descending in the west." - Walt Whitman
"A thing of beauty is a joy forever." - John Keats
"The sea is calm tonight." - Matthew Arnold
"Tread softly because you tread on my dreams." - W.B. Yeats
"I am the master of my fate." - William Ernest Henley
"I rise up and I do it again." - Maya Angelou
"I am not resigned to the shutting away." - Edna St. Vincent Millay

"Not waving but drowning." - Stevie Smith
"Two roads diverged in a yellow wood." - Robert Frost
"The mist and all its tearful mourners." - Dylan Thomas
"My heart leaps up when I behold." - William Wordsworth
"Because I could not stop for Death." - Emily Dickinson
"To see a world in a grain." - William Blake
"In the room the women come and go." - T.S. Eliot
"I cannot live with you, it would be life." - Emily Dickinson
"I was the shadow of the waxwing slain." - Sylvia Plath
"The lowing herd wind slowly o'er the lea." - John Keats
"The sedge is withered from the lake." - Alfred Lord Tennyson
"This is the way the world ends." - T.S. Eliot
"In Flanders fields the poppies blow." - John McCrae
"The woods are lovely, dark and deep." - Robert Frost
"I wandered lonely as a cloud." - William Wordsworth
"O Captain! my Captain! our fearful trip." - Walt Whitman
"Do I dare disturb the universe?" - T.S. Eliot
"Because I could not stop for Death." - Emily Dickinson
"How do I love thee? Let me count the ways." - Elizabeth Barrett Browning
"I am the master of my fate." - William Ernest Henley
"The road not taken made all difference." - Robert Frost
"I have measured out my life with coffee spoons." - T.S. Eliot
"Out of the night that covers me." - William Ernest Henley
"To be or not to be, that is the question." - William Shakespeare
"Once upon a midnight dreary." - Edgar Allan Poe
"The fog comes on little cat feet." - Carl Sandburg
"Because I could not stop for Death." - Emily Dickinson
"Shall I compare thee to a summer's day?" - William Shakespeare
"Hope is the thing with feathers." - Emily Dickinson
"I know why the caged bird sings." - Maya Angelou
"In Flanders fields the poppies blow." - John McCrae
"The sky was dark, the moon was high." - Ernest Hemingway
"To see a world in a grain." - William Blake
"It was many and many a year ago." - Edgar Allan Poe
"The soul selects her own society." - Emily Dickinson
"Let me not to the marriage of true minds." - William Shakespeare
"I am the master of my fate." - William Ernest Henley
"The woods are lovely, dark and deep." - Robert Frost
"I wandered lonely as a cloud." - William Wordsworth
"O Captain! my Captain! our fearful trip." - Walt Whitman
"Do I dare disturb the universe?" - T.S. Eliot
"Because I could not stop for Death." - Emily Dickinson
"How do I love thee? Let me count the ways." - Elizabeth Barrett Browning
"The clouds that gather round the setting sun." - Lord Byron
"To see a world in a grain." - William Blake
"A thing of beauty is a joy forever." - John Keats

"Out of the night that covers me." - William Ernest Henley
"The sea is calm tonight." - Matthew Arnold
"Hope is the thing with feathers." - Emily Dickinson
"The sedge is withered from the lake." - Alfred Lord Tennyson
"Because I could not stop for Death." - Emily Dickinson
"The sun descending in the west." - Walt Whitman
"I am the master of my fate." - William Ernest Henley
"The fog comes on little cat feet." - Carl Sandburg
"I wandered lonely as a cloud." - William Wordsworth
"O Captain! my Captain! our fearful trip." - Walt Whitman
"Do I dare disturb the universe?" - T.S. Eliot
"I have measured out my life with coffee spoons." - T.S. Eliot
"To be or not to be, that is the question." - William Shakespeare
"Once upon a midnight dreary." - Edgar Allan Poe
"The mist and all its tearful mourners." - Dylan Thomas
"I am not resigned to the shutting away." - Edna St. Vincent Millay
"Not waving but drowning." - Stevie Smith
"Two roads diverged in a yellow wood." - Robert Frost
"I rise up and I do it again." - Maya Angelou
"I was the shadow of the waxwing slain." - Sylvia Plath
"My heart leaps up when I behold." - William Wordsworth
"The lowing herd wind slowly o'er the lea." - John Keats
"Two roads diverged in a yellow wood, and sorry I could not travel both." - Robert Frost
"The sea is calm tonight, the tide is full, the moon lies fair upon the straits." - Matthew Arnold
"Let me not to the marriage of true minds admit impediments." - William Shakespeare
"I am the master of my fate, I am the captain of my soul." - William Ernest Henley
"The woods are lovely, dark and deep, but I have promises to keep, and miles to go before I sleep." - Robert Frost
"O Captain! my Captain! our fearful trip is done, the ship has weather'd every rack, the prize we sought." - Walt Whitman
"Shall I compare thee to a summer's day? Thou art more lovely and more temperate." - William Shakespeare
"Hope is the thing with feathers that perches in the soul, and sings the tune without the words." - Emily Dickinson
"How do I love thee? Let me count the ways. I love thee to the depth and breadth and height." - Elizabeth Barrett Browning
"I wandered lonely as a cloud that floats on high o'er vales and hills, when all at once I saw a crowd." - William Wordsworth
"Because I could not stop for Death, he kindly stopped for me; the carriage held but just ourselves." - Emily Dickinson
"In Flanders fields the poppies blow, between the crosses, row on row, that mark our place." - John McCrae

"Once upon a midnight dreary, while I pondered, weak and weary, over many a quaint and curious volume." - Edgar Allan Poe

"The fog comes on little cat feet. It sits looking over harbor and city on silent haunches." - Carl Sandburg

"I have measured out my life with coffee spoons; I know the voices dying with a dying fall." - T.S. Eliot

"I rise up and I do it again. I rise up and I do it a thousand times again." - Maya Angelou

"The lowing herd wind slowly o'er the lea, the plowman homeward plods his weary way." - John Keats

"To see a world in a grain, a heaven in a wild flower, hold infinity in the palm of your hand." - William Blake

"Not waving but drowning. Poor chap, he always loved larking and now he's dead." - Stevie Smith

"In the room the women come and go, talking of Michelangelo." - T.S. Eliot

"The fog comes on little cat feet. It sits looking over harbor and city on silent haunches." - Carl Sandburg

"Because I could not stop for Death, he kindly stopped for me; the carriage held but just ourselves." - Emily Dickinson

"Shall I compare thee to a summer's day? Thou art more lovely and more temperate." - William Shakespeare

"Hope is the thing with feathers that perches in the soul, and sings the tune without the words." - Emily Dickinson

"I wandered lonely as a cloud that floats on high o'er vales and hills, when all at once I saw a crowd." - William Wordsworth

"O Captain! my Captain! our fearful trip is done, the ship has weather'd every rack, the prize we sought." - Walt Whitman

"Shall I compare thee to a summer's day? Thou art more lovely and more temperate." - William Shakespeare

"Hope is the thing with feathers that perches in the soul, and sings the tune without the words." - Emily Dickinson

"How do I love thee? Let me count the ways. I love thee to the depth and breadth and height." - Elizabeth Barrett Browning

"I wandered lonely as a cloud that floats on high o'er vales and hills, when all at once I saw a crowd." - William Wordsworth

"Because I could not stop for Death, he kindly stopped for me; the carriage held but just ourselves." - Emily Dickinson

"In Flanders fields the poppies blow, between the crosses, row on row, that mark our place." - John McCrae

"Once upon a midnight dreary, while I pondered, weak and weary, over many a quaint and curious volume." - Edgar Allan Poe

"The fog comes on little cat feet. It sits looking over harbor and city on silent haunches." - Carl Sandburg

"I have measured out my life with coffee spoons; I know the voices dying with a dying fall." - T.S. Eliot

"I rise up and I do it again. I rise up and I do it a thousand times again." - Maya Angelou

"The lowing herd wind slowly o'er the lea, the plowman homeward plods his weary way." - John Keats

"To see a world in a grain, a heaven in a wild flower, hold infinity in the palm of your hand." - William Blake

"Not waving but drowning. Poor chap, he always loved larking and now he's dead." - Stevie Smith

"In the room the women come and go, talking of Michelangelo." - T.S. Eliot

"The fog comes on little cat feet. It sits looking over harbor and city on silent haunches." - Carl Sandburg

"Because I could not stop for Death, he kindly stopped for me; the carriage held but just ourselves." - Emily Dickinson

"Shall I compare thee to a summer's day? Thou art more lovely and more temperate." - William Shakespeare

"Hope is the thing with feathers that perches in the soul, and sings the tune without the words." - Emily Dickinson

"I wandered lonely as a cloud that floats on high o'er vales and hills, when all at once I saw a crowd." - William Wordsworth

"O Captain! my Captain! our fearful trip is done, the ship has weather'd every rack, the prize we sought." - Walt Whitman

"Shall I compare thee to a summer's day? Thou art more lovely and more temperate." - William Shakespeare

"Hope is the thing with feathers that perches in the soul, and sings the tune without the words." - Emily Dickinson

"How do I love thee? Let me count the ways. I love thee to the depth and breadth and height." - Elizabeth Barrett Browning

"I wandered lonely as a cloud that floats on high o'er vales and hills, when all at once I saw a crowd." - William Wordsworth

"I took the one less traveled by, and that has made all the difference." - Robert Frost

"The moon is a friend for the lonesome to talk to." - Carl Sandburg

"I hear America singing, the varied carols I hear." - Walt Whitman

"The road less traveled is the one to be embraced." - Robert Frost

"I am the master of my fate, I am the captain of my soul." - William Ernest Henley

"The fog comes on little cat feet. It sits looking over harbor and city on silent haunches." - Carl Sandburg

"Not waving but drowning. Poor chap, he always loved larking and now he's dead." - Stevie Smith

"In the room the women come and go, talking of Michelangelo." - T.S. Eliot

"The woods are lovely, dark and deep, but I have promises to keep, and miles to go before I sleep." - Robert Frost

"O Captain! my Captain! our fearful trip is done, the ship has weather'd every rack, the prize we sought." - Walt Whitman

"The moon is a friend for the lonesome to talk to." - Carl Sandburg

"I hear America singing, the varied carols I hear." - Walt Whitman

"The road less traveled is the one to be embraced." - Robert Frost

"I am the master of my fate, I am the captain of my soul." - William Ernest Henley

"The fog comes on little cat feet. It sits looking over harbor and city on silent haunches." - Carl Sandburg

"Not waving but drowning. Poor chap, he always loved larking and now he's dead." - Stevie Smith

"In the room the women come and go, talking of Michelangelo." - T.S. Eliot

"The woods are lovely, dark and deep, but I have promises to keep, and miles to go before I sleep." - Robert Frost

"O Captain! my Captain! our fearful trip is done, the ship has weather'd every rack, the prize we sought." - Walt Whitman

"The moon is a friend for the lonesome to talk to." - Carl Sandburg

"I hear America singing, the varied carols I hear." - Walt Whitman

"The road less traveled is the one to be embraced." - Robert Frost

"I am the master of my fate, I am the captain of my soul." - William Ernest Henley

"The fog comes on little cat feet. It sits looking over harbor and city on silent haunches." - Carl Sandburg

"Not waving but drowning. Poor chap, he always loved larking and now he's dead." - Stevie Smith

"In the room the women come and go, talking of Michelangelo." - T.S. Eliot

"The woods are lovely, dark and deep, but I have promises to keep, and miles to go before I sleep." - Robert Frost

"O Captain! my Captain! our fearful trip is done, the ship has weather'd every rack, the prize we sought." - Walt Whitman

"The moon is a friend for the lonesome to talk to." - Carl Sandburg

"I hear America singing, the varied carols I hear." - Walt Whitman

"The road less traveled is the one to be embraced." - Robert Frost

"I am the master of my fate, I am the captain of my soul." - William Ernest Henley

"The fog comes on little cat feet. It sits looking over harbor and city on silent haunches." - Carl Sandburg

"Not waving but drowning. Poor chap, he always loved larking and now he's dead." - Stevie Smith

"In the room the women come and go, talking of Michelangelo." - T.S. Eliot

"The woods are lovely, dark and deep, but I have promises to keep, and miles to go before I sleep." - Robert Frost

"O Captain! my Captain! our fearful trip is done, the ship has weather'd every rack, the prize we sought." - Walt Whitman

"The moon is a friend for the lonesome to talk to." - Carl Sandburg

"I hear America singing, the varied carols I hear." - Walt Whitman

"The road less traveled is the one to be embraced." - Robert Frost
"I am the master of my fate, I am the captain of my soul." - William Ernest Henley
"The fog comes on little cat feet. It sits looking over harbor and city on silent haunches." - Carl Sandburg
"Not waving but drowning. Poor chap, he always loved larking and now he's dead." - Stevie Smith
"In the room the women come and go, talking of Michelangelo." - T.S. Eliot
"The woods are lovely, dark and deep, but I have promises to keep, and miles to go before I sleep." - Robert Frost
"O Captain! my Captain! our fearful trip is done, the ship has weather'd every rack, the prize we sought." - Walt Whitman
"The moon is a friend for the lonesome to talk to." - Carl Sandburg
"I hear America singing, the varied carols I hear." - Walt Whitman
"The road less traveled is the one to be embraced." - Robert Frost
"I am the master of my fate, I am the captain of my soul." - William Ernest Henley

Or Short Poems About Fantasy, Mythology, History, Emotions, Secrets & Treasures.

In realms of fantasy, dragons soar high,
Magic whispers in the air, where dreams defy.

Gods of old, in mythology's grasp,
Tales of heroes, where legends clasp.

Ancient lands, where history breathes,
Echoes of the past, where time weaves.

Emotions swirl, in the heart's deep well,
Love's gentle touch, where souls dwell.

Secrets hidden, in shadows deep,
Whispers of mystery, where secrets sleep.

Treasures untold, in caverns vast,
Riches of the earth, where dreams amass.

A knight in armor, on a quest for glory,
Through lands of fantasy, telling tales of his story.

In the heart of the forest, nymphs dance with glee,
A magical realm, where wonders roam free.

Zeus, the king of gods, on his throne of might,
Lightning cracks, in the depths of the night.

Battles fought, in history's domain,
Heroes remembered, where valor reigns.

Tears of sorrow, in the silent night,
A broken heart, where darkness takes flight.

Locked away, in a chest of gold,
Secrets untold, where mysteries unfold.

A pirate's map, with markings obscure,
X marks the spot, where treasures allure.

Elves in the forest, with bows drawn tight,
Guardians of nature, in the moon's soft light.

Medusa's gaze, turns men to stone,
A tale of caution, in the myths we've known.

Shakespeare's words, in pages old,
Love's sweet sonnets, where emotions unfold.

Whispers in the wind, of a lost love's vow,
A heartache buried, where memories avow.

A diary's pages, filled with secrets deep,
A life unveiled, where dreams and fears creep.

Sirens' song, on the ocean's wave,
Tempting sailors, to an early grave.

A golden chalice, adorned with jewels rare,
A king's treasure, beyond compare.

Pegasus flies, with wings of white,
Across the heavens, in the sun's bright light.

King Arthur's sword, in the stone it lies,
A symbol of strength, where destiny ties.

Laughter echoes, in the halls of old,
Memories cherished, where stories are told.

A whispered promise, in the dead of night,
A secret shared, where darkness takes flight.

Aladdin's lamp, with wishes three,
A genie's magic, where dreams can be.

Fenrir's chains, in the depths of the earth,
A wolf's fury, where legends birth.

Tears of joy, in the morning dew,
A heart filled with love, where dreams come true.

A locked door, with a key of gold,
Secrets kept, where mysteries hold.

Atlantis lost, beneath the sea,
A kingdom forgotten, where myths decree.

A pirate's chest, filled with plundered gold,
A hoard of riches, where fortunes unfold.

Fairies dance, in the moonlit glen,
A world of enchantment, where magic begins.

Odin's eye, in the depths of the well,
A sacrifice made, where tales do tell.

Tears of loss, in the fading light,
A heartache felt, where shadows alight.

A hidden passage, in the castle wall,
Secrets revealed, where whispers call.

The Holy Grail, in a quest for truth,
A sacred treasure, where legends soothe.

Dragons sleep, in caverns deep,
A fiery breath, where nightmares creep.

An ancient map, with markings bold,
A path to adventure, where tales are told.

A phoenix rising, from ashes grey,
A symbol of hope, in the light of day.

Echoes of laughter, in the halls of time,
Memories cherished, in rhythm and rhyme.

A locked chest, with a key of silver,
Secrets guarded, where dreams deliver.

Apollo's lyre, in the hands of a muse,
A melody sweet, where dreams diffuse.

Tears of longing, in the night's embrace,
A yearning heart, in a silent space.

A hidden cavern, with treasures rare,
A trove of riches, beyond compare.

A phoenix's feather, in a wizard's hand,
A spell of renewal, where dreams expand.

Tears of joy, in the morning light,
A heart filled with love, in the depths of night.

A whispered vow, in the lover's ear,
A promise kept, where love is near.

A buried chest, in the sands of time,
Secrets untold, in the rhythm of rhyme.

A dragon's hoard, in a mountain cave,
Treasures untold, where dreams are brave.

A hidden path, in the forest deep,
Secrets revealed, where shadows sleep.

A golden key, in a lock of rust,
Secrets unlocked, where dreams adjust.

Using Your Creative Visual Skills, You'll Be Able To Extract Portions Of Your Favorite Poems & Turn Them Into Prompts That Create Some Amazing Images – It's Hard Work, But, The Unique Rewards Will Be Worthwhile. So, Have Fun Prompting.

You May Also Want To Play Around With Natural Or Adding Some Really Strange Configurations & Combinations

Alpha Numeric Combinations,
Beautiful Friend,
Best Friend's Name,
Book Titles,
Childhood Memory,
Current Events,
Dream Life,
Famous Architecture,
Favorite Artist,
Favorite Cities,
Favorite Foods,
Favorite Hobby,
Favorite Holidays,
Historical Events,
Ideal Date,
Month, Date & Time
Mysterious Event,
Nonsense Combinations,
Nonsense Words,
Pet's Name
Places In Nature,
Relatives Name,
Reoccurring Dream,
Song Titles,
Street Names,
Vacation Destinations,
Wishful Job Title,
Your Name,
Your Neighborhood,
Your Nickname - -

- - You get the idea!

- - - HERE ARE SOME OF MY 'SECRET SAUCE' PROMPT KEYWORDS - - -
ADD A COUPLE OF THESE AFTER YOUR PROMPT & SEE WHAT HAPPENS!

2/3 Face Angle
3D
64 Megapixels
8K Resolution
A Masterpiece
Abstract Art
Airy & Light Hearted
Architectural
Art Deco
Artstation
Asymmetrical
Atmospheric
Attractive
Beautiful
Behanced HD
Blurred
Bokeh
Brilliant
Canon Lens
Cinema 4D
Cinematic Background
Cinematic Lighting
Circuit Background
Circular
Color Depth
Color Portrait
Colorful
Complementary Colors
Complex
Concept Art
Creative
Dark Fantasy
Deep Colors
Detailed
Digital
Dramatic
Dramatic Lighting
Draw
Drawing
Elaborate
Epic
Exotic
Fantastical

Fantasy
Filigree Patterns
Flowing
Friendly
Frontal View
Full Body
Futuristic
Graffiti Art
Ground Level
Happy & Joyous
Head And Shoulder
High Contrast
High Fashion Pose
Highly Decorative
Hyper-Colorful
Hyper-Detailed
Hyper-Exotic
Hyper-Realistic
Illuminate
Imaginative
Intricate
Intricate Details
Jewelry
Line Drawing
Lush
Magical
Masks
Matte
Matte Painting
Maximalist
Mech Details
Melting
Metallic
Meticulous
Mid Shot
Neon
Oil Gouache
Oil Painting
Paint
Painterly
Paper Curls Patterns
Pen & Ink
Pencil

Pencil Drawing
Perfect
Perfect Composition
Pointillism
Polished Metal
Polished Metal
Polychromatic
Profile View
Render In Blender
Sad
Scary
Sci-Fi
Screen Art
Sharp Focus
Shot On DSLR
Side Light
Sketch
Smiling
Sparkling
Splash Art
Spray Paint
Street Art
Studio Lighting
Stunning
Stylized
Surreal
Surrealistic
Symmetrical
Torn Paper
Trending In Artsation
Triadic Colors
Tropical
Ultra Details
Ultra Quality
Ultra Realistic
Unreal Engine
Unreal Engine 5
Vibrant
Vibrant Colors
Volume

A WORD OF CAUTION:

Many Filtered Words May Be Banned And Face Prompt Rejection, Words Such As:

Bloody, Injury, Death, Guts, Gory, Gruesome, Torture, Suicide, Cannibalism, Taboo Words, Ethnic Slurs, Phobia Terminology, Slang Nicknames, Sexually Explicit, Nudity, Unclothed, Risqué, Sexual, Genitalia, Private Body Parts, Foreign Sex Words, Sex Slang, XXX, Kill, Exploitation of Children, Inflammatory, Derogatory, Blasphemy, Profanity, Prohibited, Drugs, Alcohol, Cigarettes, Terrorist, or Similar Words In Other Languages, **etc… (others may also become blocked)**

Be mindful that each generator has its own list of banned words. Avoid being banned from their image generating account platform by misuse of their terms of agreement.

Too many attempts in using banned or filtered words could result in being banned from using your selected AI generator. Carefully read the terms of your AI generators' agreement.

FEEL FREE TO CHECK OUT MY AI VIDEO COLLECTION AT:
www.ART262.com

READY TO ENJOY YOUR PROMPTING ADVENTURES? WHEN YOU ARE, STRAP YOURSELF IN FOR UNEXPECTED NEW IMAGE ADVENTURES EVEN WITH USING THESE POETIC PROMPTS.

HERE'S YOUR EXCLUSIVE GUIDE TO RICHARD'S VAULT Of *"POETIC PROMPTS – Turn Words Into Images"*
Have Fun Playing With These POETIC PROMPTS – Use Your Skill TO EXTRACT, EXCHANGE, COMBINE & ADD WORDS TO YOUR PROMPTS

READY TO ENJOY YOUR PROMPTING ADVENTURES? WHEN YOU ARE, STRAP YOURSELF IN FOR UNEXPECTED NEW IMAGE ADVENTURES EVEN WITH USING THESE POETIC PROMPTS.

HERE'S YOUR EXCLUSIVE GUIDE TO RICHARD'S VAULT
Of *"POETIC PROMPTS – Turn Words Into Images"*
Have Fun Playing With These POETIC PROMPTS – Use Your Skill TO
EXTRACT, EXCHANGE, COMBINE & ADD WORDS TO YOUR PROMPTS

SONNET:

A 14-line poem traditionally written in iambic pentameter, often focusing on themes of love or beauty.

-:|:-•:*''''''*:•.-:|:-•**•-:|:-•:*''''''*:•:*''''''*:•.-:|:-•**•-:|:--:|:-•:*''''''*:•.-:|:- •**•-:|:-•:*''''''*:•:*''''''*:•.-:|:-•**•-:|:-

Here are four Sonnet poems, 1 each about Love, Nature, Beauty & Time

Love:
In love's embrace, the world begins to sing,
A melody of passion, sweet and true,
With every heartbeat, hearts take wing,
As love's eternal flame burns bright anew.

With every touch, a symphony unfolds,
In love's embrace, we find our home,
As we explore the depths love beholds,
And let our hearts forever roam.

For love is the essence of the human soul,
A bond that ties us through eternity,
In every moment, a chance to extol,
The beauty of love's grand serenity.

So let us embrace the love we hold dear,
And let its magic banish every fear.

Nature:
In nature's realm, where wonders never cease,
We find the beauty that surrounds us all,
With every sunrise, a sense of peace,
As nature's canvas paints a vibrant thrall.

With every breeze, a whispering of grace,
In nature's embrace, we find our place,
As we connect with the earth's embrace,
And let its beauty our spirits embrace.

For nature is the teacher of the soul,
A guide that leads us to the grand design,
In every leaf, a lesson to extol,
As nature's wonders forever shine.

So let us cherish the beauty of the earth,
And let its splendor fill us with endless mirth.

Beauty:
In moments still, where silence softly sings,
We find the beauty that resides within,
With every glance, a beauty springs,
As we behold the wonders that begin.

With every smile, a beauty unfurls,
In beauty's embrace, we find our grace,
As we explore the depths, and let the pearls,
Of beauty's treasure light our face.

For beauty is the essence of the soul,
A reflection of the world's grand design,
In every moment, a chance to extol,
The beauty that forever will shine.

So let us seek the beauty that we see,
And let its radiance set our spirits free.

Time:
In moments fleeting, where time slips away,
We find the essence of life's grand design,
With every tick, a moment begins to play,
As time's eternal dance forever intertwine.

With every hour, a story starts to unfold,
In time's embrace, we find our fate,
As we navigate the mysteries, untold,
And let time's current forever sate.

For time is the river that flows through all,
A force that shapes the world we see,
In every rise, a chance to recall,
The moments that forever will be.

So let us cherish the time we hold dear,
And let its passing fill us with endless cheer.

Here are four Sonnet poems, 1 each about Death, Dreams, Hope & Despair

Death:
In shadows deep, where silence starts to reign,
We find the mystery of life's final call,
With every breath, a moment begins to wane,
As death's eternal veil begins to fall.

With every sigh, a soul begins to soar,
In death's embrace, we find our rest,
As we cross the threshold to the unknown shore,
And let the journey take us where it's best.

For death is the passage we all must take,
A journey to the realm beyond our sight,
In every goodbye, a chance to make,
The most of every moment's light.

So let us embrace the mystery of death's decree,
And let its wisdom guide us to eternity.

Dreams:
In dreams' embrace, the mind begins to soar,
A journey to the realms of endless flight,
With every vision, a new world to explore,
As dreams take hold and fill the soul with light.

With every hope, a dream begins to weave,
In dreams' embrace, we find our truth,
As we dare to believe and let our hearts believe,
And let the dreams guide us through.

For dreams are the whispers of the soul,
A promise of what could be,
In every thought, a chance to extol,
The beauty of dreams' grand decree.

So let us embrace the dreams we hold dear,
And let their magic banish every fear.

Hope:
In moments dark, where shadows start to creep,
We find the glimmer of hope's eternal light,
With every prayer, a promise to keep,
As hope takes flight and guides us through the night.

With every dawn, a new hope is born,
In hope's embrace, we find our strength,
As we face the challenges, the scars we adorn,
And let hope's flame go to any length.

For hope is the beacon that lights the way,
A torch that leads us through the darkest night,
In every prayer, a chance to say,
That hope will forever shine bright.

So let us hold onto hope's gentle thread,
And let its light guide us through the dread.

Despair
In moments bleak, where shadows start to loom,
We find the darkness of despair's embrace,
With every tear, a sense of doom,
As despair's heavy burden we must face.

With every sigh, a heart begins to break,
In despair's embrace, we find our sorrow,
As we navigate the depths, the sadness we partake,
And let the despair take hold and sorrow borrow.

For despair is the cloud that veils the sun,
A storm that rages through the soul,
In every moment, a battle must be won,
As despair takes its heavy toll.

So let us find the strength to rise above
And let the light of hope renew our love.
,

Here are four Sonnet poems, 1 each about Friendship, Loneliness, Memories & Music

Friendship:
In bonds of friendship, hearts intertwine,
A symphony of laughter, trust, and care,
With every word, a treasure we refine,
As we find solace in the love we share.

With every smile, a connection grows,
In friendship's embrace, we find our strength,
As we navigate life's highs and lows,

And find in friendship, joy at length.

For friendship is the anchor in life's sea,
A harbor safe from storms that rage,
In every moment, a chance to be,
A light for each other, in every stage.

So let us cherish the friendships we hold dear,
And let their warmth dispel every fear.

Loneliness:
In shadows deep where silence reigns supreme,
We find the solitude that pierces through,
With every sigh, a heart begins to dream,
As loneliness consumes, a bitter brew.

With every echo, a void expands,
In loneliness' embrace, we find despair,
As we reach out with trembling hands,
And find no solace in the empty air.

For loneliness is the weight we bear alone,
A burden heavy on the weary soul,
In every silence, a mournful tone,
As loneliness takes its heavy toll.

So let us reach out and bridge the divide,
And let companionship be our guide.

Memories:
In moments past, where echoes softly dwell,
We find the memories that shape our soul,
With every smile, a story to tell,
As we reminisce and let the memories roll.

With every tear, a memory blooms,
In memories' embrace, we find our past,
As we revisit old haunts and old rooms,
And let the echoes of the past ever last.

For memories are the treasures we hold dear,
A tapestry woven with threads of time,
In every moment a memory near,
As memories paint the canvas of our prime.

So let us cherish the memories we hold tight,
And let them guide us through the darkest night.

Music:
In melodies that dance upon the air,
We find the music that moves the soul,
With every note, a magic rare,
As we surrender to the music's control.

With every rhythm, a heartbeat syncs,
In music's embrace, we find our flow,
As we lose ourselves in the music's links,
And let the melodies carry us where we go.

For music is the language of the heart,
A symphony that speaks in every key,
In every chord, a chance to impart,
The emotions that words cannot decree.

So let us lose ourselves in music's sway,
And let its beauty guide us every day.

Here are four Sonnet poems, 1 each about Art, Inspiration, Creativity & Courage

Art:
In strokes of paint, where colors blend and flow,
We find the artistry that speaks to the soul,
With every stroke, a story starts to grow,
As we explore the depths of art's control.

With every canvas, a world takes shape,
In art's embrace, we find our expression,
As we delve into the depths and escape,
And let the beauty of art be our confession.

For art is the mirror of the human heart,
A reflection of the world as we perceive,
In every masterpiece, a chance to impart,
The emotions that words alone can't achieve.

So let us embrace the beauty that art brings,
And let its magic lift us on its wings.

Inspiration:
In moments still, where muses softly sing,
We find the inspiration that ignites,
With every spark, a fire starts to cling,
As we embrace the muse's guiding lights.
With every thought, a vision unfolds,
In inspiration's embrace, we find our voice,
As we tap into the endless wells untold,
And let the inspiration be our choice.

For inspiration is the wellspring of creation,
A fountain from which dreams are brought to life,
In every moment, a chance for elation,
As inspiration banishes every strife.

So let us welcome inspiration's embrace,
And let its fire ignite our creative space.

Creativity:
In moments of creation, where worlds collide,
We find the creativity that sets us free,
With every idea, a universe untied,
As we explore the depths of possibility.

With every brushstroke, a masterpiece takes form,
In creativity's embrace, we find our muse,
As we unleash the torrents of the storm,
And let the creativity be our fuse.

For creativity is the well from which we draw,
A source of endless energy and light,
In every creation, a chance to awe,
As creativity guides us through the night.

So let us embrace the creativity we hold dear,
And let its power fill us with endless cheer.

Courage:
In moments of fear, where shadows start to loom,
We find the courage that resides within,
With every step, a chance to break the gloom,
As we face the challenges, we begin.

With every trial, a strength starts to grow,
In courage's embrace, we find our might,
As we navigate the highs and lows,
And let the courage guide us through the night.

For courage is the flame that lights the way,
A beacon in the darkness of the soul,
In every challenge, a chance to say,
That courage is what makes us whole.

So let us embrace the courage that we find,
And let its strength carry us through every bind.

Here are four Sonnet poems, 1 each about Faith, Doubt, Solitude & Joy

Faith:
In moments deep, where shadows start to wane,
We find the beacon of faith's guiding light,
With every prayer, a promise to regain,
As faith restores the soul's celestial flight.

With every step, a trust begins to bloom,
In faith's embrace, we find our steadfast ground,
As we navigate life's maze, the gloom,
And let the faith in something greater be found.

For faith is the anchor in life's sea,
A compass guiding through the stormy night,
In every trial, a chance to decree,
That faith will guide us through the darkest plight.

So let us hold onto our faith so dear,
And let its grace dispel every fear.

Doubt:
In shadows deep, where doubts begin to roam,
We find the questions that haunt the mind,
With every whisper, uncertainty's tome,
As doubt's cruel fingers leave us blind.

With every thought, a seed of doubt is sown,
In doubt's embrace, we find our hesitation,
As we grapple with the unknown,
And let the doubts fuel our speculation.

For doubt is the chasm that swallows the light,
A cloud that veils the path we tread,
In every question, a chance to invite,
The doubts that linger in our head.

So let us face our doubts with open eyes,
And let them lead us to the truth, we surmise.

Solitude:
In moments still, where silence reigns supreme,
We find the solace of solitude's embrace,
With every breath, a chance to redeem,
As solitude becomes our sacred space.

With every sigh, a peace begins to bloom,
In solitude's embrace, we find our retreat,
As we find solace in the quiet room,
And let the solitude's tranquility beat.

For solitude is the sanctuary of the soul,
A refuge from life's chaotic roar,
In every moment, a chance to extol,
The beauty of the silence we adore.

So let us embrace the solitude we seek,
And let its calmness make us strong and meek.
Joy:
In moments bright, where laughter fills the air,
We find the joy that dances in the heart,
With every smile, a happiness to share,
As joy becomes the essence of our art.

With every giggle, a melody sings,
In joy's embrace, we find our delight,
As we spread our wings and let our spirits fling,
And let the joy lift us to the height.
For joy is the music that fills the soul,
A symphony of laughter, love, and glee,
In every moment, a chance to extol,
The beauty of the joy that's free.

So let us embrace the joy we find,
And let its light forever shine.

Here are four Sonnet poems, 1 each about Sorrow, Childhood, Wisdom & Innocence

Sorrow:
In shadows deep, where sorrow takes its hold,
We find the heart weighed down by heavy chains,
With every tear, a story left untold,
As grief consumes and leaves its lasting stains.

With every ache, a soul begins to weep,
In sorrow's grip, we find ourselves confined,
As memories of loss, like ghosts, do creep,
And haunt the corners of our troubled mind.

For sorrow is the burden that we bear,
A heavy cross we carry through the night,
In every sigh, a whisper of despair,
As darkness veils the once bright shining light.

So let us face the sorrow that we know,
And let our tears become the seeds we sow.

Childhood:
In days of innocence, where laughter rings,
We find the joy that fills our hearts with glee,
With every game, a new adventure springs,
As we explore the wonders that we see.

With every giggle, a world unfolds,
In childhood's embrace, we find our play,
As fantasies and dreams begin to mold,
And shape the memories of yesterday.

For childhood is the garden of the soul,
A time of magic and of pure delight,
In every moment, a chance to extol,
The beauty of life in its early light.

So let us cherish every childhood hour,
And let the memories bloom like a flower.
Wisdom:
In moments still, where silence softly speaks,
We find the wisdom that comes with the years,
With every lesson learned, a truth we seek,
As we reflect on life's joys and tears.

With every trial, a knowledge grows,
In wisdom's embrace, we find our peace,
As we navigate the highs and lows,
And let our understanding gently increase.

For wisdom is the gift that time bestows,
A treasure trove of insights to explore,
In every decision, a chance to compose,
The symphony of life's grand encore.

So let us seek the wisdom that we crave,
And let its guiding light illuminate the way.

Innocence:
In purity of heart, where dreams take flight,
We find the innocence that lights the soul,
With every smile, a world so bright,
As we embrace the innocence that makes us whole.

With every laugh, a song begins to sing,
In innocence's embrace, we find our joy,
As we dance through life, like birds on wing,
And let the wonder of innocence employ.

For innocence is the beacon in the night,
A guiding star that leads us through the dark,
In every hug, a promise to ignite,
The flame of innocence's lasting spark.

So let us hold onto our innocence dear
And let its magic banish every fear.

Here are four Sonnet poems, 1 each about Passion, Serenity, Freedom & Justice

Passion:
In flames of passion, hearts begin to burn,
With every touch, a spark ignites the fire,
In every kiss, a fervor we discern,
As passion's flames rise higher and higher.

With every beat, a rhythm starts to play,
In passion's embrace, we find our thrill,
As desires kindle and passions sway,
And let the fervor of passion fulfill.

For passion is the fuel that drives us on,
A force that propels us through the night,
In every longing, a dream is born,
As passion's fire burns ever bright.

So let us embrace the passion that we feel,
And let its flames ignite and make us real.

Serenity:
In moments still, where silence softly falls,
We find the serenity that we seek,
With every breath, a calmness enthralls,
As we embrace the peace that makes us meek.

With every sigh, a tension starts to ease,
In serenity's embrace, we find our rest,
As worries fade and anxieties cease,
And let the quietude become our quest.

For serenity is the balm for weary souls,
A sanctuary in the chaos of life,
In every moment, a chance to console,
The heart with serenity's gentle strife.

So let us seek the serenity we crave,
And let its tranquil waters be our save.

Freedom:
In open skies, where dreams take flight,
We find the freedom that we long to know,
With every step, a boundless height,
As we soar above the constraints below.

With every breath, a liberation sings,
In freedom's embrace, we find our wings,
As we break free from earthly strings,
And let the winds of freedom give us springs.

For freedom is the essence of the soul,
A birthright that we cherish and uphold,
In every dream, a chance to enroll,
The heart in freedom's story untold.

So let us embrace the freedom that we find,
And let its spirit guide us through all time.

Justice:
In halls of justice, where truth takes stand,
We find the righteousness that we seek,
With every verdict, a reprimand,
As we uphold the principles so meek.

With every trial, a judgment cast,
In justice's embrace, we find our cause,
As we fight for what is right, steadfast,
And let the scales of justice never pause.

For justice is the cornerstone of law,
A beacon in the darkness of the night,
In every act, a chance

Here are four Sonnet poems, 1 each about Change, Resilience, Gratitude & Forgiveness

Change:
In every dawn, a whisper of change's call,
A shifting tide that shapes the world anew,
With every step, we journey towards the fall,
As seasons change, so does our point of view.

With every change, a chance for growth is found,
In transformation's dance, we find our way,
As old leaves fall, new sprouts burst from the ground,
And in the cycle of change, we find our sway.

For change is constant, like the shifting tide,
A force that molds the landscape of our lives,
In every challenge, change becomes our guide,
As we embrace the change, our spirit thrives.

So let us welcome change with open arms,
And find our strength amidst life's constant charms.

Resilience:
In moments dark, where shadows start to loom,
We find the strength within to carry on,
With every storm, our resilience blooms,
As we weather trials until they're gone.

With every setback, a chance to rise,
In resilience, we find our power clear,
As we refuse to yield to compromise,
And stand strong in the face of doubt and fear.

For resilience is more than just survival,
It's the ability to thrive and grow,
In every trial, we find our revival,
As we face adversity with grace bestowed.

So let us stand tall in the face of strife,
And let resilience be the force of life.

Gratitude:
In moments still, where quietude resides,
We find the gratitude that fills our soul,
With every breath, a thankfulness abides,
As we embrace the blessings that console.

With every sunrise, gratitude's embrace,
In gratitude, we find our hearts aglow,
As we give thanks for every moment's grace,
And let appreciation freely flow.
For gratitude is more than just a feeling,
It's a way of life, a state of mind,
In every blessing, gratitude revealing,
The beauty in the moments we find.

So let us give thanks for every gift we're given,
And let gratitude be the path to heaven.

Forgiveness:
In moments fraught with anger, hurt, and pain,
We find the strength to let forgiveness reign,
With every breath, a chance to break the chain,
As we release the burdens of disdain.
With every grudge, a heart begins to wither,
In forgiveness' embrace, we find release,
As we let go of bitterness and simmer,
And find in forgiveness, our inner peace.

For forgiveness is the key to liberation,
A gift we give ourselves, as much as others,
In every act of forgiveness' salvation,
We find the freedom to uncover.

So let us forgive, and let our hearts be light,
And find in forgiveness, our eternal right.

Here are four Sonnet poems, 1 each about Longing, Belonging, Discovery & Wonder

Longing:
In moments still, where silence softly sings,
We find the longing deep within our soul,
With every beat, a heart that gently clings,
To dreams and hopes that make our spirits whole.

With every sigh, a yearning to be near,
In longing's embrace, we find our desire,
As we search for solace in the fleeting here,
And let the flames of longing never tire.

For longing is the echo of the heart,
A melody that whispers through the night,
In every longing, a chance to start,
A journey towards the distant light.

So let us embrace the longing in our breast,
And let our dreams guide us to the promised crest.

Belonging:
In moments shared, where laughter fills the air,
We find the belonging that we seek,
With every smile, a bond beyond compare,
As we find solace in the friendships we keep.

With every hug, a sense of home arrives,
In belonging's embrace, we find our place,
As we let go of fears and cast aside,
And let belonging's warmth fill every space.

For belonging is the heart's truest calling,
A connection that transcends time and space,
In every friendship, belonging enthralling,
A sanctuary in life's chaotic race.

So let us cherish every bond we hold dear,
And let belonging be our compass clear.

Discovery:
In moments bright, where wonders start to gleam,
We find the discovery that awaits,
With every step, a world unseen,
As we explore the mysteries and fates.

With every question, a journey unfolds,
In discovery's embrace, we find our way,
As we seek the truths that lie untold,
And let curiosity guide our day.

For discovery is the spark that ignites,
A flame that burns within our souls,
In every moment, a chance to alight,
And let discovery's wonders enroll.

So let us embrace the journey that unfolds,
And let discovery be our story told.

Wonder:
In moments grand, where beauty takes its stand,
We find the wonder that ignites our soul,
With every glance, a world so grand,
As we marvel at the wonders that unfold.

With every sunrise, a miracle revealed,
In wonder's embrace, we find our awe,
As we let go of doubts and fears concealed,
And let wonder's majesty open every door.

For wonder is the magic that enchants,
A spell that weaves through every day,
In every moment, a chance to dance,
And let wonder's splendor light our way.

So let us embrace the marvels that abound,
And let wonder's beauty forever astound.

Here are four Sonnet poems, 1 each about Journey, Reflection, Harmony & Imagination

Journey:
Upon the road of life, we embark,
With every step, a new adventure starts,
Through valleys low and mountains stark,
We navigate the twists and turns, the charts.

Each milestone reached, a story to be told,
With every challenge faced, we grow and learn,
In every setback, lessons do unfold,
As we press on, our inner fires burn.

For life's a journey, not a destination,
And every path we tread, a choice we make,
With courage as our guide, determination,
We face the unknown, no step we'll forsake.

So let us embrace this journey's call,
And find our purpose, as we give our all.

Reflection:
In moments quiet, where the world fades out,
We turn inward, to ponder and to muse,
Reflection's mirror, dispelling every doubt,
As we unravel mysteries, and truths peruse.

In every shadow lies a tale untold,
In every silence, echoes of the past,
As memories surface, a treasure to behold,
In reflection's gaze, we find peace at last.

For in the stillness, clarity is found,
And answers to our questions start to rise,
In every thought, a wisdom does abound,
As we unravel life's intricate disguise.

So let us pause, and ponder for a while,
In reflection's embrace, we find our smile.

Harmony:
In the symphony of life, we find our place,
Each note a melody, each chord a rhyme,
In harmony's embrace, we find our grace,
As we dance to the rhythm of the passing time.

With every beat, our hearts in unison,
In perfect sync, we move with grace and ease,
In harmony's embrace, we find communion,
As we embrace the unity, our spirits release.

For in the harmony, lies the beauty rare,
As different voices blend in perfect accord,
In every harmony, a love we share,
As we find solace in the chords restored.

So let us sing the song of life, in tune,
And find our peace, beneath the crescent moon.

Imagination:
In realms of fantasy, where dreams take flight,
Imagination soars on wings of light,
In every story spun, a world so bright,
As we journey through the realms of endless night.

With every thought, a universe unfolds,
As we explore the landscapes of the mind,
In imagination's embrace, we're bold,
As we leave reality far behind.

For in the imagination, lies the key,
To unlock the doors of possibility,
In every vision, a world set free,
As we embrace the realms of creativity.

So let us wander through the realms unknown,
In imagination's embrace, we find our own.

Here are four Sonnet poems, 1 each about Silence, Laughter, Tears & Strength

Silence:
In silence deep, where echoes softly fade,
We find a refuge from life's noisy fray,
Each moment still, a symphony is played,
In quietude, our souls begin to sway.

With every breath, the silence speaks its truth,
In whispers soft, the universe reveals,
In silence' embrace, we find our youth,
As all around us, peace gently steals.

For in the silence, lies the greatest power,
To calm the storms that rage within our soul,
In every moment, a sacred hour,
As silence' grace helps make us whole.

So let us seek the solace silence brings,
And find our peace in its gentle wings.

Laughter:
In laughter's echo, joy begins to rise,
A melody that lifts the spirits high,
With every giggle, the soul takes flight,
As laughter dances in the morning light.

With every chuckle, worries start to fade,
In laughter's embrace, we find release,
As mirth and glee become our sweet crusade,
And every moment is a moment of peace.

For in the laughter, lies the heart's delight,
A symphony of happiness, so sweet,
In every joke, a reason to unite,
As laughter's chorus fills the world complete.

So let us laugh until our sides do ache,
And let the joy of laughter never break.

Tears:
In tears that fall like raindrops from the sky,
We find the healing balm for every wound,
With every drop, a burden starts to fly,
As tears wash clean the sorrows that have loomed.

With every sob, a heart begins to mend,
In tears' release, we find our strength anew,
As every teardrop is a message sent,
From deepest wells of emotion, pure and true.

For in the tears, lies the heart's lament,
A testament to love and loss and pain,
In every drop, a memory is sent,
As tears become the music of the rain.

So let us shed our tears, without regret,
And find our solace in the tears we've met.

Strength:
In moments dark, where shadows start to creep,
We find the strength to face what lies ahead,
With every challenge, our resolve we keep,
As we rise above the doubts that fill our head.

With every trial, a lesson to be learned,
In strength's embrace, we find our courage bold,
As every obstacle is overturned,
And every victory becomes a stronghold.

For in the strength, lies the heart's resolve,
A fortress built on faith and hope and love,
In every battle, a chance to evolve,
As strength becomes the wings that lift above.

So let us find our strength in times of need,
And face the world with courage and with speed.

Here are four Sonnet poems, 1 each about Vulnerability, Renewal, Acceptance & Mystery

Vulnerability:
In moments soft, when walls begin to fade,
And tender hearts lay bare their fragile truth,
There lies a strength, though at first betrayed,
In vulnerability, we find our youth.

For only in the open, raw and real,
Do we uncover depths we long to share,
Though fear may whisper, urging us to seal
Our hearts away, vulnerability dares.

It is the pathway to connection deep,
To empathy and understanding rare,
Where wounds may heal and secrets we may keep,
In vulnerability, we find repair.

So let us not shy from this sacred space,
For in our weakness, lies our saving grace.

Renewal:
As seasons turn and leaves begin to fall,
We witness nature's wondrous, ageless dance,
For in the cycle, there's a silent call,
To let go, and embrace life's second chance.

In every ending lies a new beginning,
In every loss, a seed of hope is sown,
Renewal whispers in the wind, still spinning,
A promise of rebirth, once seeds are sown.
So let us shed our old, outgrown cocoon,
And spread our wings to greet the morning light,
For in renewal, lies the fullest boon,
As we emerge from shadows into sight.

In every sunset, lies a dawn anew,
In every ending, lies a start to pursue.

Acceptance:
In acceptance, lies the key to peace,
To let go of the battles fought in vain,
To find serenity, and grant release,
From burdens heavy, and from lingering pain.

For in acceptance, we embrace what is,
And let go of the dreams that didn't bloom,
We find contentment in life's gentle kiss,
And in the silence, we find our truest room.

Acceptance doesn't mean we passively resign,
But rather, that we choose to let things be,
To find the beauty in the grand design,
And in surrender, find our souls set free.

So let us open up our hearts to grace,
And find in acceptance, our sacred place.

Mystery:
In the shadows deep, where secrets hide,
And whispers dance in twilight's soft embrace,
There lies a world where truth and falsehoods glide,
In the realm of mystery, we find our space.

For in the unknown, lies the greatest awe,
In questions unanswered, lies our intrigue,
As we explore the depths, we find a flaw,
In the fabric of what we believe.

Yet mystery isn't just about the dark,
But also in the light that shines so bright,
In every star that twinkles, every lark,
In every moment veiled in dawning light.

So let us revel in the mystery,
For in its depths, lies life's grand tapestry.

Here are four Sonnet poems, 1 each about Transformation, Eternity, Cosmos & Happiness

Transformation:
In every moment, change begins to flow,
A metamorphosis, both subtle and profound,
From seed to tree, from rain to snow,
Transformation shapes the world around.

With every breath, a new creation born,
A butterfly emerging from its chrysalis,
A caterpillar no longer, but adorned,
With wings that carry it to realms of bliss.

But transformation isn't just for creatures small,
It's woven in the fabric of all life,
From mountains grand to rivers that enthrall,
It's in the midst of chaos and in strife.

So let us embrace this journey of transition,
For in transformation, lies our true mission.

Eternity:
In the vast expanse of time, we find,
A glimpse of eternity's enduring grace,
From dawn till dusk, from birth till decline,
Eternity's embrace leaves its trace.

For though our days may be but fleeting,
And seasons come and go like shifting sands,
Eternity's heartbeat is unrelenting,
A timeless rhythm where all life stands.

In every heartbeat, echoes of eternity,
In every breath, a whisper of the divine,
For in the midst of life's transitory,
Eternity's presence forever shines.

So let us cherish each moment we are given,
For in eternity, lies the key to living.

Cosmos:
In the vast expanse of space, we find,
A universe of wonder, vast and grand,
From galaxies that dance, to stars that shine,
The cosmos stretches out its hand.

In every constellation, a story told,
Of heroes, gods, and mysteries untold,
In every nebula, a dream unfolds,
In every black hole, secrets to behold.

For though we may be but a speck of dust,
In the grand tapestry of time and space,
Our curiosity fuels our wanderlust,
As we explore the cosmos with grace.

So let us gaze upon the stars above,
And marvel at the cosmos, full of love.

Happiness:
In laughter's echo, happiness resides,
A melody that lifts the spirit high,
In every smile, a universe abides,
In every tear, a reason to defy.

For happiness isn't just a fleeting feeling,
But a state of being, deep and true,
In every moment, joy is revealing,
The beauty of life in all that we pursue.

So let us seek happiness in every corner,
In moments simple, and in grand affairs,
For happiness is not just a foreigner,
But a friend that's with us everywhere.

So let us embrace each moment with delight,
And let happiness fill our hearts tonight.

-:|:-•:*'''''*:•.-:|:-•**•-:|:-•:*'''''*:•:*'''''*:•.-:|:-•**•-:|:--:|:-•:*'''''*:•.-:|:- •**•-:|:-•:*'''''*:•:*'''''*:•.-:|:-•**•-:|:-

HAIKU:

A traditional Japanese form consisting of three lines with a syllable pattern of 5-7-5, typically capturing a moment in nature.

Here are four Haiku poems, 1 each about Love, Nature, Beauty & Time

Love:
Hearts entwined as one,
Eternal flame in the soul,
Love's sweet melody.

Nature:
Trees sway in the breeze,
Mountains kiss the azure sky,
Nature's symphony.

Beauty:
Petals soft as silk,
Sunset's hues paint the skyline,
Beauty in each breath.

Time:
Sand slips through the glass,
Moments fleeting, never last,
Time's relentless march.

Here are four Haiku poems, 1 each about Death, Dreams, Hope & Despair

Death:
Silent whispers hush,
Eternal sleep claims the soul,
Death's final embrace.

Dreams:
Whispers in the night,
Visions dance in slumber's realm,
Dreams weave tales untold.

Hope:
Light breaks through the clouds,
A beacon in the darkest night,
Hope's gentle embrace.

Despair:
Shadows cloak the heart,
Soul consumed by endless night,
Despair's heavy weight.

Here are four Haiku poems, 1 each about Friendship, Loneliness, Memories & Music

Friendship:
Hands held in the dark,
Kindred spirits, hearts entwined,
Friendship's guiding light.

Loneliness:
Echoes in the void,
Silent tears in solitude,
Loneliness takes hold.

Memories:
Echoes of laughter,
Fragments of moments gone by,
Memories linger.

Music:
Notes dance on the air,
Melodies that touch the soul,
Music's sweet refrain.

Here are four Haiku poems, 1 each about Art, Inspiration, Creativity & Courage

Art:
Brush strokes on canvas,
Expressions of the human heart,
Art's timeless beauty.

Inspiration:
Whispers in the wind,
Creativity's gentle muse,
Inspiration's call.

Creativity:
Imagination soars,
Boundless realms of possibility,
Creativity blooms.

Courage:
Heart beats strong and true,
Facing fears with steady resolve,
Courageous spirit.

Here are four Haiku poems, 1 each about Faith, Doubt, Solitude & Joy

Faith:
Light in darkest night,
Guiding star in stormy seas,
Faith's unwavering.

Doubt:
Shadows cloud the mind,
Uncertainty's silent grip,
Doubt's endless whisper.

Solitude:
Quiet whispers soft,
In the hush, the soul finds rest,
Solitude's embrace.

Joy:
Sunshine on my face,
Heart sings with joy, spirits soar,
Joy's sweet symphony.

Here are four Haiku poems, 1 each about Sorrow, Childhood, Wisdom & Innocence

Sorrow:
Tears fall like raindrops,
Heart heavy with sorrow's weight,
Grief clouds the sunrise.

Childhood:
Laughter fills the air,
Innocence in every smile,
Childhood's precious grace.

Wisdom:
Ancient tree stands tall,
Whispering secrets of time,
Wisdom in its leaves.

Innocence:
Eyes wide with wonder,
Unspoiled by the world's harshness,
Innocence's light.

Here are four Haiku poems, 1 each about Passion, Serenity, Freedom & Justice

Passion:
Fire burns within,
Heart ablaze with fervent flame,
Passion ignites life.

Serenity:
Silent lake reflects,
Peace envelops weary soul,
Serenity reigns.

Freedom:
Wings spread wide, we soar,
Boundless skies call out to us,
Freedom in our flight.

Justice:
Scales tip with fairness,
Blindfolded lady stands tall,
Justice finds its way.

Here are four Haiku poems, 1 each about Change, Resilience, Gratitude & Forgiveness

Change:
Seasons shift and turn,
Leaves fall, buds bloom, rivers flow,
Change is constant truth.

Resilience:
Battered by the storm,
Yet still standing tall and strong,
Resilience prevails.

Gratitude:
Heart brimming with thanks,
For every blessing bestowed,
Gratitude's sweet song.

Forgiveness:
Burdens laid aside,
Hearts unburdened by grudges,
Forgiveness sets free.

Here are four Haiku poems, 1 each about Longing, Belonging, Discovery & Wonder

Longing:
Echoes in the night,
Yearning for what's out of reach,
Longing fills the void.

Belonging:
Hands clasped together,
Hearts beat in harmonious rhythm,
Belonging is found.

Discovery:
Footprints in the sand,
Unveiling treasures untold,
Discovery's joy.

Wonder:
Eyes wide with wonder,
Marveling at nature's grace,
Wonder lights the soul.

Here are four Haiku poems, 1 each about Journey, Reflection, Harmony & Imagination

Journey:
Steps echo softly,
Paths winding into the mist,
Adventure beckons.

Reflection:
Still pond mirrors sky,
Thoughts ripple through calm waters,
Self-found in stillness.

Harmony:
Birdsong fills the air,
Nature's symphony in tune,
Peace in every note.

Imagination:
Dreams painted on air,
Worlds unseen by mortal eye,
Imagination.

Here are four Haiku poems, 1 each about Silence, Laughter, Tears & Strength

Silence:
Quiet whispers soft,
In the hush, the soul finds rest,
Silence speaks volumes.

Laughter:
Giggles like raindrops,
Echoes of joy fill the air,
Laughter's melody.

Tears:
Crystal drops cascade,
Emotions flow like rivers,
Tears cleanse the soul's wounds.

Strength:
Roots firm in the earth,
Weathering storms, bending not,
Strength found in stillness.

Here are four Haiku poems, 1 each about Vulnerability, Renewal, Acceptance & Mystery

Vulnerability:
Naked soul exposed,
Raw and open to the world,
Vulnerability.

Renewal:
Spring's gentle embrace,
Life bursting forth from the earth,
Renewal's sweet kiss.

Acceptance:
Embracing flaws and scars,
Finding peace in imperfection,
Acceptance blooms bright.

Mystery:
Stars twinkle above,
Secrets whispered in the night,
Mystery untold.

Here are four Haiku poems, 1 each about Transformation, Eternity, Cosmos & Happiness

Transformation:
Caterpillar's crawl,
Emerges as butterfly,
Transformation.

Eternity:
Infinity's grasp,
Time's endless dance in the void,
Eternity's hold.

Cosmos:
Galaxies collide,
Stars twinkle in the abyss,
Cosmos unfolds wide.

Happiness:
Sunshine on my face,
Heart sings with joy, spirits soar,
Happiness abounds.

-:¦:-•:*'''''*:•.-:¦:-•**•-:¦:-•:*'''''*:•:*'''''*:•.-:¦:-•**•-:¦:--:¦:-•:*'''''*:•.-:¦:- •**•-:¦:-•:*'''''*:•:*'''''*:•.-:¦:-•**•-:¦:-

FREE VERSE:

Poetry without a fixed meter or rhyme scheme, allowing for greater freedom in expression.

Here are four Free Verse poems, 1 each about Love, Nature, Beauty & Time

Love:
Love is the gentle whisper of the heart,
The melody that soothes the soul.
It is the bond that ties us together,
And the force that makes us whole.

Love is the warmth of a tender embrace,
The sparkle in a lover's eye.
It is the laughter that fills the air,
And the tears that we cry.

Love is the eternal flame that burns,
A beacon in the darkest night.
It is the greatest gift we can give,
And the greatest joy we can find.

Nature:
Nature is the symphony of life,
The chorus of birdsong at dawn.
It is the dance of the trees in the breeze,
And the rush of the river as it flows.

Nature is the palette of colors in the sky,
The tapestry of flowers in bloom.
It is the scent of rain on the wind,
And the kiss of the sun on my skin.

Nature is the rhythm of the seasons,
The cycle of birth and rebirth.
It is the reminder that we are but a part,
Of something greater than ourselves.

Beauty:
Beauty is the softness of a rose petal,
The shimmer of sunlight on water.
It is the curve of a smile,
And the twinkle of an eye.

Beauty is the harmony of form and function,
The elegance of simplicity.
It is the feeling of awe and wonder,
That takes our breath away.

Beauty is not just what we see,
But what we feel in our hearts.
For true beauty lies in the eye of the beholder,
And in the appreciation of the world around us.

Time:
Time is the river that flows ever onward,
The constant companion on life's journey.
It is the ticking of the clock,
And the turning of the seasons.

Time is the measure of our days,
The currency of our lives.
It is the reminder that nothing lasts forever,
And that every moment is precious.

Time is the healer of wounds,
The revealer of truths.
It is the teacher that imparts wisdom,
And the force that shapes our destiny.

Here are four Free Verse poems, 1 each about Death, Dreams, Hope & Despair

Death:
Death is the final curtain call,
The closing act of life's grand play.
It is the passage into the unknown,
The journey beyond the veil.

Death is the great equalizer,
The fate that awaits us all.
It is the end of one chapter,
And the beginning of another.

But death is not the end,
But a transition into something new.
For in the cycle of life and death,
We find the promise of renewal.

Dreams:
Dreams are the whispers of the heart,
The visions that dance in the darkness.
They are the spark of inspiration,
The fuel that drives us forward.

Dreams are the blueprints of our future,
The roadmap to our destiny.
They are the canvas on which we paint,
The tapestry of our desires.

But dreams are not just fantasies,
But the seeds of possibility.
For in the pursuit of our dreams,
We find the truest expression of ourselves.

Hope:
Hope is the light that shines in the darkness,
The beacon that guides us through the storm.
It is the belief in a better tomorrow,
And the courage to keep moving forward.

Hope is the promise of possibility,
The assurance that all will be well.
It is the strength to face adversity,
And the resilience to overcome.

But hope is not just wishful thinking,
But a force to be reckoned with.
For in the power of hope,
We find the strength to persevere.

Despair:
Despair is the shadow that lurks in the corners,
The darkness that clouds the mind.
It is the feeling of being lost,
And the belief that all is hopeless.

Despair is the weight that presses down,
The anchor that keeps us from moving forward.
It is the voice that whispers in the silence,
And the hand that pulls us under.

But despair is not the end,
But a challenge to be overcome.
For in the depths of despair,
We find the strength to rise again.

Here are four Free Verse poems, 1 each about Friendship, Loneliness, Memories & Music

Friendship:
Friendship's a woven tapestry of laughter and tears,
A bond that transcends distance and years.
It is the hand that reaches out in times of need,
The shoulder to lean on, the friend indeed.

It is the shared moments of joy and sorrow,
The inside jokes that last until tomorrow.
Friendship is a treasure, rare and true,
A precious gift that enriches life anew.

Loneliness:
Loneliness a silent companion that shadows my steps,
A weight that presses down on my chest.
It is the empty room, the silent phone,
The ache in my heart when I'm all alone.

Loneliness is a cold wind that chills me to the bone,
A void that echoes with the sound of my own.
Longing for connection, the yearning for touch,
The desperate search for someone to love me much.

Memories:
Memory whispers of the past that linger in the air,
Echoes of laughter, traces of care.
They are the snapshots of moments frozen in time,
Treasures that we hold dear, the stories that we mime.

Memories are the colors that paint the canvas of lives,
Threads that weave together our joys and our strives.
The map of where we've been, to where we'll go,
The reminder that we are never truly alone.

Music:
Music is the language of soul, the melody of the heart,
The rhythm that moves us, the beat that sets us apart.
It is the symphony of life, the harmony of the spheres,
Songs that soothes sorrows, the anthem of our cheers.

The soundtrack to lives and to our dreams,
The soundtrack to our hopes, our fears, our schemes.

The bridge that connects to language that we share,
The universal language that unites us everywhere.

Here are four Free Verse poems, 1 each about Art, Inspiration, Creativity & Courage

Faith:
Faith is the whisper of the unseen,
The echo of belief in the silence of doubt.
It is the anchor in the tempest,
The unwavering compass in the storm.

Faith is the light that flickers in the darkness,
The hand that reaches out in the abyss.
It is the song of hope in the quiet night,
The promise of dawn after the longest night.

It is the trust in the unseen,
The belief in the impossible,
And the knowing that, despite the odds,
All will be well in the end.

Doubt:
Doubt is the shadow that lingers in the corners,
The whisper of uncertainty that clouds the mind.
It is the voice that questions,
The hand that trembles, unsure.

Doubt is the nagging feeling in the heart,
The hesitation in the step.
It is the fear of the unknown,
And the worry that we may not be enough.

But doubt is also the seed of growth,
The catalyst for change.
For it is in questioning that we find answers,
And in uncertainty that we find clarity.

Solitude:
Solitude is the sanctuary of the soul,
The quiet refuge in the chaos of life.
It is the space between the noise,
The pause in the cacophony.

Solitude is the stillness of the early morning,
The hush of the midnight hour.
It is the calm in the eye of the storm,
And the peace that comes with being alone.

In solitude, we find ourselves,
And in the quiet, we find our voice.
For it is in the silence that we hear the whispers of our hearts,
And in the solitude that we find our truest selves.

Joy:
Joy is the laughter that bubbles up from within,
The warmth that spreads through the chest.
It is the lightness of being,
The dance of the soul.

Joy is the smile on a stranger's face,
The hug of a loved one,
And the beauty of a sunrise.
It is the simple pleasures of life,
The moments of connection,
And the feeling of being fully alive.

In joy, we find gratitude,
And in gratitude, we find joy.
For it is in the moments of purest happiness,
That we are most truly ourselves.

Here are four Free Verse poems, 1 each about Faith, Doubt, Solitude & Joy

Faith
Faith is the whisper of hope in the darkness,
The unseen hand that guides me through the night,
And the unwavering belief that all will be well,
Even when the world seems to crumble around me.

It is the trust that I place in something greater,
A force that transcends the boundaries of the known,
And sustains me through the trials and tribulations,
With the promise of light at the end of the tunnel.

Faith is not blind obedience or unquestioning belief,
But a deep-seated conviction that carries me forward,
And gives me the strength to face whatever may come,
With courage, resilience, and unwavering resolve.

Doubt:
Doubts shadows that lurks in the corners of my mind,
The nagging voice that whispers in the silence,
And the seed of uncertainty that takes root and grows,
Casting doubt on everything I thought I knew.

It is the questioning of my beliefs and convictions,
The wrestling match between heart and mind,
And the fear of making the wrong choice,
In a world filled with endless possibilities.

Doubt is not a sign of weakness or failure,
But a natural part of the human experience,
A reminder to approach life with humility and openness,
And to embrace the uncertainty that comes with growth.

Solitude:
Solitude is the sanctuary of the soul,
The quiet refuge where I find peace,
And the space to reconnect with myself,
Away from the noise and distractions of the world.

It is the stillness of the early morning,
The gentle rustle of leaves in the breeze,
And the serenity that washes over me,
As I sink into the embrace of solitude.

Solitude is not loneliness or isolation,
But a choice to be alone with my thoughts,
And to listen to the whispers of my heart,
In a world that often feels too loud and chaotic.

Joy:
Joy is the laughter that bubbles up from within,
The warmth that spreads through my chest,
And the lightness of being that fills my soul,
When I am fully present in the moment.

It is the simple pleasures of everyday life,
The smile of a loved one, the beauty of nature,
And the sense of connection that binds us together,
In a tapestry of shared experiences and emotions.

Joy is not dependent on external circumstances,
But a state of being that arises from within,
A reflection of the gratitude and appreciation,
That fills my heart with boundless happiness.

Here are four Free Verse poems, 1 each about Sorrow, Childhood, Wisdom & Innocence

Sorrow:
Sorrow is the heavy cloak that wraps around my shoulders,
A shroud of darkness that weighs me down,
And envelops me in its suffocating embrace,
Leaving me gasping for breath in its wake.

It is the ache in my chest, the lump in my throat,
And the tears that blur my vision,
As I navigate the depths of despair,
And struggle to find my way back to the light.

Sorrow is not just a feeling, but a force,
A tidal wave of emotion that threatens to consume me,
And yet, in its depths, I find a strange kind of beauty,
A rawness and vulnerability that connects me to the heart of humanity.

Childhood:
Childhood is a patchwork quilt of memories,
A kaleidoscope of colors and textures,
That weave together to form the fabric of my identity,
And shape the person I have become.

It is the laughter that echoes through the hallways,
The games played in the backyard,
And the stories shared beneath the covers,
As we drift off to sleep.

Childhood is not just a stage of life, but a state of mind,
A time of innocence and wonder,
When the world was full of magic and possibility,
And every day held the promise of adventure.

Wisdom:
Wisdom is the steady hand that guides me,
The voice of reason in a world of chaos,
And the beacon of light that leads me through the darkness,
With grace and humility.

It is the lessons learned from mistakes made,
The insights gained from challenges faced,
And the understanding that comes with time,
And experience.

Wisdom is not just knowledge, but understanding,
A deep-seated knowing that transcends the intellect,
And touches the soul,
With the timeless truths of the universe.

Innocence:
Innocence is the purity of a child's laughter,
The twinkle in their eyes, and the joy in their heart,
As they navigate the world with wide-eyed wonder,
And open hearts.

It is the belief in the goodness of humanity,
The trust placed in the hands of strangers,
And the uncomplicated love that knows no bounds,
Or conditions.

Innocence is not naivety, but a state of being,
A precious gift that must be cherished and protected,
For in its gentle embrace,
We find the true essence of our humanity.

Here are four Free Verse poems, 1 each about Passion, Serenity, Freedom & Justice

Passion:
In the depths of my soul,
There burns a flame,
A fire that ignites my spirit,
And drives me forward.

It is the passion that fuels my dreams,
That fills my heart with purpose,
And gives me the strength
To pursue what sets my soul on fire.

For passion is not just a feeling,
But a force,
A driving energy that propels me
Towards my greatest desires.

Serenity:
In the stillness of the morning,
I find serenity,
A calmness that washes over me,
And soothes my troubled mind.

It is the peace that comes with acceptance,
With letting go of control,
And surrendering to the flow
Of life's gentle currents.

For serenity is not found in the absence of chaos,
But in the midst of it,
In the quiet moments of reflection,
And the gentle whispers of the heart.

Freedom:
Freedom is the open road,
The wind in my hair,
And the world stretched out before me,
In all its boundless possibility.

It is the ability to choose my own path,
To follow my heart's desire,
And to live my life on my own terms,
Without fear or constraint.

For freedom is not just a right,
But a privilege,
A precious gift that must be cherished,
And protected at all costs.

Justice:
In the halls of power,
I find justice,
A force for righteousness,
And a beacon of hope for the oppressed.

It is the pursuit of equality,
Of fairness and accountability,
And the unwavering commitment
To righting the wrongs of the world.

For justice is not just a concept,
But a call to action,
A rallying cry for change,
And a promise of a better tomorrow.

Here are four Free Verse poems, 1 each about Change, Resilience, Gratitude & Forgiveness

Change:
Change is the river that flows through life,
Eroding the shores of familiarity,
Carving new paths through the landscape,
And shaping the contours of our destiny.

It is the constant companion of time,
A force that sweeps away the old,
And ushers in the new,
With each passing moment.

Change is neither friend nor foe,
But a catalyst for growth,
A reminder that nothing stays the same,
And that transformation is inevitable.

Resilience:
Resilience is the steel in my spine,
The unwavering strength that lies within,
And the determination to stand tall,
No matter what life throws my way.

It is the ability to bend without breaking,
To weather the storm with grace,
And to rise again, stronger than before,
In the face of adversity.

Resilience is not about avoiding pain,
But about embracing it,
And using it as fuel for growth,
And a reminder of my own inner strength.

Gratitude:
Gratitude is the gentle rain that nourishes the soul,
The warmth of the sun on a cold winter's day,
And the embrace of loved ones after a long journey.

It is the recognition of all that I have been given,
And the acknowledgment of the blessings in my life,
Both big and small, seen and unseen,
That fill my heart with joy and appreciation.

Gratitude is not just a feeling,
But a practice,
A daily reminder to count my blessings,
And to give thanks for the abundance that surrounds me.

Forgiveness:
Forgiveness is the balm that heals the wounds of the past,
The key that unlocks the chains of resentment,
And the pathway to liberation and peace.

It is the act of letting go of anger and resentment,
And releasing the hold that past hurts have on my heart,
So that I can move forward with love and compassion,
And reclaim my own inner peace.

Forgiveness is not about condoning the actions of others,
But about freeing myself from the burden of anger,
And opening my heart to the possibility of healing,
And the transformative power of love.

Here are four Free Verse poems, 1 each about Longing, Belonging, Discovery & Wonder

Longing:
In the quiet hours of the night,
When the world is still and hushed,
I feel the tug of longing in my chest,
A yearning for something just out of reach.

It is a longing for connection,
For understanding,
For a sense of purpose that eludes me,
Like a distant star in the night sky.

I ache for the warmth of a hand in mine,
For the comfort of arms wrapped around me,
For the solace of knowing that I am not alone,
In this vast and sometimes lonely world.

Belonging:
In the embrace of community,
I find a sense of belonging,
A feeling of being seen and understood,
For who I truly am.

It is in the laughter of friends,
The shared moments of joy and sorrow,
The feeling of being part of something greater,
That I find my place in the world.

For belonging is not just about fitting in,
But about being accepted,
For the unique and wonderful individual
That I am.

Discovery:
In the uncharted depths of the unknown,
I find the thrill of discovery,
The exhilaration of uncovering secrets
That have long been hidden.

It is in the rush of adrenaline,
The tingling sensation of excitement,
The feeling of stepping into the great unknown,
And coming out forever changed.

For discovery is not just about finding new places,
But about finding new parts of myself,
And expanding the boundaries of what I thought possible,
In this vast and wondrous world.

Wonder:
In the beauty of a sunrise,
The majesty of a mountain range,
The intricacy of a snowflake,
I find wonder.

It is in the small miracles of everyday life,
The simple joys that fill my heart with gratitude,
The awe-inspiring moments that take my breath away,
And remind me of the magic that surrounds me.

For wonder is not just about seeing the world,
But about seeing it with fresh eyes,
And finding joy and amazement in the little things,
That make life worth living.

Here are four Free Verse poems, 1 each about Journey, Reflection, Harmony & Imagination

Journey:
Life is a journey,
A winding path that twists and turns,
Leading us down unexpected roads,
And through uncharted territory.

It is a journey of self-discovery,
Of growth and change,
Of triumphs and setbacks,
And of learning to embrace the unknown.

Along the way, we encounter obstacles,
And challenges that test our strength,
But also moments of joy and beauty,
That make the journey worthwhile.

For it is not the destination that matters,
But the journey itself,
And the lessons we learn,
Along the way.

Reflection:
In moments of quiet contemplation,
I find solace in reflection,
A chance to look back on where I've been,
And to ponder where I'm going.

It is a time for introspection,
For examining my thoughts and feelings,
And for gaining insight into myself,
And the world around me.

Through reflection, I come to understand,
The choices I've made,
The paths I've taken,
And the person I've become.

For it is in reflection,
That I find clarity,
And the wisdom to chart my course,
With purpose and intention.

Harmony:
In the symphony of life,
I find harmony,
A delicate balance of light and dark,
Of joy and sorrow,
Of chaos and calm.

It is in the rhythm of the seasons,
The ebb and flow of the tides,
The give and take of the natural world,
That I find peace.

For harmony is not just about balance,
But about finding unity,
In the diversity of existence,
And embracing the interconnectedness,
Of all things.

Imagination:
In the boundless expanse of the mind,
I find imagination,
A world of infinite possibilities,
Where anything is possible,
And nothing is off-limits.

It is in the flights of fancy,
The dreams that soar beyond the stars,
The visions that dance in the shadows,
That I find inspiration.

For imagination is not just about creating,
But about exploring,
And pushing the boundaries of what is known,
To discover what lies beyond.

Here are four Free Verse poems, 1 each about Silence, Laughter, Tears & Strength

Silence:
In the quiet depths of silence,
I find solace, I find peace.
No words to clutter the mind,
No noise to distract the soul.

In the stillness, I hear the whispers
Of my own heart,
And the gentle rustle of leaves
In the breeze.

Silence is not empty,
But full of possibilities,
A canvas waiting to be painted
With the colors of my thoughts.

Laughter:
Laughter dances like sunlight
Across a field of wildflowers,
Brightening even the darkest corners
Of the soul.

It bubbles up from within,
A symphony of joy,
Echoing through the chambers
Of the heart.

In laughter, I find release,
I find connection,
I find the purest expression
Of my humanity.

Tears:
Tears fall like raindrops
From a stormy sky,
Each one a testament
To the depth of my emotions.

They flow freely,
Unencumbered by shame,
For in their release,
I find healing.

Tears are not a sign of weakness,
But of strength,
A reminder that even in our darkest moments,
There is beauty to be found.

Strength:
Strength is not measured
By the size of my muscles
Or the fierceness of my gaze,
But by the resilience of my spirit.

It is the quiet determination
To keep moving forward
In the face of adversity,
To rise again after every fall.

Strength is not found
In the absence of fear,
But in the courage to face it,
And the wisdom to know
That I am capable of overcoming it.

Here are four Free Verse poems, 1 each about Vulnerability, Renewal, Acceptance & Mystery

Vulnerability:
To be vulnerable is to be human,
To open myself up to the world,
And risk being seen,
In all my imperfect glory.

It is to lay bare my soul,
And invite others to do the same,
To forge connections
That transcend the superficial.

Vulnerability is not weakness,
But a source of strength,
A testament to the courage
It takes to truly live.

Renewal:
In the quiet stillness of the dawn,
I find renewal,
A chance to begin again,
To let go of what no longer serves me,
And embrace what lies ahead.

Like a phoenix rising from the ashes,
I emerge from the darkness,
Reborn and revitalized,
Ready to face whatever challenges
Life may bring.

Renewal is not a one-time event,
But a constant process,
A journey of growth and transformation,
That leads me ever closer
To my truest self.

Acceptance:
To accept is to let go,
To release the need for control,
And surrender to the flow of life.

It is to embrace the present moment,
And all that it contains,
Without judgment or resistance.

Acceptance is not resignation,
But a profound act of love,
For myself and for others,
A recognition of our shared humanity,
And the beauty that lies within it.

Mystery:
In the depths of the unknown,
I find mystery,
A tantalizing glimpse
Of something greater than myself.

It is the unanswered questions
That drive me to explore,
To seek out the secrets
That lie just beyond my grasp.

Mystery is not something to be feared,
But embraced,
For it is the spark
That ignites my curiosity,
And fuels my sense of wonder.

Here are four Free Verse poems, 1 each about Transformation, Eternity, Cosmos & Happiness

Transformation:
In the quiet moments of becoming,
We shed our old skin, like the snake,
Embracing the unfamiliar stretch
Of new beginnings, of uncharted paths.

We bloom, not in bursts of color,
But in the slow unfurling of petals,
Each fold revealing a story of growth,
Of shedding the weight of yesterday.

Transformation is the dance of the soul,
A journey of shedding and becoming,
A metamorphosis of self and spirit,
As we embrace the ever-changing tides of life.

Eternity:
Time is but a whisper in the vast expanse
Of eternity, where stars are born and die,
And galaxies collide in cosmic ballets,
Leaving trails of stardust in their wake.

In the tapestry of eternity, we are but threads,
Woven into the fabric of the universe,
Our lives mere blinks in the eye of infinity,
Yet each moment etched into the fabric of time.

Eternity is the silent symphony of the cosmos,
A melody that echoes through the ages,
A timeless dance of light and shadow,
Where past, present, and future converge.

Cosmos:
In the vast expanse of the cosmos,
Stars twinkle like diamonds in the velvet sky,
Galaxies spiral in cosmic ballets,
And nebulae shimmer with ethereal light.

We are but specks of stardust,
Born from the heart of exploding stars,
Our souls intertwined with the fabric of space,
Our destinies written in the constellations.

The cosmos is the cradle of creation,
A tapestry of light and darkness,
Where galaxies are born and die,
And the mysteries of the universe unfold.

Happiness:
Happiness is the gentle sigh of contentment,
The warmth of sunlight on a winter's day,
The laughter that bubbles up from within,
And the embrace of loved ones after a long journey.

It is the simple pleasures of life,
A walk in the park on a sunny afternoon,
The taste of freshly baked bread,
And the sound of rain tapping on the window.

Happiness is not a destination,
But a journey of discovery,
A state of mind that blooms from within,
And radiates out into the world

-:¦:-•:*'''''*:•.-:¦:-•**•-:¦:-•:*''''''*:•:*'''''*:•.-:¦:-•**•-:¦:--:¦:-•:*'''''*:•.-:¦:- •**•-:¦:-•:*''''''*:•:*''''''*:•.-:¦:-•**•-:¦:-

LIMERICK:

A humorous poem consisting of five lines with a strict AABBA rhyme scheme, often featuring witty or nonsensical subject matter.

Here are four Limerick poems, 1 each about Love, Nature, Beauty & Time

Love:
There once was a love pure and true,
That blossomed like morning dew.
With hearts intertwined,
And souls aligned,
In love, they found skies ever blue.

Nature:
There once was a forest so grand,
With trees stretching over the land.
With birds in the air,
And creatures so rare,
In nature, they felt life's soft hand.

Beauty:
There once was a sight to behold,
With colors more precious than gold.
With a sunset so bright,
And stars in the night,
In beauty, their hearts would enfold.

Time:
There once was a clock ticking by,
With seconds that seemed to fly.
With each passing hour,
And a moment to devour,
In time, they'd embrace and comply.

Here are four Limerick poems, 1 each about Death, Dreams, Hope & Despair

Death:
There once was a soul that did roam,
Beyond the threshold of life's home.
With a sigh and a breath,
It embraced the cold death,
In death, they found peace to atone.

Dreams:
There once was a dream so bright,
That soared high like a kite.
With wings to fly,
And stars in the sky,
In dreams, they found endless flight.

Hope:
There once was a hope so true,
That whispered through the morning dew.
With each rising sun,
A new day begun,
In hope, they found dreams anew.

Despair:
There once was a heart filled with woe,
That wandered where no light could go.
With tears in their eyes,
And endless cries,
In despair, they felt the dark's blow.

Here are four Limerick poems, 1 each about Friendship, Loneliness, Memories & Music

Friendship:
There once were two pals, hand in hand,
Through thick and thin, they'd make their stand.
With laughter and cheer,
And a bond so dear,
In friendship, they found their promised land.

Loneliness:
There once was a soul all alone,
Whose heart felt like it was stone.
With nobody near,
And nothing to cheer,
In loneliness, it felt overthrown.

Memories:
There once were some memories sweet,
Of moments shared in life's fleet.
With laughter and tears,
And joys through the years,
In memories, they found their heartbeat.

Music:
There once was a song in the air,
With notes that could banish despair.
With rhythm and rhyme,
And melody prime,
In music, they found love everywhere.

Here are four Limerick poems, 1 each about Art, Inspiration, Creativity & Courage

Art:
There once was a canvas so bare,
Waiting for colors to wear.
With brushstrokes so fine,
And colors divine,
In art, they found beauty to share.

Inspiration:

There once was a spark in the dark,
That ignited a creative remark.
With passion and zest,
And dreams manifest,
In inspiration, they'd make their mark.

Creativity:
There once was an idea so grand,
That flourished with a steady hand.
With imagination's flight,
And ideas taking height,
In creativity, they'd expand.

Courage:

There once was a heart brave and bold,
That faced fears, not letting them hold.
With a step and a leap,
They'd face the steep,
In courage, they'd find their stronghold.

Here are four Limerick poems, 1 each about Faith, Doubt, Solitude & Joy

Faith:
There once was a belief so true,
That carried them through and through.
With trust in the unseen,
And a heart serene,
In faith, they knew what to pursue.

Doubt:
There once was a mind filled with doubt,
That wondered what life was about.
With questions so deep,
And worries to keep,
In doubt, they searched for a route.

Solitude:
There once was a moment of quiet,
Where thoughts danced in the hush of the night.
With a breath and a sigh,
One could hear their own heartbeat's cry,
In solitude, the world felt just right.

Joy:
There once was a heart filled with glee,
That danced like leaves on a tree.
With laughter and song,
It skipped all day long,
For in joy, they felt truly free.

Here are four Limerick poems, 1 each about Sorrow, Childhood, Wisdom & Innocence

Sorrow:
There once was a heart filled with woe,
Whose tears would often freely flow.
With a sigh and a moan,
It felt so alone,
In sorrow, it learned to let go.

Childhood:
There once was a child full of glee,
Whose laughter echoed through the tree.
With games and with toys,
And endless joys,
In childhood, they danced wild and free.

Wisdom:
There once was a sage, old and wise,
Whose words were like pearls in disguise.
With a nod and a smile,
They'd ponder awhile,
In wisdom, they found truth that flies.

Innocence:
There once was a spirit so pure,
Whose heart was forever unsure.
With eyes wide and bright,
And dreams taking flight,
In innocence, they'd always endure.

Here are four Limerick poems, 1 each about Passion, Serenity, Freedom & Justice

Passion:
There once was a flame burning bright,
With passion that soared to great height.
With fervor and heat,
It couldn't be beat,
In passion, they found their true light.

Serenity:
There once was a soul so serene,
Whose calmness was rarely seen.
With a breath and a sigh,
They'd reach for the sky,
In serenity, they felt like a queen.

Freedom:
There once was a spirit so free,
Whose wings could soar over the sea.
With wind in their hair,
And without a care,
In freedom, they felt truly glee.

Justice:
There once was a hero so bold,
Whose story was often retold.
With a fight and a stand,
They'd lend a helping hand,
For in justice, they'd never fold.

Here are four Limerick poems, 1 each about Change, Resilience, Gratitude & Forgiveness

Change:
There once was a world in a flux,
Where change would often come in trucks.
With a shift and a turn,
Things would twist and burn,
In change, they'd learn to not be stuck.

Resilience:
There once was a heart made of steel,
Whose strength would always reveal.
With a bounce and a leap,
They'd rise from the deep,
In resilience, they'd never kneel.

Gratitude:
There once was a soul full of grace,
Whose thanks could fill up all space.
With a smile and a nod,
They'd give thanks to their god,
In gratitude, they found their place.

Forgiveness:
There once was a spirit so kind,
Whose heart was so open, entwined.
With a hug and a kiss,
They'd erase all amiss,
In forgiveness, they left behind.

Here are four Limerick poems, 1 each about Longing, Belonging, Discovery & Wonder

Longing:
There once was a sailor at sea,
Who longed for the land, don't you see?
With each wave that he crossed,
His heart felt so lost,
In longing for where he'd be free.

Belonging:
There once was a bird in the sky,
Who longed for a flock flying by.
With a flap and a flutter,
It found its true mutter,
In belonging, it soared oh so high.

Discovery:
There once was an explorer bold,
Who sought treasures and stories untold.
In the depths of the unknown,
With each journey, it had shown,
Discovery was a sight to behold.

Wonder:
There once was a child with wide eyes,
Who saw magic in the starry skies.
With a heart full of awe,
And a sense of pure awe,
In wonder, the world held no lies.

Here are four Limerick poems, 1 each about Journey, Reflection, Harmony & Imagination

Journey:
There once was a traveler so keen,
Who ventured to lands yet unseen.
With a map and a pack,
And a mind that won't crack,
The journey was all he could dream.

Reflection:
There once was a thinker profound,
Who pondered the truths that he found.
In the stillness of thought,
With wisdom he sought,
Reflection turned his world around.

Harmony:
There once was a choir so grand,
Whose voices were perfectly planned.
In a melody so sweet,
Each note would repeat,
Harmony was where they would stand.

Imagination:
There once was a dreamer so wise,
Who soared through the limitless skies.
With a mind full of flight,
And colors so bright,
Imagination opened their eyes.

Here are four Limerick poems, 1 each about Silence, Laughter, Tears & Strength

Silence:
There once was a moment of quiet,
Where thoughts danced in the hush of the night.
In the calm, still and deep,
One could hear their own heartbeat,
In silence, the world felt just right.

Laughter:
There once was a jester so merry,
Whose jokes were oftentimes quite scary.
But with a chuckle and grin,
Laughter would begin,
For in mirth, the heart is never wary.

Tears:
There once was a heart filled with sorrow,
Whose tears flowed like rain tomorrow.
But with each drop that fell,
It broke through its shell,
For in tears, there's strength to borrow.

Strength:
There once was a warrior so bold,
Whose spirit could never be sold.
With courage and might,
They stood up to the fight,
For in strength, their story was told.

Here are four Limerick poems, 1 each about Vulnerability, Renewal, Acceptance & Mystery

Vulnerability:
There once was a soul soft and tender,
Whose heart, it did often surrender.
In the face of the unknown,
It would tremble and moan,
But in vulnerability, it found splendor.

Renewal:
There once was a bud in the spring,
That awaited the song birds to sing.
With each drop of rain,
It shed old, grew anew again,
In renewal, it found its truest ring.
In the mystery, the secrets did keep.

Acceptance:
There once was a soul filled with doubt,
Who feared what life's twists were about.
But with time, it learned well,
To embrace each tale it did tell,
In acceptance, it found its way out.

Mystery:
There once was a night dark and deep,
Where secrets and shadows did creep.
In the silence, whispers spoke,
Of mysteries beyond the smoke,
In the mystery, the secrets did keep.

Here are four Limerick poems, 1 each about Transformation, Eternity, Cosmos & Happiness

Transformation:
There once was a caterpillar small,
Who dreamed of soaring above it all.
It spun silk to its cocoon,
In the light of the moon,
And emerged as a butterfly, tall.

Eternity:
There once was a star in the sky,
Whose light seemed to never say bye.
It burned bright through the night,
In a dance of eternal light,
For in eternity, it would never die.

Cosmos:
There once was a cosmos so vast,
With galaxies swirling so fast.
In the depths of space,
There was no set pace,
For the cosmos, it held time in its grasp.

Happiness:
There once was a heart filled with glee,
That danced like leaves on a tree.
With laughter and song,
It skipped all day long,
For in happiness, it felt truly free.

-:¦:-•:*'''''*:•.-:¦:-•**•-:¦:-•:*'''''*:•:*'''''*:•.-:¦:-•**•-:¦:--:¦:-•:*'''''*:•.-:¦:- •**•-:¦:-•:*'''''*:•:*'''''*:•.-:¦:-•**•-:¦:-

ODE:

A lyrical poem praising a person, event, or thing, often written in a formal and elevated style.

-:¦:-•:*'''''*:•.-:¦:-•**•-:¦:-•:*''''''*:•:*'''''*:•.-:¦:-•**•-:¦:--:¦:-•:*'''''*:•.-:¦:- •**•-:¦:-•:*'''''*:•:*'''''*:•.-:¦:-•**•-:¦:-

Here are four Ode poems, 1 each about Love, Nature, Beauty & Time

Ode to Love:

Oh, love, eternal flame that warms the heart,
In thy embrace, we find our truest part.
From the tender touch of hands entwined,
To the vows spoken beneath the stars aligned.

Thou art the passion that ignites the soul,
The bond that makes us feel whole.
In thy love, we find our deepest connection,
And in thy devotion, our souls find perfection.

So let us cherish thee, oh love so divine,
For in thy love, our spirits entwine.

Ode to Nature:

Oh, nature, wondrous tapestry of life,
In thy beauty, we find solace from strife.
From the mountains that reach for the sky,
To the rivers that flow, never asking why.

Thou art the symphony that sings in the breeze,
The canvas that paints with colors that please.
In thy nature, we find our sanctuary,
And in thy majesty, our souls find clarity.

So let us honor thee, oh nature so grand,
For in thy presence, we find peace at hand.

Ode to Beauty:

Oh, beauty, ethereal essence of grace,
In thy radiance, we find our rightful place.
From the sunset that paints the sky with hues,
To the smile that brightens the darkest of blues.

Thou art the spark that lights the fire within,
The allure that captivates, drawing us in.
In thy beauty, we find our admiration,
And in thy elegance, our souls find inspiration.

So let us celebrate thee, oh beauty so rare,
For in thy beauty, life's wonders we share.

Ode to Time:

Oh, time, relentless march of the ages,
In thy passage, we turn life's pages.
From the moments fleeting like grains of sand,
To the memories etched by your steady hand.

Thou art the measure by which we live and grow,
The force that shapes us, both fast and slow.
In thy time, we find our journey's length,
And in thy wisdom, our lives find strength.

So let us embrace thee, oh time so wise,
For in thy time, all destinies arise.

Here are four Ode poems, 1 each about Death, Dreams, Hope & Despair

Oh, death, mysterious journey to the unknown,
In thy embrace, life's final chapter is shown.
From the whispers of souls departing in the night,
To the stars that guide them toward the light.

Thou art the passage from this world to the next,
The journey into the eternal rest.
In thy death, we find the cycle complete,
And in thy mystery, our fears retreat.

So let us accept thee, oh death so profound,
For in thy embrace, new beginnings are found.

Oh, dreams, ethereal visions of the night,
In thy realm, imagination takes flight.
From the fantasies that dance in our mind,
To the aspirations that make us blind.

Thou art the inspiration that fuels our desire,
The spark that sets our soul on fire.
In thy dreams, we find our true potential,
And in thy vision, our spirit is elemental.

So let us cherish thee, oh dreams so bright,
For in thy dreams, our futures ignite.

Oh, hope, steadfast beacon in life's storm,
In thy light, we find our courage to transform.
From the darkest hours to the dawn's first ray,
To the belief that guides us through the fray.

Thou art the promise of a brighter day,
The faith that guides us on our way.
In thy hope, we find our reason to strive,
And in thy promise, our hearts come alive.

So let us hold onto thee, oh hope so dear,
For in thy hope, our futures are clear.

Oh, despair, shadowy veil that clouds the soul,
In thy depths, we find our darkest hole.
From the whispers of doubt that haunt our mind,
To the anguish that leaves our hearts confined.

Thou art the storm that rages deep inside,
The darkness where our fears reside.
In thy despair, we find our deepest sorrow,
And in thy anguish, our hopes feel narrow.

So let us confront thee, oh despair so dark,
For in thy embrace, we find our spark.

Here are four Ode poems, 1 each about Friendship, Loneliness, Memories & Music

Oh, friendship, precious bond that never ends,
In thy embrace, we find our true friends.
From the laughter shared in moments bright,
To the comfort found in the darkest night.

Thou art the joy that lifts our spirits high,
The strength that helps us reach the sky.
In thy friendship, we find our loyal mate,
And in thy company, our hearts elate.

So let us cherish thee, oh friendship so dear,
For in thy friendship, there's nothing to fear.

Oh, loneliness, silent companion of the soul,
In thy solitude, we find our role.
From the quiet moments spent alone,
To the ache in the heart that's overgrown.

Thou art the echo in the empty room,
The shadow that follows in the gloom.
In thy loneliness, we find our reflection,
And in thy silence, our introspection.

So let us embrace thee, oh loneliness so deep,
For in thy solitude, our secrets we keep.

Oh, memories, timeless treasures of the past,
In thy recollection, we find memories that last.
From the snapshots captured in our mind's eye,
To the stories told beneath the evening sky.

Thou art the thread that binds us together,
The memoirs that will last forever.
In thy memories, we find our story's thread,
And in thy remembrance, our hearts are fed.

So let us hold onto thee, oh memories so true,
For in thy memories, our history we renew.

Oh, music, celestial symphony of the heart,
In thy melodies, we find our part.
From the harmonies that soothe the soul,
To the rhythms that make our spirits whole.

Thou art the language that speaks to us all,
The universal song that breaks down every wall.
In thy music, we find our joyous dance,
And in thy rhythm, our hearts advance.

So let us rejoice in thee, oh music so divine,
For in thy music, our souls entwine.

Here are four Ode poems, 1 each about Art, Inspiration, Creativity & Courage

Oh, art, majestic canvas of the soul,
In thy strokes, we find stories untold.
From the colors that dance upon the page,
To the sculptures that defy age.

Thou art the expression of human thought,
The beauty that cannot be bought.
In thy art, we find our deepest passion,
And in thy creation, eternal fashion.

So let us celebrate thee, oh art so divine,
For in thy artistry, our spirits entwine.

Oh, inspiration, elusive muse of the mind,
In thy whispers, creativity we find.
From the spark that ignites the flame within,
To the dreams that dare us to begin.

Thou art the melody that fills the air,
The vision that leads us to dare.
In thy inspiration, we find our calling,
And in thy guidance, our dreams are sprawling.

So let us embrace thee, oh inspiration so true,
For in thy inspiration, our visions renew.

Oh, creativity, boundless wellspring of innovation,
In thy depths, we find endless fascination.
From the inventions that shape our world anew,
To the stories that capture what is true.

Thou art the force that drives us to explore,
The imagination that opens every door.
In thy creativity, we find our power,
And in thy expression, our souls flower.

So let us cherish thee, oh creativity so bright,
For in thy creativity, we find our light.

Oh, courage, noble warrior of the heart,
In thy bravery, we find our part.
From the battles fought on fields of strife,
To the challenges that shape our life.

Thou art the strength that carries us through,
The resilience that makes us true.
In thy courage, we find our strength,
And in thy valor, we go to any length.

So let us honor thee, oh courage so bold,
For in thy courage, our stories are told.

Here are four Ode poems, 1 each about Faith, Doubt, Solitude & Joy

Oh, faith, unwavering anchor of the soul,
In thy embrace, we find our ultimate goal.
From the belief in unseen forces above,
To the trust that fills our hearts with love.

Thou art the light that guides us through the night,
The hope that keeps our spirits alight.
In thy faith, we find our strength to endure,
And in thy promise, our spirits soar.

So let us hold onto thee, oh faith so divine,
For in thy faith, our hearts intertwine.

Oh, doubt, shadowy whisper in the mind,
In thy questioning, truth we find.
From the uncertainty that clouds our way,
To the skepticism that leads to brighter day.

Thou art the skeptic's voice that questions all,
The skeptic's mind that does not blindly fall.
In thy doubt, we find our path to truth,
And in thy skepticism, our minds uncouth.

So let us welcome thee, oh doubt so bold,
For in thy doubt, our truths unfold.

Oh, solitude, tranquil haven of the soul,
In thy quiet, we find ourselves whole.
From the stillness of the forest's embrace,
To the solitude of the stars in outer space.

Thou art the sanctuary where we find our peace,
The refuge where our restless thoughts cease.
In thy solitude, we find our inner voice,
And in thy silence, our souls rejoice.

So let us seek thee, oh solitude so serene,
For in thy solitude, our spirits are clean.

Oh, joy, radiant beacon in life's journey,
In thy presence, we find our glee.
From the laughter that fills the air with song,
To the happiness that keeps our hearts strong.

Thou art the light that brightens every day,
The joy that drives our worries away.
In thy joy, we find our reason to smile,
And in thy happiness, life feels worthwhile.

So let us celebrate thee, oh joy so sweet,
For in thy joy, our lives are complete.

Here are four Ode poems, 1 each about Sorrow, Childhood, Wisdom & Innocence

Oh, sorrow, heavy burden of the heart,
In thy depths, we find our tearful part.
From the ache that lingers in the soul's embrace,
To the grief that colors every passing phase.

Thou art the storm that rages deep inside,
The darkness where our fears and sorrows hide.
In thy sorrow, we find our deepest pain,
And in thy mourning, we seek to regain.

So let us honor thee, oh sorrow so deep,
For in thy sorrow, our hearts do weep.

Oh, childhood, magical realm of innocence,
In thy laughter, we find our recompense.
From the days of wonder, carefree and wild,
To the dreams that danced like a whimsical child.

Thou art the treasure chest of memories sweet,
The days of play where joy and love would meet.
In thy childhood, we find our earliest delight,
And in thy innocence, our spirits take flight.

So let us cherish thee, oh childhood so dear,
For in thy innocence, there's nothing to fear.

Oh, wisdom, beacon guiding through life's maze,
In thy counsel, we find our steady gaze.
From the lessons learned through trials faced,
To the truths revealed in wisdom's embrace.

Thou art the light that shines in darkest night,
The knowledge gained from wisdom's insightful sight.
In thy wisdom, we find our guiding star,
And in thy counsel, we're never too far.

So let us heed thee, oh wisdom so wise,
For in thy wisdom, our hearts arise.

Oh, innocence, gentle purity of heart,
In thy grace, we find our fresh start.
From the innocence of a newborn's eyes,
To the trust that in innocence lies.

Thou art the purity untouched by stain,
The untainted beauty that will remain.
In thy innocence, we find our grace,
And in thy purity, we find our embrace.

So let us preserve thee, oh innocence so bright,
For in thy innocence, we find our light.

Here are four Ode poems, 1 each about Passion, Serenity, Freedom & Justice

Oh, passion, fervent flame that ignites the soul,
In thy blaze, we find our truest goal.
From the fire that burns within, fierce and bright,
To the fervor of love that takes flight.

Thou art the spark that sets our hearts aglow,
The energy that drives us, to and fro.
In thy passion, we find our purpose clear,
And in thy ardor, our dreams appear.

So let us embrace thee, oh passion so bold,
For in thy passion, our stories are told.

Oh, serenity, tranquil haven of peace,
In thy calm, all troubles cease.
From the gentle whisper of the wind in the trees,
To the stillness of the night, where silence flees.

Thou art the oasis in life's desert vast,
The sanctuary where we find rest at last.
In thy serenity, we find our refuge sweet,
And in thy quiet, our souls find retreat.

So let us seek thee, oh serenity so true,
For in thy serenity, our spirits renew.

Oh, freedom, precious gift bestowed on all,
In thy embrace, we answer the call.
From the open skies that stretch far and wide,
To the boundless seas where dreams reside.

Thou art the liberty to soar and fly,
The choice to live, to laugh, to cry.
In thy freedom, we find our wings to soar,
And in thy liberation, our spirits adore.

So let us cherish thee, oh freedom so dear,
For in thy freedom, we find no fear.

Oh, justice, noble beacon of truth,
In thy light, we find our youth.
From the scales that balance wrong and right,
To the voices that rise for justice's fight.

Thou art the fairness that rights the wrongs,
The strength that carries our voices in songs.
In thy justice, we find our unity,
And in thy righteousness, our community.

So let us uphold thee, oh justice so pure,
For in thy justice, all hearts endure.

Here are four Ode poems, 1 each about Change, Resilience, Gratitude & Forgiveness

Oh, change, eternal dance of life's embrace,
In thy shifting tides, we find our space.
From the turning of seasons, a constant flow,
To the metamorphosis within, where dreams grow.

Thou art the catalyst for growth and renewal,
The force that shapes us, forever unusual.
In thy change, we find our evolution's chance,
And in thy flux, life's endless dance.

So let us welcome thee, oh change so grand,
For in thy transformation, we find our reprimand.

Oh, resilience, sturdy fortress of the soul,
In thy strength, we find our role.
From the trials that test us, fierce and bold,
To the storms of life, where stories are told.

Thou art the unwavering spirit within,
The determination to rise, despite the din.
In thy resilience, we find our might,
And in thy endurance, our inner light.

So let us honor thee, oh resilience so true,
For in thy steadfastness, we find our breakthrough.

Oh, gratitude, gentle melody of the heart,
In thy embrace, we find our part.
From the simplest joys that light our days,
To the blessings bestowed in countless ways.

Thou art the beacon that guides us through,
The appreciation for all, old and new.
In thy gratitude, we find our peace,
And in thy thankfulness, our troubles cease.

So let us cherish thee, oh gratitude so pure,
For in thy gratitude, our hearts endure.

Oh, forgiveness, healing balm for wounds so deep,
In thy embrace, we find solace and sleep.
From the scars of past hurts, heavy and grave,
To the freedom found in the act to forgive and save.

Thou art the release from chains of pain,
The liberation from bitterness and disdain.
In thy forgiveness, we find our grace,
And in thy mercy, our souls embrace.

So let us embrace thee, oh forgiveness so divine,
For in thy forgiveness, true healing does shine.

Here are four Ode poems, 1 each about Longing, Belonging, Discovery & Wonder

Oh, longing, sweet ache of the heart's desire,
In thy yearning, passions set afire.
From the whispers of dreams unfulfilled,
To the longing for love that keeps us thrilled.

Thou art the echo of distant shores,
The call of adventure that forever implores.
In thy longing, we find our quest,
And in thy yearning, we find our zest.

So let us embrace thee, oh longing so deep,
For in thy longing, our souls doth leap.

Oh, belonging, gentle embrace of unity,
In thy warmth, we find our community.
From the bonds of friendship that hold us tight,
To the family ties that shine so bright.

Thou art the thread that weaves us together,
The shelter from life's stormy weather.
In thy belonging, we find our place,
And in thy embrace, we find our grace.

So let us celebrate thee, oh belonging so true,
For in thy embrace, we find our crew.

Oh, discovery, thrilling dance of the unknown,
In thy adventure, new worlds are shown.
From the wonders of science that unravel mysteries,
To the treasures of knowledge that unlock histories.

Thou art the spark that ignites our curiosity,
The journey that leads to boundless prosperity.
In thy discovery, we find our quest,
And in thy exploration, we find our zest.

So let us pursue thee, oh discovery so grand,
For in thy exploration, we find our stand.

Oh, wonder, enchanting melody of the soul,
In thy magic, miracles unfold.
From the beauty of nature that leaves us in awe,
To the mysteries of the cosmos that beckon and draw.

Thou art the sparkle in a child's eyes,
The joy that lifts us to the skies.
In thy wonder, we find our delight,
And in thy marvels, our spirits take flight.

So let us revel in thee, oh wonder so divine,
For in thy wonder, life's treasures shine.

Here are four Ode poems, 1 each about Journey, Reflection, Harmony & Imagination

Oh, journey, winding path of life's grand tale,
In thy twists and turns, we set sail.
From the first step ventured into the unknown,
To the roads traveled and seeds sown.

Thou art the adventure that beckons us forth,
The lessons learned, the treasures of worth.
In thy journey, we find our growth,
And in thy challenges, we find our oath.

So let us embrace thee, oh journey divine,
For in thy unfolding, our destinies intertwine.

Oh, reflection, mirror of the soul's deep well,
In thy quiet depths, truths do dwell.
From the moments paused and thoughts turned inward,
To the memories cherished and lessons conferred.

Thou art the sanctuary where wisdom resides,
The clarity gained when the heart confides.
In thy reflection, we find our clarity,
And in thy silence, our serenity.

So let us honor thee, oh reflection so clear,
For in thy stillness, our essence appears.

Oh, harmony, symphony of life's grand symposium,
In thy rhythm, all things find their equilibrium.
From the melodies that dance in the air,
To the unity found in love's tender care.

Thou art the balance that restores the soul,
The peace that makes broken spirits whole.
In thy harmony, we find our peace,
And in thy unity, our conflicts cease.

So let us celebrate thee, oh harmony sublime,
For in thy convergence, we find our prime.

Oh, imagination, boundless realm of possibility,
In thy vast expanse, creativity finds its fertility.
From the dreams that soar on wings of thought,
To the visions woven from the mind's knot.

Thou art the canvas where fantasies unfurl,
The playground where innovation swirls.
In thy imagination, we find our spark,
And in thy creativity, our worlds embark.

So let us embrace thee, oh imagination so free,
For in thy infinite horizons, we find our glee.

Here are four Ode poems, 1 each about Silence, Laughter, Tears & Strength

Oh, transformation, wondrous and profound,
In thy alchemy, new worlds are found.
From the caterpillar's crawl to the butterfly's flight,
In thy embrace, we find our true light.

Thou art the sculptor of life's grand design,
The artist who paints with strokes divine.
In thy transformation, we find our wings,
And in thy process, our spirit sings.

So let us celebrate thee, oh transformation so dear,
For in thy metamorphosis, we find our frontier.

Oh, eternity, vast and infinite,
In thy expanse, all things unite.
From the stars that shimmer in the night,
To the whispers of the wind taking flight.

Thou art the thread that weaves through time,
The melody of the universe's rhyme.
In thy eternity, we find our place,
And in thy embrace, we find our grace.

So let us marvel at thee, oh eternity so grand,
For in thy boundless expanse, we find our stand.

Oh, cosmos, majestic and sublime,
In thy vastness, we find our rhyme.
From the galaxies swirling in space,
To the planets dancing in their embrace.

Thou art the mystery beyond our sight,
The wonder that fills us with delight.
In thy cosmos, we find our awe,
And in thy stars, we find our law.

So let us ponder thee, oh cosmos so vast,
For in thy depths, we find our past.

Oh, happiness, elusive and bright,
In thy radiance, all is right.
From the laughter that fills the air,
To the smiles that banish every care.

Thou art the sunshine after the rain,
The joy that washes away the pain.
In thy happiness, we find our song,
And in thy embrace, we all belong.

So let us cherish thee, oh happiness so true,
For in thy warmth, we find our hue.

Here are four Ode poems, 1 each about Vulnerability, Renewal, Acceptance & Mystery

Oh, vulnerability, thou gentle heart's embrace,
In thy tender arms, we find our true grace.
For it is in our openness, we discover might,
And in our rawness, we shine so bright.

Thou art the courage to show our flaws,
The strength to break through life's closed doors.
In thy vulnerability, we find our power,
To rise again, like a blooming flower.

So let us embrace thee, oh vulnerability divine,
For in our openness, true strength we find.

Oh, renewal, thou gentle breeze of change,
In thy embrace, we find life rearrange.
For it is in thy touch, we shed old skin,
And in thy presence, we begin again.

Thou art the promise of a new dawn,
The chance to rise again, reborn.
In thy renewal, we find our growth,
And in thy cycle, we find our troth.

So let us welcome thee, oh renewal so dear,
For in thy embrace, we find hope clear.

Oh, acceptance, thou balm for the soul,
In thy embrace, we find ourselves whole.
For it is in thy grace, we find peace,
And in thy arms, our worries cease.

Thou art the wisdom to let things be,
The serenity to set our spirit free.
In thy acceptance, we find our rest,
And in thy love, we are truly blessed.

So let us honor thee, oh acceptance divine,
For in thy embrace, true joy we find.

Oh, mystery, thou enigmatic muse,
In thy depths, we find our clues.
For it is in thy shadows, we seek truth,
And in thy riddles, we find youth.

Thou art the whisper in the night,
The stars that guide our weary flight.
In thy mystery, we find our quest,
And in thy secrets, we find our best.

So let us embrace thee, oh mystery so grand,
For in thy mystery, we find life's hand.

Here are four Ode poems, 1 each about Transformation, Eternity, Cosmos & Happiness

Oh, transformation, wondrous and profound,
In thy alchemy, new worlds are found.
From the caterpillar's crawl to the butterfly's flight,
In thy embrace, we find our true light.

Thou art the sculptor of life's grand design,
The artist who paints with strokes divine.
In thy transformation, we find our wings,
And in thy process, our spirit sings.

So let us celebrate thee, oh transformation so dear,
For in thy metamorphosis, we find our frontier.

Oh, eternity, vast and infinite,
In thy expanse, all things unite.
From the stars that shimmer in the night,
To the whispers of the wind taking flight.

Thou art the thread that weaves through time,
The melody of the universe's rhyme.
In thy eternity, we find our place,
And in thy embrace, we find our grace.

So let us marvel at thee, oh eternity so grand,
For in thy boundless expanse, we find our stand.

Oh, cosmos, majestic and sublime,
In thy vastness, we find our rhyme.
From the galaxies swirling in space,
To the planets dancing in their embrace.

Thou art the mystery beyond our sight,
The wonder that fills us with delight.
In thy cosmos, we find our awe,
And in thy stars, we find our law.

So let us ponder thee, oh cosmos so vast,
For in thy depths, we find our past.

Oh, happiness, elusive and bright,
In thy radiance, all is right.
From the laughter that fills the air,
To the smiles that banish every care.

Thou art the sunshine after the rain,
The joy that washes away the pain.
In thy happiness, we find our song,
And in thy embrace, we all belong.

So let us cherish thee, oh happiness so true,
For in thy warmth, we find our hue.

EPIC:

A lengthy narrative poem that tells the story of heroic deeds and adventures, often featuring grand themes.

-:¦:-•:*'''''*:•.-:¦:-•**•-:¦:-•:*'''''*:•:*'''''*:•.-:¦:-•**•-:¦:--:¦:-•:*'''''*:•.-:¦:- •**•-:¦:-•:*'''''*:•:*'''''*:•.-:¦:-•**•-:¦:-

Here are four Epic poems, 1 each about Love, Nature, Beauty & Time

Epic Poem: Love
In the annals of time, a tale unfolds,
Of love that transcends the mortal bounds.
A saga of hearts entwined, through trials untold,
In the symphony of love's resounding sounds.

From ancient lands where legends were born,
To distant shores where destiny roams,
A love story woven with threads of thorn,
Yet strengthened by the fires of passion's homes.

Through tempests fierce and oceans wide,
Two souls united, side by side.
In love's embrace, they find their guide,
A bond that cannot be denied.

For love is the force that shapes the stars,
The melody that echoes near and far.
In the epic of love, we find our scars,
Yet also the strength to reach for the stars.

Epic Poem: Nature
Behold the epic saga of nature's reign,
From the dawn of time to the present domain.
A tale of forests vast and mountains high,
Of rivers that flow beneath the azure sky.

In the heart of the wilderness, secrets untold,
Whispers of ancient tales, mysteries unfold.
From the roar of thunder to the gentle breeze,
Nature's epic narrative weaves through the trees.

Through verdant valleys and rocky peaks,
Nature's symphony plays, and the earth speaks.
In every leaf that rustles, every bird that sings,
The epic of nature's glory forever rings.

For nature is the canvas where life is born,
The stage where tales of wonder are sworn.
In the epic of nature, we find our home,
A sanctuary where our spirits roam.

Epic Poem: Beauty
In the grand tapestry of life's design,
A masterpiece of beauty begins to shine.
An epic tale of grace and elegance,
Where beauty's essence weaves its presence.

From the dawn's first light to the twilight's hue,
Beauty's allure casts its spell anew.
In every petal of a flower's bloom,
And every star that lights the night's gloom.

Through valleys lush and meadows fair,
Beauty's epic journey fills the air.
In the symphony of colors, shapes, and forms,
Beauty's epic tale forever transforms.

For beauty is the essence that fills the soul,
The vision that makes the spirit whole.
In the epic of beauty, we find our bliss,
A treasure trove of wonder that we cannot miss.

Epic Poem: Time
In the realm of eternity, time reigns supreme,
An epic journey woven in the cosmic dream.
A saga of ages, of moments fleeting,
In the grand theater where destinies are meeting.

From the birth of stars to their final breath,
Time's epic tale transcends life and death.
In every heartbeat, every breath we take,
Time's relentless march we cannot forsake.

Through the corridors of history, time marches on,
Leaving behind tales of glory and song.
In the sands of time, we find our story,
A fleeting moment in time's epic inventory.

For time is the river that flows evermore,
The measure by which all things endure.
In the epic of time, we find our place,
A journey of wonder through time and space.

Here are four Epic poems, 1 each about Death, Dreams, Hope & Despair

Epic Poem: Death
In the realm of shadows where silence reigns,
Death's epic tale unfolds in whispers and refrains.
A saga of souls departing, journeys unknown,
In the symphony of life's final tone.

From the breath that fades to the eyes that close,
Death's solemn march through the cosmic prose.
In every tear shed and every heart that grieves,
Death's eternal dance, the soul perceives.

Through the veil of darkness, spirits soar,
To realms beyond where mortals explore.
In the epic of death, we find our fate,
A passage to realms beyond life's gate.

For death is the journey that all must take,
The final chapter in life's epic wake.
In the embrace of death, we find release,
And in the silence, our souls find peace.

Epic Poem: Dreams
In the realm of dreams where fantasies soar,
Dreams' epic journey unfolds forevermore.
A tale of visions born in the depths of night,
In the canvas of darkness, dreams take flight.

From the whispers of slumber to the dawn's first light,
Dreams' ethereal dance, a wondrous sight.
In every wish whispered and every desire,
Dreams' endless voyage, the soul inspires.

Through the landscapes of imagination, dreams roam,
To realms of wonder where mysteries comb.
In the epic of dreams, we find our muse,
A tapestry of fantasies, where reality defuse.

For dreams are the gateway to worlds unseen,
The canvas where life's colors convene.
In the epic of dreams, we find our quest,
A journey of the soul where dreams manifest.

Epic Poem: Hope
In the realm of possibility where dreams take flight,
Hope's epic tale unfolds in the darkest night.
A saga of resilience, of faith undeterred,
In the symphony of hope, the soul's reward.

From the depths of despair to the heights of the sky,
Hope's enduring flame, it never does die.
In every heart that beats with courage and might,
Hope's steadfast presence, a beacon in the night.

Through the trials of life where shadows loom,
To the shores of tomorrow where futures bloom.
In the epic of hope, we find our light,
A guiding star through the darkest night.

For hope is the promise that tomorrow brings,
The melody of faith where the soul sings.
In the epic of hope, we find our grace,
A sanctuary of solace in life's embrace.

Epic Poem: Despair
In the realm of darkness where shadows creep,
Despair's epic tale unfolds in the heart's deep.
A saga of anguish, of sorrow profound,
In the symphony of despair, the soul is bound.

From the depths of sorrow to the abyss of pain,
Despair's relentless grip, it leaves its stain.
In every tear shed and every heart that breaks,
Despair's haunting echo, the soul forsakes.

Through the labyrinth of torment, despair roams,
To the depths of oblivion where darkness looms.
In the epic of despair, we find our plight,
A journey through the depths of eternal night.

For despair is the shadow that follows in the gloom,
The specter of sorrow that haunts every room.
In the epic of despair, we find our sorrow,
A journey through darkness with no tomorrow.

Here are four Epic poems, 1 each about Friendship, Loneliness, Memories & Music

Epic Poem: Friendship
In the annals of time, a bond unfolds,
A tale of friendship, strong and bold.
A saga of hearts united, through trials untold,
In the symphony of friendship, love is enrolled.

From the dawn of creation to the present day,
Friendship's epic journey lights the way.
In every laugh shared and every tear shed,
Friendship's enduring bond, it spreads.

Through the storms of life where troubles arise,
To the peaks of joy where happiness flies.
In the epic of friendship, we find our kin,
A bond unbreakable, through thick and thin.

For friendship is the anchor that keeps us strong,
The melody of love, where we belong.
In the epic of friendship, we find our grace,
A sanctuary of solace in life's embrace.

Epic Poem: Loneliness
In the realm of solitude where shadows dwell,
Loneliness's epic tale, it does tell.
A saga of souls adrift, lost in the swell,
In the silence of loneliness, hearts rebel.

From the depths of isolation to the peaks of despair,
Loneliness's haunting presence, it's always there.
In every sigh uttered and every tear shed,
Loneliness's silent lament, it spreads.

Through the valleys of silence where echoes fade,
To the barren wastelands where memories evade.
In the epic of loneliness, we find our plight,
A journey through darkness, with no end in sight.

For loneliness is the void that consumes the soul,
The echo of silence, where spirits grow cold.
In the epic of loneliness, we find our sorrow,
A journey through emptiness, with no tomorrow.

Epic Poem: Memories
In the tapestry of time, a tale is woven,
A saga of memories, cherished and unbroken.
A journey through the corridors of the mind,
In the symphony of memories, life's treasures find.

From the whispers of the past to the echoes of today,
Memories epic narrative, it lights the way.
In every laugh shared and every tear shed,
Memories timeless melody, it spreads.

Through the mists of time where echoes fade,
To the shores of remembrance where dreams are made.
In the epic of memories, we find our tale,
A journey through the past, where emotions prevail.

For memories are the threads that bind us tight,
The echoes of laughter and tears in the night.
In the epic of memories, we find our trace,
A journey through time and space.

Epic Poem: Music
In the realm of sound where melodies soar,
Music's epic tale, it opens the door.
A saga of notes, harmonies, and more,
In the symphony of music, hearts implore.

From the dawn of creation to the present day,
Music's epic journey lights the way.
In every beat felt and every note heard,
Music's timeless rhythm, it's the spoken word.

Through the valleys of silence where echoes fade,
To the peaks of passion where dreams are made.
In the epic of music, we find our voice,
A journey through melody, where hearts rejoice.

For music is the language that speaks to the soul,
The melody of life, where emotions roll.
In the epic of music, we find our grace,
A sanctuary of solace in life's embrace.

Here are four Epic poems, 1 each about Art, Inspiration, Creativity & Courage

Epic Poem: Art
In the annals of creativity, a masterpiece unfurls,
A saga of imagination that spans the world.
Journey through canvas, where colors dance and swirl,
In the symphony of art, every stroke speaks its pearls.

From depths of the artist's soul to the heights of the sky,
Art's epic tale, it paints with every sigh.
In every brushstroke laid and every canvas spread,
Art's timeless expression, it fills the heart with dread.

Through the valleys of doubt where shadows dwell,
To the peaks of inspiration where dreams swell.
In the epic of art, we find our muse,
A sanctuary of solace where the soul renews.

For art is the language that speaks to every heart,
The melody of creativity, where souls depart.
In the epic of art, we find our grace,
A journey through imagination, to the soul's embrace.

Epic Poem: Inspiration
In the realm of possibility where dreams take flight,
Inspiration's epic journey unfolds in the darkest night.
A saga of visionaries who dare to ignite,
In the symphony of inspiration, every dream is a light.

From the depths of despair to the heights of the sky,
Inspiration's enduring flame, it never does die.
In every whisper heard and every idea bred,
Inspiration's guiding hand, it's the soul's thread.

Through the corridors of doubt where shadows loom,
To the shores of creativity where visions groom.
In the epic of inspiration, we find our spark,
A journey through imagination, where dreams embark.

For inspiration is the spark that ignites the flame,
The melody of possibility where dreams reclaim.
In the epic of inspiration, we find our grace,
A sanctuary of solace in life's embrace.

Epic Poem: Creativity
In the tapestry of life, a masterpiece is drawn,
A saga of innovation that inspires the dawn.
A journey through the imagination, where ideas spawn,
In the symphony of creativity, every thought is a pawn.

From the depths of the mind to the heights of the soul,
Creativity's epic tale, it reaches its goal.
In every idea conceived and every dream spun,
Creativity's boundless realm, it's never done.

Through the valleys of hesitation where doubts reign,
To the peaks of innovation where ideas train.
In the epic of creativity, we find our path,
A journey through the unknown, where dreams amass.

For creativity is the force that drives the soul,
The melody of ingenuity, where dreams enroll.
In the epic of creativity, we find our place,
A sanctuary of solace in life's embrace.

Epic Poem: Courage
In the realm of bravery where heroes rise,
Courage's epic journey unveils life's surprise.
A saga of resilience that reaches for the skies,
In the symphony of courage, every fear defies.

From the depths of fear to the heights of the peak,
Courage's enduring strength, it's what we seek.
In every step taken and every battle fought,
Courage's steadfast resolve, it cannot be bought.

Through the shadows of doubt where fears take hold,
To the light of bravery where stories are told.
In the epic of courage, we find our might,
A journey through adversity, where dreams take flight.

For courage is the flame that lights the way,
The melody of strength, where fears decay.
In the epic of courage, we find our grace,
A sanctuary of solace in life's embrace.

Here are four Epic poems, 1 each about Faith, Doubt, Solitude & Joy

Epic Poem: Faith
In the vast expanse of the universe's might,
A tale of faith emerges, a beacon of light.
A journey through the darkness, guided by sight,
In the symphony of faith, hearts take flight.

From the depths of uncertainty to the peaks of belief,
Faith's epic saga, it offers relief.
In every prayer whispered and every hope held,
Faith's unwavering strength, it cannot be quelled.

Through the valleys of despair where shadows loom,
To the mountaintops of faith where dreams bloom.
In the epic of faith, we find our grace,
A journey through uncertainty, to a brighter place.

For faith is the compass that guides us through,
The melody of trust, where dreams come true.
In the epic of faith, we find our way,
A sanctuary of solace in life's array.
Epic Poem: Doubt
In the depths of the soul where shadows dwell,
Doubt's epic tale unfolds, a haunting spell.
A journey through uncertainty, where fears swell,
In the symphony of doubt, hearts quell.

From the depths of despair to the heights of the sky,
Doubt's relentless grip, it makes us shy.
In every question asked and every fear fed,
Doubt's relentless echo, it fills the head.

Through the corridors of hesitation where shadows loom,
To the precipice of decision where doubts consume.
In the epic of doubt, we find our plight,
A journey through darkness, with no end in sight.

For doubt is the shadow that follows in the night,
The melody of uncertainty, where fears ignite.
In the epic of doubt, we find our sorrow,
A journey through uncertainty, with no tomorrow.
Epic Poem: Solitude

In the vast expanse of the world's embrace,
Solitude's epic journey finds its place.
A saga of introspection, where thoughts race,
In the symphony of solitude, hearts find grace.

From the depths of isolation to the heights of the peak,
Solitude's timeless dance, it offers what we seek.
In every moment of silence and every breath taken,
Solitude's serene embrace, it cannot be shaken.
Through the valleys of loneliness where echoes fade,
To the mountaintops of solitude where dreams are made.
In the epic of solitude, we find our peace,
A journey through introspection, where worries cease.

For solitude is the sanctuary where souls retreat,
The melody of silence, where thoughts meet.
In the epic of solitude, we find our way,
A sanctuary of solace in life's array.
Epic Poem: Joy

In the symphony of life where melodies play,
Joy's epic journey unfolds in the light of day.
A tale of laughter and smiles that never sway,
In the symphony of joy, hearts find their way.
From the depths of sorrow to the heights of the sky,
Joy's infectious embrace, it lifts us high.
In every laugh shared and every moment bright,
Joy's radiant glow, it fills the night.

Through the valleys of sadness where tears fall,
To the mountaintops of happiness where dreams call.
In the epic of joy, we find our song,
A journey through happiness, where we belong.

For joy is the melody that fills the air,
The harmony of happiness, beyond compare.
In the epic of joy, we find our grace,
A sanctuary of solace in life's embrace.

Here are four Epic poems, 1 each about Sorrow, Childhood, Wisdom & Innocence

Epic Poem: Sorrow
In the depths of despair where shadows reside,
Sorrow's epic tale unfolds, a relentless tide.
A journey through the darkness where hearts collide,
In the symphony of sorrow, tears are cried.

From the depths of grief to the heights of pain,
Sorrow's enduring grip, it leaves its stain.
In every heartache felt and every soul that mourns,
Sorrow's somber melody, it adorns.

Through the valleys of despair where shadows loom,
To the mountaintops of grief where hearts consume.
In the epic of sorrow, we find our plight,
A journey through darkness, with no end in sight.

For sorrow is the echo that lingers in the night,
The melody of pain, where hearts take flight.
In the epic of sorrow, we find our despair,
A journey through anguish, with no repair.

Epic Poem: Childhood
In the realm of innocence where dreams are spun,
Childhood's epic journey has just begun.
A tale of wonder and discovery under the sun,
In the symphony of childhood, hearts are won.

From the innocence of youth to the wisdom of age,
Childhood's carefree spirit, it turns the page.
In every laugh shared and every game played,
Childhood's joyous melody, it's conveyed.

Through meadows of imagination where dreams take flight,
To the playgrounds of adventure where hearts ignite.
In the epic of childhood, we find our delight,
A journey through innocence, where dreams alight.

For childhood is the canvas where memories are drawn,
The melody of innocence, where love is born.
In the epic of childhood, we find our bliss,
A sanctuary of solace in life's abyss.

Epic Poem: Wisdom
In the annals of time where knowledge abounds,
Wisdom's epic tale is told in solemn sounds.
A journey through the ages where truth is found,
In the symphony of wisdom, hearts are crowned.

From the depths of experience to the heights of the mind,
Wisdom's enduring light, it's what we find.
In every lesson learned and every insight gained,
Wisdom's timeless melody, it's sustained.

Through the valleys of uncertainty where doubts creep,
To the mountaintops of clarity where wisdom seeps.
In the epic of wisdom, we find our guide,
A journey through enlightenment, where truth resides.

For wisdom is the beacon that lights the way,
The melody of knowledge, where minds sway.
In the epic of wisdom, we find our grace,
A sanctuary of solace in life's embrace.

Epic Poem: Innocence
In the realm of purity where hearts are light,
Innocence's epic journey takes flight.
A tale of wonder and joy, ever bright,
In the symphony of innocence, dreams unite.

From the innocence of youth to the wisdom of age,
Innocence's carefree spirit, it takes the stage.
In every smile shared and every heart that sings,
Innocence's pure melody, it brings.

Through the meadows of wonder where dreams bloom,
To the playgrounds of imagination where hearts zoom.
In the epic of innocence, we find our truth,
A journey through purity, where dreams soothe.

For innocence is the light that guides the way,
The melody of purity, where hearts stay.
In the epic of innocence, we find our grace,
A sanctuary of solace in life's embrace.

Here are four Epic poems, 1 each about Passion, Serenity, Freedom & Justice

Epic Poem: Passion
In the fiery depths of the soul's embrace,
Passion's epic tale unfolds in boundless space.
A journey through the flames where hearts race,
In the symphony of passion, souls find grace.

From the depths of desire to the heights of ecstasy,
Passion's relentless fervor, it sets us free.
In every kiss shared and every touch felt,
Passion's fiery melody, it's the heart's belt.

Through the valleys of longing where dreams reside,
To the mountaintops of ecstasy where hearts collide.
In the epic of passion, we find our desire,
A journey through fire, where souls aspire.

For passion is the flame that lights the night,
The melody of desire, where dreams take flight.
In the epic of passion, we find our fire,
A sanctuary of solace in life's desire.

Epic Poem: Serenity
In the tranquil depths where silence reigns,
Serenity's epic journey has no chains.
A tale of peace and tranquility that sustains,
In the symphony of serenity, souls remain.

From the depths of stillness to the heights of calm,
Serenity's gentle embrace, it's the soul's balm.
In every breath taken and every moment still,
Serenity's quiet melody, it instills.

Thru the meadows of tranquility where dreams abound,
To the shores of peace where hearts are found.
In the epic of serenity, we find our rest,
A journey through calm, where hearts invest.

For serenity is the silence that soothes the soul,
The melody of peace, where spirits enroll.
In the epic of serenity, we find our grace,
A sanctuary of solace in life's embrace.

Here are four Epic poems, 1 each about Change, Resilience, Gratitude & Forgiveness

Epic Poem: Freedom
In the boundless expanse where dreams take flight,
Freedom's epic tale unfolds in the darkest night.
A journey through the winds where souls alight,
In the symphony of freedom, hearts unite.

From the chains of oppression to the wings of flight,
Freedom's relentless call, it sets things right.
In every struggle fought and every battle won,
Freedom's liberating melody, it's begun.

Through the valleys of oppression where shadows fall,
To the mountaintops of liberty where dreams call.
In the epic of freedom, we find our plight,
A journey through liberation, where souls ignite.

For freedom is the anthem that echoes in the night,
The melody of liberty, where dreams take flight.
In the epic of freedom, we find our space,
A sanctuary of solace in life's embrace.

Epic Poem: Justice
In the realm of righteousness where truth prevails,
Justice's epic journey unfurls its sails.
A tale of equality and fairness that entails,
In the symphony of justice, hearts set their trails.

From the depths of injustice to the heights of equity,
Justice's unwavering sword, it sets things free.
In every fight for right and every stand for truth,
Justice's noble melody, it soothes.

Through valleys of oppression where darkness looms,
Mountaintops of righteousness where dreams bloom.
In the epic of justice, we find our cause,
A journey through righteousness, where laws pause.

For justice is the beacon that guides the way,
The melody of fairness, where rights stay.
In the epic of justice, we find our grace,
A sanctuary of solace in life's embrace.

Epic Poem: Change
In the swirling currents of time's embrace,
Change's epic tale unfolds with grace.
A journey through the cycles of life's race,
In the symphony of change, hearts find their place.

From the depths of stagnation to the heights of transformation,
Change's relentless force, it shapes creation.
In every shift felt and every new dawn,
Change's inexorable melody, it's drawn.

Through the valleys of uncertainty where fears reside,
Mountaintops of opportunity where dreams confide.
In the epic of change, we find our fate,
A journey through evolution, where worlds create.
For change is the river that flows through life,
The melody of growth, where dreams arrive.
In the epic of change, we find our grace,
A sanctuary of solace in life's embrace.

Epic Poem: Resilience
In the crucible of adversity where trials persist,
Resilience's epic journey can't be dismissed.
A tale of strength and fortitude that exists,
In the symphony of resilience, hearts insist.

From the depths of despair to the heights of hope,
Resilience's unwavering spirit, it helps us cope.
In every setback faced and every challenge met,
Resilience's unyielding melody, we bet.
Through the valleys of hardship where struggles abide,
To the mountaintops of triumph where dreams ride.
In the epic of resilience, we find our might,
A journey through adversity, where souls take flight.

For resilience is the armor that shields the soul,
The melody of courage, where hearts console.
In the epic of resilience, we find our grace,
A sanctuary of solace in life's embrace.

Epic Poem: Gratitude
In the tapestry of life where blessings abound,
Gratitude's epic journey is profound.
A tale of thankfulness and love that's crowned,
In the symphony of gratitude, hearts are found.

From the depths of humility to the heights of grace,
Gratitude's humble spirit, it finds its place.
In every gift received and every kindness shown,
Gratitude's timeless melody, it's known.

Through the valleys of want where desires call,
To the mountaintops of abundance where blessings fall.
In the epic of gratitude, we find our joy,
A journey through thankfulness, where hearts employ.
For gratitude is the key that unlocks the soul,
The melody of appreciation, where spirits enroll.
In the epic of gratitude, we find our space,
A sanctuary of solace in life's embrace.

Epic Poem: Forgiveness
In the labyrinth of hurt where wounds reside,
Forgiveness's epic journey can't be denied.
A tale of healing and redemption that preside,
In the symphony of forgiveness, hearts collide.

From the depths of anger to the heights of peace,
Forgiveness's gentle touch, it brings release.
In every apology given and every apology received,
Forgiveness's transformative melody, it's believed.

Through the valleys of bitterness where grudges grow,
To the mountaintops of reconciliation where love flow.
In the epic of forgiveness, we find our freedom,
A journey through healing, where souls redeem.

For forgiveness is the balm that soothes the pain,
The melody of compassion, where hearts regain.
In the epic of forgiveness, we find our grace,
A sanctuary of solace in life's embrace.

Here are four Epic poems, 1 each about Longing, Belonging, Discovery & Wonder

Epic Poem: Longing
In the depths of the heart where desires dwell,
Longing's epic journey weaves its spell.
A tale of yearning and dreams that swell,
In the symphony of longing, hearts rebel.

From the depths of the soul to the heights of the sky,
Longing's relentless call, it makes us sigh.
In every whisper of hope and every tear shed,
Longing's poignant melody, it's widespread.

Through the valleys of emptiness where dreams fade,
To the mountaintops of desire where hearts are swayed.
In the epic of longing, we find our quest,
A journey through yearning, where souls invest.

For longing is the echo that lingers in the night,
The melody of desire, where dreams take flight.
In the epic of longing, we find our grace,
A sanctuary of solace in life's embrace.
Epic Poem: Belonging
In the tapestry of life where connections weave,
Belonging's epic tale, it's what we believe.
A journey through kinship where hearts cleave,
In the symphony of belonging, souls achieve.

From the depths of isolation to the heights of the clan,
Belonging's comforting embrace, it's our plan.
In every bond forged and every love found,
Belonging's harmonious melody, it's profound.

Through the valleys of loneliness where hearts ache,
To the mountaintops of community where souls awake.
In the epic of belonging, we find our tribe,
A journey through unity, where hearts imbibe.

For belonging is the thread that ties us tight,
The melody of connection, where souls take flight.
In the epic of belonging, we find our space,
A sanctuary of solace in life's embrace.

Epic Poem: Discovery
In the vast expanse of the unknown where mysteries lie,
Discovery's epic journey takes flight in the sky.
A tale of exploration and wonder that defy,
In the symphony of discovery, hearts amplify.

From the depths of the earth to the stars above,
Discovery's relentless quest, it's driven by love.
In every step taken and every new horizon,
Discovery's adventurous melody, it's surprising.

Through the valleys of ignorance where shadows dwell,
To the mountaintops of enlightenment where stories swell.
In the epic of discovery, we find our path,
A journey through exploration, where knowledge hath.

For discovery is the quest that fuels the soul,
The melody of curiosity, where dreams enroll.
In the epic of discovery, we find our grace,
A sanctuary of solace in life's embrace.

Epic Poem: Wonder
In the realm of awe where magic reigns,
Wonder's epic tale, it knows no chains.
A journey through the marvels where beauty stains,
In the symphony of wonder, hearts contain.

From the depths of the forest to the oceans blue,
Wonder's endless marvel, it brings us anew.
In every sunset witnessed and every star above,
Wonder's captivating melody, it's love.

Through the valleys of routine where eyes grow dull,
To the mountaintops of enchantment where hearts pull.
In the epic of wonder, we find our awe,
A journey through amazement, where dreams thaw.

For wonder is the spark that ignites the flame,
The melody of enchantment, where dreams reclaim.
In the epic of wonder, we find our grace,
A sanctuary of solace in life's embrace.

Here are four Epic poems, 1 each about Journey, Reflection, Harmony & Imagination

Epic Poem: Journey
In the vast expanse of time's embrace,
Journey's epic tale takes its place.
A saga of adventure in every space,
In the symphony of journey, souls race.

From the depths of the earth to the stars above,
Journey's relentless call, it whispers of love.
In every step taken and every road unwound,
Journey's adventurous melody, it resounds.

Through the valleys of doubt where fears ensnare,
To the mountaintops of triumph where dreams declare.
In the epic of journey, we find our quest,
A voyage through life, where hearts invest.

For journey is the path that leads us home,
The melody of exploration, where dreams roam.
In the epic of journey, we find our grace,
A sanctuary of solace in life's embrace.

Epic Poem: Reflection
In the quiet depths of the soul's retreat,
Reflection's epic journey finds its seat.
A tale of introspection where thoughts meet,
In the symphony of reflection, hearts beat.

From the depths of the mind to the heights of the sky,
Reflection's endless dance, it can't deny.
In every question pondered and every truth sought,
Reflection's thoughtful melody, it's wrought.

Through the valleys of confusion where shadows loom,
To the mountaintops of clarity where minds groom.
In the epic of reflection, we find our light,
A journey through introspection, where insights ignite.

For reflection is the mirror that shows the way,
The melody of introspection, where souls sway.
In the epic of reflection, we find our grace,
A sanctuary of solace in life's embrace.

Epic Poem: Harmony
In the symphony of life where rhythms entwine,
Harmony's epic journey is divine.
A tale of unity where souls align,
In the symphony of harmony, hearts define.

From the depths of discord to the heights of peace,
Harmony's soothing embrace, it brings release.
In every note played and every chord struck,
Harmony's melodious melody, it's luck.

Through the valleys of discord where chaos reigns,
To the mountaintops of concord where hearts reclaim.
In the epic of harmony, we find our song,
A journey through unity, where souls belong.

For harmony is the song that fills the air,
The melody of peace, where souls repair.
In the epic of harmony, we find our grace,
A sanctuary of solace in life's embrace.

Epic Poem: Imagination
In the realm of dreams where fantasies fly,
Imagination's epic journey takes its high.
A saga of creativity that touches the sky,
In the symphony of imagination, hearts vie.

From the depths of the mind to the expanse of space,
Imagination's boundless reach, it's our embrace.
In every idea conceived and every world created,
Imagination's wondrous melody, it's celebrated.

Through the valleys of doubt where fears reside,
To the mountaintops of possibility where dreams confide.
In the epic of imagination, we find our muse,
A journey through creativity, where thoughts amuse.

For imagination is the canvas where dreams unfold,
The melody of possibility, where stories are told.
In the epic of imagination, we find our grace,
A sanctuary of solace in life's embrace.

Here are four Epic poems, 1 each about Silence, Laughter, Tears & Strength

Epic Poem: Silence
In the hush of the night where whispers wane,
Silence's epic journey begins its reign.
A tale of stillness where peace remains,
In the symphony of silence, hearts refrain.

From the depths of the soul to the heights of the sky,
Silence's serene embrace, it cannot deny.
In every breath taken and every moment stilled,
Silence's tranquil melody, it's fulfilled.

Through the valleys of chaos where noise invades,
To the mountaintops of tranquility where dreams cascade.
In the epic of silence, we find our rest,
A journey through quietude, where souls invest.

For silence is the refuge that soothes the soul,
The melody of serenity, where spirits enroll.
In the epic of silence, we find our grace,
A sanctuary of solace in life's embrace.

Epic Poem: Laughter
In the chorus of joy where laughter rings,
Laughter's epic journey takes flight on wings.
A tale of mirth where hearts sing,
In the symphony of laughter, souls bring.

From the depths of the belly to the heights of the sky,
Laughter's infectious embrace, it makes us fly.
In every chuckle shared and every smile bright,
Laughter's jubilant melody, it's the heart's delight.

Through the valleys of sorrow where tears may fall,
To the mountaintops of happiness where hearts enthrall.
In the epic of laughter, we find our joy,
A journey through hilarity, where hearts deploy.

For laughter is the medicine that heals the soul,
The melody of happiness, where spirits enroll.
In the epic of laughter, we find our grace,
A sanctuary of solace in life's embrace.

Epic Poem: Tears
In the well of emotion where rivers flow,
Tears' epic journey finds its ebb and flow.
A tale of sorrow where hearts bestow,
In the symphony of tears, souls know.

From the depths of pain to the heights of release,
Tears' cathartic embrace, it brings peace.
In every drop shed and every heartache felt,
Tears' poignant melody, it's heartfelt.

Through the valleys of grief where shadows loom,
To the mountaintops of healing where hearts resume.
In the epic of tears, we find our solace,
A journey through emotion, where hearts encase.

For tears are the language that speaks the soul,
The melody of empathy, where spirits enroll.
In the epic of tears, we find our grace,
A sanctuary of solace in life's embrace.
Epic Poem: Strength
crucible of adversity where trials test,
Strength's epic journey proves its best.
A tale of resilience where hearts invest,
In the symphony of strength, souls attest.

From the depths of despair to the heights of might,
Strength's indomitable spirit, it takes flight.
In every trial faced and every battle won,
Strength's resolute melody, it's begun.

Through the valleys of doubt where fears persist,
To the mountaintops of triumph where dreams enlist.
In the epic of strength, we find our might,
A journey through adversity, where souls take flight.

For strength is the fortress that shields the soul,
The melody of perseverance, where spirits enroll.
In the epic of strength, we find our grace,
A sanctuary of solace in life's embrace.

Here are four Epic poems, 1 each about Vulnerability, Renewal, Acceptance & Mystery

Epic Poem: Vulnerability
In the depths of the heart where walls crumble,
Vulnerability's epic journey starts to rumble.
A tale of openness where fears may stumble,
In the symphony of vulnerability, souls assemble.

From the depths of insecurity to the heights of trust,
Vulnerability's courageous embrace, it's a must.
In every tear shed and every mask removed,
Vulnerability's honest melody, it's proved.

Through the valleys of doubt where shadows loom,
To the mountaintops of authenticity where hearts bloom.
In the epic of vulnerability, we find our strength,
A journey through openness, where souls length.
For vulnerability is the gateway to connection,
The melody of truth, where hearts find affection.
In the epic of vulnerability, we find our grace,
A sanctuary of solace in life's embrace.

Epic Poem: Renewal
In the cycle of life where seasons turn,
Renewal's epic journey begins to churn.
A tale of rebirth where hearts yearn,
In the symphony of renewal, souls discern.

From the depths of winter to the heights of spring,
Renewal's relentless force, it brings.
In every bud bloomed and every seed sown,
Renewal's rejuvenating melody, it's grown.

Through the valleys of darkness where shadows creep,
To the mountaintops of light where dreams leap.
In the epic of renewal, we find our hope,
A journey through transformation, where souls elope.

For renewal is the promise of a new day,
The melody of growth, where dreams find their way.
In the epic of renewal, we find our grace,
A sanctuary of solace in life's embrace.
Epic Poem: Acceptance
Here are four Epic poems, 1 each about Transformation, Eternity, Cosmos & Happiness
Epic Poem: Transformation
In the crucible of change where souls are tested,
In the realm of the heart where judgments cease,
Acceptance's epic journey finds its peace.
A tale of surrender where conflicts cease,
In the symphony of acceptance, souls release.

From the depths of resistance to the heights of surrender,
Acceptance's gentle embrace, it's tender.
In every apology given and every apology received,
Acceptance's healing melody, it's believed.

Through the valleys of denial where shadows reign,
To the mountaintops of understanding where hearts gain.
In the epic of acceptance, we find our serenity,
A journey through forgiveness, where hearts align.

For acceptance is the key that unlocks the door,
The melody of harmony, where judgments restore.
In the epic of acceptance, we find our grace,
A sanctuary of solace in life's embrace.

Epic Poem: Mystery
In the enigma of the universe where secrets hide,
Mystery's epic journey begins to glide.
A tale of intrigue where truths confide,
In the symphony of mystery, souls decide.

From the depths of the cosmos to the expanse of the mind,
Mystery's elusive embrace, it's undefined.
In every question asked and every answer sought,
Mystery's elusive melody, it's sought.

Through the valleys of uncertainty where shadows play,
To the mountaintops of revelation where truths sway.
In the epic of mystery, we find our wonder,
A journey through curiosity, where minds plunder.

For mystery is the spark that ignites the flame,
The melody of wonder, where souls reclaim.
In the epic of mystery, we find our grace,
A sanctuary of solace in life's embrace.
Transformation's epic journey is manifested.
A tale of growth where hearts are invested,
In the symphony of transformation, souls are attested.

From the depths of darkness to the heights of light,
Transformation's relentless might, it takes flight.
In every trial faced and every obstacle overcome,
Transformation's empowering melody, it drums.

Through the valleys of despair where shadows loom,
To the mountaintops of enlightenment where dreams consume.
In the epic of transformation, we find our rebirth,
A journey through evolution, where souls unearth.

For transformation is the phoenix that rises from the ashes,
The melody of renewal, where spirits rehash.
In the epic of transformation, we find our grace,
A sanctuary of solace in life's embrace.

Epic Poem: Eternity

In the infinite expanse where time has no hold,
Eternity's epic journey is told.
A tale of forever where stories unfold,
In the symphony of eternity, souls behold.

From the depths of the past to the heights of the future,
Eternity's timeless embrace, it's our nurture.
In every moment lived and every memory stored,
Eternity's everlasting melody, it's adored.

Through the valleys of mortality where time fades,
To the mountaintops of immortality where dreams cascade.
In the epic of eternity, we find our legacy,
A journey through infinity, where souls preside.

For eternity is the echo that resonates through time,
The melody of forever, where dreams align.
In the epic of eternity, we find our grace,
A sanctuary of solace in life's embrace.

Epic Poem: Cosmos

In the boundless expanse where stars collide,
Cosmos's epic journey is wide.
A tale of creation where wonders reside,
In the symphony of cosmos, souls confide.

From the depths of the void to the heights of the heavens,
Cosmos's cosmic dance, it beckons.
In every galaxy spun and every planet formed,
Cosmos's celestial melody, it's performed.

Through the valleys of darkness where mysteries dwell,
To the mountaintops of brilliance where wonders swell.
In the epic of cosmos, we find our awe,
A journey through infinity, where dreams thaw.

For cosmos is the canvas where worlds are born,
The melody of creation, where souls adorn.
In the epic of cosmos, we find our grace,
A sanctuary of solace in life's embrace.

Epic Poem: Happiness

In the heart's embrace where joy resides,
Happiness's epic journey abides.
A tale of bliss where dreams collide,
In the symphony of happiness, souls confide.

From the depths of despair to the heights of elation,
Happiness's radiant embrace, it's salvation.
In every smile shared and every laughter heard,
Happiness's uplifting melody, it's stirred.

Through the valleys of sorrow where tears may fall,
To the mountaintops of joy where hearts enthrall.
In the epic of happiness, we find our delight,
A journey through euphoria, where souls ignite.

For happiness is the beacon that lights the way,
The melody of joy, where spirits sway.
In the epic of happiness, we find our grace,
A sanctuary of solace in life's embrace.

-:¦:-•:*'''''*:•.-:¦:-•**•-:¦:-•:*'''''*:•:*'''''*:•.-:¦:-•**•-:¦:--:¦:-•:*'''''*:•.-:¦:- •**•-:¦:-•:*'''''*:•:*'''''*:•.-:¦:-•**•-:¦:-

BALLAD:

A narrative poem that tells a story, often focusing on themes of love, tragedy, or adventure, typically written in a simple, rhythmic style.

-:|:-•:*''''*:•.-:|:-•**•-:|:-•:*''''*:•:*''''*:•.-:|:-•**•-:|:--:|:-•:*''''*:•.-:|:- •**•-:|:-•:*''''*:•:*''''*:•.-:|:-•**•-:|:-

Here are four Ballad poems, 1 each about Love, Nature, Beauty & Time

Ballad of Love
In the meadows green where flowers bloom,
Lies a tale of love, in the sweet perfume.
A maiden fair, with eyes like stars,
Captured the heart of a knight from afar.

Through trials and tribulations, they did stray,
Yet their love endured, come what may.
In moonlit nights and sun-kissed days,
Their love blossomed in myriad ways.

Though storms may rage and tempests roar,
Their love remained steadfast, forevermore.
For in each other's arms, they found their home,
Bound together, never to roam.

So let this ballad of love resound,
A testament to the love they found.
In each other's hearts, they'll eternally shine,
A love so pure, a love divine.

Ballad of Nature
In the whispering woods where trees stand tall,
Lies a ballad of nature, heard by all.
The babbling brook and the rustling leaves,
Sing a melody that forever weaves.

From the mountains high to the valleys low,
Nature's wonders, they ebb and flow.
The song of the birds and the dance of the breeze,
Paint a picture of tranquility, a masterpiece.

In fields of gold and skies of blue,
Nature's beauty, it shines anew.
For in every leaf and every flower,
Nature reveals its timeless power.

So let this ballad of nature ring,
A symphony of life in everything.
In nature's embrace, we find our rhyme,
A harmony that withstands all time.

Ballad of Beauty
In the canvas of life where colors blend,
Lies a ballad of beauty that never ends.
The graceful dance of the butterfly's flight,
The radiant glow of the stars at night.

From the delicate petals of a rose in bloom,
To the vast expanse of an ocean's plume.
Beauty surrounds us, everywhere we look,
In nature's embrace, in every nook.

In the laughter of children and the touch of a friend,
Beauty's presence, it knows no end.
For in every smile and every tear,
Beauty's essence, it's always near.

So let this ballad of beauty resound,
A celebration of the beauty we've found.
In each moment lived, in every rhyme,
Beauty's presence, it stands the test of time.

Ballad of Time

In the sands of time where moments pass,
Lies a ballad of time, a looking glass.
The ticking clock and the turning tide,
Remind us of time's relentless ride.

From the dawn of life to the twilight years,
Time's journey, it's filled with hopes and fears.
The memories made and the lessons learned,
Shape our lives, in every turn.

In the bonds of friendship and the bonds of love,
Time's passage, it's written above.
For in every heartbeat and every breath,
Time's rhythm, it leads us to our death.

So let this ballad of time be sung,
A reminder of the race we've run.
In each fleeting moment, in every chime,
Time's echo, it withstands all time.

Here are four Ballad poems, 1 each about Death, Dreams, Hope & Despair

Ballad of Death

In the shadowed realm where darkness reigns,
Lies a ballad of death, with sorrow's stains.
The tolling bell and the mournful wail,
Echoes of loss, they fill the vale.

From the first breath drawn to the final sigh,
Death's embrace, it beckons nigh.
The cycle of life, it comes to an end,
As souls depart, to realms unknown they wend.

In the depths of grief where tears flow free,
Death's cold touch, it takes its fee.
Yet in the stillness of the night,
We find solace, in memories bright.

So let this ballad of death be told,
A tribute to those we've lost, so bold.
In the tapestry of life, they'll forever weave,
In our hearts, their spirits never leave.

Ballad of Dreams

In the land of dreams where fantasies roam,
Lies a ballad of dreams, a heart's sweet home.
The whispered wish and the secret desire,
Fuel the flames of dreams, ever higher.

From the first glimmer of hope to the last sigh,
Dreams take flight, reaching for the sky.
The stars above, they guide the way,
As dreams unfold, in the light of day.

In the depths of sleep where visions play,
Dreams lead us, on a wondrous array.
For in each dream, a world is spun,
Where hearts find solace, under the sun.

So let this ballad of dreams resound,
A testament to the dreams we've found.
In the canvas of night, they'll forever gleam,
For dreams are the stuff from which we dream.

Ballad of Hope

In the darkest night where shadows creep,
Lies a ballad of hope, where hearts do leap.
The flickering flame and the whispered prayer,
Illuminate the path, through despair.

From the depths of despair to the heights of grace,
Hope's embrace, it finds its place.
The beacon of light in the stormy sea,
Guides us home, to where we're meant to be.

In the depths of sorrow where tears may fall,
Hope's gentle touch, it heals us all.
For in each trial faced and each challenge met,
Hope's flame, it never shall set.

So let this ballad of hope be sung,
A hymn to the hope that's never undone.
In the hearts of the weary, it finds its scope,
For hope is the anchor in life's tempestuous slope.

Ballad of Despair

In the abyss of despair where darkness dwells,
Lies a ballad of despair, where sadness swells.
The heavy heart and the weary soul,
Lost in despair's relentless toll.

From the depths of anguish to the heights of grief,
Despair's grip, it offers no relief.
The shadows cast, they cloak the light,
As despair consumes, day turns to night.

In the depths of sorrow where tears may flow,
Despair's icy touch, it lays its woe.
Yet in the depths of despair's bleak night,
We find solace, in the morning light.

So let this ballad of despair be known,
A lament for the sadness we've sown.
In the depths of despair, we find our plea,
For redemption's grace, to set us free.

Here are four Ballad poems, 1 each about Friendship, Loneliness, Memories & Music

Ballad of Friendship
In the golden light of the setting sun,
Lies a ballad of friendship, forever spun.
The bond so strong, it never fades,
Through trials and triumphs, in the shade.

From the laughter shared to the tears we cry,
Friendship's embrace, it lifts us high.
The hand to hold in times of need,
A steadfast anchor, in word and deed.

In the heart's embrace where trust resides,
Friendship's melody, it gently guides.
For in each friend, a treasure found,
A bond unbroken, forever bound.

So let this ballad of friendship ring,
A celebration of the joy they bring.
In the tapestry of life, they'll forever weave,
In our hearts, their spirits never leave.

Ballad of Loneliness
In the silent hours of the lonely night,
Lies a ballad of loneliness, a ghostly sight.
The empty room and the hollow heart,
Echoes of solitude, tearing apart.

From the crowded streets to the empty hall,
Loneliness's shadow, it covers all.
The ache within, it knows no end,
As solitude becomes a faithful friend.

In the quietude where silence reigns,
Loneliness's lament, it bears the stains.
For in the depths of solitude's embrace,
We find solace, in empty space.

So let this ballad of loneliness be sung,
A haunting melody, for hearts undone.
In the depths of despair, they'll forever roam,
For loneliness is the burden of the lone.

Ballad of Memories
In the corners of the mind where shadows dwell,
Lies a ballad of memories, where stories tell.
The laughter shared and the tears we shed,
Echoes of the past, in our heads.

From the days of youth to the twilight years,
Memories linger, through joy and tears.
The moments captured, forever kept,
In the tapestry of time, they're tightly swept.

In the quiet moments where thoughts reside,
Memories's melody, it cannot hide.
For in each memory, a story's told,
A cherished treasure, in days of old.

So let this ballad of memories resound,
A tribute to the past, where love is found.
In the tapestry of time, they'll forever weave,
In our hearts, their spirits never leave.

Ballad of Music
In the symphony of life where rhythms play,
Lies a ballad of music, in every way.
The melody sweet and the harmony clear,
Music's embrace, it draws us near.

From the gentle lullaby to the anthem bold,
Music's power, it cannot be controlled.
The notes that soar and the chords that ring,
Music's magic, it makes us sing.

In the quietude where silence falls,
Music's melody, it enthralls.
For in each note, a soul's released,
A symphony of love, in perfect peace.

So let this ballad of music ring,
A celebration of the songs we sing.
In the heart's embrace, they'll forever stay,
For music is the language where souls play.

Here are four Ballad poems, 1 each about Art, Inspiration, Creativity & Courage

Ballad of Art
In the canvas of life where colors blend,
Lies a ballad of art, where souls transcend.
The strokes so bold, the colors bright,
Art's embrace, it brings us light.

From the master's hand to the novice's touch,
Art's beauty, it means so much.
The stories told and the emotions stirred,
In art's reflection, our hearts are heard.

In the gallery halls where masterpieces hang,
Art's melody, it echoes, it sang.
For in each stroke, a tale is spun,
A masterpiece of life, forever won.

So let this ballad of art be sung,
A tribute to the beauty we've found.
In the tapestry of life, it'll forever weave,
In our hearts, its spirit will never leave.

Ballad of Inspiration
In the quiet moments where thoughts reside,
Lies a ballad of inspiration, a rising tide.
The spark so bright, the flame so strong,
Inspiration's embrace, it guides us along.

From the depths of doubt to the heights of dreams,
Inspiration's fire, it ignites, it gleams.
The whispers heard and the visions seen,
In inspiration's embrace, we find our sheen.

In the darkest night where shadows loom,
Inspiration's melody, it lights up the room.
For in each idea, a dream takes flight,
A beacon of hope, in the darkest night.

So let this ballad of inspiration resound,
A tribute to the dreams we've found.
In the tapestry of life, it'll forever weave,
In our hearts, its spirit will never leave.

Ballad of Creativity
In the realm of imagination where wonders soar,
Lies a ballad of creativity, forevermore.
The ideas that flow, the dreams that bloom,
Creativity's embrace, it clears the gloom.

From the blank page to the empty stage,
Creativity's magic, it knows no age.
The stories told and the songs sung,
In creativity's embrace, we find our rung.

In the quiet moments where ideas take flight,
Creativity's melody, it shines so bright.
For in each creation, a piece of us,
A masterpiece of life, without fuss.

So let this ballad of creativity ring,
A tribute to the beauty we bring.
In the tapestry of life, it'll forever weave,
In our hearts, its spirit will never leave.

Ballad of Courage
In the face of fear where shadows loom,
Lies a ballad of courage, in the gloom.
The strength to stand, the will to fight,
Courage's embrace, it brings us light.

From the depths of despair to the heights of grace,
Courage's flame, it sets the pace.
The battles fought and the victories won,
In courage's embrace, we find our run.

In the darkest night where fears prevail,
Courage's melody, it breaks the veil.
For in each step taken, a path unfolds,
A journey of bravery, where hearts enfold.

So let this ballad of courage resound,
A tribute to the strength we've found.
In the tapestry of life, it'll forever weave,
In our hearts, its spirit will never leave.

Here are four Ballad poems, 1 each about Faith, Doubt, Solitude & Joy

Ballad of Faith
In the depths of the soul where shadows wane,
Lies a ballad of faith, in the heart's domain.
The light that guides, the hope that stays,
Faith's embrace, in its warmth we sway.

From the trials faced to the dreams we chase,
Faith's steadfast hand, it finds its place.
The prayers whispered and the trust we hold,
In faith's sanctuary, we're consoled.

In the darkest hour where doubts may creep,
Faith's melody, it sings us to sleep.
For in each belief, a soul finds peace,
A beacon of hope, where doubts cease.

So let this ballad of faith resound,
A testament to the trust we've found.
In the tapestry of life, it'll forever weave,
In our hearts, its spirit will never leave.

Ballad of Doubt
In the depths of the mind where shadows lie,
Lies a ballad of doubt, where fears multiply.
The questions asked, the answers lost,
Doubt's embrace, it comes at a cost.

From the uncertainties faced to the fears we hide,
Doubt's relentless grip, it grips us wide.
The voices whispered and the shadows cast,
In doubt's shadow, our hopes are outlast.

In the quiet moments where doubts arise,
Doubt's melody, it sings us lies.
For in each uncertainty, a soul finds strife,
A labyrinth of fears, where doubts thrive.

So let this ballad of doubt be known,
A lament for the fears we've sown.
In the depths of despair, it'll forever roam,
For doubt is the burden of the lone.

Ballad of Solitude
In the quietude where silence reigns
Lies a ballad of solitude, where hearts sustain.
The moments spent, the thoughts that roam,
Solitude's embrace, it finds its home.

From the crowded streets to the empty room,
Solitude's gentle touch, it brings us to bloom.
The introspection found and the peace we seek,
In solitude's sanctuary, we find our peak.

In the stillness of the night where silence sings,
Solitude's melody, it spreads its wings.
For in each moment alone, a soul finds rest,
A refuge of calm, in solitude's nest.

So let this ballad of solitude resound,
A hymn to the quietude we've found.
In the tapestry of life, it'll forever weave,
In our hearts, its spirit will never leave.

Ballad of Joy
In the heart's embrace where happiness resides,
Lies a ballad of joy, where spirits rise.
The laughter shared, the smiles wide,
Joy's embrace, in its warmth we glide.

From the moments cherished to the dreams we chase,
Joy's infectious spirit, it finds its place.
The memories made and the bonds we form,
In joy's embrace, we weather the storm.

In the brightest day where happiness gleams,
Joy's melody, it fills our dreams.
For in each moment of bliss, a soul finds delight,
A symphony of happiness, in the heart's delight.

So let this ballad of joy be sung,
A tribute to the happiness we've won.
In the tapestry of life, it'll forever spin
In a universe where everyone wins.

Here are four Ballad poems, 1 each about Sorrow, Childhood, Wisdom & Innocence

Ballad of Sorrow
In the depths of the heart where shadows dwell,
Lies a ballad of sorrow, a somber knell.
The tears that fall, the sighs that heave,
Sorrow's embrace, it never leaves.

From the moments lost to the dreams unfulfilled,
Sorrow's heavy burden, it's never stilled.
The pain endured and the scars we bear,
In sorrow's shadow, we find despair.

In the quiet moments where grief resides,
Sorrow's melody, it softly glides.
For in each heartache, a soul finds lament,
A mournful melody, in sorrow's descent.

So let this ballad of sorrow resound,
A tribute to the sadness we've found.
In the tapestry of life, it'll forever weave,
In our hearts, its spirit will never leave.

Ballad of Childhood
In the land of innocence where dreams take flight,
Lies a ballad of childhood, in the soft moonlight.
The laughter shared, the games we'd play,
Childhood's embrace, it lights the way.

From the days of wonder to the nights of sleep,
Childhood's magic, it's ours to keep.
The memories made and the joys we knew,
In childhood's realm, our dreams renew.

In the innocence of youth where dreams are born,
Childhood's melody, it sings at dawn.
For in each moment of play, a soul finds glee,
A symphony of innocence, forever free.

So let this ballad of childhood be sung,
A tribute to the innocence we've sprung.
In the tapestry of life, it'll forever weave,
In our hearts, its spirit will never leave.

Ballad of Wisdom
In the halls of knowledge where truths are found,
Lies a ballad of wisdom, with echoes profound.
The lessons learned, the paths we've trod,
Wisdom's embrace, it points to God.

From the trials faced to the choices made,
Wisdom's guiding hand, it doesn't fade.
The insights gained and the journeys made,
In wisdom's sanctuary, we find our shade.

In the depths of thought where silence reigns,
Wisdom's melody, it soothes our pains.
For in each truth revealed, a soul finds grace,
A symphony of wisdom, in life's embrace.

So let this ballad of wisdom resound,
A tribute to the lessons we've found.
In the tapestry of life, it'll forever weave,
In our hearts, its spirit will never leave.

Ballad of Innocence
In the purity of heart where dreams take flight,
Lies a ballad of innocence, in the soft moonlight.
The wonder felt, the dreams that soar,
Innocence's embrace, it opens the door.

From the days of youth to the nights of sleep,
Innocence's magic, it's ours to keep.
The moments shared and the joys we knew,
In innocence's realm, our dreams renew.

In the purity of spirit where hearts are light,
Innocence's melody, it sings at night.
For in each moment of wonder, a soul finds peace,
A symphony of innocence, forever released.

So let this ballad of innocence be sung,
A tribute to the purity we've sprung.
In the tapestry of life, it'll forever weave,
In our hearts, its spirit will never leave.

Here are four Ballad poems, 1 each about Passion, Serenity, Freedom & Justice

Ballad of Passion
In the fiery depths of the heart's embrace,
Lies a ballad of passion, in its grace.
The flames that burn, the desires untamed,
Passion's embrace, forever inflamed.

From the fervent kiss to the ardent touch,
Passion's fervor, it means so much.
The dreams that soar and the hearts that race,
In passion's storm, we find our place.

In the depths of desire where yearning gleams,
Passion's melody, it fuels our dreams.
For in each moment of love, a soul finds fire,
A symphony of passion, in desire's choir.

So let this ballad of passion resound,
A tribute to the ardor we've found.
In the tapestry of life, it'll forever weave,
In our hearts, its spirit will never leave.

Ballad of Serenity
In the tranquil depths where calmness flows,
Lies a ballad of serenity, where peace bestows.
The gentle breeze and the stillness deep,
Serenity's embrace, in its silent sweep.

From the quiet dawn to the peaceful night,
Serenity's calm, it guides us right.
The moments cherished and the spirits free,
In serenity's haven, we find our plea.

In the peaceful silence where worries cease,
Serenity's melody, it brings release.
For in each moment of peace, a soul finds rest,
A symphony of serenity, in life's quest.

So let this ballad of serenity be sung,
A tribute to the calmness we've sprung.
In the tapestry of life, it'll forever weave,
In our hearts, its spirit will never leave.

Ballad of Freedom
In the open expanse where skies are wide,
Lies a ballad of freedom, in the open stride.
The winds that blow and the horizons vast,
Freedom's embrace, it holds us fast.

From the chains released to the dreams unbound,
Freedom's spirit, it knows no bound.
The choices made and the paths we take,
In freedom's grasp, we find our wake.

In the boundless sky where eagles soar,
Freedom's melody, it sings for more.
For in each breath of liberty, a soul finds flight,
A symphony of freedom, in life's bright light.

So let this ballad of freedom resound,
A tribute to the liberty we've found.
In the tapestry of life, it'll forever weave,
In our hearts, its spirit will never leave.

Ballad of Justice
In the halls of righteousness where fairness reigns,
Lies a ballad of justice, where equity maintains.
The scales that balance and the truth unveiled,
Justice's embrace, it never failed.

From the rights restored to the wrongs made right,
Justice's hand, it guides the fight.
The voices heard and the rights defended,
In justice's court, the wrongs amended.

In the halls of truth where justice gleams,
Justice's melody, it fights for dreams.
For in each victory for right, a soul finds peace,
A symphony of justice, where justice's cease.

So let this ballad of justice be sung,
A tribute to the fairness we've sprung.
In the tapestry of life, it'll forever weave,
In our hearts, its spirit will never leave.

Here are four Ballad poems, 1 each about Change, Resilience, Gratitude & Forgiveness

Ballad of Change
In the dance of life, a constant sway,
Lies a ballad of change, come what may.
From the dawn's first light to the twilight's gleam,
Change's whisper is heard in every stream.

Through the winding paths, we find our way,
Embracing transformation, day by day.
With every turn, a new story to unfold,
In the tale of change, our destiny's mold.

So let us sing of change's refrain,
A melody of growth through joy and pain.
For in the tapestry of life, it weaves,
Change, the constant, in which we believe.

Ballad of Resilience
In the crucible of hardship's might,
Lies a ballad of resilience, shining bright.
Through storms endured and battles fought,
Resilience's flame, it cannot be bought.

In the face of adversity, we stand tall,
Meeting each challenge, we give our all.
With every trial, a strength revealed,
In the heart of resilience, wounds are healed.

So let us sing of resilience's song,
A chorus of courage, in times long.
For in the tapestry of life, it's clear,
Resilience, the beacon, we hold dear.

Ballad of Gratitude
In the quiet moments of reflection deep,
Lies a ballad of gratitude, ours to keep.
For every blessing, both big and small,
Gratitude's whisper, it touches all.

With hearts full of thanks, we find our grace,
In the warmth of gratitude, we embrace.
For every kindness, a debt we owe,
In gratitude's embrace, our spirits grow.

So let us sing of gratitude's hymn,
A chorus of thanks, both light and dim.
For in the tapestry of life, we see,
Gratitude, the key to feeling free.

Ballad of Forgiveness
In the chambers of the heart, forgiveness lies,
A ballad of healing, beneath the skies.
With every hurt, a chance to mend,
In forgiveness's embrace, we find our friend.

Through wounds deep and scars unseen,
Forgiveness's touch, it washes clean.
For every apology, a door unlocked,
In forgiveness's sanctuary, love is stocked.

So let us sing of forgiveness's grace,
A melody of peace, in every place.
For in the tapestry of life, we find,
the joyful place for spirit of mind.

Here are four Ballad poems, 1 each about Longing, Belonging, Discovery & Wonder

Ballad of Longing
In the depths of night where shadows creep,
Lies a ballad of longing, in dreams we keep.
The whispers heard and the yearning felt,
Longing's embrace, where hearts melt.

From the distant shores to the starlit sky,
Longing's echo, it whispers by.
The memories cherished and the moments missed,
In longing's sigh, our souls insist.

So let us sing of longing's tale,
A melody of desire, in every gale.
For in the tapestry of life, we find,
Longing, the thread, that binds our mind.

Ballad of Belonging
In the heart's embrace where love abounds,
Lies a ballad of belonging, in the sounds.
The bonds we form and the ties we share,
Belonging's embrace, beyond compare.

From the friendships forged to the family near,
Belonging's warmth, it draws us near.
The laughter shared and the tears we shed,
In belonging's realm, our souls are led.

So let us sing of belonging's song,
A chorus of unity, where we belong.
For in the tapestry of life, we find,
Belonging, the anchor, in hearts entwined.

Ballad of Discovery
In the realm of curiosity where wonders lie,
Lies a ballad of discovery, soaring high.
The mysteries unraveled and the truths revealed,
Discovery's embrace, in awe we yield.

From the distant stars to the depths below,
Discovery's call, it bids us go.
The journeys taken and the paths unknown,
In discovery's wake, our spirits are shown.

So let us sing of discovery's quest,
A symphony of knowledge, in every test.
For in the tapestry of life, we find,
Discovery, the spark, that lights the mind.

Ballad of Wonder
In the moments of awe where beauty shines,
Lies a ballad of wonder, in nature's lines.
The sights beheld and the dreams we chase,
Wonder's embrace, in every space.

From the gentle breeze to the mountain's peak,
Wonder's magic, it makes us seek.
The colors painted and the songs sung,
In wonder's realm, our souls are stung.

So let us sing of wonder's grace,
A tribute to the awe we face.
For in the tapestry of life, we find,
Wonder, the magic, that enchants our mind.

Here are four Ballad poems, 1 each about Journey, Reflection, Harmony & Imagination

Ballad of the Journey
In the vast expanse where roads divide,
Lies a ballad of journey, our hearts abide.
With every step, a story unfolds,
Journey's embrace, in adventures untold.

From the hills we climb to the valleys deep,
Journey's song, it never sleeps.
The trials faced and the victories won,
In journey's path, our dreams are spun.

So let us sing of the journey's call,
A melody of courage, through rise and fall.
For in the tapestry of life, we find,
Journey, the compass, that guides our mind.

Ballad of Harmony
In the symphony of life where notes align,
Lies a ballad of harmony, in rhythms divine.
With every chord, a melody sings,
Harmony's embrace, in music's wings.

From the chords we strum to the songs we sing,
Harmony's magic, it makes hearts ring.
The voices raised and the souls entwined,
In harmony's chorus, our spirits find.

So let us sing of harmony's song,
A chorus of unity, where we belong.
For in the tapestry of life, we find,
Harmony, the bond, that makes us kind.

Ballad of Reflection
In the quiet moments where silence reigns,
Lies a ballad of reflection, where wisdom gains.
With every thought, a truth is found,
Reflection's embrace, in silence profound.

From the memories cherished to the lessons learned,
Reflection's fire, it brightly burned.
The paths we've walked and the choices made,
In reflection's mirror, our souls are laid.

So let us sing of reflection's grace,
A hymn of understanding, in every space.
For in the tapestry of life, we find,
Reflection, the guide, that clears our mind.

Ballad of Imagination
In the realm of dreams where thoughts take flight,
Lies a ballad of imagination, in the starry night.
With every vision, a world is born,
Imagination's embrace, in dreams adorned.

From the tales we weave to the skies we soar,
Imagination's fire, it opens doors.
The fantasies spun and the hopes unfurled,
In imagination's canvas, our dreams swirl.

So let us sing of imagination's tale,
A symphony of wonder, where dreams prevail.
For in the tapestry of life, we find,
Imagination, the spark, that fuels our mind.

Here are four Ballad poems, 1 each about Silence, Laughter, Tears & Strength

Ballad of Silence
In the hush of night where whispers cease,
Lies a ballad of silence, a moment of peace.
With every breath, a calm descends,
Silence's embrace, where solace mends.

From the stillness deep to the quiet calm,
Silence's song, it holds a charm.
The thoughts that roam and the hearts that yearn,
In silence's sanctuary, we discern.

So let us sing of silence's grace,
A melody of quiet in every space.
For in the tapestry of life, we find,
Silence, the solace, that soothes the mind.

Ballad of Laughter
In the echo of joy where hearts align,
Lies a ballad of laughter, a gift divine.
With every chuckle, a bond is sealed,
Laughter's embrace, in joy revealed.

From the jokes we share to the smiles bright,
Laughter's magic, it brings delight.
The memories made and the moments dear,
In laughter's echo, our spirits cheer.

So let us sing of laughter's song,
A chorus of joy, where we belong.
For in the tapestry of life, we find,
Laughter, the harmony, that makes us kind.

Ballad of Tears
In the depths of sorrow where emotions flow,
Lies a ballad of tears, in sadness's glow.
With every drop, a heart breaks free,
Tears' embrace, in sorrow's sea.

From the pains endured to the losses felt,
Tears' melody, in grief we've dwelt.
The wounds that heal and the scars remain,
In tears' release, our souls regain.

So let us sing of tears' lament,
A hymn of healing, in moments spent.
For in the tapestry of life, we find,
Tears, the catharsis, that cleanses the mind.

Ballad of Strength
In the forge of struggle where trials arise,
Lies a ballad of strength, in courage's guise.
With every challenge, a soul withstands,
Strength's embrace, where resilience expands.

From the battles fought to the wars won,
Strength's anthem, it's never done.
The spirits lifted and the wills unbroken,
In strength's embrace, our hearts outspoken.

So let us sing of strength's refrain,
A chorus of fortitude, through joy and pain.
For in the tapestry of life, we find,
Strength, the cornerstone, of the human mind.

Here are four Ballad poems, 1 each about Vulnerability, Renewal, Acceptance & Mystery

Ballad of Vulnerability
In the quiet chambers where fears reside,
Lies a ballad of vulnerability, where hearts confide.
With every trembling step, a soul reveals,
Vulnerability's embrace, where truth heals.

From the walls we build to the masks we wear,
Vulnerability's song, it strips us bare.
The wounds exposed and the scars we hide,
In vulnerability's gaze, we find our guide.

So let us sing of vulnerability's tale,
A melody of courage, in every gale.
For in the tapestry of life, we find,
Vulnerability, the strength, that binds our mind.

Ballad of Renewal
In the dawn's first light where hope ignites,
Lies a ballad of renewal, in nature's rites.
With every bud that blooms, a spirit soars,
Renewal's embrace, where life restores.

From the ashes of yesterday to the seeds we sow,
Renewal's magic, it makes hearts glow.
The seasons turn and the cycles spin,
In renewal's cycle, we begin again.

So let us sing of renewal's song,
A chorus of rebirth, where we belong.
For in the tapestry of life, we find,
Renewal, the promise, of a soul refined.

Ballad of Acceptance
In the open fields where judgments wane,
Lies a ballad of acceptance, without disdain.
With every hand extended, a bridge is built,
Acceptance's embrace, where hearts are stilled.

From the differences embraced to the wounds forgiven,
Acceptance's grace, it makes us driven.
The barriers broken and the love professed,
In acceptance's arms, we find our rest.

So let us sing of acceptance's grace,
A hymn of unity, in every place.
For in the tapestry of life, we find,
Acceptance, the peace, that eases the mind.

Ballad of Mystery
In the shadows deep where secrets lie,
Lies a ballad of mystery, in whispers sly.
With every enigma, a story untold,
Mystery's embrace, where wonders unfold.

From the riddles unsolved to the dreams we chase,
Mystery's allure, it leaves no trace.
The questions asked and the answers sought,
In mystery's allure, our minds are caught.

So let us sing of mystery's intrigue,
A symphony of wonder, in every league.
For in the tapestry of life, we find,
Mystery, the magic, that enchants the mind.

Here are four Ballad poems, 1 each about Transformation, Eternity, Cosmos & Happiness

Ballad of Transformation
In the heart's deepest chambers, where shadows lie,
Lies a ballad of transformation, where dreams defy.
With every whispered wish, a soul takes flight,
Transformation's embrace, in the darkest night.

From the cocoon's shell to the butterfly's wing,
Transformation's magic, it makes hearts sing.
The metamorphosis complete, the journey's end,
In transformation's dance, we find our mend.

So let us sing of transformation's tale,
A melody of rebirth, where dreams prevail.
For in the tapestry of life, we find,
Transformation, the key, to the soul's bind.

Ballad of Eternity
In the endless expanse where time stands still,
Lies a ballad of eternity, beyond the thrill.
With every beat of the heart, a soul transcends,
Eternity's embrace, where life never ends.

From the stars that twinkle to the oceans wide,
Eternity's echo, it's a timeless ride.
The moments cherished and the memories stored,
In eternity's realm, our spirits soared.

So let us sing of eternity's hymn,
A chorus of forever, where light is dim.
For in the tapestry of life, we find,
Eternity, the promise, of the soul's bind.

Ballad of the Cosmos
In the boundless universe where galaxies dance,
Lies a ballad of the cosmos, in cosmic trance.
With every shimmering star, a story weaves,
Cosmos's embrace, where wonder conceives.

From the black hole's maw to the supernova's glow,
Cosmos's grandeur, it's a cosmic show.
The mysteries unveiled and the planets spun,
In cosmos's ballet, our journey's begun.

So let us sing of the cosmos's song,
A symphony of stardust, where we belong.
For in the tapestry of life, we find,
Cosmos, the infinite, in the mind's bind.

Ballad of Happiness
In the laughter's echo where joy abounds,
Lies a ballad of happiness, in life's rounds.
With every smile shared, a heart takes flight,
Happiness's embrace, in the darkest night.

From the friendships forged to the love we hold,
Happiness's magic, it never grows old.
The moments cherished and the dreams we chase,
In happiness's embrace, we find our grace.

So let us sing of happiness's tale,
A melody of joy, where hearts prevail.
For in the tapestry of life, we find,
Happiness, the light, in the soul's bind.

-:|:-•:*'''''*:•.-:|:-•**•-:|:-•:*'''''*:•:*'''''*:•.-:|:-•**•-:|:--:|:-•:*'''''*:•.-:|:- •**•-:|:-•:*'''''*:•:*'''''*:•.-:|:-•**•-:|:-

VILLANELLE:

A 19-line poem consisting of five tercets followed by a quatrain, with a specific rhyme scheme and repeated lines.

Here are four Vaillanelle poems, 1 each about Love, Nature, Beauty & Time

Vaillanelle of Love
In love's embrace, two hearts beat as one,
Bound by the threads of fate, they entwine.
Through laughter and tears, their journey's begun.

In passion's flame, where dreams are spun,
In whispered words and kisses divine,
In love's embrace, two hearts beat as one.

Through trials and triumphs, when day is done,
In moments shared, their souls align.
Through laughter and tears, their journey's begun.

In the dance of love beneath the sun,
In each other's arms, they find the sign.
In love's embrace, two hearts beat as one.

Through the years, when all is said and done,
Their love endures, an eternal shrine.
Through laughter and tears, their journey's begun.

In the symphony of love, where hearts won,
In the tapestry of life, their bond is fine.
In love's embrace, two hearts beat as one,
Through laughter and tears, their journey's begun.

Vaillanelle of Nature
In nature's arms, where serenity's spun,
Among the trees, under the azure sky.
Through whispers of leaves, the day's begun.

In the meadows green, where flowers shun,
The constraints of time as they sway and sigh.
In nature's arms, where serenity spun.

Through the rivers' flow, where dreams overrun,
And mountains rise, reaching so high.
Through whispers of leaves, the day's begun.

In the songs of birds, where melodies stun,
And the breeze carries secrets that mystify.
In nature's arms, where peace is found

In the dance of seasons, where cycles run,
And the stars adorn the night's supply.
Through whispers of leaves, the day's begun.

In nature's embrace, where all is won,
In the tapestry of life, where dreams lie.
In nature's arms, where serenity's spun,
Through whispers of leaves, the day's begun.

Vaillanelle of Beauty
In beauty's realm, where wonders are spun,
In the petals of flowers, in the butterfly.
Through the colors of dawn, the day's begun.

In the symphony of art, where dreams are done,
In the strokes of the brush, in the artist's eye.
In beauty's realm, where wonders are spun.

Through the eyes of a lover, where hearts are won,
In the grace of a dancer, as she takes to the sky.
Through the colors of dawn, the day's begun.

In the depths of the ocean, where mysteries run,
And the mountains' peaks reach so high.
In beauty's realm, where wonders are spun.

In the laughter of children, where innocence shun,
In the starry nights, where dreams can't die.
Through the colors of dawn, the day's begun.

In beauty's embrace, where all is won,
In the tapestry of life, where dreams lie.
In beauty's realm, where wonders are spun,
Through the colors of dawn, the day's begun.

Vaillanelle of Time
In the flow of time, where destinies run,
In the ticking clock, where moments fly.
Through the passage of hours, the day's begun.

In the memories held, when all is done,
And the echoes of the past, they amplify.
In the flow of time, where destinies run.

Through the sands of the hourglass, where all's spun,
And the seasons change, under the endless sky.
Through the passage of hours, the day's begun.

In the wrinkles of age, where stories are won,
And the wisdom of years, they testify.
In the flow of time, where destinies run.

In the cycle of life, where all's begun,
In the tapestry of existence, where we lie.
Through the passage of hours, the day's begun.

In the embrace of time, where all is done,
In the fading light, where dreams comply.
In the flow of time, where destinies run,
Through the passage of hours, the day's begun.

Here are four Vaillanelle poems, 1 each about Death, Dreams, Hope & Despair

Vaillanelle of Death
In the silent realm where shadows roam,
Death's vaillanelle sings its mournful tune.
With every breath, a journey home.

Through the veil of night, where spirits comb,
In the quiet chamber, where stars attune.
In the silent realm where shadows roam.

From the cradle to the final tome,
In the cycle of life, where souls commune.
With every breath, a journey home.

In the embrace of darkness, where all succumb,
In the realm of silence, where silence looms.
In the silent realm where shadows roam.

Through the whispers of the wind, a solemn tome,
In the stillness of the grave, where all exhume.
With every breath, a journey home.

In the dance of eternity, where hearts become,
In the tapestry of existence, where we resume.
In the silent realm where shadows roam,
With every breath, a journey home.

Vaillanelle of Dreams
In the realm of dreams, where visions soar,
Dreams' vaillanelle weaves a tapestry grand.
With every wish, a soul yearns for more.

Through the depths of night, where fantasies pour,
In the slumber's embrace, where we stand.
In the realm of dreams, where visions soar.

From the stars that twinkle to the oceans' roar,
In the canvas of night, where dreams command.
With every wish, a soul yearns for more.

In the whispers of the moon, secrets store,
In the ethereal dance, where dreams expand.
In the realm of dreams, where visions soar.

Through the corridors of time, where dreams implore,
In the labyrinth of thought, where minds disband.
With every wish, a soul yearns for more.

In the embrace of dreams, where we explore,
In the boundless expanse, where dreams withstand.
In the realm of dreams, where visions soar,
With every wish, a soul yearns for more.

Vaillanelle of Hope
In the darkest night, where shadows creep,
Hope's vaillanelle sings a hopeful song.
With every dawn, a promise to keep.

Through the storms that rage and the oceans deep,
In the heart's respite, where dreams belong.
In the darkest night, where shadows creep.

From the mountaintops to the valleys steep,
In the soul's ascent, where fears prolong.
With every dawn, a promise to keep.

In the whispers of the wind, secrets seep,
In the whispers of the wind, secrets seep.
In the darkest night, where shadows creep.

Through the echoes of time, where spirits leap,
In the echoes of time, where spirits leap.
With every dawn, a promise to keep.

In the realm of possibilities, where dreams leap,
In the realm of possibilities, where dreams leap.
In the darkest night, where shadows creep,
With every dawn, a promise to keep.

Vaillanelle of Despair
In the depths of despair, where darkness reigns,
Despair's vaillanelle echoes a mournful cry.
With every tear shed, a soul's chains.

Through the labyrinth of sorrow, where no light gains,
In the heart's abyss, where dreams defy.
In the depths of despair, where darkness reigns.

From the shattered dreams to the silent plains,
In the echoes of pain, where hearts lie.
With every tear shed, a soul's chains.

In the shadow's embrace, where hope wanes,
In the shadows of doubt, where hope sighs.
In the depths of despair, where darkness reigns.

Through the silence of night, where nothing explains,
In the silence of night, where nothing explains.
With every tear shed, a soul's chains.

In the realm of desolation, where all stains,
In the depths of despair, where sorrow tries.
In the depths of despair, where darkness reigns,
With every tear shed, a soul's chains.

Here are four Vaillanelle poems, 1 each about Friendship, Loneliness, Memories & Music

Vaillanelle of Friendship
In the garden of bonds where hearts unite,
Friendship's vaillanelle weaves a tale so true.
With every laugh shared, the world feels bright.

Through the highs and lows, in the day's light,
In the embrace of trust, where dreams accrue.
In the garden of bonds where hearts unite.

From the whispered secrets to the stars' height,
In the friendship's embrace, where spirits renew.
With every laugh shared, the world feels bright.

In the symphony of souls, where wrongs take flight,
In the harmony of love, where kindness ensues.
In the garden of bonds where hearts unite.

Through the years, when days turn to night,
In the labyrinth of life, where paths pursue.
With every laugh shared, the world feels bright.

In the embrace of friendship, where burdens light,
In the friendship's embrace, where hearts pursue.
In the garden of bonds where hearts unite,
With every laugh shared, the world feels bright.

Vaillanelle of Loneliness
In the empty spaces where silence dwells,
Loneliness's vaillanelle weaves its tune.
With every echo, a heart rebels.

Through the silent nights where darkness swells,
In the depths of solitude, where dreams prune.
In the empty spaces where silence dwells.

From the distant echoes to the distant bells,
In the void of despair, where hope balloons.
With every echo, a heart rebels.

In the shadow's embrace, where sorrow wells,
In the echoes of longing, where souls commune.
In the empty spaces where silence dwells.

Through the whispers of the wind, where truth tells,
In the whispers of the wind, where thoughts impugn.
With every echo, a heart rebels.

In the realm of solitude, where sadness dwells,
In the realm of solitude, where thoughts accrue.
In the empty spaces where silence dwells,
With every echo, a heart rebels.

Vaillanelle of Memories
In the halls of time where memories wane,
Memories' vaillanelle whispers its tale.
With every thought, a heart feels the strain.

Through the photographs faded, where shadows reign,
In the albums of yesteryears, where dreams pale.
In the halls of time where memories wane.

From the laughter shared to the tears' disdain,
In the echoes of the past, where voices trail.
With every thought, a heart feels the strain.

In the whispers of nostalgia, where echoes feign,
In the whispers of nostalgia, where hearts impale.
In the halls of time where memories wane.

Through the stories told and the stories retain,
In the tapestry of life, where stories hail.
With every thought, a heart feels the strain.

In the embrace of memories, where hearts maintain,
In the embrace of memories, where love entails.
In the halls of time where memories wane,
With every thought, a heart feels the strain.

Vaillanelle of Music
In the symphony of notes where dreams take flight,
Music's vaillanelle paints a canvas grand.
With every chord struck, the world feels bright.

Through the melody's sway in the depths of night,
In the rhythm's embrace, where souls expand.
In the symphony of notes where dreams take flight.

From the crescendo's roar to the lull's respite,
In the harmony of love, where souls withstand.
With every chord struck, the world feels bright.

In the whispers of the wind, where spirits unite,
In the echoes of harmony, where hearts demand.
In the symphony of notes where dreams take flight.

Through the strings' vibrations, where emotions incite,
In the tapestry of sound, where dreams command.
With every chord struck, the world feels bright.

In the embrace of music, where spirits alight,
In the embrace of music, where souls expand.
In the symphony of notes where dreams take flight,
With every chord struck, the world feels bright.

Here are four Vaillanelle poems, 1 each about Art, Inspiration, Creativity & Courage

Vaillanelle of Art
In the strokes of the brush where colors blend,
Art's vaillanelle whispers a tale divine.
With every stroke, a masterpiece penned.

Through the canvas of life, where dreams ascend,
In the depths of creation, where visions shine.
In the strokes of the brush where colors blend.

From the sculptures carved to the verses penned,
In the soul's expression, where truths align.
With every stroke, a masterpiece penned.

In the beauty captured, where souls suspend,
In the depths of emotion, where hearts intertwine.
In the strokes of the brush where colors blend.

Through the artist's eyes, where dreams transcend,
In the artist's hands, where worlds combine.
With every stroke, a masterpiece penned.

In the dance of creation, where souls contend,
In the tapestry of art, where dreams refine.
In the strokes of the brush where colors blend,
With every stroke, a masterpiece penned.

Vaillanelle of Inspiration
In the whispers of the muse where dreams take flight,
Inspiration's vaillanelle weaves its spell.
With every spark, the world feels bright.

Through the moments of silence and the depths of night,
In the heart's recesses, where ideas dwell.
In the whispers of the muse where dreams take flight.

From the pages filled with words to the artist's sight,
In the realm of creation, where stories swell.
With every spark, the world feels bright.

In the depths of the soul, where thoughts ignite,
In the echoes of inspiration, where hearts compel.
In the whispers of the muse where dreams take flight.

Through the streams of thought that intertwine tight,
In the tapestry of imagination, where dreams excel.
With every spark, the world feels bright.

In the embrace of inspiration, where dreams alight,
In the embrace of inspiration, where stories tell.
In the whispers of the muse where dreams take flight,
With every spark, the world feels bright.

Vaillanelle of Creativity
In the dance of ideas where minds collide,
Creativity's vaillanelle paints its hue.
With every thought, a new world is tied.

Through the blank pages where dreams abide,
In the labyrinth of thought, where visions brew.
In the dance of ideas where minds collide.

From the symphonies composed to the tales untied,
In the wellsprings of imagination, where dreams accrue.
With every thought, a new world is tied.

In the sparks of innovation, where dreams abide,
In the sparks of innovation, where truths pursue.
In the dance of ideas where minds collide.

Through the canvases of life where dreams reside,
In the strokes of creation, where passions ensue.
With every thought, a new world is tied.

In the embrace of creativity, where dreams abide,
In the embrace of creativity, where visions renew.
In the dance of ideas where minds collide,
With every thought, a new world is tied.

Vaillanelle of Courage
In the heart's deepest caverns where fears reside,
Courage's vaillanelle whispers its decree.
With every step taken, a soul finds its stride.

Through the tempest's rage and the ocean's tide,
In the depths of adversity, where doubts flee.
In the heart's deepest caverns where fears reside.

From the battles fought to the wounds that bide,
In the crucible of bravery, where souls plea.
With every step taken, a soul finds its stride.

In the face of darkness, where hopes abide,
In the depths of the soul, where dreams decree.
In the heart's deepest caverns where fears reside.

Through the trials endured and the tears dried,
In the crucible of strength, where hearts decree.
With every step taken, a soul finds its stride.

In the embrace of courage, where dreams abide,
In the embrace of courage, where fears flee.
In the heart's deepest caverns where fears reside,
With every step taken, a soul finds its stride

.

Here are four Vaillanelle poems, 1 each about Faith, Doubt, Solitude & Joy

Vaillanelle of Faith
In the depths of faith, where spirits ascend,
Faith's vaillanelle sings a sacred hymn.
With every prayer whispered, doubts amend.

Through the trials faced, where paths unbend,
In the sanctuary of belief, where lights dim.
In the depths of faith, where spirits ascend.

From the shadows cast, where doubts contend,
In the heart's cathedral, where doubts skim.
With every prayer whispered, doubts amend.

In the light of hope, where fears transcend,
In the embrace of trust, where souls trim.
In the depths of faith, where spirits ascend.

Through the valleys of despair, where hearts lend,
In the echoes of grace, where souls swim.
With every prayer whispered, doubts amend.

In the embrace of faith, where doubts suspend,
In the tapestry of belief, where souls skim.
In the depths of faith, where spirits ascend,
With every prayer whispered, doubts amend.

Vaillanelle of Doubt
In the shadows cast, where fears entwine,
Doubt's vaillanelle whispers its refrain.
With every question posed, the soul incline.

Through the labyrinth of uncertainty, thoughts recline,
In the heart's abyss, where doubts obtain.
In the shadows cast, where fears entwine.

From the whispers of hesitation to the dreams malign,
In the echoes of disbelief, where doubts constrain.
With every question posed, the soul incline.

In the depths of skepticism, where doubts align,
In the maze of confusion, where doubts abstain.
In the shadows cast, where fears entwine.

Through the whispers of reason, where doubts design,
In the whispers of doubt, where doubts retain.
With every question posed, the soul incline.

In the embrace of doubt, where minds decline,
In the embrace of doubt, where truths remain.
In the shadows cast, where fears entwine,
With every question posed, the soul incline.

Vaillanelle of Solitude
In the quiet hours where silence reigns,
Solitude's vaillanelle murmurs its song.
With every sigh, a soul finds its plains.

Through the empty spaces, where echoes contain,
In the depths of introspection, where dreams prolong.
In the quiet hours where silence reigns.

From the distant echoes to the whispered strains,
In the embrace of solitude, where thoughts throng.
With every sigh, a soul finds its plains.

In the depths of solitude, where serenity feigns,
In the solitude's embrace, where hearts belong.
In the quiet hours where silence reigns.

Through the labyrinth of thoughts where minds abstain,
In the whispers of solitude, where dreams prolong.
With every sigh, a soul finds its plains.

In the embrace of solace, where solitudes detain,
In the embrace of solace, where souls prolong.
In the quiet hours where silence reigns,
With every sigh, a soul finds its plains.

Vaillanelle of Joy
In the laughter shared, where hearts entwine,
Joy's vaillanelle sings a merry tune.
With every smile bestowed, the soul aligns.

Through the moments cherished, where dreams combine,
In the embrace of happiness, where spirits commune.
In the laughter shared, where hearts entwine.

From the jubilant cries to the tears benign,
In the realm of ecstasy, where hearts attune.
With every smile bestowed, the soul aligns.

In the dance of delight, where worlds entwine,
In the tapestry of joy, where love cocoon.
In the laughter shared, where hearts entwine.

Through the echoes of mirth, where souls recline,
In the echoes of laughter, where spirits croon.
With every smile bestowed, the soul aligns.

In the embrace of joy, where hearts define,
In the embrace of joy, where dreams commune.
In the laughter shared, where hearts entwine,
With every smile bestowed, the soul aligns.

Here are four Vaillanelle poems, 1 each about Sorrow, Childhood, Wisdom & Innocence

Vaillanelle of Sorrow
In the depths of sorrow, where tears run free,
Sorrow's vaillanelle sings its mournful song.
With every ache, a soul seeks to flee.

Through the darkness of night, where shadows spree,
In the heart's abyss, where dreams belong.
In the depths of sorrow, where tears run free.

From the silent screams to the whispered plea,
In the echoes of pain, where hearts prolong.
With every ache, a soul seeks to flee.

In the emptiness felt, where hearts decree,
In the depths of despair, where doubts throng.
In the depths of sorrow, where tears run free.

Through the mist of grief, where souls decree,
In the depths of anguish, where sorrows prolong.
With every ache, a soul seeks to flee.

In the embrace of sorrow, where hearts agree,
In the embrace of sorrow, where hearts prolong.
In the depths of sorrow, where tears run free,
With every ache, a soul seeks to flee.

Vaillanelle of Childhood
In the fields of innocence, where dreams ignite,
Childhood's vaillanelle sings a playful tune.
With every giggle, the world feels bright.

Through the days of wonder and the nights of flight,
In the heart's playground, where joys festoon.
In the fields of innocence, where dreams ignite.

From the laughter shared to the stars' delight,
In the realms of make-believe, where fantasies strewn.
With every giggle, the world feels bright.

In the secret hideaways where hopes alight,
In the tapestry of youth, where dreams cocoon.
In the fields of innocence, where dreams ignite.

Through the memories held, where hearts incite,
In the echoes of childhood, where dreams commune.
With every giggle, the world feels bright.

In the embrace of innocence, where hearts unite,
In the embrace of innocence, where dreams impugn.
In the fields of innocence, where dreams ignite,
With every giggle, the world feels bright.

Vaillanelle of Wisdom
In the depths of wisdom, where truths entwine,
Wisdom's vaillanelle whispers its decree.
With every lesson learned, the soul aligns.

Through the trials faced, where paths define,
In the heart's sanctuary, where insights decree.
In the depths of wisdom, where truths entwine.

From the whispers of sages to the stars that shine,
In the echelons of knowledge, where minds agree.
With every lesson learned, the soul aligns.

In the tapestry of life, where paths incline,
In the echoes of eternity, where souls flee.
In the depths of wisdom, where truths entwine.

Through silent contemplation, where thoughts refine,
In the labyrinth of understanding, where souls decree.
With every lesson learned, the soul aligns.

In the embrace of wisdom, where truths refine,
In the embrace of wisdom, where insights decree.
In the depths of wisdom, where truths entwine,
With every lesson learned, the soul aligns.

Vaillanelle of Innocence
In the purity of heart where dreams ignite,
Innocence's vaillanelle sings its refrain.
With every smile, the world feels bright.

Through the wonder-filled days and the starry night,
In the soul's haven, where hopes sustain.
In the purity of heart where dreams ignite.

From the laughter shared to the tears contrite,
In the realm of purity, where souls abstain.
With every smile, the world feels bright.

In the dance of innocence, where hearts unite,
In the tapestry of youth, where dreams ordain.
In the purity of heart where dreams ignite.

Through the echoes of laughter, where hearts excite,
In the echoes of innocence, where dreams remain.
With every smile, the world feels bright.

In the embrace of innocence, where souls alight,
In the embrace of innocence, where's love's terrain.
In the purity of heart where dreams ignite,
With every smile, the world feels bright.

Here are four Vaillanelle poems, 1 each about Passion, Serenity, Freedom & Justice

Vaillanelle of Passion
In the fire of passion, where hearts collide,
Passion's vaillanelle sings its fervent song.
With every touch, a soul finds its pride.

Through the flames of desire, where dreams abide,
In the depths of longing, where souls belong.
In the fire of passion, where hearts collide.

From the whispered promises to the vows untied,
In the embrace of ecstasy, where love is strong.
With every touch, a soul finds its pride.

In the heat of the moment, where love is allied,
In the dance of ardor, where desires prolong.
In the fire of passion, where hearts collide.

Through the tempest of emotions, where truths confide,
In the echoes of desire, where passions throng.
With every touch, a soul finds its pride.

In the embrace of passion, where love's tide,
In the embrace of passion, where hearts prolong.
In the fire of passion, where hearts collide,
With every touch, a soul finds its pride.

Vaillanelle of Serenity
In the calm embrace where peace resides,
Serenity's vaillanelle whispers its decree.
With every breath, a soul gently glides.

Through the tranquil waters and the mountainsides,
In the heart's haven, where dreams roam free.
In the calm embrace where peace resides.

From the stillness of dawn to the eventide,
In the serenade of silence, where souls agree.
With every breath, a soul gently glides.

In the sanctuary of solitude, where solace abides,
In the tranquil expanse, where spirits flee.
In the calm embrace where peace resides.

Through the echoes of nature, where tranquility guides,
In the whispers of serenity, where dreams decree.
With every breath, a soul gently glides.

In the embrace of calm, where worries subside,
In the embrace of calm, where hearts decree.
In the calm embrace where peace resides,
With every breath, a soul gently glides.

Vaillanelle of Freedom
In the open skies where dreams take flight,
Freedom's vaillanelle sings its anthem bold.
With every step, a soul embraces its light.

Through the winds of change and the darkest night,
In the heart's expanse, where truths unfold.
In the open skies where dreams take flight.

From the chains released to the soul's respite,
In the echoes of liberation, where spirits hold.
With every step, a soul embraces its light.

In the vast expanse where souls ignite,
In the realm of possibility, where destinies mold.
In the open skies where dreams take flight.

Through the echoes of courage, where hearts excite,
In the echoes of emancipation, where truths retold.
With every step, a soul embraces its light.

In the embrace of freedom, where hearts unite,
In the embrace of freedom, where dreams enfold.
In the open skies where dreams take flight,
With every step, a soul embraces its light.

Vaillanelle of Justice
In the halls of justice, where truths abide,
Justice's vaillanelle sings its solemn decree.
With every verdict rendered, a soul is tied.

Through the scales of balance and the laws applied,
In the heart's tribunal, where fairness decree.
In the halls of justice, where truths abide.

From the cries of the oppressed to the wrongs defied,
In the quest for equality, where rights decree.
With every verdict rendered, a soul is tied.

In the pursuit of fairness, where rights collide,
In the echoes of righteousness, where justice plea.
In the halls of justice, where truths abide.

Through the echoes of integrity, where souls confide,
In the echoes of righteousness, where justice plea.
With every verdict rendered, a soul is tied.

In the embrace of justice, where wrongs denied,
In the embrace of justice, where truths decree.
In the halls of justice, where truths abide,
With every verdict rendered, a soul is tied.

Here are four Vaillanelle poems, 1 each about Change, Resilience, Gratitude & Forgiveness

Vaillanelle of Change
In the dance of change, where paths unwind,
Change's vaillanelle sings its transformative song.
With every shift, a new world we find.

Through the seasons' cycle and the ties that bind,
In the heart's evolution, where dreams belong.
In the dance of change, where paths unwind.

From the echoes of growth to the dreams refined,
In the embrace of transformation, where souls prolong.
With every shift, a new world we find.

In the whispers of transition, where destinies align,
In the echoes of renewal, where hearts are strong.
In the dance of change, where paths unwind.

Through the winds of fate and the dreams enshrined,
In the tapestry of life, where destinies throng.
With every shift, a new world we find.

In the embrace of change, where souls remind,
In the embrace of change, where spirits long.
In the dance of change, where paths unwind,
With every shift, a new world we find.

Vaillanelle of Resilience
In the depths of adversity, where trials combine,
Resilience's vaillanelle whispers its decree.
With every challenge faced, a soul does shine.

Through the storms endured and the mountains climbed,
In the heart's fortress, where courage is free.
In the depths of adversity, where trials combine.

From the scars embraced to the dreams refined,
In the echoes of perseverance, where strength decree.
With every challenge faced, a soul does shine.

In the face of darkness, where hopes enshrine,
In the echoes of fortitude, where dreams agree.
In the depths of adversity, where trials combine.

Through the echoes of determination, where spirits incline,
In the whispers of resilience, where souls plea.
With every challenge faced, a soul does shine.

In the embrace of resilience, where hearts intertwine,
In the embrace of resilience, where souls decree.
In the depths of adversity, where trials combine,
With every challenge faced, a soul does shine.

Vaillanelle of Gratitude
In the heart's embrace where blessings align,
Gratitude's vaillanelle sings its thankful song.
With every grace received, a soul does shine.

Through the trials endured and the stars that align,
In the depths of appreciation, where dreams belong.
In the heart's embrace where blessings align.

From the whispered thanks to the joys refined,
In the echoes of thankfulness, where hearts prolong.
With every grace received, a soul does shine.

In the moments cherished and the dreams enshrined,
In the tapestry of gratitude, where souls belong.
In the heart's embrace where blessings align.

Through the echoes of appreciation, where souls incline,
In the whispers of gratitude, where hearts prolong.
With every grace received, a soul does shine.

In the embrace of gratitude, where hearts entwine,
In the embrace of gratitude, where souls belong.
In the heart's embrace where blessings align,
With every grace received, a soul does shine.

Vaillanelle of Forgiveness
In the depths of forgiveness, where wounds unbind,
Forgiveness's vaillanelle whispers its decree.
With every pardon given, a soul does find.

Through the scars embraced and the hearts aligned,
In the realm of reconciliation, where hearts are free.
In the depths of forgiveness, where wounds unbind.

From the tears shed to the peace designed,
In the echoes of mercy, where souls plea.
With every pardon given, a soul does find.

In the grace bestowed and the love enshrined,
In the echoes of compassion, where souls decree.
In the depths of forgiveness, where wounds unbind.

Through the echoes of healing, where souls remind,
In the whispers of forgiveness, where souls agree.
With every pardon given, a soul does find.

In the embrace of forgiveness, where hearts align,
In the embrace of forgiveness, where souls decree.
In the depths of forgiveness, where wounds unbind,
With every pardon given, a soul does find.

Here are four Vaillanelle poems, 1 each about Longing, Belonging, Discovery & Wonder

Vaillanelle of Change
In the dance of change, where paths unwind,
Change's vaillanelle sings its transformative song.
With every shift, a new world we find.

Through the seasons' cycle and the ties that bind,
In the heart's evolution, where dreams belong.
In the dance of change, where paths unwind.

From the echoes of growth to the dreams refined,
In the embrace of transformation, where souls prolong.
With every shift, a new world we find.

In the whispers of transition, where destinies align,
In the echoes of renewal, where hearts are strong.
In the dance of change, where paths unwind.

Through the winds of fate and the dreams enshrined,
In the tapestry of life, where destinies throng.
With every shift, a new world we find.

In the embrace of change, where souls remind,
In the embrace of change, where spirits long.
In the dance of change, where paths unwind,
With every shift, a new world we find.

Vaillanelle of Resilience
In the depths of adversity, where trials combine,
Resilience's vaillanelle whispers its decree.
With every challenge faced, a soul does shine.

Through the storms endured and the mountains climbed,
In the heart's fortress, where courage is free.
In the depths of adversity, where trials combine.

From the scars embraced to the dreams refined,
In the echoes of perseverance, where strength decree.
With every challenge faced, a soul does shine.

In the face of darkness, where hopes enshrine,
In the echoes of fortitude, where dreams agree.
In the depths of adversity, where trials combine.

Through the echoes of determination, where spirits incline,
In the whispers of resilience, where souls plea.
With every challenge faced, a soul does shine.

In the embrace of resilience, where hearts intertwine,
In the embrace of resilience, where souls decree.
In the depths of adversity, where trials combine,
With every challenge faced, a soul does shine.

Vaillanelle of Gratitude
In the heart's embrace where blessings align,
Gratitude's vaillanelle sings its thankful song.
With every grace received, a soul does shine.

Through the trials endured and the stars that align,
In the depths of appreciation, where dreams belong.
In the heart's embrace where blessings align.

From the whispered thanks to the joys refined,
In the echoes of thankfulness, where hearts prolong.
With every grace received, a soul does shine.

In the moments cherished and the dreams enshrined,
In the tapestry of gratitude, where souls belong.
In the heart's embrace where blessings align.

Through the echoes of appreciation, where souls incline,
In the whispers of gratitude, where hearts prolong.
With every grace received, a soul does shine.

In the embrace of gratitude, where hearts entwine,
In the embrace of gratitude, where souls belong.
In the heart's embrace where blessings align,
With every grace received, a soul does shine.

Vaillanelle of Forgiveness
In the depths of forgiveness, where wounds unbind,
Forgiveness's vaillanelle whispers its decree.
With every pardon given, a soul does find.

Through the scars embraced and the hearts aligned,
In the realm of reconciliation, where hearts are free.
In the depths of forgiveness, where wounds unbind.

From the tears shed to the peace designed,
In the echoes of mercy, where souls plea.
With every pardon given, a soul does find.

In the grace bestowed and the love enshrined,
In the echoes of compassion, where souls decree.
In the depths of forgiveness, where wounds unbind.

Through the echoes of healing, where souls remind,
In the whispers of forgiveness, where souls agree.
With every pardon given, a soul does find.

In the embrace of forgiveness, where hearts align,
In the embrace of forgiveness, where souls decree.
In the depths of forgiveness, where wounds unbind,
With every pardon given, a soul does find.

Here are four Vaillanelle poems, 1 each about Journey, Reflection, Harmony & Imagination

Vaillanelle of Journey
In the winding road of life, where dreams unfold,
Journey's vaillanelle sings its traveler's song.
With every step taken, a new story is told.

Through the valleys deep and the mountains cold,
In the heart's wanderlust, where desires prolong.
In the winding road of life, where dreams unfold.

From the whispered echoes to the tales retold,
In the tapestry of adventure, where souls belong.
With every step taken, a new story is told.

In the embrace of uncertainty, where destinies enfold,
In the echoes of exploration, where dreams are strong.
In the winding road of life, where dreams unfold.

Through the echoes of discovery, where mysteries hold,
In the whispers of wanderlust, where souls abscond.
With every step taken, a new story is told.

In the embrace of the journey, where dreams mold,
In the embrace of the journey, where destinies respond.
In the winding road of life, where dreams unfold,
With every step taken, a new story is told.

Vaillanelle of Reflection
In the stillness of time, where thoughts evolve,
Reflection's vaillanelle whispers its introspective tune.
With every pondered moment, a new truth resolves.

Through the depths of contemplation and the questions unsolved,
In the heart's introspection, where insights commune.
In the stillness of time, where thoughts evolve.

From the whispers of wisdom to the stories absolved,
In the tapestry of understanding, where minds attune.
With every pondered moment, a new truth resolves.

In the echo of silence, where souls revolve,
In the echoes of introspection, where spirits cocoon.
In the stillness of time, where thoughts evolve.

Through the echoes of retrospection, where truths dissolve,
In the whispers of reflection, where souls festoon.
With every pondered moment, a new truth resolves.

In the embrace of clarity, where minds absolve,
In the embrace of reflection, where souls commune.
In the stillness of time, where thoughts evolve,
With every pondered moment, a new truth resolves.

Vaillanelle of Harmony
In the symphony of life, where souls unite,
Harmony's vaillanelle sings its melodic song.
With every note played, the world feels right.

Through the chords of unity and the stars that ignite,
In the heart's orchestra, where dreams prolong.
In the symphony of life, where souls unite.

From the whispered melodies to the dreams in flight,
In the tapestry of melodies, where hearts belong.
With every note played, the world feels right.

In the dance of rhythm and the souls in sight,
In the echoes of resonance, where spirits throng.
In the symphony of life, where souls unite.

Through the echoes of melody and the hearts ignite,
In the whispers of harmony, where dreams abscond.
With every note played, the world feels right.

In the embrace of music, where souls incite,
In the embrace of music, where hearts respond.
In the symphony of life, where souls unite,
With every note played, the world feels right.

Vaillanelle of Imagination
In the realm of dreams, where thoughts take flight,
Imagination's vaillanelle whispers its fanciful tune.
With every creation spun, the soul's delight.

Through the landscapes painted and the stars that ignite,
In the heart's canvas, where fantasies commune.
In the realm of dreams, where thoughts take flight.

From the whispered musings to the tales that excite,
In the tapestry of creativity, where dreams festoon.
With every creation spun, the soul's delight.

In the dance of whimsy and the visions bright,
In the echoes of inspiration, where minds attune.
In the realm of dreams, where thoughts take flight.

Through the echoes of imagination, where dreams unite,
In the whispers of creativity, where souls cocoon.
With every creation spun, the soul's delight.

In the embrace of wonder, where dreams ignite,
In the embrace of imagination, where souls respond.
In the realm of dreams, where thoughts take flight,
With every creation spun, the soul's delight.

Here are four Vaillanelle poems, 1 each about Silence, Laughter, Tears & Strength

Vaillanelle of Silence
In the embrace of silence, where peace resides,
Silence's vaillanelle whispers its tranquil song.
With every hushed breath, a soul confides.

Through the echoes of quiet and the stillness inside,
In the heart's sanctuary, where serenity prolong.
In the embrace of silence, where peace resides.

From the whispered murmurs to the truths implied,
In the tapestry of tranquility, where dreams belong.
With every hushed breath, a soul confides.

In the depths of stillness, where fears subside,
In the echoes of solitude, where solace is strong.
In the embrace of silence, where peace resides.

Through the echoes of contemplation, where souls confide,
In the whispers of tranquility, where spirits prolong.
With every hushed breath, a soul confides.

In the embrace of silence, where dreams coincide,
In the embrace of silence, where hearts respond.
In the embrace of silence, where peace resides,
With every hushed breath, a soul confides.

Vaillanelle of Laughter
In the symphony of laughter, where joy presides,
Laughter's vaillanelle sings its jubilant song.
With every shared chuckle, a soul confides.

Through the echoes of merriment and the smiles wide,
In the heart's celebration, where happiness prolong.
In the symphony of laughter, where joy presides.

From the whispered jokes to the happiness implied,
In the tapestry of humor, where dreams belong.
With every shared chuckle, a soul confides.

In the dance of amusement and the hearts allied,
In the echoes of hilarity, where spirits respond.
In the symphony of laughter, where joy presides.

Through the echoes of glee and the tears dried,
In the whispers of mirth, where bonds grow strong.
With every shared chuckle, a soul confides.

In the embrace of laughter, where hearts collide,
In the embrace of laughter, where spirits abscond.
In the symphony of laughter, where joy presides,
With every shared chuckle, a soul confides.

Vaillanelle of Tears
In the cascade of tears, where emotions collide,
Tears' vaillanelle sings its melancholic song.
With every drop shed, a soul finds its guide.

Through the echoes of sorrow and the pain inside,
In the heart's lamentation, where sadness prolong.
In the cascade of tears, where emotions collide.

From the whispered cries to the anguish implied,
In the tapestry of grief, where dreams belong.
With every drop shed, a soul finds its guide.

In the depths of despair, where hope is denied,
In the echoes of anguish, where souls abscond.
In the cascade of tears, where emotions collide.

Through the echoes of sorrow and the truths implied,
In the whispers of lament, where souls respond.
With every drop shed, a soul finds its guide.

In the embrace of tears, where hearts confide,
In the embrace of tears, where healing is found.
In the cascade of tears, where emotions collide,
With every drop shed, a soul finds its guide.

Vaillanelle of Strength
In the heart's fortress, where resilience resides,
Strength's vaillanelle sings its empowering song.
With every trial faced, a soul's resolve abides.

Through the storms weathered and the battles untied,
In the tapestry of fortitude, where dreams prolong.
In the heart's fortress, where resilience resides.

From the whispered courage to the fears defied,
In the echoes of endurance, where spirits respond.
With every trial faced, a soul's resolve abides.

In the face of adversity, where hopes collide,
In the echoes of bravery, where hearts abscond.
In the heart's fortress, where resilience resides.

Through the echoes of tenacity and the tears dried,
In the whispers of strength, where souls respond.
With every trial faced, a soul's resolve abides.

In the embrace of fortitude, where hearts confide,
In the embrace of strength, where spirits abscond.
In the heart's fortress, where resilience resides,
With every trial faced, a soul's resolve abides.

Here are four Vaillanelle poems, 1 each about Vulnerability, Renewal, Acceptance & Mystery

Vaillanelle of Vulnerability
In the tender space where fears reside,
Vulnerability's vaillanelle whispers its plea.
With every exposed truth, a soul finds its stride.

Through the layers peeled back and the masks untied,
In the heart's openness, where honesty is key.
In the tender space where fears reside.

From the whispered confessions to the tears dried,
In the tapestry of authenticity, where souls are free.
With every exposed truth, a soul finds its stride.

In the vulnerability embraced, where courage is supplied,
In the echoes of transparency, where spirits decree.
In the tender space where fears reside.

Through the echoes of confession and the wounds wide,
In the whispers of vulnerability, where souls foresee.
With every exposed truth, a soul finds its stride.

In the embrace of vulnerability, where hearts confide,
In the embrace of vulnerability, where souls agree.
In the tender space where fears reside,
With every exposed truth, a soul finds its stride.

Vaillanelle of Renewal
In the cycle of rebirth, where dreams reside,
Renewal's vaillanelle sings its hopeful song.
With every transformation, a soul abides.

Through the ashes of the past and the dreams implied,
In the heart's regeneration, where strength prolong.
In the cycle of rebirth, where dreams reside.

From the whispered whispers to the phoenix's glide,
In the tapestry of rejuvenation, where spirits throng.
With every transformation, a soul abides.

In the embrace of renewal, where hopes collide,
In the echoes of revival, where souls respond.
In the cycle of rebirth, where dreams reside.

Through the echoes of transformation, where truths confide,
In the whispers of revival, where dreams abscond.
With every transformation, a soul abides.

In the embrace of renewal, where hearts confide,
In the embrace of renewal, where souls respond.
In the cycle of rebirth, where dreams reside,
With every transformation, a soul abides.

Vaillanelle of Acceptance
In the embrace of acceptance, where truths confide,
Acceptance's vaillanelle whispers its comforting song.
With every embraced flaw, a soul finds its guide.

Through the doubts dismissed and the shadows untied,
In the heart's surrender, where belonging is strong.
In the embrace of acceptance, where truths confide.

From the whispered affirmations to the fears defied,
In the tapestry of inclusion, where souls belong.
With every embraced flaw, a soul finds its guide.

In the embrace of understanding, where judgments hide,
In the echoes of tolerance, where hearts abscond.
In the embrace of acceptance, where truths confide.

Through the echoes of compassion and the fears denied,
In the whispers of acceptance, where spirits respond.
With every embraced flaw, a soul finds its guide.

In the embrace of acceptance, where hearts collide,
In the embrace of acceptance, where souls abscond.
In the embrace of acceptance, where truths confide,
With every embraced flaw, a soul finds its guide.

Vaillanelle of Mystery
In the shadows cast where secrets reside,
Mystery's vaillanelle sings its enigmatic song.
With every hidden truth, a soul's curiosity is pried.

Through the depths explored and the veils untied,
In the heart's intrigue, where wonder prolong.
In the shadows cast where secrets reside.

From the whispered riddles to the dreams implied,
In the tapestry of the unknown, where dreams belong.
With every hidden truth, a soul's curiosity is pried.

In the dance of shadows and the mysteries beside,
In the echoes of enigma, where spirits abscond.
In the shadows cast where secrets reside.

Through the echoes of uncertainty and the questions implied,
In the whispers of intrigue, where minds respond.
With every hidden truth, a soul's curiosity is pried.

In the embrace of mystery, where souls confide,
In the embrace of mystery, where minds respond.
In the shadows cast where secrets reside,
With every hidden truth, a soul's curiosity is pried.

Here are four Vaillanelle poems, 1 each about Transformation, Eternity, Cosmos & Happiness

Vaillanelle of Transformation
In the crucible of change, where dreams collide,
Transformation's vaillanelle sings its evolving song.
With every shift, a soul's journey is amplified.

Through the fires of growth and the barriers defied,
In heart's metamorphosis, where strengths prolong.
In the crucible of change, where dreams collide.

From the whispered whispers to the self-inside,
In the tapestry of rebirth, where spirits are strong.
With every shift, a soul's journey is amplified.

In the embrace of evolution, where fears subside,
In the echoes of renewal, where dreams respond.
In the crucible of change, where dreams collide.

Through the echoes of transition and the self-denied,
In whispers of transformation, where souls abscond.
With every shift, a soul's journey is amplified.

In the embrace of growth, where souls confide,
In the embrace of transformation, where spirits respond.
In the crucible of change, where dreams collide,
With every shift, a soul's journey is amplified.

Vaillanelle of Eternity
In the timeless expanse, where dreams reside,
Eternity's vaillanelle sings its eternal song.
With every moment lived, a soul's journey's stride.

Through vastness of space and the stars that guide,
In the heart's infinity, where love belongs.
In the timeless expanse, where dreams reside.

From the whispered echoes to the heavens wide,
In the tapestry of forever, where souls prolong.
With every moment lived, a soul's journey's stride.

In the embrace of eternity, where dreams confide,
In the echoes of immortality, where souls respond.
In the timeless expanse, where dreams reside.

Through the echoes of forever and the universe wide,
In the whispers of eternity, where souls abscond.
With every moment lived, a soul's journey's stride.

In the embrace of infinity, where dreams coincide,
In the embrace of eternity, where spirits respond.
In the timeless expanse, where dreams reside,
With every moment lived, a soul's journey's stride.

Vaillanelle of Cosmos
In the cosmic dance, where dreams collide,
Cosmos's vaillanelle sings its celestial song.
With every star's twinkle, a soul's wonder implied.

Through the galaxies vast and the mysteries beside,
In the heart's exploration, where knowledge prolong.
In the cosmic dance, where dreams collide.

From the whispered secrets to the universe wide,
In the tapestry of cosmos, where souls belong.
With every star's twinkle, a soul's wonder implied.

In the embrace of infinity, where dreams confide,
In echoes of cosmic harmony, where spirits abscond.
In the cosmic dance, where dreams collide.

Through echoes of exploration and the cosmos' guide,
In the whispers of stardust, where souls respond.
With every star's twinkle, a soul's wonder implied.

In the embrace of the cosmos, where dreams reside,
In the embrace of the cosmos, where spirits respond.
In the cosmic dance, where dreams collide,
With every star's twinkle, a soul's wonder implied.

Vaillanelle of Happiness
In the joyous moments, where dreams reside,
Happiness's vaillanelle sings its joyful song.
With every smile shared, a soul's happiness implied.

Through the laughter echoed and the love applied,
In the heart's elation, where spirits prolong.
In the joyous moments, where dreams reside.

From the whispered giggles to the dreams beside,
In the tapestry of bliss, where hearts belong.
With every smile shared, a soul's happiness implied.

In the embrace of joy, where hearts confide,
In the echoes of laughter, where spirits respond.
In the joyous moments, where dreams reside.

Through the echoes of joy and the love untied,
In the whispers of happiness, where souls abscond.
With every smile shared, a soul's happiness implied.

In the embrace of laughter, where dreams coincide,
In the embrace of happiness, where spirits respond.
In the joyous moments, where dreams reside,
With every smile shared, a soul's happiness implied.

-:|:-●:*''''''*:●.-:|:-●**●-:|:-●:*''''''*:●:*''''''*:●.-:|:-●**●-:|:--:|:-●:*''''''*:●.-:|:- ●**●-:|:-●:*''''''*:●:*''''''*:●.-:|:-●**●-:|:-

SESTINA:

A highly structured poem consisting of six six-line stanzas followed by a three-line stanza, with the same six end words repeated in a specific pattern.

Here are four Sestina poems, 1 each about Love, Nature, Beauty & Time

Sestina: Love
In twilight's glow, love whispers soft and true,
Entwining hearts in an eternal dance,
A bond that weathers storms and trials through,
With every beat, a rhythm of romance.
In tender moments, love's sweet melody,
Resounds within, a symphony so grand.

Yet love can lead us to a distant land,
Where shadows lurk, and doubts begin to brew.
But in the darkest hour, love's harmony
Guides us back to where our dreams advance,
Through highs and lows, the essence of romance,
Endures, unbroken, steadfast and true.

For love's embrace is steadfast and true,
A beacon shining in the darkest land.
In its embrace, we find our true romance,
Embraced by love's enduring, endless dance,
It blossoms like a flower in advance,
Blooming in life's evergreen melody.

So let us revel in love's melody,
Embrace its song, unwavering and true,
For in its cadence lies our best advance,
Guiding us through the valleys and the land,
In every step, a graceful, flowing dance,
A testament to love's enduring romance.

For love's endurance is the heart of romance,
A melody that echoes in life's dance,
With each embrace, it grows ever true,
Guiding us through trials, a steady advance.
In nature's embrace, love finds fertile land,
Where hearts entwine in eternal harmony.

Sestina: Nature
In nature's arms, we find tranquility,
Beneath the boughs, where whispers softly dance,
A symphony of life's serene melody,
Where every leaf and blade sways in advance.
Through sunlit glades and shadowed forest land,
Nature's beauty blooms in hues so grand.

From dawn to dusk, the sky's hues are grand,
Painting a portrait of tranquility,
In every stroke, the artist's graceful dance,
A masterpiece of earth's divine advance.
The river's flow, a timeless melody,
Carving its path through valleys and through land.

In meadows green, where life abounds on land,
Each flower's bloom a testament so grand,
To nature's artistry, its vibrant melody,
A canvas painted with tranquility,
In every stroke, a subtle advance,
As seasons waltz in a perpetual dance.

In twilight's glow, the creatures start to dance,
Amidst the wonders of this fertile land,
In harmony, they move and they advance,
Celebrating life's abundance so grand,
In nature's embrace, finding tranquility,
United in earth's eternal melody.

For in nature's dance lies true tranquility,
A symphony of life's eternal melody,
Where every creature, every leaf, every grain of land,
Contributes to the canvas, so vast and grand,
In unity, we find our true advance,
Amidst the beauty of nature's graceful dance.

Sestina: Beauty
In every dawn, beauty's light does dance,
Illuminating skies with hues so grand,
A symphony of colors in advance,
A tapestry woven with delicate melody.
In every petal, every leaf, beauty's hand,
Creates a masterpiece across the land.

From mountains high to valleys low, the land
Bears witness to the grace of beauty's dance,
In every vista, every view, beauty's hand,
Crafts scenes of awe-inspiring grand,
In every whisper of the breeze, a melody,
Serenading the world in gentle advance.

But beauty's true essence lies not in advance,
Nor solely in the landscape of the land,
It dwells within, a soulful melody,
An inner radiance that inspires dance,
Transcending the limits of the grand,
A reflection of divinity's hand.

For in the heart's depths, beauty finds its hand,
Guiding us forward in graceful advance,
Transforming the mundane into the grand,
Infusing every corner of the land,
With love's eternal, everlasting dance,
A symphony of life's enduring melody.

So let us embrace beauty's gentle hand,
And let its melody lead us in advance,
Across the landscapes of this wondrous land,
In a dance of grace, both delicate and grand.

Sestina: Time
Through the passage of time, we see the dance,
A relentless march, an unyielding advance,
In every moment, echoes of a melody,
That weaves through the tapestry of the land,
A reminder of the fleeting nature of the grand,
As seconds slip away like grains through hand.

In youth, we dream of futures vast and grand,
Unaware of the relentless passage of time,
But as the years unfurl, we come to understand,
That every moment is a precious dance,
A chance to leave our mark upon the land,
And compose our own symphony's melody.

Yet time's relentless march can bring melody,
To moments both mundane and those most grand,
A reminder to cherish the beauty of the land,
For as the seasons change, so does time,
In an eternal cycle of birth and dance,
A reminder of life's fragile advance.

So let us heed the lessons time does hand,
Embrace each moment, whether small or grand,
And in life's dance, find our own melody,
As we journey through this ever-changing land,
For in the end, it's not the speed of time's advance,
But the richness of each moment's dance.

Through time's passage, leave a mark upon the land,
In every step, a graceful advance,
And let our lives compose a timeless melody,
both gentle and grand.

Here are four Sestina poems, 1 each about Death, Dreams, Hope & Despair

Sestina: Death
In shadows deep, where whispers of death dance,
A solemn waltz, a haunting melody,
Echoes through the void, a chilling advance,
As time stands still in this spectral land.
A somber symphony of finality,
Where souls depart in silent reverence.

Through veils of mist, cloaked in solemn reverence,
We navigate the labyrinth where shadows dance,
Seeking solace in the echoes of eternity,
In the whispered secrets of mortality's melody,
For in the end, we all return to the land,
Embraced by darkness, in death's final advance.

Yet in the stillness, there's a subtle advance,
A glimmer of peace, a quiet reverence,
For in the cycle of life, death claims its land,
But from its grasp, new beginnings dance,
And in the silence, a hopeful melody,
A reminder of life's enduring eternity.

Though death may come, it cannot erase eternity,
For from its grasp, new life will advance,
In the cadence of existence, a resilient melody,
A symphony of rebirth and reverence,
For even in the shadows, hope can dance,
And light can pierce through death's somber land.

So let us face death with courage and reverence,
Embracing the dance of life's eternal melody,
And in the end, may hope advance, and despair be banished from the land.

Sestina: Dreams
In the realm of dreams, where fantasies dance,
We find escape from life's harsh advance,
In every shadow, whispers of possibility,
A symphony of hopes in sweet melody,
Guiding us through the night with reverence,

In the tapestry of dreams, a boundless land.

In dreams, we wander through an endless land,
Where wishes take flight and ambitions dance,
In the depths of slumber, we find reverence,
For the power of imagination's advance,
In the dreamer's heart, a hopeful melody,
A reminder of life's infinite possibility.

Though reality may shatter our possibility,
In dreams, we craft our own enchanted land,
Where dreams take root and blossom into melody,
And in the starlit skies, our aspirations dance,
Defying the limitations of time's advance,
With each dream, a prayer whispered in reverence.

But dreams can also carry a weight of reverence,
For they hold within them fragile possibility,
In the face of failure and relentless advance,
We seek refuge in the sanctuary of dreamland,
Where broken hearts find solace in the dance,
And shattered hopes are mended by melody.

So let us cherish the power of dreams' melody,
With reverence for their boundless possibility,
For in their dance lies hope's eternal advance,
Guiding us through the labyrinth of life's land.

Sestina: Hope
In the depths of despair, where shadows dance,
And darkness shrouds the land in bleak advance,
There lies a flicker, a fragile melody,
A whisper of hope amid the echoes of reverence.
In the heart of despair blooms possibility,
For even in the darkest night, hope can advance.

Through trials and tribulations, hope can advance,
A beacon shining bright amidst despair's dance,
Guiding us through the storm with possibility,
And filling the void with its hopeful melody,
In the silence, a prayer whispered in reverence,
For the light that banishes darkness from the land.

Though despair may cast its shadow over the land,
With every step forward, hope can advance,
In the depths of our souls, a quiet reverence,
For the resilience of the human spirit's dance,
And the power of hope's transformative melody,
To breathe life into the barren soil of possibility.

So let us embrace hope's possibility,
And let its melody echo across the land,
A symphony of resilience and advance,
A testament to the triumph of hope's dance,
And in its presence, let us bow in reverence,
For the miracle of hope amid despair's possibility.

Sestina: Despair
In the depths of despair, where shadows dance,
And darkness reigns over the desolate land,
There echoes a mournful, haunting melody,
A symphony of sorrow without advance,
In the heart of despair, there is no possibility,
Only the relentless rhythm of despair's dance.

Through tear-stained eyes, we witness the dance,
Of souls lost in the abyss of despair's trance,
For in its grip, there is no possibility,
No escape from the suffocating land,
Only the endless echo of despair's melody,
A dirge that drowns out any hope of advance.

Yet even in the grip of despair's advance,
There lies a sliver of light amidst the dance,
A fragile thread woven into the melody,
A whisper of redemption within the trance,
For even in the darkest depths of the land,
There lingers a glimmer of possibility.

So let us cling to that thread of possibility,
And let it guide us through despair's advance,
For in its presence, there is hope for the land,
A chance to break free from despair's dance,
And rewrite the sorrowful melody,
With notes of resilience and possibility.

Here are four Sestina poems, 1 each about Friendship, Loneliness, Memories & Music

Sestina: Friendship
In the tapestry of life, where friendships dance,
We find solace in the warmth of true connection,
A bond that weaves hearts in a melody,
Through laughter and tears, a symphony of trust,
In the embrace of friendship, we find advance,
Navigating the journey with unwavering affection.

Through trials and triumphs, affection
Blossoms in the garden where friendships dance,
In the echo of laughter, we find advance,
For in the company of friends, there's connection,
A lifeline woven with threads of trust,
Binding souls together in harmonious melody.

In the silence of understanding, a melody
Resonates, a testament to affection,
For in the heart of friendship lies trust,
A beacon guiding us through life's dance,
In the ebb and flow of human connection,
We find strength to weather any advance.

As time unfolds, we cherish the advance,
In the symphony of shared memories, a melody,
Echoes of laughter, whispers of connection,
A testament to enduring affection,
For in the rhythm of friendship's dance,
We find sanctuary in the shelter of trust.

Through distance and time, we nurture trust,
A foundation upon which we advance,
In the cadence of reunion, we dance,
Recalling the harmonious melody,
Of friendship's embrace and affection,
Rekindling the flame of connection.

So let us celebrate the power of connection,
And nurture the bonds of trust,
For in the tapestry of life, affection
Is the key to our collective advance,
Guiding us through the highs and lows with melody,
In the eternal dance of friendship's affection.

Sestina: Loneliness
In the silence of solitude, shadows dance,
A somber waltz in the chamber of loneliness,
Echoes of emptiness, devoid of connection,
In the depths of despair, where trust
Is but a distant memory, a fading melody,
Lost in the caverns of isolation's affection.

Through the veil of tears, devoid of affection,
We navigate the labyrinth where shadows dance,
Seeking solace in the echoes of a melody,
In the haunting embrace of loneliness,
For in the absence of trust,
We find ourselves adrift, severed from connection.

In the void of isolation, we crave connection,
Longing for the comfort of affection,
But in the absence of trust,
We stumble through the darkness, where shadows dance,
Bound by the chains of loneliness,
Lost in the echoes of a melancholic melody.

Yet amidst the silence, there lingers a melody,
A whisper of hope, a glimmer of connection,
For even in the depths of loneliness,
There lies the potential for affection,
In the symphony of solitude's dance,
A fragile bridge that leads us back to trust.

So let us embrace the possibility of trust,
And weave a new melody of connection,
Breaking free from the chains of loneliness,
And finding solace in the embrace of affection.

Sestina: Memories
In the vault of time, where memories dance,
We find solace in the echoes of melody,
A symphony of moments, woven with affection,
Each note a tribute to cherished connection,
In the tapestry of life, where trust
Guides us through the passage of advance.

Through the corridors of time, we advance,
Navigating the labyrinth where memories dance,
Each step a testament to enduring trust,
For in the melody of remembrance, affection
Blossoms anew, reigniting connection,
And illuminating the darkness of forgetfulness.

In the tapestry of our minds, memories dance,
In the flicker of nostalgia, a bittersweet melody,
A tribute to the bonds of connection,
Forged in the crucible of time's advance,
For in the depths of recollection, affection
Resides, a testament to enduring trust.

Though time may fade, trust
Endures, a beacon guiding us through advance,
In the heart's treasury, affection
Lingers, painting the canvas where memories dance,
For in the symphony of remembrance, melody
Resonates, bridging the gap of connection.

So let us cherish the treasure of connection,
And honor the bonds forged in trust,
For in the tapestry of memories, melody
Weaves its magic, guiding us through advance,
And in the dance of recollection, affection
Blossoms anew, nourishing our souls with melody.

Sestina: Music
In the symphony of life, where music dance,
We find solace in the harmony of melody,
A timeless echo of connection,
Uniting hearts in a bond of trust,
In the rhythm of existence, we advance,
Nourished by the soulful embrace of affection.

Through the notes of joy and sorrow, affection
Blooms, in the garden where music dance,
In the cadence of the soul, we advance,
Immersed in the beauty of melody,
For in the language of music, trust
Resides, forging unbreakable connection.

In the sanctuary of sound, where connection
Flourishes, we bask in the glow of affection,
In the embrace of melody, trust
Blossoms, guiding us through the dance
Of life's symphony, where music
Serves as the conductor of advance.

Through the ebb and flow of advance,
We find strength in the power of connection,
And solace in the healing embrace of music,
For in its harmonious melody, affection
Finds expression, and in its rhythmic dance,
We discover the essence of trust.
So let us surrender to the dance of advance,
And embrace the sacred bond of connection,
For in the language of music, we find trust,
And in its timeless melody, the truest affection.

Here are four Sestina poems, 1 each about Art, Inspiration, Creativity & Courage

Sestina: Art
In the gallery of life, where colors dance,
We find solace in the strokes of artistry,
A canvas painted with boundless inspiration,
Each brushstroke a testament to creativity,
In the depths of expression, we discover courage,
And in the masterpiece, we glimpse eternity.

Through the eyes of the beholder, eternity
Resides, captured within the frames of dance,
In the symphony of hues, we find courage,
For in the realm of creation, artistry
Thrives, fueled by the fire of creativity,
Guiding us through the labyrinth of inspiration.

In the silence of creation, inspiration
Whispers, a gentle reminder of eternity,
For in the wellspring of imagination, creativity
Flows, igniting the flames of dance,
In the tapestry of expression, artistry
Blooms, a testament to fearless courage.

Through the storm of doubt, courage
Prevails, a beacon guiding us to inspiration,
In the crucible of creation, artistry
Blooms, transcending the boundaries of eternity,
For in the rhythm of expression, dance
Resonates, fueled by the spark of creativity.

In the heart of the creator, creativity
Throbs, a pulse of unyielding courage,
In the symphony of creation, dance
Unfolds, a graceful manifestation of inspiration,
For in the sanctuary of imagination, eternity
Resides, immortalized by artistry.

So let us embrace the power of creativity,
And summon the strength of courage,
For in the wellspring of inspiration, eternity
Awaits, in the timeless dance of artistry.

Sestina: Inspiration
In the silence of the soul, where dreams dance,
We find solace in the whispers of inspiration,
A guiding light in the darkness of creativity,
Each spark igniting the flames of courage,
In the depths of imagination, eternity
Resides, beckoning us to embrace inspiration.

Through the labyrinth of life, inspiration
Guides us, like a compass in the dance,
In the symphony of existence, eternity
Echoes, in the harmonious melody of creativity,
For in the depths of the heart, courage
Burns bright, fueled by the fire of inspiration.

In the tapestry of dreams, inspiration
Blooms, a testament to the power of dance,
In the canvas of creation, courage
Thrives, nurtured by the wellspring of creativity,
For in the infinite expanse of possibility, eternity
Resides, waiting to be discovered through inspiration.

Through the trials of life, inspiration
Uplifts us, like a gentle breeze in the dance,
In the sanctuary of the mind, creativity
Flourishes, nurturing the seeds of courage,
For in the depths of the universe, eternity
Awaits, revealed through the lens of inspiration.

So let us embrace the gift of inspiration,
And surrender to the rhythm of the dance,
For in the pursuit of creativity, courage
Guides us towards the shores of eternity.

Sestina: Creativity
In the realm of imagination, where dreams dance,
We find solace in the boundless expanse of creativity,
A universe of possibilities fueled by inspiration,
Each idea a brushstroke in the canvas of eternity,
In the depths of the soul, courage
Resides, guiding us through the dance of creation.

Through the corridors of the mind, creation
Unfolds, a kaleidoscope of colors in the dance,
In the symphony of expression, courage
Echoes, driving us towards the shores of creativity,
For in the depths of the soul, eternity
Awaits, illuminated by the light of inspiration.

In the sanctuary of the heart, inspiration
Throbs, a pulse of unyielding creation,
In the labyrinth of the mind, eternity
Resides, beckoning us to join the dance,
For in the tapestry of existence, creativity
Blooms, nurtured by the flames of courage.

Through the storms of doubt, courage
Prevails, a beacon guiding us towards inspiration,
In the crucible of expression, creativity
Flourishes, birthing new realms of creation,
For in the rhythm of life, the dance
Unfolds, revealing the secrets of eternity.

So let us embrace the power of creativity,
And summon the strength of courage,
For in the dance of creation, inspiration
Awaits, leading us towards the shores of eternity.

Sestina: Courage
In the depths of the soul, where fears dance,
We find solace in the flames of courage,
A beacon guiding us through the labyrinth of creativity,
Each step a testament to the power of inspiration,
In the symphony of existence, eternity
Resides, awaiting our fearless creation.

Through the trials of life, creation
Unfolds, a testament to the strength of courage,
In the tapestry of dreams, eternity
Awaits, illuminated by the dance,
For in the depths of the heart, inspiration
Throbs, fueling the flames of creativity.

In the crucible of expression, creativity
Blooms, a symphony of fearless creation,
For in the wellspring of the soul, inspiration
Resides, igniting the flames of courage,
In the dance of life, the rhythm of eternity
Echoes, guiding us towards fearless creation.

Through the storms of doubt, courage
Prevails, a beacon leading us towards inspiration,
In the sanctuary of the mind, creativity
Flourishes, nurtured by the flames of creation,
For in the depths of the soul, eternity
Awaits, beckoning us towards fearless dance.

So let us embrace the power of creativity,
And summon the strength of courage,
For in the dance of existence, inspiration
Guides us towards the shores of eternity.

Here are four Sestina poems, 1 each about Faith, Doubt, Solitude & Joy

Sestina: Faith
In the sanctuary of the heart, where faith resides,
We find solace in the whispers of divine grace,
A guiding light in the darkness of uncertainty,
Each prayer a testament to unwavering belief,
In the depths of the soul, a steadfast trust,
For in the embrace of faith, hope blossoms.

Through the trials of life, hope blossoms,
A beacon of light in the shadows where faith resides,
In the symphony of existence, we place our trust,
For in the tapestry of destiny, grace
Unfolds, revealing the beauty of belief,
Guiding us through the labyrinth of uncertainty.

In the silence of the night, uncertainty
Looms, casting shadows where joy once blossoms,
Yet in the depths of despair, we find belief,
For in the sanctuary of the soul, faith resides,
In the embrace of love's eternal grace,
We surrender to the rhythm of divine trust.

Through the storms of doubt, we cling to trust,
A lifeline in the sea of uncertainty,
In the gentle breeze of grace, we find solace,
And in the warmth of the sun, hope blossoms,
For in the depths of our being, faith resides,
Nurtured by the nourishing waters of belief.

In the dance of existence, belief
Guides us, like a compass pointing towards trust,
In the symphony of life, where faith resides,
We find courage to face the waves of uncertainty,
And in the blooming flowers of hope, joy blossoms,
Filling our hearts with divine grace.

So let us embrace the power of belief,
And surrender to the embrace of faith's trust,
For in the depths of our souls, joy blossoms,
And we find solace in the midst of uncertainty.

Sestina: Doubt
In the depths of the mind, where shadows of doubt reside,
We find solace in the whispers of uncertainty,
A haunting echo in the chambers of belief,
Each question a testament to wavering trust,
In the labyrinth of thought, doubt blossoms,
Casting a pall over the once vibrant joy.

Through the corridors of uncertainty, joy
Fades, overshadowed by the specter of doubt,
In the garden of the soul, where hope once blossoms,
We find ourselves lost in the fog of doubt's reside,
For in the tapestry of existence, trust
Unravels, leaving behind shards of shattered belief.

In the silence of the night, belief
Wavers, like a flickering flame in the wind of doubt,
In the depths of the heart, where faith once reside,

We find ourselves grappling with uncertainty,
Caught in the web of doubt's insidious joy,
As the petals of hope wither and doubt blossoms.

Through the haze of uncertainty, trust
Falters, like a ship adrift in the sea of doubt,
In the echo of silence, joy remains a distant belief,
Lost in the shadows where doubt resides.

So let us confront the shadows of doubt with trust,
And banish uncertainty with the light of belief,
For in the embrace of faith, joy blossoms.

Sestina: Solitude
In the quiet of solitude, where silence resides,
We find solace in the stillness of our own belief,
A sanctuary of peace where joy blossoms,
Each moment a testament to the power of trust,
In the depths of introspection, uncertainty
Fades, leaving behind the serenity of solitude.

Through the solitude of self-reflection, trust
Deepens, like roots anchoring belief,
In the sanctuary of the soul, uncertainty
Recedes, replaced by the calm of solitude,
For in the depths of silence, joy
Finds its home, and blossoms.

In the embrace of solitude, belief
Grows stronger, like a tree reaching towards trust,
In the quiet of contemplation, joy
Unfolds, like petals opening to the sun of solitude,
For in the stillness of the moment, uncertainty
Melts away, leaving behind the beauty of belief.

Through the whispers of solitude, trust
Echoes, like a gentle breeze carrying the fragrance of belief,
In the heart's sanctuary, uncertainty
Fades, yielding to the peace of solitude,
For in the depths of introspection, joy
Blooms, nourished by the roots of belief.

So let us embrace the gift of solitude with trust,
And find solace in the sanctuary of belief,
For in the quietude of the soul, joy blossoms.

Sestina: Joy
In the dance of existence, where joy resides,
We find solace in the laughter of belief,
A melody that echoes through the halls of trust,
Each note a testament to the power of solitude,
In the symphony of life, uncertainty
Fades, giving way to the radiance of joy.

Through the tapestry of experience, joy
Weaves its thread, a vibrant hue where hope resides,
In the chorus of celebration, uncertainty
Dissolves, washed away by the flood of belief,
For in the sanctuary of the heart, solitude
Beckons, offering respite from doubt's trust.

In the embrace of joy, trust
Flourishes, like a flower basking in the sun of solitude,
In the tapestry of emotion, belief
Guides us, like a compass pointing towards joy,
For in the depths of the soul, where love resides,
There is no room for fear or uncertainty.

Through the lens of gratitude, uncertainty
Fades, replaced by the warmth of trust,
In the cathedral of the spirit, where faith resides,
We find ourselves immersed in the river of joy,
For in the sanctuary of the heart, solitude
Becomes a sacred temple of belief.

So let us embrace the dance of joy with trust,
And find solace in the sanctuary of belief,
For in the depths of the soul, where love resides,
There is eternal solace and radiant joy.

Here are four Sestina poems, 1 each about Sorrow, Childhood, Wisdom & Innocence

Sestina: Sorrow
In the shadowed corners of the heart, sorrow dwells,
A heavy burden that weighs upon the soul's dance,
Echoes of pain reverberate in the chambers of grief,
Each tear a testament to the depth of despair,
In the labyrinth of emotions, sorrow holds sway,
Casting a pall over the once vibrant landscape.

Through the veil of tears, the landscape
Transforms, cloaked in the shadow of sorrow's dwell,
In the depths of the soul, melancholy holds sway,
A mournful refrain in the symphony of life's dance,
In the silence of the night, the echoes of despair
Resound, enveloping the spirit in the shroud of grief.

In the crucible of loss, the flames of grief
Burn bright, scorching the tender landscape,
Leaving scars etched with the mark of sorrow's despair,
In the recesses of memory, where sadness dwells,
We find ourselves lost in the mournful dance,
Enveloped in the embrace of sorrow's sway.

Yet amidst the darkness, a glimmer of hope holds sway,
A flickering light in the depths of grief,
A reminder that even in sorrow's dance,
There exists beauty in the desolate landscape,
For in the tears of mourning, love's presence dwells,
A beacon guiding us through the shadows of despair.

So let us embrace the shadows, for even in despair,
There lies a path illuminated by sorrow's sway,
Leading us towards the light where wisdom dwells,
In the crucible of suffering, where grief
Transforms the barren landscape,
And plants seeds of resilience in the dance.

In the rhythm of life's dance, sorrow finds its sway,
But within grief's embrace lies the wisdom of despair,
For in the landscape of the soul, every sorrowful moment is a chance.

Sestina: Childhood
In the golden haze of innocence, childhood thrives,
A magical realm where dreams dance and laughter dwells,
In the playground of imagination, joy holds sway,
Each moment a treasure in the vibrant landscape,
In the heart of every child, wonder and curiosity reside,
Guiding them through the wondrous dance of discovery.

Through eyes of a child, the world is full of discovery,
Every corner a new adventure where excitement thrives,
In the simple pleasures of play, happiness resides,
And in the bonds of friendship, love and laughter dwell,
In the kaleidoscope of memories, a vivid landscape,
Painted with the colors of innocence and joy's sway.

In the embrace of family, security holds sway,
A comforting presence in the journey of discovery,
In the nurturing arms of parents, a sheltered landscape,
Where dreams take flight and ambition thrives,
In the innocent laughter of children, love dwells,
A bond unbreakable, where happiness resides.

But as time passes, innocence fades and wisdom lie,
In bittersweet nostalgia of memories, regret holds sway,
Yet within every heart, the spirit of childhood still dwells,
A timeless essence that fuels the flames of discovery,
In the pursuit of dreams, where resilience thrives,
And in the cherished moments that shape life's landscape.

So let us embrace the magic of childhood's sway,
And treasure each moment of discovery,
For within the landscape of innocence, joy still dwells.

Sestina: Wisdom
In the depths of the soul, where silence reigns,
Wisdom resides, a guiding light in the darkness,
In the quiet moments of reflection, clarity holds sway,
Each revelation a treasure in the landscape of the mind,
In the tapestry of experience, lessons thrive,
And in the whispers of intuition, truth dwells.
Through the trials of life, the wisdom of the ages dwells,
A timeless beacon shining through the fog of mundane reigns,
In the crucible of adversity, resilience thrives,
And in the face of uncertainty, courage banishes darkness,
In the wellspring of knowledge, understanding holds sway,
Guiding us through the labyrinth of existence's dance.

In the chambers of the heart, compassion holds sway,
A gentle force that softens the edges of wisdom's dwell,
In the embrace of empathy, kindness thrives,
And in the echoes of forgiveness, healing reigns,
In the symphony of emotions, love dispels darkness,
And in the essence of compassion, humanity thrives.

But wisdom not confined to age, innocence that reigns,
There's purity that transcends the barriers of time's sway,
In the unfiltered perspective of youth, truth still dwells,
A reminder in every heart, potential for wisdom thrives,
For within the depths of the soul, the light of enlightenment holds sway.

Embrace wisdom that resides within, for in its reigns,
With power to navigate the landscape of life's dance,
And to thrive in the presence of darkness,
where resilience dwells.

Sestina: Innocence
In the purity of innocence, where light reigns,
We find solace in the simplicity of youth's sway,
In the laughter of children, joy still dwells,
Each smile a beacon of hope in the darkness,
In the carefree days of youth, freedom thrives,
And in the wonder of discovery, innocence holds sway.

Through lens of innocence, a worlds vibrant landscape,
Every moments adventure where imagination reigns,
In the boundless expanse of possibility, creativity thrives,
And in the heart of every child, love still holds sway,
In gentle embrace of innocence, beauty dispels darkness,
And in the sparkle of their eyes, magic still dwells.

But as time passes, innocence fades and reality reigns,
In harsh light of adulthood, responsibility holds sway,
And complexities of life, innocence is lost in darkness,
Yet within every heart, the spirit of youth still dwells,
A reminder of purity and wonder of innocence's sway,
And in the memories of childhood, nostalgia thrives.

Let's cherish fleeting moments where innocence reigns,
And embrace the childlike wonder that still holds sway,
For within the depths of the soul, the light of innocence still dwells.

Here are four Sestina poems, 1 each about Passion, Serenity, Freedom & Justice

Sestina: Passion
In the fiery depths of the heart, passion ignites,
A relentless flame that consumes the soul's dance,
In the fervent embrace of desire, intensity holds sway,
Each heartbeat a testament to the power of passion,
In the tumultuous storm of emotion, chaos reigns,
And in the throes of ecstasy, ecstasy dwells.

Through the tempest of desire, ecstasy dwells,
A euphoric state where passion ignites,
In the symphony of love, chaos reigns,
Every touch a spark that fuels the soul's dance,
In the throbbing pulse of longing, passion
Guides us, like a beacon in the night's sway.

In the whirlwind of romance, passion holds sway,
A force of nature that defies reason, where ecstasy dwells,
In the tangled web of attraction, passion
Weaves its spell, igniting the flames of desire,
In the delicate balance of give and take, the soul's dance
Unfolds, amidst the chaos where love reigns.

But passion is not confined to love's reign,
In the pursuit of dreams, its fervor holds sway,
In the depths of creativity, the soul's dance
Unfolds, and in the ecstasy of creation, genius dwells,
For in the heart of every artist, desire
Burns bright, fueling the flames of passion.

So let us embrace the power of passion's sway,
And surrender to the ecstasy where love dwells,
For in the pursuit of dreams, the soul's dance ignites.

Sestina: Serenity
In the stillness of the soul, serenity dwells,
A tranquil oasis where peace holds sway,
In the gentle embrace of calm, clarity reigns,
Each breath a reminder of the beauty of serenity,
In the symphony of nature, harmony ignites,
And in the quiet moments, the spirit's dance.

Through the whispers of the wind, the spirit's dance
Unfolds, amidst the tranquility where wisdom dwells,
In the embrace of the earth, serenity ignites,
A gentle force that soothes the soul's sway,
In the tranquil waters of reflection, clarity reigns,
And in the depths of meditation, peace reigns.

In the sanctuary of the heart, peace reigns,
A sacred haven where the spirit's dance
Finds solace, and in the silence, wisdom dwells,
For in the depths of stillness, serenity
Blooms, guiding us through life's sway,
And in the embrace of grace, love ignites.

But serenity is not confined to love's reign,
In the pursuit of truth, its power holds sway,
In the moments of solitude, where silence ignites,
The spirit's dance finds expression, and in the quiet, wisdom dwells,
For in the heart of every seeker, serenity
Resides, a beacon guiding us through life's sway.

So let us embrace the beauty of serenity's reign,
And surrender to the peace where wisdom dwells,
For in the stillness of the soul, the spirit's dance ignites.

Sestina: Freedom

In the boundless expanse of the sky, freedom reigns,
A canvas where dreams take flight and hope holds sway,
In the endless horizon, possibility ignites,
Each breath a reminder of the power of freedom,
In the dance of liberation, courage dwells,
And in the pursuit of justice, passion ignites.

Through the trials of oppression, passion ignites,
A fierce flame that fuels the fight where justice reigns,
In the hearts of the oppressed, resilience dwells,
A strength that cannot be quenched, where hope holds sway,
In the relentless pursuit of equality, freedom
Blooms, and in the face of adversity, courage ignites.

In the chorus of dissent, courage ignites,
A rallying cry that echoes where injustice reigns,
In the struggle for liberation, freedom
Resides, a beacon guiding us through the fray where hope holds sway,
In the tapestry of resistance, solidarity dwells,
And in the hearts of the righteous, passion ignites.

But freedom is not confined to passion's reign,
In the pursuit of dreams, its power holds sway,
In the unyielding spirit of adventure, courage dwells,
A fearless force that defies boundaries where justice reigns,
In the boundless expanse of the human soul, hope ignites,
And in the pursuit of truth, freedom finds its sway.

So let us embrace the power of freedom's sway,
And stand united in the fight where justice reigns,
For in the hearts of the righteous, courage ignites.

Sestina: Justice
In the pursuit of righteousness, justice reigns,
A guiding principle that upholds the sway,
In the halls of power, integrity ignites,
Each action a testament to cause where truth holds sway,

In the fight for equality, righteousness dwells,
And in the hearts of the just, compassion ignites.

Through the trials of adversity, compassion ignites,
A flame that fuels the fight where justice reigns,
In the face of injustice, courage dwells,
A steadfast resolve cannot be swayed where hope holds its way,
In the pursuit of righteousness, integrity ignites,
And in the chorus of dissent, passion ignites.

In the struggle for reform, passion ignites,
A fervor that drives the movement where justice reigns,
In the depths of the soul, empathy dwells,
A force bridges the divide where understanding sways,
In the pursuit of fairness, empathy ignites,
And in the hearts of the righteous, righteousness dwells.

But justice is not confined to righteousness's reign,
In the pursuit of truth, its power holds sway,
In the unyielding spirit of compassion, empathy ignites,
A flame that burns bright where justice reigns,
In the halls of power, integrity dwells,
And in the hearts of the just, righteousness ignites.

So let us embrace the cause where justice reigns,
And stand united in the fight where truth holds sway.

Here are four Sestina poems, 1 each about Change, Resilience, Gratitude & Forgiveness

Sestina: Change
In the ever-shifting currents of life, change abounds,
A constant force that shapes the landscape of existence,
In the dance of transformation, uncertainty reigns,
Each moment a crossroads of possibility and fear,
In the depths of transition, courage holds sway,
And in the embrace of evolution, growth ignites.

Through the ebb and flow of time, growth ignites,
A relentless pursuit that propels us through change's bounds,
In the crucible of adversity, resilience holds sway,
A strength forged in the fires of life's persistence,
In the face of challenges, determination reigns,
And in the depths of struggle, hope still abounds.

In the tapestry of experience, hope abounds,
A thread that weaves through the fabric of growth's ignite,
In the symphony of resilience, faith reigns,
A melody that carries us beyond life's bounds,
In the echo of perseverance, courage holds sway,
And in the heart's journey, transformation ignites.

But change is not without its challenges, and fear reigns,
In the uncertainty of the unknown, doubt abounds,
In the face of obstacles, perseverance holds sway,
A steadfast resolve that fuels growth's ignite,
In the depths of adversity, resilience reigns,
And in the process of healing, forgiveness ignites.

Sestina: Resilience
In the crucible of struggle, resilience thrives,
A sturdy fortress that withstands life's storms and reigns,
In the face of adversity, strength abounds,
Each trial a testament to the power of resilience,
In the depths of hardship, hope ignites,
And in the heart's resilience, courage holds sway.

Through the darkest nights, courage holds sway,
A guiding light that illuminates the path where resilience thrives,
In the shadows of despair, hope ignites,
A flame that banishes darkness and reigns,
In the sanctuary of the soul, resilience abounds,
And in the embrace of love, healing abounds.

But resilience is not without its trials, and doubt ignites,
In the face of uncertainty, fear holds sway,
In the depths of pain, grief abounds,
A heavy burden that tests the limits of resilience,
Yet even in the depths of sorrow, hope still reigns,
And in the process of healing, forgiveness ignites.

Sestina: Gratitude
In the garden of the heart, gratitude blooms,
A fragrant blossom that colors the landscape of existence,
In the symphony of blessings, joy reigns,
Each moment a gift to be cherished, where gratitude thrives,
In the depths of appreciation, love holds sway,
And in the dance of abundance, generosity ignites.

Through the lens of gratitude, generosity ignites,
A ripple of kindness that flows through the garden where love blooms,
In the embrace of community, unity holds sway,
A bond that strengthens the fabric of existence,
In the tapestry of connection, compassion thrives,
And in the hearts of the grateful, peace reigns.

But gratitude is not without its challenges, and doubt ignites,
In the face of adversity, faith holds sway,
In the depths of loss, grief abounds,
A heavy burden that tests the resilience of gratitude,
Yet even in the darkest moments, hope still blooms,
And in the process of healing, forgiveness ignites.

Sestina: Forgiveness
In the healing embrace of forgiveness, peace reigns,
A balm that soothes the wounds of the past and ignites,
In the depths of the soul, compassion blooms,
A gentle reminder of the power of forgiveness,
In the face of hurt, love holds sway,
And in the heart's journey, healing abounds.

Through the process of healing, transformation ignites,
A phoenix rising from the ashes, where forgiveness reigns,
In the crucible of redemption, redemption holds sway,
A second chance that restores the spirit and ignites,
In the depths of reconciliation, understanding abounds,
And in the dance of forgiveness, grace blooms.

But forgiveness is not without its challenges, and pain reigns,
In the face of betrayal, anger holds sway,
In the depths of resentment, bitterness abounds,
A poison that corrodes the soul and stifles forgiveness,
Yet even in the darkest moments, light ignites,
And in the process of letting go, freedom blooms.

So let us embrace the power of forgiveness, where peace reigns,
And surrender to the grace that ignites the soul's transformation.

Here are four Sestina poems, 1 each about Longing, Belonging, Discovery & Wonder

Sestina: Longing
In the quiet hours of night, longing lingers,
A whispered yearning that haunts the soul's dance,
In the depths of desire, the heart's ache reigns,
Each moment a reminder of what's missing,
In the shadows of absence, loneliness holds sway,
And in the echo of silence, longing ignites.

Through the corridors of memory, longing ignites,
A flame that flickers in the darkness where hope lingers,
In the labyrinth of longing, nostalgia holds sway,
A bittersweet melody that echoes in the soul's dance,
In the tapestry of longing, longing holds sway,
And in the depths of yearning, desire reigns.

In the embrace of dreams, desire reigns,
A beacon of light in the darkness where longing ignites,
In the symphony of longing, passion holds sway,
A fervent melody that crescendos where love lingers,
In the heart's sanctuary, longing fuels the soul's dance,
And in the pursuit of fulfillment, hope reigns.

But longing is not without its trials, and doubt reigns,
In the face of uncertainty, fear holds sway,
In the depths of longing, despair lingers,
A shadow that threatens to extinguish the flame where longing ignites,
Yet even in the darkest moments, faith holds sway,
And in the depths of longing, resilience reigns.

Sestina: Belonging
In the warmth of connection, belonging thrives,
A sense of home that comforts the soul's dance,
In the embrace of community, unity holds sway,
Bonding thread that weaves a tapestry where love reigns,
In the symphony of belonging, acceptance ignites,
And in the heart's sanctuary, peace lingers.

Through the ups and downs of life, peace lingers,
A serene presence that anchors where belonging thrives,
In the chorus of voices, harmony ignites,
A melody that resonates in the soul's dance,
In the sanctuary of friendship, trust holds sway,
And in the depths of camaraderie, loyalty reigns.

In the beauty of diversity, inclusivity reigns,
A celebration of differences where unity holds sway,
In the embrace of acceptance, understanding ignites,
A bridge that spans the divides where belonging lingers,
In the tapestry of humanity, compassion thrives,
And in the heart's sanctuary, kindness reigns.

But belonging is not without its challenges, and doubt reigns,
In the face of exclusion, loneliness holds sway,
In the depths of isolation, despair lingers,
A shadow that threatens to obscure where belonging thrives,
Yet even in the darkest moments, hope reigns,
And in the pursuit of connection, resilience ignites.

Sestina: Discovery
In the journey of exploration, discovery reigns,
A quest for knowledge that fuels the soul's dance,
In the depths of curiosity, wonder ignites,
Each revelation a spark that illuminates where curiosity holds sway,
In the vast expanse of possibility, potential thrives,
And in the heart's sanctuary, curiosity lingers.

Through the lens of imagination, curiosity lingers,
A flame that burns bright in the darkness where discovery reigns,
In the pursuit of truth, curiosity ignites,
A relentless pursuit that propels the soul's dance,
In the labyrinth of inquiry, inquiry holds sway,
And in the depths of exploration, adventure thrives.

In the beauty of nature, wonder reigns,
A symphony of awe that echoes where discovery lingers,
In the tapestry of creation, creativity holds sway,
A palette of colors that paints the soul's dance,
In the embrace of wonder, inspiration ignites,
And in the depths of revelation, revelation thrives.

But discovery not without its challenges, and fear reigns,
In the face of the unknown, uncertainty holds sway,
In the depths of doubt, hesitation lingers,
A shadow threatens to obscure where discovery reigns,
Yet even in the darkest moments, courage ignites,
And in the pursuit of enlightenment, perseverance thrives.

Sestina: Wonder
In the magic of the moment, wonder reigns,
A sense of awe that captivates the soul's dance,
In the depths of fascination, curiosity ignites,
Each discovery a treasure that delights where curiosity holds sway,
In the symphony of exploration, adventure thrives,
And in the heart's sanctuary, wonder lingers.

Through the lens of imagination, wonder lingers,
A spark that ignites the flames of creativity where wonder reigns,
In the pursuit of beauty, appreciation thrives,
A reverence for the world that enchants the soul's dance,
In the embrace of gratitude, joy holds sway,
And in the depths of admiration, inspiration ignites.

In the wonder of nature, inspiration ignites,
A spark that fuels the fire of creation where wonder reigns,
In the tapestry of existence, diversity holds sway,
A kaleidoscope of experiences where wonder lingers,
In the symphony of life, harmony thrives,
And in the heart's sanctuary, wonder reigns.

But wonder is not without its mysteries, and curiosity reigns,
In the face of the unknown, exploration holds sway,
In the depths of inquiry, fascination lingers,
A hunger for knowledge that drives where wonder reigns,
Yet even in the pursuit of answers, awe ignites,
And in the depths of wonder, the soul's dance thrives.

Here are four Sestina poems, 1 each about Journey, Reflection, Harmony & Imagination

Sestina: Journey
In the vast expanse of the unknown, a journey begins,
A path unfurls before us, winding through the landscape,
In the depths of anticipation, excitement ignites,
Each step a new adventure in the dance of life's journey,
In the tapestry of experiences, growth holds sway,
And in the heart's sanctuary, courage lingers.

Through the twists and turns of fate, courage lingers,
A steadfast companion that guides us on our journey,
In the face of uncertainty, resilience holds sway,
A strength that carries us through the rugged landscape,
In the depths of perseverance, determination ignites,
And in the pursuit of dreams, passion reigns.

In the pursuit of dreams, passion reigns,
A fire that burns bright in the darkness where hope lingers,
In the realm of possibility, imagination ignites,
A spark that propels us forward on our journey,
In the symphony of existence, purpose holds sway,
And in the heart's sanctuary, faith ignites.

But the journey is not without its challenges, and doubt reigns,
In the face of adversity, fear holds sway,
In the depths of despair, loneliness lingers,
A shadow that threatens to obscure where hope reigns,
Yet even in the darkest moments, love ignites,
And in the pursuit of truth, wisdom holds sway.

Sestina: Reflection
In the stillness of the soul, reflection begins,
A moment of introspection in the sanctuary where peace reigns,
In the depths of contemplation, clarity ignites,
Each thought a ripple in the pool where serenity lingers,
In the tapestry of memories, nostalgia holds sway,
And in the heart's sanctuary, gratitude reigns.

Through the lens of gratitude, gratitude reigns,
A lens that illuminates the beauty of life where reflection begins,
In the mirror of the mind, truth holds sway,
A revelation that resonates where wisdom ignites,
In the echoes of silence, introspection lingers,
A dialogue with the self where insight ignites.

In the pursuit of insight, inspiration reigns,
A muse that sparks the flames of creativity where imagination ignites,
In the depths of the subconscious, magic lingers,
A whisper of possibility where dreams begin,
In the symphony of ideas, innovation holds sway,
And in the heart's sanctuary, wonder ignites.

Reflection is not without its challenges, and doubt reigns,
In the face of uncertainty, fear holds sway,
In the depths of self-doubt, insecurity lingers,

A shadow that threatens to obscure where confidence reigns,
Yet even in the darkest moments, belief ignites,
And in the pursuit of self-discovery, authenticity holds sway.

Sestina: Harmony
In the melody of existence, harmony reigns,
A symphony of interconnectedness where unity holds sway,
In the dance of coexistence, compassion ignites,
Each act a note in the chorus where love reigns,
In the tapestry of relationships, empathy lingers,
And in the heart's sanctuary, acceptance ignites.

Through the embrace of acceptance, peace reigns,
A tranquility that settles where serenity holds sway,
In the rhythm of connection, understanding ignites,
A bridge that spans the divides where harmony reigns,
In the symphony of diversity, tolerance lingers,
And in the heart's sanctuary, respect ignites.

In the pursuit of respect, justice reigns,
A beacon of fairness that shines where equality holds sway,
In the depths of fairness, integrity ignites,
A moral compass that guides where righteousness reigns,
In the pursuit of balance, equilibrium lingers,
And in the heart's sanctuary, compassion ignites.

But harmony is not without its discord, and conflict reigns,
In the face of disagreement, strife holds sway,
In the depths of discord, resentment lingers,
A poison that corrodes where harmony reigns,
Yet even in the midst of turmoil, reconciliation ignites,
And in the pursuit of peace, forgiveness holds sway.

Sestina: Imagination
In the realm of possibility, imagination reigns,
A boundless expanse where creativity holds sway,
In the depths of invention, innovation ignites,
Each idea a spark that ignites the flames where inspiration begins,
In the tapestry of dreams, curiosity lingers,
And in the heart's sanctuary, wonder ignites.

Through the lens of wonder, curiosity reigns,
A hunger for knowledge that drives where exploration holds sway,
In the pursuit of discovery, adventure ignites,
A spirit that embarks on the journey where imagination reigns,
In the symphony of ideas, innovation lingers,
And in the heart's sanctuary, creativity ignites.

In the pursuit of creativity, passion reigns,
A fire that burns bright in the darkness where doubt holds sway,
In the depths of expression, authenticity ignites,
A voice that resonates where originality reigns,
In the canvas of creation, expression lingers,
And in the heart's sanctuary, imagination ignites.

But imagination is not without its constraints, and fear reigns,
In the face of criticism, insecurity holds sway,
In the depths of self-doubt, hesitation lingers,
A shadow that threatens to obscure where confidence reigns,
Yet even in the darkest moments, belief ignites,
And in the pursuit of self-expression, freedom holds sway.

Here are four Sestina poems, 1 each about Silence, Laughter, Tears & Strength

Sestina: Silence
In the hushed embrace of silence, secrets dwell,
A sanctuary where whispers echo and linger,
In the depths of solitude, tranquility reigns,
Each moment a pause in life's chaotic dance,
In the tapestry of stillness, peace ignites,
And in the heart's sanctuary, wisdom holds sway.

Through the corridors of thought, wisdom holds sway,
A guiding light that illuminates where truths dwell,
In the sanctuary of the mind, clarity ignites,
A beacon that pierces through the shadows that linger,
In the symphony of silence, introspection reigns,
And in the depths of reflection, insight ignites.

In the canvas of dreams, inspiration ignites,
A spark that kindles the flames of creativity where passion holds sway,
In the depths of imagination, possibility reigns,
A realm where fantasies come alive and dreams dwell,
In the tapestry of visions, hope still lingers,
And in the heart's sanctuary, ambition ignites.

But silence is not without its power, and fear reigns,
In the face of the unknown, uncertainty holds sway,
In the depths of solitude, loneliness lingers,
Shadows threatens to obscure as strength holds sway,
Yet even in the darkest moments, resilience ignites,
And in the pursuit of solace, courage reigns.

Sestina: Laughter
In the chorus of mirth, joy holds sway,
A symphony of laughter that echoes and ignites,
In the hearts of the merry, happiness reigns,
Each chuckle a note in life's jubilant dance,
In the tapestry of humor, camaraderie holds sway,
And in the echo of giggles, love still lingers.

Through the cacophony of glee, love lingers,
A bond that strengthens where laughter holds sway,
In the embrace of friendship, unity ignites,
A connection that deepens as laughter reigns,
In the heart's sanctuary, trust holds sway,
And in the ripple of amusement, kindness reigns.

In the melody of jest, kindness reigns,
A harmony that resonates where compassion lingers,
In the chorus of jesters, empathy holds sway,
A camaraderie that flourishes where laughter ignites,
In the tapestry of anecdotes, friendship reigns,
And in the echo of guffaws, loyalty holds sway.

But laughter is not without its shadows, and pain reigns,
In the face of adversity, sorrow holds sway,
In the depths of despair, grief lingers,
A heaviness that threatens to silence where laughter reigns,
Yet even in the darkest moments, resilience ignites,
And in the pursuit of joy, strength holds sway.

Sestina: Tears
In the cascade of tears, emotions hold sway,
A torrent of feelings that overflow where vulnerability ignites,
In the depths of sorrow, grief reigns,
Each drop a testament to the depth of pain that lingers,
In the tapestry of memories, loss holds sway,
And in the heart's sanctuary, healing ignites.

Through the rivers of anguish, healing ignites,
A process of renewal that begins where acceptance holds sway,
In the embrace of empathy, comfort reigns,
A solace that soothes where compassion ignites,
In the labyrinth of mourning, nostalgia lingers,
And in the echo of sobs, resilience reigns.

In the journey of recovery, resilience reigns,
A strength that emerges from the ashes where hope ignites,
In the depths of adversity, courage holds sway,
A bravery that persists where fear lingers,
In the symphony of emotions, perseverance ignites,
And in the pursuit of solace, faith reigns.

But tears are not without their purpose, and growth reigns,
In the face of pain, transformation ignites,
In the depths of loss, wisdom holds sway,
A clarity that emerges where insight ignites,
In the tapestry of experience, gratitude reigns,
And in the heart's sanctuary, strength holds sway.

Sestina: Strength
In the crucible of trials, resilience reigns,
A fortitude that emerges from the depths where determination ignites,
In the face of adversity, courage holds sway,
A bravery that persists where fear lingers,
In the symphony of struggles, perseverance ignites,
And in the pursuit of victory, hope reigns.

Through the battles of life, hope reigns,
A beacon that guides us through the darkness where resilience holds sway,
In the depths of despair, determination ignites,
A fire that burns bright in the soul where passion lingers,
In the tapestry of challenges, endurance reigns,
And in the heart's sanctuary, strength holds sway.

In the embrace of support, strength holds sway,
A pillar of support that lifts us up where love reigns,
In the depths of compassion, empathy ignites,
A connection that strengthens where understanding holds sway,
In the symphony of relationships, unity reigns,
And in the heart's sanctuary, resilience ignites.

But strength is not without its vulnerabilities, and doubt reigns,
In the face of uncertainty, faith holds sway,
In the depths of insecurity, courage ignites,
A bravery that defies the shadows where confidence reigns,
Yet even in the darkest moments, belief ignites,
And in the pursuit of greatness, resilience holds sway.

Here are four Sestina poems, 1 each about Vulnerability, Renewal, Acceptance & Mystery

Sestina: Vulnerability
In the rawness of emotions, vulnerability lies,
A tender openness that exposes the soul's core,
In the depths of honesty, courage holds sway,
Each moment a tightrope walk between fear and trust,
In the labyrinth of feelings, uncertainty reigns,
And in the heart's sanctuary, authenticity ignites.

Through the cracks in the armor, authenticity ignites,

A flame that burns bright in the darkness where vulnerability lies,
In the vulnerability of exposure, growth holds sway,
A process of transformation that shapes the soul's core,
In the embrace of vulnerability, connection finds trust,
And in the depths of intimacy, love reigns.

In the vulnerability of love, passion reigns,
A force that binds hearts together where vulnerability ignites,
In the sanctuary of intimacy, security holds sway,
A refuge that shelters the fragile where vulnerability lies,
In the dance of relationships, communication forms the core,
And in the rhythm of partnership, mutual trust.

But vulnerability is not without its risks, and doubt reigns,
In the face of rejection, insecurity holds sway,
In the depths of fear, hesitation lingers,
A shadow that threatens to obscure where vulnerability lies,
Yet even in the darkest moments, resilience ignites,
And in the pursuit of connection, courage reigns.

Sestina: Renewal
In the cycle of seasons, renewal begins,
A rebirth that follows the death where hope ignites,
In the depths of winter, dormant life lies,
Each frost a blanket that covers the earth's core,
In the tapestry of nature, regeneration holds sway,
And in the heart's sanctuary, optimism reigns.

Through the thaw of spring, optimism reigns,
A blossoming of life that heralds new beginnings,
In the symphony of growth, rejuvenation holds sway,
A flourishing of beauty where vitality ignites,
In the embrace of change, transformation finds its core,
And in the cycle of rebirth, resilience lies.

In the promise of summer, resilience lies,
A strength that endures where perseverance reigns,
In the depths of the sun's warmth, vitality holds sway,
A vitality that pulses through the veins of life's core,
In the dance of abundance, gratitude ignites,
And in the harvest of abundance, fulfillment reigns.

But renewal is not without its challenges, and fear reigns,
In the face of uncertainty, doubt holds sway,
In the depths of change, hesitation lingers,
A shadow that threatens to obscure where renewal begins,
Yet even in the darkest moments, faith ignites,
And in the pursuit of transformation, courage reigns.

Sestina: Acceptance
In the realm of understanding, acceptance lies,
A willingness to embrace what is where peace reigns,
In the depths of surrender, tranquility ignites,
Each moment a surrender to the flow of life's core,
In the tapestry of existence, harmony holds sway,
And in the heart's sanctuary, serenity lingers.

Through the embrace of imperfection, serenity lingers,
A contentment that arises from the acceptance of flaws where love lies,
In the depths of forgiveness, reconciliation reigns,
A bridge that spans the divides where compassion ignites,
In the dance of connection, unity holds sway,
And in the symphony of relationships, trust ignites.

In the sanctuary of self, trust ignites,
A confidence that emerges from the acceptance of oneself where peace reigns,
In the depths of self-love, empowerment holds sway,
A strength that radiates from within where resilience lies,
In the pursuit of authenticity, liberation ignites,
And in the heart's sanctuary, acceptance finds its core.

But acceptance is not without its challenges, and doubt reigns,
In the face of resistance, judgment holds sway,
In the depths of denial, hesitation lingers,
A shadow that threatens to obscure where acceptance lies,
Yet even in the darkest moments, compassion ignites,
And in the pursuit of understanding, empathy reigns.

Sestina: Mystery
In the enigma of existence, mystery lies,
A veil that shrouds the unknown where wonder ignites,
In the depths of curiosity, fascination holds sway,
Each question a key that unlocks the secrets where intrigue lies,
In the tapestry of discovery, adventure reigns,
And in the heart's sanctuary, awe lingers.

Through the lens of imagination, awe lingers,
A sense of wonder that captivates where magic lies,
In the embrace of possibility, creativity ignites,
A spark that kindles the flames of exploration where mystery holds sway,
In the pursuit of enlightenment, curiosity reigns,
Symphony of wonder, fascination finds its core.

In the sanctuary of the mind, fascination finds its core,
A fascination that lingers,
In the pursuit of truth, curiosity reigns,
A hunger for knowledge that drives where mystery lies,
In the depths of inquiry, innovation ignites,
And in the dance of ideas, imagination holds sway.

But mystery is not without its allure, and fear reigns,
In the face of the unknown, uncertainty holds sway,
In the depths of doubt, hesitation lingers,
A shadow that threatens to obscure where mystery lies,
Yet even in the darkest moments, curiosity ignites,
And in the pursuit of discovery, courage reigns.

Here are four Sestina poems, 1 each about Transformation, Eternity, Cosmos & Happiness

Sestina: Transformation
In the crucible of change, transformation begins,
A metamorphosis that shapes the essence of being,
In the depths of growth, evolution holds sway,
Each moment a step towards a new reality,
In the tapestry of life, adaptation ignites,
And in the heart's sanctuary, resilience lingers.

Through the trials of adversity, resilience lingers,
A strength that endures in the face of transformation,
In the symphony of challenges, perseverance ignites,
A determination that fuels the journey of being,
In the pursuit of self-discovery, authenticity holds sway,
And in the depths of self-awareness, wisdom reigns.

In the embrace of wisdom, wisdom reigns,
A clarity that guides where resilience lingers,
In the depths of introspection, introspection holds sway,
A journey inward that leads to transformation,
In the sanctuary of self, truth holds the key to being,
And in the pursuit of enlightenment, enlightenment ignites.

But transformation is not without its shadows, and fear reigns,
In the face of uncertainty, doubt holds sway,
In the depths of insecurity, hesitation lingers,
A shadow that threatens to obscure where wisdom reigns,
Yet even in the darkest moments, courage ignites,
And in the pursuit of growth, faith holds the power of being.

Sestina: Eternity
In the vast expanse of time, eternity lies,
A timeless realm beyond the grasp of being,
In the depths of infinity, eternity holds sway,
Each moment a drop in the ocean of existence,
In the tapestry of forever, immortality ignites,
And in the heart's sanctuary, peace lingers.

Through the cycles of creation, peace lingers,
A serenity that transcends the bounds of time where eternity lies,
In the dance of eternity, eternity reigns,
A symphony of permanence amidst the fleeting nature of being,
In the pursuit of infinity, eternity holds sway,
And in the depths of the cosmos, eternity ignites.

In the cosmic symphony, eternity ignites,
A spark that illuminates the mysteries where wonder lingers,
In the fabric of the universe, eternity holds sway,
A force that binds the stars to the sky where eternity lies,
In the depths of the cosmos, cosmic being,
And in the dance of eternity, eternity reigns.

But eternity is not without its enigmas, and mystery reigns,
In the face of the unknown, curiosity holds sway,
In the depths of the cosmos, wonder lingers,
A fascination that fuels the quest where eternity lies,
Yet even in the cosmic expanse, understanding ignites,
And in the pursuit of enlightenment, wisdom holds the key to being.

Sestina: Cosmos
In the vast expanse of the cosmos, mystery reigns,
A tapestry of stars that illuminates the unknown where wonder ignites,
In the depths of space, exploration holds sway,
Each journey a voyage into the unknown of being,
In the dance of galaxies, cosmic energy lingers,
And in the heart of the universe, creation ignites.

Through the nebulae of existence, creation ignites,
A process of birth that shapes the cosmos where mystery reigns,
In the symphony of stardust, magic lingers,
A spark that ignites the flames of curiosity where wonder lies,
In the pursuit of knowledge, discovery holds sway,
And in the depths of exploration, adventure ignites.

In the cosmic dance, adventure ignites,
A quest for understanding that spans the ages where curiosity reigns,
In the depths of the universe, possibility holds sway,
A realm of infinite potential where creativity ignites,
In the tapestry of galaxies, diversity lingers,
And in the heart of creation, beauty reigns.

But the cosmos is not without its secrets, and enigma reigns,
In the face of the unknown, uncertainty holds sway,
In the depths of space, mystery lingers,
A puzzle that challenges the limits of comprehension where wonder ignites,
Yet even in the cosmic expanse, enlightenment reigns,

And in the pursuit of truth, wisdom holds the key to being.

Sestina: Happiness

In the pursuit of joy, happiness reigns,
A state of bliss that permeates the soul where contentment ignites,
In the depths of fulfillment, satisfaction holds sway,
Each moment a treasure in the journey of being,
In the tapestry of emotions, joyfulness lingers,
And in the heart's sanctuary, serenity reigns.

Through the laughter of life, serenity reigns,
A tranquility that soothes the spirit where happiness ignites,
In the embrace of love, harmony holds sway,
A connection that nurtures the soul where joyfulness lies,
In the dance of relationships, companionship lingers,
And in the symphony of affection, affection ignites.

In the warmth of connection, affection ignites,
A bond that strengthens where happiness reigns,
In the depths of empathy, compassion lingers,
A kindness that uplifts the spirit where love ignites,
In the pursuit of fulfillment, purpose holds sway,
And in the heart's sanctuary, gratitude reigns.

But happiness is not without its challenges, and sadness reigns,
In the face of adversity, despair holds sway,
In the depths of sorrow, grief lingers,
A shadow that threatens to obscure where happiness reigns,
Yet even in the darkest moments, resilience ignites,
And in the pursuit of positivity, optimism holds the power of being.

-:|:-•:*'''''*:•.-:|:-•**•-:|:-•:*'''''*:•:*'''''*:•.-:|:-•**•-:|:--:|:-•:*'''''*:•.-:|:- •**•-:|:-•:*'''''*:•:*'''''*:•.-:|:-•**•-:|:-

CONCRETE POETRY:

Poetry in which the visual arrangement of words on the page enhances meaning or imagery, often taking on shapes related to the poem's subject matter.

We won't do them all, but here are examples of Concrete poetic forms: Love, Nature, Beauty & Time

Love

    L
   O O
  V   V
 E   E
L   L   L
O   O   O
V E   E V

Nature

 N A T U R E
N   E
A   R
T   U
U   T
R   A
E   N
 N R U T A N

Beauty

B E A U T Y
B   Y
E   T
A   U
U   A
T   E
Y   B
 Y T U A E B

Time

   T
  I M
 M   E
E   T
M   I
E M I T

Here are four more Concrete poetic forms: Art, Dreams, Hope & Joy

Art

   A
  R R
 T   T
A   A
R   R
T   T
  T A R

Dreams

 D R E A M S
D   S
R   M
E   A
A   E
M   R
S M A E R D

Hope

  O
 O O
H   E
O   P
P   O
E P O H

Joy

 J O Y
J   Y
O   O
Y   J
 Y O Y

You get the idea. Try making some yourself

ACROSTIC:

A poem in which the first letter of each line spells out a word or message when read vertically.

Here are four Acrostic poems, 1 each about Love, Nature, Beauty & Time

Love

Like a gentle breeze, it soothes the soul,
Opening hearts to warmth and affection,
Vows exchanged in whispers, binding spirits,
Embracing flaws, nurturing growth.

Nature

Nurturing life in its vast embrace,
A symphony of beauty, a canvas divine,
Taking breath away with its wonders,
Unfolding mysteries in every leaf and vine,
Radiant sunsets, majestic mountains, serene rivers,
Eternal dance of seasons, nature's eternal grace.

Beauty

Blossoming in the soul, a radiant glow,
Embracing imperfections with tender care,
A reflection of grace, a whisper of hope,
Unveiling wonders in the simplest of things,
Transforming darkness into light,
Yearning hearts find solace in its embrace.

Time

Ticking away, relentless and unyielding,
In its embrace, memories are woven,
Moments cherished, fleeting yet eternal,
Evolving, shaping destinies in its wake.

Here are four Acrostic poems, 1 each about Death, Dreams, Hope & Despair

Death

Dawn fades, shadows lengthen, the final journey begins,
Eternal sleep awaits, a silent passage into the unknown,
A somber farewell, a whisper in the wind, a silent hymn,
Taking with it memories, leaving behind echoes of what has been,
Heralding the end of one chapter, the beginning of another.

Dreams

Dancing in the realm of imagination, limitless possibilities unfold,
Reaching for stars, chasing shadows of desires untold,
Echoes of hopes, whispers of aspirations in the night,
Awakening the spirit, igniting the flames of inner light,
Manifesting fantasies, shaping destinies dreams' might,
Sailing on the waves of reverie, where fantasies take flight.

Hope

Holding onto dreams, even when skies are gray,
Offering solace in the darkest of days,
Painting rainbows amidst life's storms,
Embracing hearts with its gentle warmth.

Despair

Darkness descends, swallowing the light,
Eroding hope, suffocating in its might,
Sinking deeper into the abyss of despair,
Pain echoes, consuming with its glare,
A relentless shadow, a haunting nightmare,
In its grip, hearts falter, souls tear.

Here are four Acrostic poems, 1 each about Friendship, Loneliness, Memories & Music

Friendship

Forever by your side, through thick and thin,
Radiating warmth, like the sun's gentle grin,
In laughter and tears, we find solace within,
Endless support, a bond that will never dim,
Navigating life's journey, together we win,
Diverse souls united, our friendship akin.

Loneliness

Lost in the silence, echoes of solitude,
Outcast from the crowd, in the shadows brood,
Navigating the emptiness, a solitary mood,
Echoes of laughter, a distant interlude,
Longing for connection, misunderstood,
In the depths of loneliness, spirits subdued.

Memories

Moments etched in time, treasures to hold dear,
Echoes of laughter, whispers of yesteryear,
Moments shared, like stars in the night sky,
Opulent tapestry, where memories lie,
Reflections of the past, nostalgia's lullaby,
In the heart's sanctuary, memories reside.

Music

Melodies weave through the air, a symphony divine,
Unraveling emotions, like threads of time,
Soothing the soul, like a gentle chime,
Inspiring hearts to dance, in rhythm and rhyme,
Captivating spirits, transcending the mundane,
In the language of music, emotions reign.

Here are four Acrostic poems, 1 each about Art, Inspiration, Creativity & Courage

Art

A canvas blank, awaiting the artist's touch,
Reflecting visions, emotions, a story to clutch,
Transcending boundaries, expressing much,
Imagination unleashed, creativity's crutch.

Inspiration

Igniting the flame, a spark in the dark,
Nourishing creativity, like a vibrant spark,
Sparking ideas, a journey to embark,
Paving the way, like a guiding mark,
In the heart's sanctuary, where dreams embark,
Radiating light, inspiration leaves its mark.

Creativity

Crafting wonders, from visions unseen,
Radiant expressions, from the artist's dream,
Evolving ideas, like a flowing stream,
A dance of imagination, a vibrant beam,
Transcending limits, like a sunbeam,
In the realm of creativity, possibilities teem.

Courage

Confronting fears, with a steadfast heart,
Overcoming obstacles, making a new start,
Unfurling wings, ready to depart,
Radiating strength, like a work of art,
A beacon of hope, in the realm of dark,
Gathering courage, to embark on life's chart.

Here are four Acrostic poems, 1 each about Faith, Doubt, Solitude & Joy

Faith

Firm belief in the unseen, guiding light,
Assurance in the face of darkness, burning bright,
In the heart's sanctuary, it takes flight,
Trusting in divine providence, day and night,
Holding onto hope, through every plight.

Doubt

Dwindling confidence, shadows creeping near,
Outpouring skepticism, clouding vision clear,
Uncertainty's grip, tightening its hold here,
Besieging thoughts, drowning in fear,
Testing faith, in the crucible of doubt, dear.

Solitude

Silent echoes, whispers in the breeze,
Outpouring emotions, like autumn leaves,
Lonely hearts, seeking refuge in the trees,
In the depths of silence, the soul grieves,
Treading pathways of solitude, where sorrows heave.

Joy

Jubilant laughter, ringing in the air,
Overflowing hearts, free from despair,
Yearning souls find solace there,
In the dance of joy, worries repair,
Celebrating life, in its beauty rare.

Here are four Acrostic poems, 1 each about Sorrow, Childhood, Wisdom & Innocence

Sorrow

Sullen skies, weep with heavy rain,
Outpouring tears, washing away the pain,
Reflecting darkness, like an endless chain,
Rending hearts, with grief's refrain,
Overwhelmed by sorrow, where hopes wane.

Childhood

Carefree days, laughter in the sun,
Holding onto innocence, until day is done,
In the realm of dreams, adventures begun,
Lingering memories, of games and fun,
Delighting in the wonder, where childhood's won.

Wisdom

Wise counsel, from years of insight,
Insightful reflections, shining bright,
Seeking truth, in the darkest night,
Delving into knowledge, like a guiding light,
Overcoming challenges, with wisdom's might.

Innocence

Innocent eyes, filled with wonder and delight,
Never tainted by the shadows of the night,
Nurtured by love, in the heart's pure flight,
Oblivious to darkness, in the realm of light,
Capturing hearts, with innocence so bright.

Here are four Acrostic poems, 1 each about Passion, Serenity, Freedom & Justice

Passion

Pulsating hearts, ablaze with fiery desire,
Ardent flames, igniting dreams to aspire,
Soulful melodies, like a soaring lyre,
Seeking fulfillment, in passion's fire,
Overflowing spirits, with fervent ire.

Serenity

Soothing whispers, in the gentle breeze,
Embracing tranquility, amidst life's unease,
Radiant calm, like the stillness of seas,
Elevating souls, to a state of peace,
Nurturing hearts, where serenity flees.

Freedom

Fleeting wings, soaring in the sky,
Releasing chains, bidding constraints goodbye,
Evolving spirits, like a butterfly,
Embracing liberation, with a joyous cry,
Dancing in the winds, where freedom flies high.

Justice

Judging impartially, with a discerning eye,
Unyielding fairness, where truth won't lie,
Steadfast principles, that never shy,
Taking a stand, against wrongs that pry,
In the pursuit of righteousness, justice won't die.

Here are four Acrostic poems, 1 each about Change, Resilience, Gratitude & Forgiveness

Change

Challenging the status quo, embracing the new,
Heralding transformation, in all that we pursue,
Adapting to the shifts, in the winds that blew,
Navigating uncertainties, with courage to imbue,
Grasping opportunities, in the change's ensue,
Evolving and growing, in the journey we accrue.

Resilience

Rebounding from setbacks with steadfast grace,
Enduring trials with a determined face.
Steady in storms, never losing sight,
Indomitable spirit, shining bright.
Living through challenges, finding new ways,
Illuminating paths through darkest days.

Gratitude

Grateful hearts, overflowing with praise,
Reflecting on blessings, in myriad ways,
Acknowledging kindness, through life's maze,
Traversing paths of gratitude, with grace,
Invoking thankfulness, in every phase,
Tranquility found, where gratitude stays.

Forgiveness

Finding peace, in letting go of the past,
Overcoming resentments, that everlast,
Releasing burdens, that hold us fast,
Granting compassion, where hurts amass,
Initiating healing, where wounds contrast,
Vowing to forgive, where love is vast.

Here are four Acrostic poems, 1 each about Longing, Belonging, Discovery & Wonder

Longing

Lingering desires, echoing in the heart,
Outpouring yearnings, tearing souls apart,
Navigating the abyss, where longings start,
Grasping for solace, in love's impart,
In the depths of longing, passions dart,
Never-ending cravings, where emotions chart.

Belonging

Bonding hearts, in a tapestry divine,
Embracing unity, like the stars align,
Lifting spirits, where connections entwine,
Navigating friendships, in life's design,
Granting solace, in the family line,
In the sanctuary of belonging, souls intertwine.

Discovery

Delving into the unknown, with eager eyes,
Unraveling mysteries, beneath the skies,
Seeking revelations, where truth lies,
Covering horizons, where dreams arise,
Observing wonders, in nature's guise,
Venturing forth, where discovery flies.

Wonder

Wandering in awe, through nature's grand display,
Observing miracles, in the light of day,
Navigating wonders, in every way,
Dancing with curiosity, in the cosmic ballet,
Exploring marvels, in the vast array,
Revering beauty, where wonder holds sway.

Here are four Acrostic poems, 1 each about Journey, Reflection, Harmony & Imagination

Journey

Journeying through life, with steps unknown,
Understanding pathways, uniquely shown,
Reveling in adventures, where seeds are sown,
Nurturing dreams, in the heart's own,
Embarking on odysseys, where stories are honed,
Yielding to the flow, where destinies are grown.

Reflection

Reveling in stillness, where thoughts are clear,
Evaluating experiences, both far and near,
Considering lessons, in the mirror's leer,
Treading pathways of introspection, without fear,
Listening to whispers, that the soul may hear,
Exploring depths of self, where truth appears.

Harmony

Heralding unity, in the symphony of life,
Aligning hearts, in serenity's strife,
Radiating peace, amidst worldly strife,
Melodies of oneness, free from strife,
Optimizing balance, in the ebb and rife,
Navigating rhythms, where harmony is rife.

Imagination

Inspiring visions, in the mind's vast scope,
Manifesting fantasies, where dreams elope,
Adventuring in realms, beyond life's trope,
Gathering musings, where fantasies rope,
Inventing worlds, where imagination can cope,
Navigating wonders, where creativity's slope.

Here are four Acrostic poems, 1 each about Silence, Laughter, Tears & Strength

Silence

Soothing whispers in the stillness of the night,
Inner peace found in the absence of sound,
Listening to the quiet, where thoughts take flight,
Embracing serenity, in silence profound,
Navigating the depths, where silence is found,
Calmness reigns in the hush, where silence is crowned,
Endless solace in the sanctuary of silence.

Laughter

Light-hearted echoes, ringing in the air,
Amidst joyous moments, banishing despair,
Uplifting spirits, with a gleeful flair,
Giggles and chuckles, beyond compare,
Happiness resounding, in laughter's snare,
Tears of joy, in laughter's rare.

Tears

Tumbling down cheeks, like raindrops from the sky,
Expressing emotions, without needing to comply,
Aching hearts finding release, as tears flow by,
Releasing pain, allowing healing to apply,
Shedding burdens, letting sorrows fly,
Streaming emotions, tears do not lie.

Strength

Standing tall in the face of adversity's test,
Tenacious spirit, refusing to rest,
Resilient hearts, enduring life's zest,
Empowered souls, facing each quest,
Navigating challenges, with fortitude blessed,
Graceful warriors, strength at their behest.

Here are four Acrostic poems, 1 each about Vulnerability, Renewal, Acceptance & Mystery

Vulnerability

Venturing into the unknown, with an open heart,
Unveiling truths, tearing walls apart,
Leaning into discomfort, where vulnerabilities start,
Navigating uncertainties, with courage to impart,
Embracing authenticity, in every part,
Radiating strength, where vulnerability imparts.

Renewal

Rising from the ashes, like a phoenix in flight,
Embracing change, with all its might,
Nurturing growth, in the darkness of night,
Evolving and transforming, in the morning light,
Welcoming rebirth, after the long night,
Awakening to possibilities, in renewal's sight.

Acceptance

Acknowledging realities, without resistance,
Cultivating peace, in the absence of insistence,
Choosing serenity, in the face of persistence,
Embracing imperfections, with gentle persistence,
Navigating life's twists, with calm resilience,
Trusting in the journey, with graceful subsistence.

Mystery

Mesmerizing enigmas, shrouded in the unknown,
Yearning souls, seeking answers to be shown,
Seeking revelations, where wonders are sown,
Traversing the abyss, where mysteries are grown,
Enigmatic riddles, in secrets yet unblown,
Revering the magic, where mystery has flown.

Here are four Acrostic poems, 1 each about Transformation, Eternity, Cosmos & Happiness

Transformation

Transcending limitations, like a butterfly's flight,
Rising from the ashes, to embrace the light,
A metamorphosis, in the depths of night,
Navigating change, with all its might,
Sculpting new beginnings, with insight,
Manifesting growth, in transformation's height.

Eternity

Endless expanse, beyond the scope of time,
Traversing the cosmos, in an endless climb,
Eternal realms, where stars forever shine,
Radiant light, in the tapestry divine,
Navigating infinity, in eternity's prime,
Immersed in the timeless, where eternity chimes.
In the embrace of happiness, hearts dance with glee,

Cosmos

Celestial wonders, dancing in the night,
Orbiting galaxies, in a cosmic flight,
Starry constellations, weaving patterns bright,
Majestic planets, in the void's sight,
Orbiting suns, in the cosmic light,
Spectacular vistas, in the cosmic height.

Happiness

Harmonious laughter, filling hearts with glee,
Abundant joy, in every moment we see,
Prosperous souls, living life carefree,
Pervasive smiles, like the waves of the sea,

-:¦:-•:*'''''*:•.-:¦:-•**•-:¦:-•:*''''''*:•:*''''''*:•.-:¦:-•**•-:¦:--:¦:-•:*'''''*:•.-:¦:- •**•-:¦:-•:*''''''*:•:*''''''*:•.-:¦:-•**•-:¦:-

ELEGY:

A mournful poem lamenting the death of a person or reflecting on loss and mortality.

-:¦:-•:*'''''*:•.-:¦:-•**•-:¦:-•:*'''''*:•:*'''''*:•.-:¦:-•**•-:¦:--:¦:-•:*'''''*:•.-:¦:- •**•-:¦:-•:*'''''*:•:*'''''*:•.-:¦:-•**•-:¦:-

Here are four Elegy poems, 1 each about Love, Nature, Beauty & Time

Elegy for Love

In the garden of our hearts, love once bloomed,
A vibrant tapestry of emotions entwined,
But now, like petals scattered by the wind,
Our love has faded, lost in time's cruel tide.
Memories linger, like echoes of a forgotten tune,
In the silent chambers where our love once resided.

Elegy for Nature

In the whispering woods and fields of green,
Nature's beauty once adorned the land,
But now, the trees stand silent, stripped and lean,
The rivers run dry, no longer grand.
Gone are the melodies of birds unseen,
Lost to the ravages of man's careless hand.

Elegy for Beauty

Once, beauty adorned the world with grace,
In the symmetry of flowers and sunset's glow,
But now, the shadows deepen, obscuring its face,
The passing of time has dimmed its wondrous show.
Gone are the days of beauty's embrace,
Lost to the relentless march of time's cruel flow.

Elegy for Time

In the hourglass of eternity, time once flowed,
A steady stream, relentless and true,
But now, its sands are scattered, its rhythm slowed,
The echoes of moments, fading from view.
Gone are the days when time freely flowed,
Lost to the abyss where all things are due.

Here are four Elegy poems, 1 each about Death, Dreams, Hope & Despair

Elegy for Death

In the silence of the night, death's shadow falls,
A solemn reminder of life's transient breath,
Gone are the voices, the laughter, the calls,
In the realm of shadows, where all things rest.
Memories linger, within these hallowed halls,
In the wake of death's embrace, we mourn our loss.

Elegy for Dreams

Once, dreams soared high on wings of hope,
A symphony of possibilities, unfurled,
But now, the dreams lie shattered, beyond scope,
In the depths of despair, where shadows whirl.
Gone are the visions, the dreams we once strove,
Lost to the abyss, where dreams unfurl.

Elegy for Hope

In the heart's sanctuary, hope once thrived,
A beacon of light in the darkest night,
But now, the flame flickers, barely alive,
In the depths of despair, where shadows alight.
Gone are the dreams, the hopes that once strived,
Lost to the echoes of a fading plight.

Elegy for Despair

In the depths of darkness, despair holds sway,
A haunting specter, casting shadows deep,
Gone are the hopes, the dreams of yesterday,
In the realm of sorrow, where tears do weep.
Memories linger, in the silence of decay,
In the embrace of despair, where sorrows seep.

Here are four Elegy poems, 1 each about Friendship, Loneliness, Memories & Music

Elegy for Friendship

In the garden of camaraderie, friendship once bloomed,
A tapestry woven with laughter and shared delight,
But now, the silence echoes, where once voices boomed,
Gone are the moments of companionship, warm and bright.
Memories linger, like shadows in a deserted room,
In the absence of friendship's comforting light.

Elegy for Loneliness

In the empty chambers of solitude, loneliness resides,
A silent companion, in the darkness of the night,
Gone are the echoes of laughter, where once joy presides,
In the depths of isolation, where shadows alight.
Memories linger, like whispers of lost tides,
In the solitude's embrace, where sorrows ignite.

Elegy for Memories

Once, memories danced like fireflies in the night,
A kaleidoscope of moments, bright and clear,
But now, they fade into shadows, out of sight,
Gone are the echoes of laughter, once so near.
In the silence of forgetting, where shadows alight,
Memories linger, like ghosts of yesteryear.

Elegy for Music

In the symphony of life, music once played,
A harmony of melodies, sweet and pure,
But now, the notes are silent, the rhythm frayed,
Gone are the songs that made our spirits soar.
Memories linger, like echoes in the glade,
In the absence of music, our hearts implore.

Here are four Elegy poems, 1 each about Art, Inspiration, Creativity & Courage

Elegy for Art

Once, art adorned the world with vibrant hues,
A canvas of expression, bold and bright,
But now, the colors fade, the canvas stews,
Gone are the strokes that brought our hearts delight.
In the silence of creation, where shadows ensue,
Art's legacy lingers, in the depths of night.

Elegy for Inspiration

In the realm of imagination, inspiration once thrived,
A fountain of creativity, flowing free,
But now, the well runs dry, the flame deprived,
Gone are the sparks that ignited our reverie.
In the absence of inspiration, where shadows connive,
Memories linger, in the depths of creativity.

Elegy for Creativity

Once, creativity danced like fire in the mind,
A symphony of innovation, bold and bright,
But now, the flames have dimmed, the muses resigned,
Gone are the visions that once took flight.
In the silence of stagnation, where shadows bind,
Creativity's echo lingers, in the depths of night.

Elegy for Courage

In the crucible of adversity, courage once stood,
A beacon of strength, steadfast and true,
But now, the flames flicker, misunderstood,
Gone are the heroes who dared to pursue.
In the absence of courage, where shadows brood,
Memories linger, in the depths of virtue.

Here are four Elegy poems, 1 each about Faith, Doubt, Solitude & Joy

Elegy for Faith

Once, faith illuminated the path ahead,
A guiding light in the darkest of days,
But now, doubts cast shadows, where fears spread,
Gone are the prayers, the hopeful displays.
In the absence of faith, where shadows embed,
Memories linger, in the echoes of praise.

Elegy for Doubt

In the depths of uncertainty, doubt once reigned,
Casting shadows on hopes and dreams,
But now, clarity emerges, where truth is gained,
Gone are the fears, the stifling screams.
In the absence of doubt, where confidence unchained,
Memories linger, in the river's streams.

Elegy for Solitude

Once, solitude was a sanctuary, serene and still,
A refuge from the chaos of the world,
But now, it's a prison, where shadows fill,
Gone are the moments of solace, unfurled.
In the absence of solitude, where silence spills,
Memories linger, in the void unfurled.

Elegy for Joy

In the heart's embrace, joy once resided,
A fountain of happiness, flowing free,
But now, it's a memory, where shadows collided,
Gone are the smiles, the laughter's spree.
In the absence of joy, where sorrows confided,
Memories linger, in the depths of glee.

Here are four Elegy poems, 1 each about Sorrow, Childhood, Wisdom & Innocence

Elegy for Sorrow

In the depths of despair, sorrow once dwelled,
A heavy burden, weighing down the soul,
But now, its grip has loosened, where shadows meld,
Gone are the tears, the heartache's toll.
In the absence of sorrow, where peace excelled,
Memories linger, in the void's black hole.

Elegy for Childhood

Once, childhood was a sanctuary, innocent and pure,
A realm of wonder, where dreams took flight,
But now, it's a memory, where shadows obscure,
Gone are the days of laughter, shining bright.
In the absence of childhood, where memories endure,
Nostalgia lingers, in the fading light.

Elegy for Wisdom

In the halls of knowledge, wisdom once reigned,
A beacon of guidance, in the darkest night,
But now, its voice is silent, where shadows feigned,
Gone are the lessons, the insights bright.
In the absence of wisdom, where truth is strained,
Memories linger, in the fading light.

Elegy for Innocence

Once, innocence adorned the soul with purity,
A shield against the world's harsh reality,
But now, it's a memory, tainted by maturity,
Gone are the days of naivety, carefree.
In the absence of innocence, where shadows flee,
Nostalgia lingers, in the fading sea.

Here are four Elegy poems, 1 each about Passion, Serenity, Freedom & Justice

Elegy for Passion

In the heart's embrace, passion once burned,
A fire of desire, igniting dreams,
But now, its flames have dwindled, where shadows churned,
Gone are the fervor, the vibrant streams.
In the absence of passion, where yearnings yearned,
Memories linger, in the fading beams.

Elegy for Serenity

Once, serenity enveloped the soul with peace,
A tranquil haven, in the chaos of life,
But now, its calm is shattered, where shadows cease,
Gone are the moments, free from strife.
In the absence of serenity, where turmoil's increase,
Nostalgia lingers, in the fading rife.

Elegy for Freedom

In the realm of liberty, freedom once soared,
A soaring eagle, in the boundless sky,
But now, its wings are clipped, where shadows roared,
Gone are the liberties, once held high.
In the absence of freedom, where chains hoard,
Memories linger, in the fading cry.

Elegy for Justice

Once, justice was a beacon, guiding the way,
A moral compass, in the tumultuous sea,
But now, its light is dimmed, where shadows sway,
Gone are the rights, the fairness decree.
In the absence of justice, where darkness may,
Nostalgia lingers, in the fading spree.

Here are four Elegy poems, 1 each about Change, Resilience, Gratitude & Forgiveness

Elegy for Change

In the flow of time, change once prevailed,
A constant force, shaping destinies,
But now, its currents have shifted, where shadows veiled,
Gone are the transformations, the unseen remedies.
In the absence of change, where dreams derailed,
Memories linger, in the fading reveries.

Elegy for Resilience

Once, resilience fortified the spirit's core,
A sturdy fortress, against life's storms,
But now, its walls are breached, where shadows tore,
Gone are the triumphs, the brave reforms.
In the absence of resilience, where courage swore,
Nostalgia lingers, in the fading norms.

Elegy for Gratitude

In the heart's sanctuary, gratitude once thrived,
A fountain of thankfulness, overflowing,
But now, its waters are still, where shadows contrived,
Gone are the blessings, the moments glowing.
In the absence of gratitude, where blessings arrived,
Memories linger, in the fading showing.

Elegy for Forgiveness

Once, forgiveness healed the wounds of the past,
A balm of mercy, soothing the soul,
But now, its touch is distant, where shadows amassed,
Gone are the reconciliations, making whole.
In the absence of forgiveness, where grievances amassed,
Nostalgia lingers, in the fading toll.

Here are four Elegy poems, 1 each about Longing, Belonging, Discovery & Wonder

Elegy for Longing

In the depths of yearning, longing once resided,
A constant ache, echoing through the soul,
But now, its echoes fade, where shadows divided,
Gone are the desires, beyond control.
In the absence of longing, where dreams collided,
Memories linger, in the fading shoal.

Elegy for Belonging

Once, belonging was a refuge, a sanctuary,
A place of acceptance, amidst the crowd,
But now, its embrace is distant, where shadows vary,
Gone are the connections, once avowed.
In the absence of belonging, where solitude tarry,
Nostalgia lingers, in the fading shroud.

Elegy for Discovery

In the quest for knowledge, discovery once thrived,
A journey of enlightenment, in the vast expanse,
But now, its spark is dimmed, where shadows contrived,
Gone are the revelations, the cosmic dance.
In the absence of discovery, where mysteries arrived,
Memories linger, in the fading trance.

Elegy for Wonder

Once, wonder adorned the world with awe,
A tapestry of marvels, in the eyes of youth,
But now, its magic is fading, where shadows draw,
Gone are the miracles, the eternal truth.
In the absence of wonder, where echoes gnaw,
Nostalgia lingers, in the fading sleuth.

Here are four Elegy poems, 1 each about Journey, Reflection, Harmony & Imagination

Elegy for Journey

In the winding roads of life, journey once prevailed,
A path of twists and turns, leading to the unknown,
But now, its trails grow cold, where shadows unveiled,
Gone are the adventures, the stories sown.
In the absence of journey, where paths curtailed,
Memories linger, in the fading drone.

Elegy for Reflection

Once, reflection was a mirror, revealing truth,
A moment of introspection, in the quietude of mind,
But now, its surface is murky, where shadows sleuth,
Gone are the insights, once intertwined.
In the absence of reflection, where doubts soothe,
Nostalgia lingers, in the fading find.

Elegy for Harmony

In the symphony of existence, harmony once reigned,
A melody of unity, in the cosmic dance,
But now, its chords are discordant, where shadows feigned,
Gone are the symphonies, the divine trance.
In the absence of harmony, where chaos reigned,
Memories linger, in the fading glance.

Elegy for Imagination

Once, imagination was a canvas, boundless and free,
A realm of endless possibilities, in the mind's eye,
But now, its colors fade, where shadows decree,
Gone are the fantasies, the dreams that fly.
In the absence of imagination, where reality bleeds,
Nostalgia lingers, in the fading sky.

Here are four Elegy poems, 1 each about Silence, Laughter, Tears & Strength

Elegy for Silence

In the realm of quiet, silence once reigned,
A sanctuary of peace, in the stillness of the night,
But now, its tranquility fades, where shadows feigned,
Gone are the whispers, the calming light.
In the absence of silence, where chaos detained,
Memories linger, in the fading sight.

Elegy for Laughter

Once, laughter filled the air with joy,
A symphony of mirth, in the hearts of friends,
But now, its echoes fade, where shadows deploy,
Gone are the chuckles, the laughter that mends.
In the absence of laughter, where sorrows cloy,
Nostalgia lingers, in the fading bends.

Elegy for Tears

In the river of emotions, tears once flowed,
A cleansing release, in the depths of sorrow,
But now, its currents ebb, where shadows crowed,
Gone are the torrents, the tears that borrow.
In the absence of tears, where sorrows stowed,
Memories linger, in the fading morrow.

Elegy for Strength

Once, strength fortified the soul's resolve,
A pillar of resilience, in the face of strife,
But now, its foundation crumbles, where shadows absolve,
Gone are the triumphs, the battles of life.
In the absence of strength, where shadows revolve,
Nostalgia lingers, in the fading rife.

Here are four Elegy poems, 1 each about Vulnerability, Renewal, Acceptance & Mystery

Elegy for Vulnerability

In the depths of exposure, vulnerability once lay,
A tender openness, in the heart's embrace,
But now, its walls are fortified, where shadows betray,
Gone are the confessions, the intimate space.
In the absence of vulnerability, where fears stray,
Memories linger, in the fading grace.
Elegy for Renewal

Once, renewal breathed life into weary souls,
A rejuvenating force, in the cycle of existence,
But now, its breath grows faint, where shadows control,
Gone are the rebirths, the moments of persistence.
In the absence of renewal, where despair patrols,
Nostalgia lingers, in the fading instance.

Elegy for Acceptance

A realm of understanding, acceptance once prevailed,
A gentle embrace, in the heart's sanctuary,
But now, its arms grow cold, where shadows availed,
Gone are the compromises, the peace's emissary.
In the absence of acceptance, where doubts hailed,
Memories linger, in the fading quandary.

Elegy for Mystery

Once, mystery enshrouded the world in wonder,
A veil of intrigue, in the unknown's domain,
But now, its secrets unravel, where shadows plunder,
Gone are the enigmas, the mystique's reign.
In the absence of mystery, where truths sunder,
Nostalgia lingers, in the fading lane.

Here are four Elegy poems, 1 each about Transformation, Eternity, Cosmos & Happiness

Elegy for Transformation

The crucible of change, transformation once thrived,
A metamorphosis of being, in the crucible of time,
Its essence wanes, where shadows contrived,
Gone are the evolutions, the rhythms sublime.
Absence of transformation, where illusions arrived,
Memories linger, in the fading chime.

Elegy for Eternity

Once, eternity stretched beyond the horizon's gaze,
A timeless expanse, in the cosmic symphony,
But now, its infinity dims, where shadows graze,
Gone are the forever's, the immortality.
In the absence of eternity, where destinies daze,
Nostalgia lingers, in the fading spree.

Elegy for Cosmos

In the celestial expanse, cosmos once shimmered,
A tapestry of stars, in the galaxy's embrace,
Its brilliance fades, where shadows glimmered,
Gone are the constellations, the celestial space.
In the absence of cosmos, where darkness simmered,
Memories linger, in the fading grace.

Elegy for Happiness

Once, happiness illuminated the soul with light,
A radiant glow, in life's jubilant dance,
But now, its radiance dims, where shadows alight,
Gone are the smiles, the joy's expanse.
In the absence of happiness, where sorrows bite,
Nostalgia lingers, in the fading trance.

-:|:-•:*'''''*:•.-:|:-•**•-:|:-•:*'''''*:•:*'''''*:•.-:|:-•**•-:|:--:|:-•:*'''''*:•.-:|:- •**•-:|:-•:*'''''*:•:*'''''*:•.-:|:-•**•-:|:-

PASTORAL:

A poem that idealizes rural life or the simplicity of nature, often depicting shepherds or rural settings.

Here are four Pastoral poems, 1 each about Love, Nature, Beauty & Time

Pastoral Poem: Love

In fields adorned with blooms of every hue,
Where whispers of the breeze dance with delight,
Two hearts entwined, their bond forever true,
Underneath the canvas of the starry night.
Their love, a melody that sweetly sings,
In nature's embrace, where passion springs.

Pastoral Poem: Nature

Oh, nature's splendor, vast and free,
Where rolling hills meet the azure sky,
The melody of birds, the rustle of the tree,
In the quiet glen, where the brook runs by.
Here, harmony reigns, in every sight,
A symphony of beauty, pure and bright.

Pastoral Poem: Beauty

In the meadow's expanse, beauty abounds,
Where wildflowers bloom in vibrant array,
The sun's golden rays, where warmth surrounds,
Casting a radiant glow, on the canvas of the day.
Oh, beauty's grace, in every hue,
In nature's embrace, forever anew.

Pastoral Poem: Time

Through the fields of time, we wander on,
Beneath the canopy of the ageless sky,
Seasons come and go, their melodies drawn,
In the tapestry of life, where moments fly.
Yet amidst the passing years, we find,
Eternal beauty, in the heart and mind.

Here are four Pastoral poems, 1 each about Death, Dreams, Hope & Despair

Pastoral Poem about Death:

In fields where the golden wheat does sway,
Beneath the arch of the cerulean sky,
Where whispering winds with gentle sighs do play,
Lies a quiet spot where souls bid goodbye.

Amidst the meadows where wildflowers bloom,
And the river softly murmurs its lament,
Underneath the canopy of nature's tomb,
Rest those who've journeyed to the final event.

Their spirits linger in the rustling leaves,
Their memories etched in every blade of grass,
In this pastoral scene where the heart believes,
That death is but a pause, not the final pass.

Pastoral Poem about Dreams:

In the pastures where the moonlight falls,
And stars dance in a sky painted blue,
Dreams roam free within nature's halls,
In the realm where imagination brews.

Amidst the gentle rustle of the trees,
Where the brook whispers secrets untold,
Lies a world where fantasies tease,
And the dreamer's story begins to unfold.

Here, amidst the fragrance of wildflowers,
And the melody of the nightingale's song,
Dreams take flight in magical towers,
Where reality and fantasy belong.

Pastoral Poem about Hope:

In the meadows where the sun's first rays alight,
And dew-kissed petals glisten with morning's grace,
Hope blossoms anew in the soft morning light,
In this tranquil sanctuary, a sacred space.

Amidst the fields where the breeze softly sighs,
And the earth awakens with a gentle stir,
Hope takes root beneath the cerulean skies,
A beacon of light, a promise to confer.

Here, amidst nature's evergreen embrace,
Where the whispers of hope softly resound,
In the boundless expanse of time and space,
Hope springs eternal, forever unbound.

Pastoral Poem about Despair:

In the shadows where the moonlight fades away,
And the whispers of the night grow dark and deep,
Despair lurks in the corners where shadows sway,
In this somber landscape, where sorrows sleep.

Amidst the silent woods where shadows dwell,
And the echoes of lost dreams linger on,
Despair casts its shroud like a haunting spell,
A silent specter, where hope is gone.

Here, amidst the haunting cries of the night,
Where the darkness reigns with a solemn air,
In the depths of despair's relentless blight,
The soul finds solace in the silence there.

Here are four Pastoral poems, 1 each about Friendship, Loneliness, Memories & Music

Pastoral Poem about Friendship:

In the meadows where the wildflowers bloom,
And the breeze carries whispers of camaraderie,
Friendship blossoms like a fragrant perfume,
In this idyllic haven of unity.

Amidst the verdant fields where laughter rings,
And the sun bathes all in its golden light,
Friends gather, their voices like songbirds' wings,
In this tranquil retreat, hearts take flight.

Here, amidst nature's harmonious embrace,
Where the bonds of friendship forever endure,
In the embrace of love and grace,
Friendship blooms like a rose, pure and sure.

Pastoral Poem about Loneliness:

In the quiet valleys where shadows creep,
And the echo of solitude fills the air,
Loneliness wanders, like a lost sheep,
In this desolate landscape, devoid of care.

Amidst the rolling hills where silence reigns,
And the moon casts its silver glow,
Loneliness lingers, its presence pains,
In this solitary realm, where sorrows flow.

Here, amidst nature's unyielding embrace,
Where the heartache of loneliness abides,
In the depths of despair's endless chase,
Loneliness haunts, where hope hides.

Pastoral Poem about Memories:

In the meadows where the tall grass sways,
And the sun sets with a golden hue,
Memories dance in the twilight's blaze,
In this timeless haven where dreams come true.

Amidst the whispering leaves where stories are told,
And the river reflects the sky's serene,
Memories linger, like treasures of old,
In this sacred sanctuary, serene.

Here, amidst nature's gentle embrace,
Where the echoes of the past softly call,
In the depths of time's eternal grace,
Memories linger, beloved by all.

Pastoral Poem about Music:

In the groves where the melodies reside,
And the harmony of nature fills the air,
Music flows like a timeless tide,
In this symphony of life, beyond compare.

Amidst the rustling leaves where rhythms play,
And the songbirds sing their sweet refrain,
Music dances, in the light of day,
In this blissful sanctuary, free from pain.

Here, amidst nature's enchanting embrace,
Where the soul finds solace in every chord,
In the melodies that time cannot erase,
Music lifts the spirit, forever adored.

Here are four Pastoral poems, 1 each about Art, Inspiration, Creativity & Courage

Pastoral Poem about Art:

In the meadows where the colors dance,
And the canvas of nature unfolds,
Artistry blooms in every glance,
In this masterpiece of stories untold.

Amidst the fields where the brushstrokes play,
And the sun paints the sky with its brush,
Art whispers secrets in the light of day,
In this sanctuary where dreams rush.

Here, amidst nature's endless embrace,
Where the muse finds solace in every hue,
In the strokes of beauty that time can't erase,
Art reigns supreme, forever anew.

Pastoral Poem about Inspiration:

In the meadows where the dreams take flight,
And the whispers of possibility abound,
Inspiration dances in the soft moonlight,
In this fertile ground where ideas are found.

Amidst the fields where the imagination roams,
And the stars illuminate the night,
Inspiration sparks in the hearts' quiet homes,
In this realm of endless insight.

Here, amidst nature's boundless embrace,
Where the soul finds solace in every thought,
In the whispers of inspiration's grace,
Dreams take flight, forever sought.
The heart prevails, forever worthwhile.

Pastoral Poem about Creativity:

In the meadows where the muses sing,
And the echoes of creation resound,
Creativity blooms like the flowers in spring,
In this fertile ground where ideas abound.

Amidst the fields where the ideas grow,
And the sun ignites the spark of imagination,
Creativity flows like the rivers' flow,
In this sanctuary of endless fascination.

Here, amidst nature's nurturing embrace,
Where the mind finds solace in every creation,
In the depths of creativity's space,
The spirit thrives, forever in elation.

Pastoral Poem about Courage:

In the meadows where the brave hearts roam,
And the echoes of courage fill the air,
Courage shines like the brightest beacon,
In this sanctuary where fears lay bare.

Amidst the fields where the battles are fought,
And the sun sets on the warriors' quest,
Courage rises, in the face of what's sought,
In this realm where the brave are blessed.

Here, amidst nature's steadfast embrace,
Where the spirit finds solace in every trial,
In the depths of courage's grace,

Here are four Pastoral poems, 1 each about Faith, Doubt, Solitude & Joy

Pastoral Poem about Faith:

In the meadows where the light breaks through,
And the whispers of faith fill the air,
Faith blooms like the flowers in dew,
In this sacred sanctuary, beyond compare.

Amidst the fields where the spirits soar,
And the sun casts its golden glow,
Faith guides, like a beacon on the shore,
In this realm where believers grow.

Here, amidst nature's loving embrace,
Where the soul finds solace in every prayer,
In the depths of faith's endless grace,
The heart finds peace, forever there.
Pastoral Poem about Doubt:
In the meadows where shadows play,

And the echoes of doubt linger long,
Doubt creeps in like the fading day,
In this realm where uncertainty belongs.

Amidst the fields where the questions rise,
And the moon casts its haunting glow,
Doubt whispers secrets in silent sighs,
In this sanctuary of ebb and flow.

Here, amidst nature's vast embrace,
Where the mind finds solace in the unknown,
In the depths of doubt's endless space,
The soul finds strength, to stand alone.

Pastoral Poem about Solitude:

In the meadows where silence reigns,
And the echoes of solitude resound,
Solitude blooms like the wildflowers' stains,
In this sacred sanctuary, profound.

Amidst the fields where the heart finds peace,
And the breeze carries whispers soft and low,
Solitude offers a sweet release,
In this realm where the soul can grow.

Here, amidst nature's gentle embrace,
Where the spirit finds solace in quiet grace,
In the depths of solitude's endless space,
The mind finds clarity, in this tranquil place.

Pastoral Poem about Joy:

In the meadows where laughter rings,
And the echoes of joy fill the air,
Joy blossoms like the flowers in spring,
In this magical sanctuary, beyond compare.

Amidst the fields where the heart sings,
And the sun dances in the azure sky,
Joy spreads its wings with radiant flings,
In this realm where spirits soar high.

Here, amidst nature's loving embrace,
Where the soul finds solace in every smile,
In the depths of joy's endless grace,
The spirit dances, free from guile

.

Here are four Pastoral poems, 1 each about Sorrow, Childhood, Wisdom & Innocence

Pastoral Poem about Sorrow:

In the meadows where the shadows weep,
And the echoes of sorrow fill the air,
Sorrow lurks like a secret to keep,
In this somber sanctuary, beyond compare.

Amidst the fields where tears softly fall,
And the moon casts its melancholy glow,
Sorrow whispers tales of a heart's call,
In this realm where emotions ebb and flow.

Here, amidst nature's tender embrace,
Where the soul finds solace in quiet grace,
In the depths of sorrow's endless space,
The heart finds healing, in this tranquil place.

Pastoral Poem about Childhood:

In the meadows where innocence reigns,
And the echoes of laughter fill the air,
Childhood dances like the wind in the lanes,
In this magical sanctuary, beyond compare.

Amidst the fields where dreams take flight,
And the sun paints the sky with hues so bright,
Childhood skips along in the golden light,
In this realm where imagination takes flight.

Here, amidst nature's loving embrace,
Where the soul finds solace in every smile,
In the depths of childhood's endless grace,
The heart finds joy, free from guile.

Pastoral Poem about Wisdom:

In the meadows where the wise trees stand,
And the echoes of ancient whispers fill the air,
Wisdom flows like the rivers' grand,
In this sacred sanctuary, beyond compare.

Amidst the fields where the old stones lay,
And the stars shine with their eternal glow,
Wisdom guides like a light on the way,
In this realm where the learned minds grow.

Here, amidst nature's vast embrace,
Where the spirit finds solace in every thought,
In the depths of wisdom's endless grace,
The mind finds peace, with lessons taught.

Pastoral Poem about Innocence:

In the meadows where purity dwells,
And the echoes of innocence fill the air,
Innocence thrives like the sweetest of spells,
In this precious sanctuary, beyond compare.

Amidst the fields where the flowers bloom,
And the sun casts its golden glow,

Innocence dances like a butterfly's plume,
In this realm where the young hearts grow.

Here, amidst nature's tender embrace,
Where the soul finds solace in every smile,
In the depths of innocence's endless grace,
The heart finds joy, free from guile.

Here are four Pastoral poems, 1 each about Passion, Serenity, Freedom & Justice

Pastoral Poem about Passion:

In the meadows where fervor ignites,
And the echoes of desire fill the air,
Passion blazes like a thousand lights,
In this fervent sanctuary, beyond compare.

Amidst the fields where hearts entwine,
And the moon casts its amorous glow,
Passion dances like the grapevine,
In this realm where love's currents flow.

Here, amidst nature's ardent embrace,
Where the soul finds solace in every kiss,
In the depths of passion's endless grace,
The heart finds bliss, in the sweet abyss.

Pastoral Poem about Serenity:

In the meadows where tranquility reigns,
And the echoes of peace fill the air,
Serenity whispers like gentle rains,
In this tranquil sanctuary, beyond compare.

Amidst the fields where the grasses sway,
And the sun sets with a golden hue,
Serenity soothes like the end of day,
In this realm where troubles are few.

Here, amidst nature's calming embrace,
Where the spirit finds solace in every sigh,
In the depths of serenity's endless grace,
The mind finds rest, under the azure sky.

Pastoral Poem about Freedom:

In the meadows where liberty sings,
And the echoes of liberation fill the air,
Freedom soars on unfettered wings,
In this boundless sanctuary, beyond compare.

Amidst the fields where dreams take flight,
And the stars shimmer with their radiant light,
Freedom dances like the fire's bright,
In this realm where hopes ignite.

Here, amidst nature's unyielding embrace,
Where the soul finds solace in every breeze,
In the depths of freedom's endless grace,
The heart finds ease, in the open seas.

Pastoral Poem about Justice:

In the meadows where fairness prevails,
And the echoes of righteousness fill the air,
Justice stands tall, unfurling its sails,
In this noble sanctuary, beyond compare.

Amidst the fields where truth takes root,
And the moon casts its unwavering gaze,
Justice blooms like the ripening fruit,
In this realm where virtue stays.

Here, amidst nature's impartial embrace,
Where the spirit finds solace in every verdict,
In the depths of justice's endless grace,
The mind finds peace, where righteousness is affirmed.

Here are four Pastoral poems, 1 each about Change, Resilience, Gratitude & Forgiveness

Pastoral Poem about Change:

In the meadows where transformation blooms,
And the echoes of renewal fill the air,
Change whispers secrets in nature's rooms,
In this shifting sanctuary, beyond compare.

Amidst the fields where seasons dance,
And the sun sets with a golden glow,
Change weaves its tale of circumstance,
In this realm where transitions flow.

Here, amidst nature's ever-changing embrace,
Where the soul finds solace in every shift,
In the depths of change's endless grace,
The heart finds peace, in the rhythm's drift.

Pastoral Poem about Resilience:

In the meadows where strength abounds,
And the echoes of fortitude fill the air,
Resilience stands tall on sacred grounds,
In this sturdy sanctuary, beyond compare.

Amidst the fields where storms may rage,
And the winds howl with relentless might,

Resilience weathers every stage,
In this realm where resilience takes flight.

Here, amidst nature's unwavering embrace,
Where the spirit finds solace in every trial,
In the depths of resilience's endless grace,
The mind finds peace, amidst the storm's dial.

Pastoral Poem about Gratitude:

In the meadows where thankfulness resides,
And the echoes of appreciation fill the air,
Gratitude flourishes like the rising tides,
In this grateful sanctuary, beyond compare.

Amidst the fields where blessings abound,
And the sun shines with its radiant light,
Gratitude's melody sweetly resounds,
In this realm where gratitude takes flight.

Here, amidst nature's bountiful embrace,
Where the soul finds solace in every gift,
In the depths of gratitude's endless grace,
The heart finds peace, in the grateful drift.

Pastoral Poem about Forgiveness:

In the meadows where mercy blooms,
And the echoes of compassion fill the air,
Forgiveness heals old wounds,
In this forgiving sanctuary, beyond compare.

Amidst the fields where scars may dwell,
And the moon casts its forgiving glow,
Forgiveness whispers tales to tell,
In this realm where forgiveness bestows.

Here, amidst nature's compassionate embrace,
Where the spirit finds solace in every release,
In the depths of forgiveness's endless grace,
The mind finds peace, in the forgiven peace

Here are four Pastoral poems, 1 each about Longing, Belonging, Discovery & Wonder

Pastoral Poem about Longing:

In the meadows where the heartache dwells,
And the echoes of yearning fill the air,
Longing whispers in the distant swells,
In this pining sanctuary, beyond compare.

Amidst the fields where dreams take flight,
And the stars shimmer with their tender light,
Longing dances in the shadows of the night,
In this realm where longings take flight.

Here, amidst nature's embracing grace,
Where the soul finds solace in every sigh,
In the depths of longing's endless chase,
The heart finds peace, beneath the endless sky.

Pastoral Poem about Belonging:

In the meadows where acceptance thrives,
And the echoes of unity fill the air,
Belonging offers solace in our lives,
In this comforting sanctuary, beyond compare.

Amidst the fields where friendships grow,
And the sun sets with its golden glow,
Belonging blossoms like the flowers aglow,
In this realm where hearts overflow.

Here, amidst nature's welcoming embrace,
Where the spirit finds solace in every embrace,
In the depths of belonging's endless grace,
The mind finds peace, in the warmest embrace.

Pastoral Poem about Discovery:

In the meadows where secrets hide,
And the echoes of curiosity fill the air,
Discovery beckons with mysteries wide,
In this adventurous sanctuary, beyond compare.

Amidst the fields where wonders unfold,
And the moon casts its enchanting glow,
Discovery's tale is forever told,
In this realm where explorations bestow.

Here, amidst nature's captivating embrace,
Where the soul finds solace in every find,
In the depths of discovery's endless chase,
The heart finds peace, in the seeker's mind.

Pastoral Poem about Wonder:

In the meadows where awe abounds,
And the echoes of marvel fill the air,
Wonder sparkles in nature's profound,
In this mystical sanctuary, beyond compare.

Amidst the fields where dreams take flight,
And the stars twinkle with their radiant light,
Wonder dances in the realm of the night,
In this realm where magic takes flight.
Here, amidst nature's enchanting embrace,
Where the spirit finds solace in every sight,
In the depths of wonder's endless grace,
The mind finds peace, in the wondrous light.

Here are four Pastoral poems, 1 each about Journey, Reflection, Harmony & Imagination

Pastoral Poem about Journey:

In the meadows where paths diverge,
And the echoes of adventure fill the air,
Journey beckons with promises to emerge,
In this wanderlust sanctuary, beyond compare.

Amidst the fields where dreams take flight,
And the sun sets with its golden light,
Journey leads us to realms bright,
In this realm where paths intertwine.

Here, amidst nature's embracing grace,
Where the soul finds solace in every stride,
In the depths of journey's endless pace,
The heart finds peace, in the road less tried.

Pastoral Poem about Reflection:

In the meadows where the waters still,
And the echoes of introspection fill the air,
Reflection invites with its quiet thrill,
In this contemplative sanctuary, beyond compare.

Amidst the fields where the mind finds ease,
And the moon casts its silvery glow,
Reflection reveals what the heart sees,
In this realm where serenity flows.

Here, amidst nature's tranquil embrace,
Where the spirit finds solace in every musing,
In the depths of reflection's endless grace,
The mind finds peace, in the soul's perusing.

Pastoral Poem about Harmony:

In the meadows where the melodies weave,
And the echoes of unity fill the air,
Harmony sings with voices interleave,
In this symphonic sanctuary, beyond compare.

Amidst the fields where notes ascend,
And the stars twinkle with their cosmic grace,
Harmony unites, without end,
In this realm where rhythms embrace.

Here, amidst nature's melodic embrace,
Where the soul finds solace in every chord,
In the depths of harmony's endless grace,
The heart finds peace, in the music adored.

Pastoral Poem about Imagination:

In the meadows where dreams take flight,
And the echoes of creativity fill the air,
Imagination dances with colors bright,
In this fantastical sanctuary, beyond compare.

Amidst the fields where ideas bloom,
And the sunsets with its fiery glow,
Imagination paints the world's room,
In this realm where wonders grow.

Here, amidst nature's imaginative embrace,
Where the spirit finds solace in every dream,
In the depths of imagination's endless grace,
The mind finds peace, in the endless stream.

Here are four Pastoral poems, 1 each about Silence, Laughter, Tears & Strength

Pastoral Poem about Silence:

In the meadows where stillness reigns supreme,
And the echoes of quiet fill the air,
Silence whispers softly like a dream,
In this tranquil sanctuary, beyond compare.

Amidst the fields where peace abounds,
And the moon casts its silver glow,
Silence blankets the earth with profound,
In this realm where serenity flows.

Here, amidst nature's embracing grace,
Where the soul finds solace in tranquil space,
In the depths of silence's endless embrace,
The heart finds peace, in this sacred place.

Pastoral Poem about Laughter:

In the meadows where joy takes flight,
And the echoes of mirth fill the air,
Laughter dances with pure delight,
In this jubilant sanctuary, beyond compare.

Amidst the fields where happiness blooms,
And the sun shines with its golden glow,
Laughter echoes like the sweetest of tunes,
In this realm where spirits aglow.

Here, amidst nature's joyful embrace,
Where the soul finds solace in every chime,
In the depths of laughter's endless grace,
The heart finds peace, in the laughter's prime.

Pastoral Poem about Tears:

In the meadows where sorrows reside,
And the echoes of grief fill the air,
Tears flow like rivers, a soul's tide,
In this mournful sanctuary, beyond compare.

Amidst the fields where sadness prevails,
And the moon casts its mournful glow,
Tears fall like raindrops, a mournful wail,
In this realm where emotions flow.

Here, amidst nature's compassionate embrace,
Where the soul finds solace in every tear,
In the depths of tears' endless grace,
The heart finds peace, in the healing sphere.

Pastoral Poem about Strength:

In the meadows where courage stands tall,
And the echoes of resilience fill the air,
Strength rises like a fortress wall,
In this steadfast sanctuary, beyond compare.

Amidst the fields where challenges lie,
And the sun sets with its fiery glow,
Strength prevails beneath the endless sky,
In this realm where the brave hearts grow.

Here, amidst nature's unwavering embrace,
Where the soul finds solace in every fight,
In the depths of strength's endless grace,
The heart finds peace, in the warrior's might.

Here are four Pastoral poems, 1 each about Vulnerability, Renewal, Acceptance & Mystery

Pastoral Poem about Vulnerability:

In the meadows where hearts lay bare,
And the echoes of openness fill the air,
Vulnerability whispers secrets with care,
In this tender sanctuary, beyond compare.

Amidst the fields where souls unite,
And the moon casts its gentle glow,
Vulnerability shines in the soft light,
In this realm where emotions flow.

Here, amidst nature's compassionate embrace,
Where the soul finds solace in being true,
In the depths of vulnerability's grace,
The heart finds peace, in the openness anew.

Pastoral Poem about Renewal:

In the meadows where new life springs,
And the echoes of rebirth fill the air,
Renewal dances on gentle wings,
In this rejuvenating sanctuary, beyond compare.

Amidst the fields where hope takes root,
And the sun rises with its golden glow,
Renewal blossoms from the seed to fruit,
In this realm where transformations grow.

Here, amidst nature's nurturing embrace,
Where the spirit finds solace in every bloom,
In the depths of renewal's endless grace,
The mind finds peace, in the cycle's loom.

Pastoral Poem about Acceptance:

In the meadows where differences unite,
And the echoes of understanding fill the air,
Acceptance shines with its gentle light,
In this harmonious sanctuary, beyond compare.

Amidst the fields where hearts align,
And the stars twinkle with their cosmic glow,
Acceptance bridges the divide, divine,
In this realm where compassion flows.

Here, amidst nature's embracing grace,
Where the soul finds solace in every embrace,
In the depths of acceptance's endless embrace,
The heart finds peace, in the unity's trace.

Pastoral Poem about Mystery:

In the meadows where shadows dance,
And the echoes of intrigue fill the air,
Mystery weaves its elusive trance,
In this enigmatic sanctuary, beyond compare.

Amidst the fields where secrets lie,
And the moon hides behind its shroud,
Mystery whispers tales that fly,
In this realm where enigmas are endowed.

Here, amidst nature's mystifying embrace,
Where the spirit finds solace in the unknown,
In the depths of mystery's endless grace,
The mind finds peace, in the mysteries shown.

Here are four Pastoral poems, 1 each about Transformation, Eternity, Cosmos & Happiness

Pastoral Poem about Transformation:

In the meadows where change takes hold,
And the echoes of metamorphosis fill the air,
Transformation weaves its story bold,
In this ever-changing sanctuary, beyond compare.

Amidst the fields where growth unfolds,
And the sun rises with its golden flare,
Transformation shapes the paths untold,
In this realm where destinies dare.

Here, amidst nature's embracing grace,
Where the soul finds solace in every mold,
In the depths of transformation's endless chase,
The heart finds peace, in the change foretold.

Pastoral Poem about Eternity:

In the meadows where time stands still,
And the echoes of infinity fill the air,
Eternity whispers with tranquil will,
In this timeless sanctuary, beyond compare.

Amidst the fields where dreams fulfill,
And the stars twinkle with celestial flair,
Eternity beckons with promises to instill,
In this realm where moments flare.

Here, amidst nature's eternal embrace,
Where the spirit finds solace in every thrill,
In the depths of eternity's endless grace,
The mind finds peace, in the cosmic quill.

Pastoral Poem about Cosmos:

In the meadows where galaxies twirl,
And the echoes of celestial dance fill the air,
Cosmos reveals its cosmic swirl,
In this vast sanctuary, beyond compare.

Amidst the fields where stardust whirls,
And the moon casts its silvery glare,
Cosmos whispers of mysteries unfurl,
In this realm where wonders fare.

Here, amidst nature's cosmic embrace,
Where the soul finds solace in every celestial curl,
In the depths of cosmos's endless grace,
The heart finds peace, in the universal pearl.

Pastoral Poem about Happiness:

In the meadows where joy takes flight,
And the echoes of laughter fill the air,
Happiness glows with radiant light,
In this joyful sanctuary, beyond compare.

Amidst the fields where hearts unite,
And the sun sets with its golden glare,
Happiness blooms in the day or night,
In this realm where smiles share.

Here, amidst nature's joyful embrace,
Where the spirit finds solace in every delight,
In the depths of happiness's endless grace,
The mind finds peace, in the happiness so bright.

SATIRE:

Poetry that uses humor, irony, or exaggeration to criticize society or human behavior.

Here are four Satire poems, 1 each about Love, Nature, Beauty & Time

Satire Poem about Love:

Oh, love, that fickle beast we chase,
With heart in hand, we make our plea,
But Cupid's arrow hits with grace,
Then leaves us in calamity.

We sing of passion, sweet and true,
Yet behind closed doors, we fumble and fight,
Love's facade reveals a different view,
A game of deceit, both day and night.

In love's name, we make grand schemes,
But in reality, it's all a ruse,
For love's a tale of shattered dreams,
A mockery of the hearts we abuse.

Satire Poem about Nature:

Nature, that pristine wonderland,
Where birds sing sweet and trees sway,
But behind the facade lies something bland,
A twisted joke on display.

For nature's beauty is but a lie,
Beneath the surface, chaos reigns,
With creatures that bite and clouds that cry,
A farce of tranquility that never wanes.

So let's not romanticize the land,
For nature's satire is dark and grand.

Satire Poem about Beauty:

Beauty, that elusive prize we seek,
With creams and powders, we try to cheat,
But beneath the layers, we're still weak,
A façade of glamour, oh so neat.

We chase perfection, skin so fair,
But wrinkles come and beauty fades,
And what's left is a mask we wear,
A satire of the accolades.

For beauty's standards shift like sand,
A cruel joke played by an unseen hand.

Satire Poem about Time:

Time, that relentless thief of youth,
We chase its fleeting moments with dread,
But no matter our protest or truth,
It marches on, leaving us misled.

We try to grasp its slippery hold,
But time slips through our fingers fast,
Leaving us weary, tired, and old,
A satire of our efforts vast.

For time's grip tightens without fail,
A mockery of our futile wail.

Here are four Satire poems, 1 each about Death, Dreams, Hope & Despair

Satire Poem about Death:

Oh, Death, that grand finale show,
With curtains drawn, we take our bow,
But what's the use, we'll never know,
The punchline of this final vow.

We dress it up in somber tones,
With flowers, tears, and mournful cries,
But Death cares not for earthly loans,
A farce of sorrow in disguise.

For Death's the ultimate comedian,
A joke on us, forever unseen.

Satire Poem about Dreams:

Dreams, those fleeting flights of fancy,
We chase them like elusive ghosts,
But reality's grip is cold and chancy,
A mockery of our heartfelt boasts.

We dream of riches, fame, and bliss,
But wake to bills and mundane chores,
Dreams, oh dreams, a cruel abyss,
A satire of our longing cores.

For dreams are but illusions grand,
A jest upon our outstretched hand.

Satire Poem about Hope:

Hope, that beacon in the night,
We cling to it with desperate might,
But in the end, it takes its flight,
A farce of promises, oh so trite.

We hope for change, for better days,
But reality scoffs at our pleas,
Hope's cruel joke, a twisted maze,
A satire of our desperate pleas.

For hope's illusion fades with time,
A mockery of the uphill climb.

Satire Poem about Despair:

Despair, that shadow in our soul,
We drown in it, we lose control,
But in the end, it takes its toll,
A farce of darkness, an endless scroll.

We wallow in our misery,
But despair laughs at our pain,
A satire of our tragedy,
A joke played by the insane.

For despair's grip is cold and grim,
A mockery of life's fleeting whim.

Here are four Satire poems, 1 each about Friendship, Loneliness, Memories & Music

Satire Poem about Friendship:

Friendship, that elusive charm we seek,
With smiles and hugs, we play our part,
But beneath the surface, we're so weak,
A mockery of trust, a brittle heart.

We pledge allegiance, hand in hand,
Yet behind backs, we stab and jeer,
Friendship's vow, a shifting sand,
A farce of loyalty, insincere.

For friendship's bond is but a show,
A façade we wear, a tale of woe.

Satire Poem about Loneliness:

Loneliness, that silent thief we dread,
We wrap ourselves in solitude's embrace,
But in the end, we're left misled,
A satire of emptiness, a bitter chase.
We crave connection, longing for a friend,
But loneliness haunts our every move,
In solitude's grip, our hopes descend,
A farce of solitude, we can't improve.

For loneliness is a cruel jest,
A mocking laugh at our quest for rest.

Satire Poem about Memories:

Memories, those shadows of our past,
We hold them dear, we treasure each,
But in the end, they cannot last,
A satire of nostalgia, just out of reach.

We reminisce, with smiles and tears,
But memories fade, they slip away,
In the end, they're lost to years,
A farce of recollection, in disarray.

For memories are a fleeting dream,
A jest upon our tenuous scheme.

Satire Poem about Music:

Music, that soothing balm we crave,
We lose ourselves in its sweet refrain,
But in the end, it cannot save,
A satire of harmony, a twisted game.

We seek solace in its melody,
But music mocks our futile plea,
In the end, it's just a parody,
A farce of rhythm, a mockery.

For music's symphony is a cruel joke,
A mockery of the hearts it broke.

Here are four Satire poems, 1 each about Art, Inspiration, Creativity & Courage

Satire Poem about Art:

Art, that lofty pursuit we adore,
We gaze upon it with awe and praise,
But beneath the surface, there's more,
A satire of pretension, a tangled maze.

We marvel at its colors and forms,
But art laughs at our futile chase,
In the end, it's just a storm,
A farce of expression, a hollow space.

For art's allure is but a game,
A mockery of the fame we claim.

Satire Poem about Inspiration:

Inspiration, that elusive muse we seek,
We chase its whispers with eager ears,
But in the end, we're left meek,
A satire of motivation, drowning in tears.

We long for flashes of brilliance bright,
But inspiration mocks our feeble plea,
In the end, it's just a fleeting light,
A farce of creativity, a mockery.

For inspiration's spark is but a jest,
A mockery of the dreams we invest.

Satire Poem about Creativity:

Creativity, that boundless well we mine,
We strive to tap into its endless flow,
But in the end, it's just a line,
A satire of originality, a feeble show.

We seek to innovate, to break the mold,
But creativity scoffs at our attempts,
In the end, it's just a story told,
A farce of ingenuity, a lament.

For creativity's spark is but a joke,
A mockery of the risks we invoke.

Satire Poem about Courage:

Courage, that noble virtue we extol,
We praise its bravery, its fearless might,
But in the end, it's just a toll,
A satire of valor, a darkened light.

We admire those who dare to fight,
But courage laughs at our admiration,
In the end, it's just a flight,
A farce of heroism, a strained relation.

For courage's valor is but a ruse,
A mockery of the risks we choose.

Here are four Satire poems, 1 each about Faith, Doubt, Solitude & Joy

Satire Poem about Faith:

Faith, that steadfast belief we claim,
We cling to it with desperate hands,
But in the end, it's all the same,
A satire of certainty, in shifting sands.

We pray for miracles, for divine grace,
But faith mocks our futile plea,
In the end, it's just an empty space,
A farce of devotion, a mockery.

For faith's assurance is but a lie,
A jest upon the faithful eye.
Satire Poem about Doubt:

Doubt, that nagging voice we hear,
We wrestle with it day and night,
But in the end, it's always near,
A satire of certainty, a blinding light.

We question truths, we challenge belief,
But doubt laughs at our feeble quest,
In the end, it's just a thief,
A farce of skepticism, a futile test.

For doubt's uncertainty is but a game,
A mockery of the doubts we name.
Satire Poem about Solitude:

Solitude, that silent refuge we seek,
We long for peace, for quiet rest,
But in the end, we're left bleak,
A satire of serenity, a futile quest.

We yearn for solitude, for tranquil space,
But solitude mocks our desperate plea,
In the end, it's just an empty place,
A farce of isolation, a mockery.

For solitude's silence is but a joke,
A mockery of the solace we invoke.

Satire Poem about Joy:
Joy, that elusive feeling we chase,
We seek it in laughter, in gleeful cheer,
But in the end, it's a fleeting embrace,
A satire of happiness, in joyless fear.

We pursue joy with fervent zeal,
But joy laughs at our futile quest,
In the end, it's just a reel,
A farce of elation, a hollow jest.

For joy's ecstasy is but a tease,
A mockery of the joy we seize.

Here are four Satire poems, 1 each about Sorrow, Childhood, Wisdom & Innocence

Satire Poem about Sorrow:

Sorrow, that heavy burden we bear,
We wallow in its depths, we drown in tears,
But in the end, it's just despair,
A satire of sadness, echoing fears.

We mourn our losses, we wear grief's cloak,
But sorrow mocks our somber plea,
In the end, it's just a cruel joke,
A farce of mourning, a mockery.

For sorrow's weight is but a jest,
A mockery of the tears we invest.

Satire Poem about Childhood:

Childhood, that golden age we recall,
We reminisce with rose-tinted hue,
But in the end, it's not all,
A satire of innocence, a skewed view.

We long for innocence, for carefree days,
But childhood laughs at our longing heart,
In the end, it's just a haze,
A farce of nostalgia, a childhood apart.

For childhood's innocence is but a dream,
A mockery of the innocence we deem.

Satire Poem about Wisdom:

Wisdom, that noble virtue we revere,
We seek its counsel, its guiding light,
But in the end, it's not so clear,
A satire of knowledge, a twisted plight.

We strive for wisdom, for sage advice,
But wisdom mocks our earnest quest,
In the end, it's just a roll of the dice,
A farce of enlightenment, a wisdom detest.

For wisdom's insight is but a jest,
A mockery of the truths we test.

Satire Poem about Innocence:

Innocence, that pure state we praise,
We cherish its purity, its untainted grace,
But in the end, it's just a phase,
A satire of naivety, a mask we embrace.

We yearn for innocence, for unspoiled hearts,
But innocence laughs at our longing plea,
In the end, it's just a fleeting dart,
A farce of purity, a truth to see.

For innocence's purity is but a lie,
A mockery of the innocence we imply.

Here are four Satire poems, 1 each about Passion, Serenity, Freedom & Justice

Satire Poem about Passion:

Passion, that fiery flame we adore,
We chase it with reckless abandon,
But in the end, it's just a chore,
A satire of desire, a fruitless grandstand.

We burn with fervor, with heated zeal,
But passion mocks our fervent plea,
In the end, it's just a deal,
A farce of intensity, a mockery.

For passion's fire is but a joke,
A mockery of the flames we stoke.

Satire Poem about Serenity:

Serenity, that tranquil state we crave,
We seek it in silence, in peaceful calm,
But in the end, it's just a wave,
A satire of tranquility, a soothing balm.

We yearn for serenity, for quiet reprieve,
But serenity laughs at our earnest plea,
In the end, it's just a naive belief,
A farce of tranquility, a mockery.

For serenity's peace is but a jest,
A mockery of the calm we request.

Satire Poem about Freedom:

Freedom, that cherished prize we hold,
We fight for it with all our might,
But in the end, it's just a mold,
A satire of liberation, a freedom slight.
We long for freedom, for unbound wings,
But freedom mocks our desperate plea,
In the end, it's just a fleeting fling,
A farce of liberty, a mockery.

For freedom's promise is but a lie,
A mockery of the freedoms we imply.

Satire Poem about Justice:

Justice, that noble ideal we proclaim,
We strive for it with righteous might,
But in the end, it's just a game,
A satire of fairness, a twisted sight.

We seek justice, for the oppressed,
But justice laughs at our earnest plea,
In the end, it's just a jest,
A farce of equality, a mockery.

For justice's scales are but a ruse,
A mockery of the justice we choose.

Here are four Satire poems, 1 each about Change, Resilience, Gratitude & Forgiveness

Satire Poem about Change:

Change, that elusive force we chase,
We yearn for it with hopeful eyes,
But in the end, it's just a race,
A satire of progress, a truth we despise.

We clamor for change, for a brighter day,
But change mocks our fervent plea,
In the end, it's just a delay,
A farce of transformation, a mockery.

For change's promise is but a jest,
A mockery of the change we request.

Satire Poem about Resilience:

Resilience, that sturdy armor we wear,
We boast of it with proud chest,
But in the end, it's just a snare,
A satire of strength, a facade at best.

We endure hardships, we weather storms,
But resilience laughs at our vain boast,
In the end, it's just a norm,
A farce of fortitude, a mockery.

For resilience's shield is but a joke,
A mockery of the strength we invoke.

Satire Poem about Gratitude:

Gratitude, that noble virtue we extol,
We preach it with pious tongue,
But in the end, it's just a toll,
A satire of thankfulness, a song unsung.

We offer thanks, with humble grace,
But gratitude scoffs at our humble plea,
In the end, it's just a misplaced chase,
A farce of appreciation, a mockery.

For gratitude's virtue is but a lie,
A mockery of the thanks we imply.

Satire Poem about Forgiveness:

Forgiveness, that lofty ideal we preach,
We preach it with righteous tone,
But in the end, it's just out of reach,
A satire of absolution, a sin we condone.

We seek forgiveness, with contrite heart,
But forgiveness laughs at our desperate plea,
In the end, it's just a shallow part,
A farce of reconciliation, a mockery.

For forgiveness's grace is but a joke,
A mockery of the mercy we invoke.

Here are four Satire poems, 1 each about Longing, Belonging, Discovery & Wonder

Satire Poem about Longing:

Longing, that persistent ache we bear,
We yearn for it with desperate sighs,
But in the end, it's just despair,
A satire of desire, a truth we despise.
We long for what we cannot reach,
But longing mocks our futile plea,
In the end, it's just a breach,
A farce of yearning, a mockery.

For longing's promise is but a jest,
A mockery of the dreams we invest.

Satire Poem about Belonging:

Belonging, that elusive sense we seek,
We crave it with desperate eyes,
But in the end, we're left weak,
A satire of unity, a truth we despise.

We yearn for connection, for a place to fit,
But belonging laughs at our earnest plea,
In the end, it's just a pit,
A farce of acceptance, a mockery.

For belonging's embrace is but a joke,
A mockery of the bonds we invoke.

Satire Poem about Discovery:

Discovery, that grand adventure we crave,
We seek it with eager eyes,
But in the end, it's just a grave,
A satire of exploration, a truth we despise.

We search for truths, for hidden gems,
But discovery mocks our fervent plea,
In the end, it's just a whim,
A farce of revelation, a mockery.

For discovery's promise is but a jest,
A mockery of the secrets we invest.

Satire Poem about Wonder:

Wonder, that magical feeling we cherish,
We revel in it with wide eyes,
But in the end, it's just perish,
A satire of awe, a truth we despise.

We marvel at the world, at its grand design,
But wonder laughs at our naive plea,
In the end, it's just a decline,
A farce of admiration, a mockery.

For wonder's spell is but a joke,
A mockery of the awe we invoke

.

Here are four Satire poems, 1 each about Journey, Reflection, Harmony & Imagination

Satire Poem about Journey:

Oh, the journey, how grand it sounds,
With maps and plans, we'll take our rounds,
But in the end, it's just a ride,
A satire of wanderlust, we can't abide.

We pack our bags, we hit the road,
But journey's end, we're left in woe,
For every step is just a chase,
A farce of adventure, a frantic race.

And though we seek, with eager eyes,
In every mile, a new surprise,
In the end, it's all the same,
A mockery of the journey's game.

Satire Poem about Reflection:

Reflection, that solemn art we claim,
With pens and journals, we'll lay our claim,
But in the end, it's just a show,
A satire of introspection, a superficial glow.

We ponder life, we ponder fate,
But reflection's mirror, it lies in wait,
For every thought is just a trick,
A farce of insight, a shallow flick.

And though we strive, with earnest might,
In every moment, a futile fight,
In the end, it's all a jest,
A mockery of reflection's quest.

Satire Poem about Harmony:

Harmony, that symphony we seek,
With chords and strings, we'll make it sleek,
But in the end, it's just a tune,
A satire of unity, a discordant moon.

We sing our songs, we play our parts,
But harmony's grace, it falls apart,
For every note is just a lie,
A farce of unity, a mournful cry.

And though we strive, with harmonious grace,
In every melody, a misplaced place,
In the end, it's all a sham,
A mockery of harmony's grand slam.

Satire Poem about Imagination:

Imagination, that boundless realm we claim,
With dreams and visions, we'll stake our aim,
But in the end, it's just a game,
A satire of creativity, a whimsical flame.

We paint our worlds, we weave our tales,
But imagination's grip, it often fails,
For every idea is just a ruse,
A farce of innovation, a creative abuse.
And though we dream, with hopeful eyes,
In every fantasy, a truth belies,
In the end, it's all a farce,
A mockery of imagination's brass.

Here are four Satire poems, 1 each about Silence, Laughter, Tears & Strength

Satire Poem about Silence:

Silence, that hallowed state we venerate,
With lips sealed tight, we meditate,
But in the end, it's just a bore,
A satire of tranquility, we can't ignore.

We seek solace in its quiet embrace,
But silence's grip, it leaves no trace,
For every moment is just a waste,
A farce of serenity, a misplaced haste.

And though we crave, with desperate need,
In every hush, a mockery indeed,
In the end, it's all a sham,
A mockery of silence's calm.

Satire Poem about Laughter:

Laughter, that joyful sound we revere,
With smiles wide, we hold it dear,
But in the end, it's just a show,
A satire of happiness, a laughter's blow.

We chuckle and giggle, with hearty cheer,
But laughter's ring, it often veers,
For every joke is just a jest,
A farce of amusement, a laughter's quest.

And though we laugh, with gleeful mirth,
In every chuckle, a cynical birth,
In the end, it's all a game,
A mockery of laughter's claim.

Satire Poem about Tears:

Tears, those salty drops we shed,
With mournful eyes, we bow our head,
But in the end, it's just a ploy,
A satire of sorrow, a tear's decoy.

We weep and wail, with heartache deep,
But tears' cascade, it often seeps,
For every sob is just a mask,
A farce of grief, a tear's flask.

And though we cry, with bitter pain,
In every tear, a truth we feign,
In the end, it's all a fraud,
A mockery of tears' facade.

Satire Poem about Strength:

Strength, that sturdy virtue we applaud,
With muscles flexed, we stand tall and broad,
But in the end, it's just a show,
A satire of resilience, a strength's blow.

We boast of might, with chest puffed high,
But strength's façade, it often lies,
For every muscle is just a flex,
A farce of power, a strength's hex.

And though we strive, with steadfast might,
In every muscle, a weakness slight,
In the end, it's all a facade,
A mockery of strength's applaud.

Here are four Satire poems, 1 each about Vulnerability, Renewal, Acceptance & Mystery

Satire Poem about Vulnerability:

Vulnerability, that tender state we loathe,
With hearts exposed, we tremble and we clothe,
But in the end, it's just a ruse,
A satire of weakness, a vulnerability's abuse.

We bare our souls, we shed our armor,
But vulnerability's charm, it brings no glamour,
For every tear is just a plea,
A farce of openness, a vulnerability's spree.

And though we fear, with trembling fear,
In every vulnerability, a mockery near,
In the end, it's all a game,
A mockery of vulnerability's shame.

Satire Poem about Renewal:

Renewal, that hopeful theme we chant,
With new beginnings, we take our stance,
But in the end, it's just a ploy,
A satire of rebirth, a renewal's decoy.

We seek redemption, with hopeful hearts,
But renewal's promise, it often departs,
For every change is just a facade,
A farce of transformation, a renewal's façade.

And though we strive, with earnest plea,
In every renewal, a cynic's decree,
In the end, it's all a show,
A mockery of renewal's glow.

Satire Poem about Acceptance:

Acceptance, that noble grace we preach,
With open arms, we strive to reach,
But in the end, it's just a dance,
A satire of tolerance, a painful trance.

We embrace differences, with open mind,
But acceptance's virtue, it's hard to find,
For every embrace is just a mask,
A farce of tolerance, a tolerance's task.

And though we preach, with fervent zeal,
In every acceptance, a skeptic's spiel,
In the end, it's all a facade,
A mockery of acceptance's nod.

Satire Poem about Mystery:

Mystery, that enigmatic puzzle we ponder,
With curious minds, we wonder and wander,
But in the end, it's just a tease,
A satire of secrets, a mystery's frieze.

We chase after clues, with eager eyes,
But mystery's allure, it often defies,
For every revelation is just a game,
A farce of intrigue, a mystery's name.

And though we seek, with endless quest,
In every mystery, a skeptic's jest,
In the end, it's all a hoax,
A mockery of mystery's cloak.

Here are four Satire poems, 1 each about Transformation, Eternity, Cosmos & Happiness

Satire Poem about Transformation:

Transformation, that wondrous change we praise,
With hopeful hearts, we seek to raise,
But in the end, it's just a guise,
A satire of growth, a transformation's lies.

We strive for change, with eager might,
But transformation's promise, it takes flight,
For every shift is just a sham,
A farce of progress, a transformation's scam.

And though we yearn, with earnest plea,
In every transformation, a cynic's decree,
In the end, it's all a game,
A mockery of transformation's acclaim.

Satire Poem about Eternity:

Eternity, that timeless expanse we revere,
With lofty dreams, we hold it near,
But in the end, it's just a myth,
A satire of immortality, a hopeless pith.

We chase after forever, with desperate strive,
But eternity's grasp, it leaves us deprived,
For every moment is just a fleeting sigh,
A farce of permanence, a lifetime's lie.

And though we long, with fervent breath,
In every eternity, a skeptic's death,
In the end, it's all a hoax,
A mockery of eternity's spokes.

Satire Poem about Cosmos:

Cosmos, that vast expanse we explore,
With starry eyes, we yearn for more,
But in the end, it's just a dream,
A satire of infinity, a cosmic scheme.

We gaze upon the heavens, with awe and wonder,
But cosmos' mysteries, they only sunder,
For every galaxy is just a charade,
A farce of grandeur, a universe's façade.

And though we ponder, with curious quest,
In every cosmos, a skeptic's jest,
In the end, it's all a show,
A mockery of cosmos' glow.

Satire Poem about Happiness:

Happiness, that elusive state we chase,
With smiles wide, we try to embrace,
But in the end, it's just a game,
A satire of joy, a happiness's shame.

We seek contentment, with eager strive,
But happiness' pursuit, it leaves us deprived,
For every laughter is just a guise,
A farce of bliss, a happiness's rise.

And though we long, with hopeful plea,
In every happiness, a cynic's decree,
In the end, it's all a sham,
A mockery of happiness's glam.

-:¦:-•:*'''''*:•.-:¦:-•**•-:¦:-•:*'''''*:•:*'''''*:•.-:¦:-•**•-:¦:--:¦:-•:*'''''*:•.-:¦:- •**•-:¦:-•:*'''''*:•:*'''''*:•.-:¦:-•**•-:¦:-

LYRIC POETRY:

Short, musical poems that express the poet's emotions or thoughts, often focusing on personal experiences and feelings.

-:¦:-•:*'''''*:•.-:¦:-•**•-:¦:-•:*'''''*:•:*'''''*:•.-:¦:-•**•-:¦:--:¦:-•:*'''''*:•.-:¦:- •**•-:¦:-•:*'''''*:•:*'''''*:•.-:¦:-•**•-:¦:-

Here are four Lyrik poems, 1 each about Love, Nature, Beauty & Time

Lyric Poem about Love:

In love's embrace, we find our home,
A sanctuary, where hearts freely roam.
With tender touch and whispered vow,
We navigate the seas of love, here and now.

Through stormy nights and sun-kissed days,
Love's gentle melody forever plays.
In every glance, a story told,
In every beat, a love to behold.

For love is timeless, love is pure,
A flame that forever shall endure.
In love's embrace, we find our rhyme,
A symphony of hearts, forever in time.

Lyric Poem about Nature:

In nature's arms, we find our peace,
Where troubles cease, and worries release.
With every breeze and rustling leaf,
We find solace in nature's relief.

Through whispering trees and babbling brooks,
Nature paints its picture with skillful strokes.
In every bloom, a story told,
In every sunset, a sight to behold.

For nature's beauty knows no end,
A tapestry of colors that forever blend.
In nature's embrace, we find our grace,
A sacred connection, in every space.

Lyric Poem about Beauty:

Beauty, that elusive grace we seek,
In every sunset and mountain peak.
With every smile and twinkling eye,
We find beauty in the earth and sky.

Through laughter's ring and gentle sigh,
Beauty's touch forever nigh.
In every song, a beauty's note,
In every face, a beauty's vote.

For beauty lies in every soul,
In every moment, it takes its toll.
In beauty's embrace, we find our light,
A radiant glow, forever in sight.

Lyric Poem about Time:

Time, that relentless force we face,
In every moment, a fleeting trace.
With every tick and tock it chimes,
We dance along the thread of time.

Through days of joy and nights of woe,
Time's steady march, it continues to grow.
In every sunrise, a new beginning,
In every moonrise, a tale worth spinning.

For time is fleeting, time is swift,
A constant reminder of life's gift.
In time's embrace, we find our story,
A journey of love, nature, and glory.

Here are four Lyrik poems, 1 each about Death, Dreams, Hope & Despair

Lyric Poem about Death:

In death's embrace, we find our rest,
A journey to the unknown, where souls attest.
With every breath, a step we take,
Towards the eternal slumber, we forsake.

Through shadows deep and silent sighs,
Death's gentle touch, forever lies.
In every goodbye, a tear is shed,
In every farewell, a soul is led.

For death is but a passage, a doorway,
To realms beyond, where spirits sway.
In death's embrace, we find our peace,
A final release, where sorrows cease.

Lyric Poem about Dreams:

In dreams we wander, free and light,
Through realms of wonder, in the silent night.
With every whisper and gentle sigh,
We soar through the stars, beyond the sky.

Through fantasies wild and wishes untold,
Dreams weave their magic, in stories bold.
In every slumber, a journey begins,
In every reverie, a world within.

For dreams are the canvas, where hopes reside,
A tapestry of visions, where hearts confide.
In dreams we find, our soul's delight,
A flight of fancy, in the depths of night.

Lyric Poem about Hope:

In hope's embrace, we find our strength,
A beacon of light, in times of length.
With every prayer and whispered plea,
We cling to hope, when shadows flee.

Through trials faced and battles won,
Hope's gentle touch, forever spun.
In every setback, a lesson learned,
In every setback, a hope returned.

For hope is the fire, that burns within,
A guiding star, where dreams begin.
In hope's embrace, we find our way,
A promise of a brighter day.

Lyric Poem about Despair:

In despair's grip, we find our plight,
A darkness deep, where fears alight.
With every sigh and bitter tear,
We sink into despair, with doubts severe.

Through nights of anguish and days of sorrow,
Despair's heavy burden, we must borrow.
In every shadow, a demon hides,
In every silence, despair resides.

For despair is a prison, with walls so high,
A relentless foe, that makes us sigh.
In despair's embrace, we lose our way,
A journey through darkness, with no light of day.

Here are four Lyrik poems, 1 each about Friendship, Loneliness, Memories & Music

Lyric Poem about Friendship:

In friendship's bond, we find our kin,
A sacred tie that lies within.
With every laugh and shared delight,
We journey together, through day and night.

Through trials faced and joys we share,
Friendship's embrace, forever there.
In every moment, a hand to hold,
In every story, a tale untold.

For friendship is a treasure, rare and true,
A bond that binds, me and you.
In friendship's warmth, we find our light,
A beacon of love, forever bright.

Lyric Poem about Loneliness:

In loneliness' grip, we find our plight,
A solitary path, where shadows alight.
With every sigh and silent cry,
We wander alone, beneath the sky.

Through empty rooms and vacant halls,
Loneliness' echo, forever calls.
In every silence, a hollow sound,
In every tear, loneliness is found.

For loneliness is a burden, heavy to bear,
A weight that crushes, with despair.
In loneliness' embrace, we lose our way,
A solitary journey, with no light of day.

Lyric Poem about Memories:

In memories' embrace, we find our past,
A tapestry of moments, forever cast.
With every smile and bittersweet tear,
We cherish the memories, so dear.

Through faded photographs and whispered sighs,
Memories' echo, forever lies.
In every heartbeat, a memory's song,
In every dream, a memory's throng.

For memories are treasures, timeless and true,
A legacy of love, from me to you.
In memories' embrace, we find our light,
A guiding star, through the darkest night.

Lyric Poem about Music:
In music's rhythm, we find our soul,
A melody that makes us whole.
With every note and harmonious chord,
We dance to the rhythm, with hearts adored.

Through symphonies grand and ballads sweet,
Music's magic, forever we meet.
In every lyric, a story to tell,
In every beat, a rhythm to dwell.

For music is a language, universal and pure,
A symphony of sound, that will endure.
In music's embrace, we find our voice,
A song of love, that makes us rejoice.

Here are four Lyrik poems, 1 each about Art, Inspiration, Creativity & Courage

Lyric Poem about Art:

In strokes of color, we find our soul,
A canvas of emotions, where stories unfold.
With every brushstroke and hue so bright,
We paint the world with pure delight.

Through swirling lines and shapes so bold,
Art's beauty, forever told.
In every masterpiece, a glimpse of truth,
In every stroke, a fountain of youth.

For art is a language, spoken with grace,
A symphony of expression, in every space.
In art's embrace, we find our voice,
A canvas of dreams, where hearts rejoice.

Lyric Poem about Inspiration:

In moments of inspiration, we find our light,
A spark of creativity, burning bright.
With every idea and whispered thought,
We journey into realms, yet to be sought.

Through dreams that dance and muses that sing,
Inspiration's song, forever rings.
In every moment, a vision so clear,
In every whisper, inspiration near.

For inspiration is a flame, that never dies,
A beacon of hope, in endless skies.
In inspiration's embrace, we find our way,
A path of possibilities, come what may.

Lyric Poem about Creativity:

In the depths of creativity, we find our spark,
A fountain of ideas, lighting the dark.
With every creation and work of art,
We weave together, soul and heart.

Through words that flow and colors that blend,
Creativity's journey, has no end.
In every expression, a story to tell,
In every creation, a magic spell.

For creativity is a force, wild and free,
A river of imagination, to set us free.
In creativity's embrace, we find our power,
A canvas of dreams, to bloom and flower.

Lyric Poem about Courage:

In acts of courage, we find our strength,
A fearless heart, going to great lengths.
With every step and leap of faith,
We rise above, in the face of fate.

Through trials faced and battles won,
Courage's journey, has just begun.
In every fear, a courage to face,
In every challenge, a courage to embrace.

For courage is a fire, burning bright,
A beacon of hope, in the darkest night.
In courage's embrace, we find our way,
A path of bravery, come what may.

Here are four Lyrik poems, 1 each about Faith, Doubt, Solitude & Joy

Lyric Poem about Faith:

In faith's embrace, we find our light,
A guiding star, in the darkest night.
With every prayer and whispered plea,
We trust in the unseen, to set us free.

Through trials faced and storms we weather,
Faith's gentle touch, binds us together.
In every doubt, a seed of trust,
In every challenge, a faith robust.

For faith is a journey, deep and true,
A steadfast belief, in all we do.
In faith's embrace, we find our grace,
A sanctuary of hope, in every place.

Lyric Poem about Doubt:

In doubt's shadow, we find our fears,
A whispering voice, that lingers near.
With every question and uncertain thought,
We wander through doubts, where answers sought.

Through cloudy skies and restless seas,
Doubt's heavy burden, brings us to our knees.
In every hesitation, a seed of fear,
In every uncertainty, doubt draws near.

For doubt is a storm, raging within,
A tempest of thoughts, where doubts begin.
In doubt's embrace, we find our strife,
A battle of faith, in the journey of life.

Lyric Poem about Solitude:

In solitude's embrace, we find our peace,
A quiet refuge, where troubles cease.
With every breath and whispered sigh,
We embrace the silence, beneath the sky.

Through tranquil forests and empty halls,
Solitude's gentle touch, softly calls.
In every moment, a soul laid bare,
In every silence, solitude's care.

For solitude is a sanctuary, serene and still,
A sacred space, where hearts can fill.
In solitude's embrace, we find our way,
A path of introspection, day by day.

Lyric Poem about Joy:

In joy's embrace, we find our song,
A melody of laughter, pure and strong.
With every smile and gleeful cry,
We dance through joy, beneath the sky.

Through sunny days and starlit nights,
Joy's radiant glow, forever ignites.
In every moment, a heart set free,
In every laughter, joy's decree.

For joy is a gift, precious and rare,
A beacon of light, beyond compare.
In joy's embrace, we find our bliss,
A celebration of life, in every kiss.

Here are four Lyrik poems, 1 each about Sorrow, Childhood, Wisdom & Innocence

Lyric Poem about Sorrow:

In sorrow's depths, we find our tears,
A river of grief, through the passing years.
With every sigh and heavy heart,
We navigate the darkness, never apart.

Through stormy nights and lonely days,
Sorrow's heavy burden, forever stays.
In every loss, a soul laid bare,
In every ache, sorrow's despair.

For sorrow is a shadow, haunting the soul,
A weight that takes its toll.
In sorrow's embrace, we find our pain,
A journey through darkness, where hearts remain.

Lyric Poem about Childhood:

In childhood's innocence, we find our joy,
A world of wonder, free to enjoy.
With every laugh and playful grin,
We dance through childhood, where dreams begin.

Through sunny days and carefree nights,
Childhood's magic, forever alights.
In every adventure, a story to tell,
In every memory, childhood's spell.

For childhood is a treasure, pure and bright,
A time of innocence, in the morning light.
In childhood's embrace, we find our truth,
A journey of discovery, in the days of youth.

Lyric Poem about Wisdom:

In wisdom's gaze, we find our guide,
A beacon of light, in the vast divide.
With every lesson and word of sage,
We journey through wisdom, with every age.

Through trials faced and mountains climbed,
Wisdom's wisdom, forever enshrined.
In every insight, a truth revealed,
In every wisdom, a soul healed.

For wisdom is a journey, deep and wise,
A path of understanding, beneath the skies.
In wisdom's embrace, we find our way,
A journey of enlightenment, day by day.

Lyric Poem about Innocence:

In innocence' embrace, we find our purity,
A gentle innocence, in every plea.
With every smile and trusting gaze,
We navigate through innocence, in wonderous days.

Through starlit skies and moonlit nights,
Innocence' glow, forever ignites.
In every heart, a spirit pure,
In every laughter, innocence' allure.

For innocence is a treasure, untarnished and true,
A world of wonder, for me and you.
In innocence' embrace, we find our grace,
A sanctuary of light, in every place.

Here are four Lyrik poems, 1 each about Passion, Serenity, Freedom & Justice

Lyric Poem about Passion:

In passion's fire, we find our flame,
A burning desire, with no one to blame.
With every touch and fervent kiss,
We dance through passion, in eternal bliss.

Through fiery nights and ardent days,
Passion's embrace, forever stays.
In every heartbeat, a rhythm wild,
In every caress, passion's child.

For passion is a tempest, raging strong,
A force of nature, where hearts belong.
In passion's embrace, we find our power,
A symphony of desire, in every hour.

Lyric Poem about Serenity:

In serenity's calm, we find our peace,
A tranquil refuge, where troubles cease.
With every breath and gentle sigh,
We drift through serenity, beneath the sky.

Through quiet forests and still waters,
Serenity's touch, forever falters.
In every moment, a soul at rest,
In every silence, serenity's quest.

For serenity is a sanctuary, serene and pure,
A haven of tranquility, to endure.
In serenity's embrace, we find our grace,
A journey of calmness, in every space.

Lyric Poem about Freedom:

In freedom's flight, we find our wings,
A boundless sky, where the spirit sings.
With every leap and daring dream,
We soar through freedom, in a fearless stream.

Through open fields and endless horizons,
Freedom's call, forever mesmerizes.
In every breath, a taste of the wild,
In every choice, freedom's child.

For freedom is a birthright, cherished and true,
A beacon of hope, in all we pursue.
In freedom's embrace, we find our voice,
A symphony of liberation, to rejoice.

Lyric Poem about Justice:

In justice' embrace, we find our truth,
A guiding light, in the pursuit of youth.
With every fight and righteous stand,
We strive for justice, hand in hand.

Through darkened alleys and city streets,
Justice' call, forever meets.
In every heart, a longing for right,
In every fight, justice' might.

For justice is a beacon, shining bright,
A symbol of fairness, in the darkest night.
In justice' embrace, we find our way,
A path of equality, in every day.

Here are four Lyrik poems, 1 each about Change, Resilience, Gratitude & Forgiveness

Lyric Poem about Change:

In change's tide, we find our flow,
A shifting landscape, where dreams grow.
With every turn and twist of fate,
We embrace the change, before it's too late.

Through seasons passed and winds of time,
Change's rhythm, forever chime.
In every transition, a new dawn,
In every transformation, change is drawn.

For change is the river, flowing free,
A journey of growth, for you and me.
In change's embrace, we find our way,
A path of evolution, come what may.

Lyric Poem about Resilience:

In resilience' heart, we find our strength,
A steadfast spirit, that goes to great lengths.
With every fall and rise again,
We stand tall in resilience, despite the pain.

Through trials endured and battles fought,
Resilience' courage, forever sought.
In every setback, a lesson learned,
In every challenge, resilience earned.

For resilience is the armor, that shields the soul,
A beacon of hope, that makes us whole.
In resilience' embrace, we find our power,
A testament to our strength, hour by hour.

Lyric Poem about Gratitude:

In gratitude's embrace, we find our light,
A radiant glow, that shines so bright.
With every thank you and heartfelt smile,
We bask in gratitude, mile after mile.

Through blessings counted and kindness shared,
Gratitude's warmth, forever declared.
In every sunrise, a gift to behold,
In every sunset, gratitude unfolds.

For gratitude is the magic, that fills the heart,
A treasure of appreciation, from the start.
In gratitude's embrace, we find our grace,
A journey of thankfulness, in every space.

Lyric Poem about Forgiveness:

In forgiveness' embrace, we find our peace,
A gentle release, where conflicts cease.
With every apology and healing touch,
We let go in forgiveness, oh so much.

Through wounds healed and scars made whole,
Forgiveness' grace, forever extol.
In every apology, a bridge rebuilt,
In every forgiveness, a heart uplifted.

For forgiveness is the balm, that soothes the soul,
A pathway to healing, to make us whole.
In forgiveness' embrace, we find our way,
A journey of reconciliation, day by day.

Here are four Lyrik poems, 1 each about Longing, Belonging, Discovery & Wonder

Lyric Poem about Journey:

In every step, a tale unfolds,
Each road a chapter, yet untold,
Through valleys deep and mountains high,
We journey on beneath the sky.

With every dawn, a new beginning,
Each day a canvas for the winning,
Through trials faced and battles won,
We journey forth until day is done.

And though the path may twist and turn,
With every step, we live and learn,
For in the journey, we find our way,
Towards the light of a brighter day.

Lyric Poem about Harmony:

In harmony, the world takes flight,
A symphony of day and night,
In every note, a melody,
A song of love, a reverie.

Through harmony, the stars align,
In perfect balance, they entwine,
With every chord, a dance begins,
A dance of life, where joy begins.

And in the rhythm of the earth's embrace,
We find our place, our sacred space,
For in harmony, we find our voice,
In the chorus of the world, we rejoice.

Lyric Poem about Reflection:

In moments quiet, thoughts take flight,
Reflecting on the day's delight,
In stillness found, the mind takes pause,
To ponder life's uncertain cause.

Through memories old and dreams anew,
Reflection brings the past in view,
In the mirror of the soul's deep gaze,
We find the wisdom of bygone days.

And as we ponder, lost in thought,
Reflection brings the lessons taught,
For in the stillness, truth is found,
In the echoes of reflection's sound.

Lyric Poem about Imagination:

In the realm of imagination, dreams take flight,
Where thoughts wander in the dead of night,
In every whisper, a story told,
In every vision, a world unfold.

Through the eyes of imagination, we see,
The endless possibilities that could be,
In every fantasy, a truth revealed,
In every dream, a heart unsealed.

And in the depths of imagination's sea,
We find the key to set us free,
For in the realm of dreams, we find our power,
In the magic of imagination's hour.

Here are four Lyrik poems, 1 each about Journey, Reflection, Harmony & Imagination

Lyric Poem about Journey:

In the journey of life, we find our way,
A winding road, come what may.
With every step and path we tread,
We journey onward, where dreams are led.

Through valleys low and mountains high,
The journey unfolds beneath the sky.
In every twist, a story to tell,
In every turn, a journey to propel.

For the journey is a tapestry, woven with delight,
A path of discovery, in the morning light.
In the journey's embrace, we find our grace,
A voyage of adventure, in every space.

Lyric Poem about Reflection:

In reflection's mirror, we find our soul,
A tranquil pool, where memories roll.
With every thought and whispered prayer,
We reflect on life, with gentle care.

Through quiet moments and silent sighs,
Reflection's wisdom, forever lies.
In every pause, a moment to ponder,
In every silence, reflection's wonder.

For reflection is a journey, deep and wide,
A mirror of the heart, where truth resides.
In reflection's embrace, we find our truth,
A path of introspection, from our youth.

Lyric Poem about Harmony:

In harmony's embrace, we find our song,
A symphony of voices, singing strong.
With every note and chord so clear,
We blend in harmony, with hearts sincere.

Through melodies sweet and rhythms bold,
Harmony's beauty, forever told.
In every harmony, a balance found,
In every chord, harmony's sound.

For harmony is a dance, graceful and pure,
A union of voices, that will endure.
In harmony's embrace, we find our peace,
A sanctuary of sound, where troubles cease.

Lyric Poem about Imagination:

In the realm of imagination, we find our wings,
A boundless sky, where the mind sings.
With every dream and whispered wish,
We soar through imagination, in an endless swish.

Through fantasy lands and tales untold,
Imagination's magic, forever bold.
In every thought, a world to explore,
In every vision, imagination's door.

For imagination is a canvas, waiting to be filled,
A palette of colors, where dreams are willed.
In imagination's embrace, we find our muse,
A journey of creation, where hearts enthuse.

Here are four Lyrik poems, 1 each about Silence, Laughter, Tears & Strength

Lyric Poem about Silence:

In silence' embrace, we find our peace,
A tranquil refuge, where worries cease.
With every breath and whispered sigh,
We embrace the silence, beneath the sky.

Through quiet forests and still waters,
Silence' touch, forever falters.
In every moment, a soul at rest,
In every silence, silence' quest.

For silence is a sanctuary, serene and pure,
A haven of tranquility, to endure.
In silence' embrace, we find our grace,
A journey of calmness, in every space.

Lyric Poem about Laughter:

In laughter's echo, we find our joy,
A symphony of mirth, without a ploy.
With every chuckle and belly laugh,
We dance through laughter, along the path.

Through sunny days and starlit nights,
Laughter's magic, forever ignites.
In every giggle, a heart set free,
In every guffaw, laughter's decree.

For laughter is a melody, merry and bright,
A chorus of happiness, in the darkest night.
In laughter's embrace, we find our light,
A celebration of life, in every delight.

Lyric Poem about Tears:

In tears' embrace, we find our release,
A cleansing rain, that brings us peace.
With every drop and heartfelt cry,
We let go in tears, as time goes by.

Through stormy nights and gentle showers,
Tears' healing touch, forever empowers.
In every sob, a heart laid bare,
In every tear, a burden to share.

For tears are the language, of the soul's plight,
A river of emotion, in the dead of night.
In tears' embrace, we find our solace,
A journey through sorrow, with every trace.

Lyric Poem about Strength:

In strength's embrace, we find our might,
A fortress of courage, shining bright.
With every trial and challenge faced,
We stand tall in strength, with hearts embraced.

Through storms endured and battles won,
Strength's resilience, forever spun.
In every setback, a lesson learned,
In every obstacle, strength discerned.

For strength is a beacon, in the darkest night,
A pillar of resolve, to face the fight.
In strength's embrace, we find our way,
A path of resilience, come what may.

Here are four Lyrik poems, 1 each about Vulnerability, Renewal, Acceptance & Mystery

Lyric Poem about Vulnerability:

In vulnerability's touch, we find our truth,
A raw openness, without a sleuth.
With every sigh and whispered plea,
We embrace vulnerability, to set us free.

Through moments shared and fears revealed,
Vulnerability's embrace, forever sealed.
In every tear, a heart laid bare,
In every vulnerability, a soul to care.

For vulnerability is a strength, not a weakness,
A bridge to connection, in the midst of bleakness.
In vulnerability's embrace, we find our light,
A journey of authenticity, shining bright.

Lyric Poem about Renewal:

In renewal's embrace, we find our grace,
A fresh beginning, in life's embrace.
With every sunrise and morning dew,
We embrace renewal, to start anew.

Through seasons passed and cycles turned,
Renewal's spirit, forever churned.
In every ending, a new chapter begun,
In every farewell, renewal's sun.

For renewal is a rebirth, in every day,
A chance to grow, in every way.
In renewal's embrace, we find our power,
A journey of transformation, hour by hour.

Lyric Poem about Acceptance:

In acceptance' embrace, we find our peace,
A tranquil surrender, where worries cease.
With every breath and gentle sigh,
We embrace acceptance, beneath the sky.

Through trials faced and battles lost,
Acceptance' serenity, forever embossed.
In every flaw, a beauty found,
In every acceptance, a heart unbound.

For acceptance is a journey, deep and true,
A pathway to healing, for me and you.
In acceptance' embrace, we find our way,
A path of liberation, come what may.

Lyric Poem about Mystery:

In mystery's allure, we find our wonder,
A captivating enigma, to ponder.
With every question and quest for truth,
We delve into mystery, in the quest for youth.

Through shadowed forests and starlit skies,
Mystery's magic, forever lies.
In every riddle, a secret to unveil,
In every mystery, a story to regale.

For mystery is a journey, into the unknown,
A realm of fascination, where dreams are sown.
In mystery's embrace, we find our awe,
A journey of exploration, without a flaw.

Here are four Lyrik poems, 1 each about Transformation, Eternity, Cosmos & Happiness

Lyric Poem about Transformation:

In transformation's dance, we find our wings,
A metamorphosis, where the soul sings.
With every change and inner shift,
We embrace transformation, to uplift.

Through trials faced and lessons learned,
Transformation's fire, forever burns.
In every challenge, a chance to grow,
In every transformation, a new glow.

For transformation is a journey, deep and wide,
A path of evolution, where hearts abide.
In transformation's embrace, we find our way,
A journey of becoming, day by day.

Lyric Poem about Eternity:

In eternity's embrace, we find our peace,
A timeless realm, where worries cease.
With every breath and whispered prayer,
We journey through eternity, beyond compare.

Through endless days and boundless skies,
Eternity's beauty, forever lies.
In every moment, a glimpse of forever,
In every eternity, a love to endeavor.

For eternity is a horizon, beyond our sight,
A realm of endless possibility, shining bright.
In eternity's embrace, we find our grace,
A journey of infinity, in every space.

Lyric Poem about Cosmos:

In the cosmos' expanse, we find our awe,
A celestial wonder, beyond all law.
With every star and distant galaxy,
We journey through the cosmos, endlessly free.

Through nebulous clouds and astral streams,
The cosmos' beauty, forever gleams.
In every constellation, a story told,
In every cosmos, a mystery to unfold.

For the cosmos is a tapestry, woven with light,
A canvas of wonder, in the darkest night.
In the cosmos' embrace, we find our place,
A journey through infinity, through time and space.

Lyric Poem about Happiness:

In happiness' embrace, we find our joy,
A boundless elation, without alloy.
With every laugh and heartfelt smile,
We bask in happiness, mile after mile.

Through sunny days and moonlit nights,
Happiness' glow, forever ignites.
In every moment, a bliss to find,
In every happiness, a peace of mind.

For happiness is a journey, within and without,
A state of being, beyond all doubt.
In happiness' embrace, we find our light,
A celebration of life, in every delight.

GHAZAL:

A poetic form with rhyming couplets and a refrain, typically dealing with themes of love, loss, and longing.

Here are four Ghazal poems, 1 each about Love, Nature, Beauty & Time

Ghazal on Love:

In love's embrace, our hearts unite,
Two souls entwined, in passion's flight.

Through whispers soft and tender sighs,
In love's sweet dance, our spirits rise.

In every glance, a world revealed,
In love's embrace, all wounds are healed.

With every beat, a love song sung,
In love's eternal dance, we're forever young.

Though storms may rage and stars may fall,
In love's embrace, we conquer all.

Ghazal on Nature:

In nature's arms, we find our peace,
Where gentle winds and waters cease.

Through forests deep and mountains high,
In nature's realm, we learn to fly.

In every leaf and flower's bloom,
Nature's symphony, dispels all gloom.

With every dawn, a new refrain,
In nature's embrace, we're born again.

Though seasons change and years may pass,
In nature's beauty, we find our compass.

Ghazal on Beauty:

In beauty's gaze, we find our grace,
A timeless allure, in every trace.

Through eyes that see and hearts that feel,
In beauty's presence, all is real.

In every form and every hue,
Beauty's essence, forever true.

With every smile, a masterpiece,
In beauty's embrace, we find release.

Though time may fade and shadows fall,
In beauty's light, we stand tall.

Ghazal on Time:

In time's relentless march, we tread,
Through moments fleeting, swiftly led.

Through sands that slip and hours that fly,
In time's embrace, we live and die.

In every heartbeat, time's refrain,
A reminder of its silent reign.

With every tick, a tale untold,
In time's embrace, our fate unfolds.

Though days may pass and years may fade,
In time's embrace, we find our shade.

Here are four Ghazal poems, 1 each about Death, Dreams, Hope & Despair

Ghazal on Death:

In shadows deep, Death's whisper near,
A silent vow, its secrets veer.

In twilight's hush, life's flame doth wane,
Eternal sleep, its silent reign.

Oh, mortal soul, embrace the night,
In Death's embrace, find silent flight.

Through realms unknown, we journey far,
In Death's embrace, our guiding star.

Though fears may rise, and tears may fall,
In Death's sweet call, find peace in all.

Ghazal on Dreams:

In dreams, we roam where stars alight,
Through veils of time, in darkest night.

In whispers soft, the dreams unfold,
A world of wonders, yet untold.

In dreams, we chase the fleeting light,
Through realms of magic, taking flight.

With every breath, a dream takes form,
In whispers soft, our hearts transform.

Though morning breaks, and dreams depart,
In memories sweet, they leave their mark.

Ghazal on Hope:

In darkest night, a flicker glows,
Hope's gentle whisper, softly flows.

Through trials fierce, and storms that rage,
Hope's steady hand, our fears assuage.

In shadows deep, a beacon bright,
Hope's guiding star, in endless flight.

With every dawn, new hope takes wing,
In hearts that dare, hope's song shall sing.

Though storms may rage, and tempests blow,
In hope's embrace, we find our glow.

Ghazal on Despair:

In shadows deep, despair takes hold,
A silent scream, in darkness bold.

Through tears that fall, and hearts that break,
Despair's cold touch, our souls forsake.

In silence deep, despair doth weep,
A mournful dirge, in shadows steep.

With every sigh, despair takes flight,
In hearts weighed down, by endless night.

Though shadows linger, and darkness reign,
In despair's grip, we rise again.

Here are four Ghazal poems, 1 each about Friendship, Loneliness, Memories & Music

Ghazal on Friendship:

In friendship's bond, our hearts entwine,
A sacred trust, a love divine.

Through laughter shared and tears we mend,
In friendship's embrace, our souls transcend.

In shadows deep, a friend's true light,
Guides us through the darkest night.

With every step, together we stride,
In friendship's warmth, our fears subside.

Though time may pass and miles may part,
In friendship's glow, we're never apart.

Ghazal on Loneliness:

In solitude's embrace, I dwell alone,
A silent ache, an empty tone.

Through silent nights and silent tears,
Loneliness whispers all my fears.

In echoes deep, my voice unheard,
Loneliness wraps around like a shroud.

With every sigh, the void expands,
Loneliness grips with icy hands.

Though crowds may swarm and voices call,
In loneliness, I stand small.

Ghazal on Memories:

In memories' embrace, we wander free,
Through time's vast tapestry, we flee.

Through laughter shared and tears we've shed,
In memories' embrace, we're never dead.

In whispers soft, the past unfolds,
A treasure trove, of stories untold.

With every glance, a memory's spark,
In memories' embrace, we leave our mark.

Though time may fade and years may fly,
In memories' embrace, we never say goodbye.

Ghazal on Music:

In melodies sweet, our souls take flight,
Through notes that dance in the still of night.

In rhythms soft, our hearts entwine,
As music weaves its spell divine.

In symphonies grand, we find our peace,
As music's magic shall never cease.

With every chord, a story told,
In music's embrace, our spirits unfold.

Though silence falls and fades away,
In music's echo, we forever sway.

Here are four Ghazal poems, 1 each about Art, Inspiration, Creativity & Courage

Ghazal on Art:

In strokes of paint, the canvas sings,
A symphony of colors, wild wings.

Through eyes that see, the artist's hand,
In art's embrace, we understand.

In every line, a story weaves,
In art's reflection, beauty cleaves.

With every brush, a soul's ascent,
In art's domain, all barriers relent.

Though critics scorn and doubts may rise,
In art's embrace, our spirit flies.

Ghazal on Inspiration:

In whispers soft, inspiration calls,
A muse's touch, as night befalls.

Through dreams that dance and thoughts that soar,
In inspiration's grasp, we explore.

In every word, a spark ignites,
In inspiration's glow, we take flight.

With every breath, a new creation,
In inspiration's realm, we find elation.

Though doubts may linger and fears may haunt,
In inspiration's embrace, we boldly flaunt.

Ghazal on Creativity:

In boundless realms, creativity thrives,
A force of nature, that forever strives.

Through chaos born and order formed,
In creativity's dance, we're transformed.

In every idea, a world takes shape,
In creativity's realm, there's no escape.

With every act, a masterpiece unfolds,
In creativity's fire, all barriers erode.

Though doubts may linger and fears may rise,
In creativity's embrace, we realize.

Ghazal on Courage:

In the face of fear, courage stands tall,
A beacon bright, amidst the squall.

Through trials faced and battles won,
In courage's embrace, we find the sun.

In every step, a leap of faith,
In courage's realm, we rewrite our fate.

With every choice, a path revealed,
In courage's fire, our fate is sealed.

Though shadows loom and doubts may creep,
In courage's embrace, we dare to leap.

Here are four Ghazal poems, 1 each about Faith, Doubt, Solitude & Joy

Ghazal on Faith:

In faith's embrace, the soul finds peace,
A guiding light, that will never cease.

Through trials faced and storms endured,
In faith's sanctuary, our hearts secured.

In every prayer, a whisper heard,
In faith's refuge, hope is stirred.

With every step, a leap of trust,
In faith's embrace, we find robust.

Though doubts may linger and fears may rise,
In faith's embrace, our spirit flies.

Ghazal on Doubt:

In shadows deep, doubt takes hold,
A whisper soft, in stories told.

Through questions asked and answers sought,
In doubt's domain, our minds are caught.

In every pause, a voice resounds,
In doubt's silence, truth confounds.

With every thought, a seed of fear,
In doubt's embrace, confusion nears.

Though doubts may linger and shadows fall,
In doubt's embrace, we stand tall.

Ghazal on Solitude:

In solitude's embrace, the soul finds rest,
A silent refuge, in nature's nest.

Through whispers of the wind and rustling leaves,
In solitude's realm, the heart believes.

In every moment, a sacred pause,
In solitude's silence, the soul thaws.

With every breath, a quiet peace,
In solitude's embrace, worries cease.

Though crowds may swarm and voices call,
In solitude's embrace, we find it all.

Ghazal on Joy:

In joy's embrace, the heart takes flight,
A melody sweet, in the darkest night.

Through laughter shared and tears of glee,
In joy's symphony, we dance carefree.

In every smile, a sunbeam's kiss,
In joy's radiance, we find bliss.

With every step, a dance of grace,
In joy's embrace, we find our place.

Though storms may rage and shadows may loom,
In joy's embrace, we dispel gloom.

Here are four Ghazal poems, 1 each about Sorrow, Childhood, Wisdom & Innocence

Ghazal on Sorrow:

In sorrow's grasp, the heart weighs heavy,
A burden borne in shadows unsteady.

Through tears that fall like gentle rain,
In sorrow's realm, we bear the pain.

In every sigh, a mournful wail,
In sorrow's silence, we set sail.

With every ache, a heart's lament,
In sorrow's embrace, we're bent.

Though storms may rage and darkness cling,
In sorrow's embrace, we find our wings.

Ghazal on Childhood:

In childhood's realm, the world's a dream,
A playground vast, with streams that gleam.

Through laughter pure and mischief's spree,
In childhood's innocence, we're free.

In every game, a tale untold,
In childhood's wonder, hearts unfold.

With every hug, a love so deep,
In childhood's embrace, memories keep.

Though time may pass and years may flee,
In childhood's heart, we forever be.

Ghazal on Wisdom:

In wisdom's gaze, the soul finds light,
A guiding star in the darkest night.

Through trials faced and lessons learned,
In wisdom's embrace, our paths discerned.

In every silence, a truth revealed,
In wisdom's whisper, hearts are healed.

With every choice, a path well trod,
In wisdom's embrace, we find our God.

Though doubts may linger and shadows loom,
In wisdom's embrace, we find our room.

Ghazal on Innocence:
In innocence's glow, the heart is pure,
A gentle breeze, forever sure.

Through eyes that see with wonder wide,
In innocence's realm, we abide.

In every smile, a glimpse of grace,
In innocence's laughter, we find our place.

With every touch, a world untamed,
In innocence's embrace, we're unashamed.

Though time may pass and innocence wane,
In innocence's heart, we'll remain.

Here are four Ghazal poems, 1 each about Passion, Serenity, Freedom & Justice

Ghazal on Passion:

In passion's fire, the heart ignites,
A burning flame in the darkest nights.

Through kisses fierce and longing sighs,
In passion's embrace, our spirits rise.

In every touch, a spark of desire,
In passion's dance, we never tire.

With every heartbeat, a wild beat,
In passion's storm, we find retreat.

Though doubts may linger and fears may taunt,
In passion's embrace, we relentlessly flaunt.

Ghazal on Serenity:

In serenity's calm, the soul finds peace,
A tranquil lake where worries cease.

Through whispers soft and gentle breeze,
In serenity's embrace, we find release.

In every breath, a quiet sigh,
In serenity's silence, we learn to fly.

With every moment, a tranquil pause,
In serenity's haven, we find our cause.

Though storms may rage and chaos reign,
In serenity's embrace, we remain.

Ghazal on Freedom:

In freedom's breeze, the spirit soars,
A boundless sky, where dreams explore.

Through open fields and open minds,
In freedom's embrace, we leave behind.

In every step, a choice unfurled,
In freedom's dance, we shape the world.

With every breath, a new beginning,
In freedom's realm, there's no sinning.

Though chains may bind and shackles hold,
In freedom's embrace, we break the mold.

Ghazal on Justice:

In justice's call, the heart beats strong,
A righteous path, where we belong.

Through voices raised and truths unveiled,
In justice's embrace, we never fail.

In every fight, a cause to defend,
In justice's name, we make amends.

With every verdict, a balance restored,
In justice's eyes, we're never ignored.

Though darkness falls and injustice reigns,
In justice's embrace, we break the chains.

Here are four Ghazal poems, 1 each about Change, Resilience, Gratitude & Forgiveness

Ghazal on Change:

In change's embrace, the world evolves,
A shifting dance, where time resolves.

Through seasons turned and tides that flow,
In change's realm, we learn to grow.

In every shift, a new frontier,
In change's whispers, we shed our fear.

With every dawn, a promise new,
In change's embrace, we bid adieu.

Though uncertainty may cast its spell,
In change's embrace, we learn it well.

Ghazal on Resilience:

In resilience's strength, we find our might,
A steadfast courage in the darkest night.

Through trials faced and battles won,
In resilience's embrace, we carry on.

In every setback, a lesson learned,
In resilience's flame, our spirits burn.

With every scar, a story told,
In resilience's embrace, we unfold.

Though storms may rage and shadows fall,
In resilience's embrace, we stand tall.

Ghazal on Gratitude:

In gratitude's embrace, the heart finds peace,
A gentle whisper that never cease.

Through blessings counted and kindness shown,
In gratitude's realm, we find our own.

In every smile, a treasure found,
In gratitude's dance, our souls abound.

With every thank you, a bond is formed,
In gratitude's embrace, love is adorned.

Though challenges may come and fortunes wane,
In gratitude's embrace, we find our gain.

Ghazal on Forgiveness:

In forgiveness's grace, we find release,
A healing balm, that brings us peace.

Through wounds endured and scars that bind,
In forgiveness's embrace, we leave behind.

In every pardon, a burden shed,
In forgiveness's light, our souls are led.

With every act, a bridge rebuilt,
In forgiveness's embrace, guilt is wilt.

Though bitterness may linger and anger flare,
In forgiveness's embrace, we find repair

.

Here are four Ghazal poems, 1 each about Longing, Belonging, Discovery & Wonder

Ghazal on Longing:

In longing's ache, the heart does yearn,
A silent plea, for love's return.

Through endless nights and lonely sighs,
In longing's embrace, dreams arise.

In every whisper, a lover's name,
In longing's depths, we play the game.

With every tear, a river flows,
In longing's silence, the heart knows.

Though distance separates and time may steal,
In longing's embrace, our love we feel.

Ghazal on Belonging:

In belonging's warmth, the soul finds rest,
A gentle embrace, among the blessed.

Through bonds formed and hearts entwined,
In belonging's realm, we're defined.

In every smile, a family's face,
In belonging's grace, we find our place.

With every hug, a home's embrace,
In belonging's haven, we find solace.

Though paths may diverge and worlds collide,
In belonging's embrace, we find our tribe.
Ghazal on Discovery:

In discovery's quest, the spirit soars,
A journey wild, to distant shores

Through mysteries untold and secrets kept,
In discovery's embrace, our fears are swept.

In every step, a world revealed,
In discovery's path, our fate's sealed.

With every wonder, a truth unveiled,
In discovery's realm, our thirst is quelled.

Though challenges may rise and doubts may loom,
In discovery's embrace, we find our bloom.

Ghazal on Wonder:

In wonder's gaze, the world unfolds,
A tapestry rich, of stories untold.

Through starlit skies and ocean's deep,
In wonder's embrace, our souls do leap.

In every sunrise, a miracle found,
In wonder's whispers, our hearts astound.

With every breath, a universe anew,
In wonder's embrace, dreams come true.

Though doubts may linger and fears may cower,
In wonder's embrace, we find our power.

Here are four Ghazal poems, 1 each about Journey, Reflection, Harmony & Imagination

Ghazal on Journey:

In journeys vast, the heart finds its way,
Through winding paths, night and day.

Through valleys deep and mountains high,
In journey's embrace, we learn to fly.

In every step, a story told,
In journey's rhythm, we unfold.

With every mile, a new horizon,
In journey's embrace, our spirit's risin'.

Though storms may rage and winds may blow,
In journey's embrace, we boldly go.

Ghazal on Reflection:

In reflections deep, the soul finds peace,
A quiet pool where worries cease.

Through memories held and dreams untold,
In reflection's embrace, we find gold.

In every moment, a chance to see,
In reflection's mirror, we find the key.

With every thought, a truth revealed,
In reflection's silence, our fate's sealed.

Though shadows dance and doubts may rise,
In reflection's embrace, we find our guise.

Ghazal on Harmony:

In harmony's tune, the world is one,
A symphony played by moon and sun.

Through melodies sweet and rhythms pure,
In harmony's embrace, we endure.

In every chord, a unity,
In harmony's grace, we find serenity.

With every note, a balance found,
In harmony's realm, we're tightly bound.

Though discord may sound and chaos may reign,
In harmony's embrace, we find refrain.

Ghazal on Imagination:

In imagination's realm, the mind takes flight,
A boundless canvas, infinite.

Through dreams that dance and visions soar,
In imagination's embrace, we explore.

In every thought, a world conceived,
In imagination's magic, we believe.

With every idea, a spark ignited,
In imagination's fire, we're delighted.

Though reality may dim and logic may confine,
In imagination's embrace, we redefine.

Here are four Ghazal poems, 1 each about Silence, Laughter, Tears & Strength

Ghazal on Silence:

In silence deep, the soul finds solace,
A tranquil refuge, in the quiet's embrace.

Through whispers soft and echoes still,
In silence's realm, we find our fill.

In every breath, a symphony of calm,
In silence's embrace, we find our psalm.

With every pause, a story untold,
In silence's sanctuary, secrets unfold.

Though words may fail and noise may deafen,
In silence's embrace, we find heaven.

Ghazal on Laughter:

In laughter's echo, the heart takes flight,
A melody sweet, in the darkest night.

Through joyful tears and merry cries,
In laughter's embrace, our spirits rise.

In every joke, a bond is formed,
In laughter's dance, we're transformed.

With every chuckle, a burden shed,
In laughter's realm, worries fled.

Though life may challenge and troubles may loom,
In laughter's embrace, we find our room.

Ghazal on Tears:

In tears that fall, the heart reveals,
A language deep, that sorrow seals.

Through gentle streams and silent cries,
In tears' embrace, emotions rise.

In every drop, a story told,
In tears' release, we find our hold.

With every sob, a burden eased,
In tears' passage, wounds appeased.

Though pain may linger and darkness fall,
In tears' embrace, we stand tall.

Ghazal on Strength:

In strength's embrace, the spirit rises,
A mighty force, that never disguises.

Through trials faced and battles won,
In strength's sanctuary, we are undone.

In every trial, a lesson learned,
In strength's embrace, our fate discerned.

With every challenge, a chance to grow,
In strength's presence, we glow.

Though doubts may linger and fears may taunt,
In strength's embrace, we boldly flaunt.

Here are four Ghazal poems, 1 each about Vulnerability, Renewal, Acceptance & Mystery

Ghazal on Vulnerability:

In vulnerability's embrace, the heart is bared,
A delicate dance, where souls are shared.

Through walls dismantled and defenses down,
In vulnerability's realm, truth is found.

In every tear, a strength revealed,
In vulnerability's touch, wounds are healed.

With every sigh, a fear released,
In vulnerability's grace, we find peace.

Though fears may rise and doubts may cling,
In vulnerability's embrace, we sing.

Ghazal on Renewal:

In renewal's embrace, the world begins anew,
A fresh canvas painted with morning dew.

Through cycles turned and seasons changed,
In renewal's dance, life's rearranged.

In every sunrise, a promise bright,
In renewal's rhythm, we take flight.

With every bloom, a hope restored,
In renewal's embrace, dreams are stored.

Though darkness falls and shadows may loom,
In renewal's embrace, we find our bloom.
Ghazal on Acceptance:

In acceptance's embrace, the soul finds peace,
A quiet surrender, where troubles cease.

Through trials faced and scars borne,
In acceptance's sanctuary, we're reborn.

In every flaw, a beauty seen,
In acceptance's light, we're serene.

With every flaw, a strength revealed,
In acceptance's embrace, wounds are healed.

Though doubts may linger and fears may taunt,
In acceptance's embrace, we confront.

Ghazal on Mystery:
In mystery's shroud, the world unfolds,
A tapestry woven with secrets untold.

Through whispers heard and shadows cast,
In mystery's embrace, we're steadfast.

In every question, a journey begins,
In mystery's realm, truth wins.

With every enigma, a wonder blooms,
In mystery's allure, we find our rooms.

Though answers elude and riddles persist,
In mystery's embrace, we coexist.

Here are four Ghazal poems, 1 each about Transformation, Eternity, Cosmos & Happiness

Ghazal on Transformation:

In transformation's dance, the soul takes flight,
A journey of becoming, in the darkest night.

Through trials faced and fears embraced,
In transformation's realm, we find our grace.

In every change, a new beginning,
In transformation's fire, we're winning.

With every step, a metamorphosis,
In transformation's embrace, we find our bliss.

Though doubts may linger and shadows loom,
In transformation's embrace, we rise and bloom.

Ghazal on Eternity:

In eternity's grasp, time stands still,
A boundless expanse, where dreams fulfill.

Through cycles turned and stars that gleam,
In eternity's embrace, we find our dream.

In every moment, a forever told,
In eternity's silence, we unfold.

With every heartbeat, a pulse divine,
In eternity's realm, we intertwine.

Though days may fade and years may flee,
In eternity's embrace, we forever be.

Ghazal on Cosmos:

In the cosmos vast, stars alight,
A symphony of galaxies, in the silent night.

Through cosmic dance and celestial sway,
In the cosmos' embrace, we find our way.

In every nebula, a story unfurled,
In the cosmos' tapestry, we're swirled.

With every planet, a song sung,
In the cosmos' grandeur, we belong.

Though mysteries abound and wonders enthrall,
In the cosmos' embrace, we stand tall.

Ghazal on Happiness:

In happiness' glow, the heart takes flight,
A joyous melody, in the darkest night.

Through laughter shared and tears of glee,
In happiness' embrace, we're wild and free.

In every smile, a sunbeam's kiss,
In happiness' dance, we find our bliss.

With every hug, a warmth revealed,
In happiness' realm, our hearts are healed.

Though challenges may come and sorrows may befall,
In happiness' embrace, we conquer all.

TANKA:

A traditional Japanese form similar to haiku but longer, consisting of five lines with a syllable pattern of 5-7-5-7-7.

-:|:-•:*'''''*:•.-:|:-•**•-:|:-•:*'''''*:•:*'''''*:•.-:|:-•**•-:|:--:|:-•:*'''''*:•.-:|:- •**•-:|:-•:*'''''*:•:*'''''*:•.-:|:-•**•-:|:-

Here are four Tanka poems, 1 each about Love, Nature, Beauty & Time

Tanka on Love:

Embrace tenderly,
Heartbeats sync in harmony,
Love's whispered promise,
Two souls bound in sweet embrace,
Eternal flame, love's embrace.

Tanka on Nature:

Beneath azure skies,
Majestic mountains stand tall,
Whispering rivers,
Nature's symphony of peace,
Earth's beauty never to cease.

Tanka on Beauty:

In petals unfurl,
Nature's artistry revealed,
Each bloom a masterpiece,
Beauty's essence pure and true,
In every hue, life anew.

Tanka on Time:

Moments slip away,
Like sand through an hourglass,
Time's relentless march,
Each tick a reminder clear,
Of life's transient frontier.

Here are four Tanka poems, 1 each about Death, Dreams, Hope & Despair

Tanka on Death:

In silent repose,
Life's journey finds its closure,
Beyond mortal coil,
Soul's passage to unknown realms,
In death's embrace, peace prevails.

Tanka on Dreams:

In dreams' gentle hold,
Fantasies take flight, soaring,
Beyond earthly bounds,
Visions dance in starlit skies,
Dreams whisper of endless ties.

Tanka on Hope:

In darkest of nights,
Hope's flicker lights the pathway,
Guiding weary souls,
Through trials and tribulations,
Hope's flame fuels aspirations.

Tanka on Despair:

In shadows profound,
Despair's grip holds tight and firm,
Choking out the light,
Yet in despair's darkest hour,
Seeds of resilience may flower.

Here are four Tanka poems, 1 each about Friendship, Loneliness, Memories & Music

Tanka on Friendship:

In bonds forged by time,
Friendship's warmth lights up the soul,
A beacon of light,
Through joys shared and sorrows borne,
Friendship's embrace, never torn.

Tanka on Loneliness:

In solitude's depths,
Echoes of silence resound,
A solitary
Heart's longing for connection,
Loneliness' silent reflection.

Tanka on Memories:

In whispers of time,
Memories weave tapestries,
Threads of days gone by,
Each moment a precious gem,
In memory's embrace, a hymn.

Tanka on Music:

In melodies sweet,
Music's cadence touches souls,
Harmonies entwine,
A symphony of emotion,
Music's gift, pure devotion.

Here are four Tanka poems, 1 each about Art, Inspiration, Creativity & Courage

Tanka on Art:

Brush strokes on canvas,
Colors swirl in harmony,
Art speaks without words,
A masterpiece of the soul,
Infinite stories untold.

Tanka on Inspiration:

Inspirations spark,
Igniting creative flames,
Fueling dreams to life,
In the whispers of the muse,
Imagination takes flight.

Tanka on Creativity:

Mind's vast playground calls,
Creativity's dance begins,
Ideas unfurling,
From chaos, new worlds emerge,
Creation's endless surge.

Tanka on Courage:

In the face of fear,
Courage stands tall and steadfast,
A beacon of strength,
Defying doubts, forging on,
In courage's embrace, we rise.

Here are four Tanka poems, 1 each about Faith, Doubt, Solitude & Joy

Tanka on Faith:

In faith's gentle hold,
Heart finds solace, spirits soar,
Trusting in unseen,
Guiding light in darkest hours,
Faith's embrace, eternal power.

Tanka on Doubt:

In shadows of doubt,
Questions linger, fears arise,
Challenging beliefs,
Yet within doubt's silent storm,
Seeds of wisdom may be born.

Tanka on Solitude:

In solitude's calm,
Echoes of self softly speak,
A sacred retreat,
Where hearts find solace and peace,
In solitude's gentle release.

Tanka on Joy:

In laughter's ripple,
Joy's melody fills the air,
Hearts dancing in light,
Embracing life's precious gift,
In joy's embrace, spirits lift.

Here are four Tanka poems, 1 each about Sorrow, Childhood, Wisdom & Innocence

Tanka on Sorrow:

Tears trace silent paths,
Sorrow's weight upon the soul,
Aching hearts whisper,
In grief's shadow, solace sought,
Sorrow's touch, a bittersweet knot.

Tanka on Childhood:

In innocence's glow,
Childhood's dreams take flight on wings,
Laughter fills the air,
Memories of carefree days,
Childhood's magic forever stays.

Tanka on Wisdom:

In wisdom's embrace,
Lessons learned, truths revealed,
Ageless knowledge flows,
In the depths of seasoned souls,
Wisdom's light guides and consoles.

Tanka on Innocence:

In innocence pure,
Heart's gentle whispers are heard,
Untouched by the world,
In the embrace of innocence,
Life's beauty finds resonance.

Here are four Tanka poems, 1 each about Passion, Serenity, Freedom & Justice

Tanka on Passion:

Flames of passion burn,
Hearts ablaze with fervent fire,
Desire's embrace,
In the heat of love's embrace,
Passion's dance, wild and free.

Tanka on Serenity:

In tranquil waters,
Serenity finds its home,
Calmness in the soul,
Amidst life's chaotic storm,
Serenity's peace prevails.

Tanka on Freedom:

Wings spread wide, we soar,
Freedom's breeze beneath our wings,
Boundless sky above,
In freedom's vast expanse,
Dreams take flight, limitless.

Tanka on Justice:

In the pursuit of,
Justice, fairness, equality,
Voices rise in song,
Championing rights for all,
In justice's embrace, we stand.

Here are four Tanka poems, 1 each about Change, Resilience, Gratitude & Forgiveness

Tanka on Change:

Seasons come and go,
Change sweeps through life's shifting sands,
Embrace the unknown,
For in change's constant flow,
Opportunities unfold.

Tanka on Resilience:

In the face of storms,
Resilience stands unyielding,
Strength born from within,
Bouncing back, standing tall,
Resilience conquers all.

Tanka on Gratitude:

Heartfelt gratitude,
Fills the soul with warmth and light,
Counting blessings dear,
In each moment, grace is found,
Gratitude's sweet embrace.

Tanka on Forgiveness:

In forgiveness' grace,
Hearts find healing, wounds are soothed,
Letting go of pain,
Forgiveness sets spirits free,
In its embrace, peace restored.

Here are four Tanka poems, 1 each about Longing, Belonging, Discovery & Wonder

Tanka on Longing:

Echoes of longing,
Whispers in the silent night,
Heartache fills the air,
In the depths of yearning souls,
Longing's ache, timeless and true.

Tanka on Belonging:

In belonging's arms,
Soul finds solace, heart finds home,
Connected in love,
In the embrace of kinship,
Belonging's warmth, pure and deep.

Tanka on Discovery:

In the quest for truth,
Discovery's light reveals,
Hidden worlds unfold,
In the journey of seeking,
Discovery's wonders gleam.

Tanka on Wonder:

In wonder's embrace,
Eyes behold the mysteries,
Of the universe,
Marveling at life's beauty,
Wonder's magic, pure delight.

Here are four Tanka poems, 1 each about Journey, Reflection, Harmony & Imagination

Tanka on Journey:

Path unfolds ahead,
Each step a new adventure,
Journey of the soul,
Embracing twists and turns,
Seeking treasures yet unknown.

Tanka on Reflection:

In silent repose,
Mind's eye gazes inward,
Reflection's embrace,
Echoes of moments gone by,
Wisdom found in quietude.

Tanka on Harmony:

Notes in perfect sync,
Harmony's sweet melody,
Echoes through the air,
Instruments blend in rhythm,
Unity in diversity.

Tanka on Imagination:

In dreams' boundless realm,
Imagination takes flight,
Worlds born from the mind,
Visions of infinite scope,
Where possibilities reign.

Here are four Tanka poems, 1 each about Silence, Laughter, Tears & Strength

Tanka on Silence:

In silence profound,
Echoes of the soul resound,
Peace in quietude,
A sanctuary for the heart,
Where whispers hold great power.

Tanka on Laughter:

Laughter fills the air,
Joy's infectious melody,
Hearts dance in delight,
In shared moments of mirth,
Laughter binds us together.

Tanka on Tears:

Tears trace silent paths,
Emotions overflow,
Release in each drop,
Cleansing the soul's inner depths,
Healing through salty waters.

Tanka on Strength:

In moments of trial,
Strength rises from within,
Resilience revealed,
Each challenge a testament,
To the power of the soul.

Here are four Tanka poems, 1 each about Vulnerability, Renewal, Acceptance & Mystery

Tanka on Vulnerability:

In vulnerability,
Courage resides in the heart,
Embracing flaws whole,
Strength found in openness,
Where authenticity thrives.

Tanka on Renewal:

From ashes we rise,
Renewal's sweet promise blooms,
Each dawn brings new light,
In the cycle of rebirth,
Hope springs eternal once more.

Tanka on Acceptance:

In acceptance' hold,
Surrender to what is true,
Peace in letting go,
Embracing life's ebb and flow,
Finding grace in every moment.

Tanka on Mystery:

In the shadows deep,
Mystery's allure beckons,
Whispers of the unknown,
In the dance of light and dark,
Secrets of the cosmos lie.

Here are four Tanka poems, 1 each about Transformation, Eternity, Cosmos & Happiness

Tanka on Transformation:

From cocoon to wing,
Metamorphosis unfolds,
Transformation's dance,
Emerging from the shadows,
New beginnings, life reborn.

Tanka on Eternity:

Eternal cosmos,
Stars shine in timeless expanse,
Infinite realms span,
In the tapestry of time,
Eternity's song resounds.

Tanka on Cosmos:

Galaxies alight,
In the vastness of the void,
Cosmic symphony,
Planets dance in harmony,
Cosmos' wonders revealed.

Tanka on Happiness:

In laughter's embrace,
Joy blossoms like springtime flowers,
Hearts sing in delight,
In happiness' gentle glow,
Life's beauty fully embraced.

-:¦:-•:*'''''*:•.-:¦:-•**•-:¦:-•:*''''''*:•:*'''''*:•.-:¦:-•**•-:¦:--:¦:-•:*'''''*:•.-:¦:- •**•-:¦:-•:*''''''*:•:*'''''*:•.-:¦:-•**•-:¦:-

CINQUAIN:

A five-line poem with a specific syllable pattern (2-4-6-8-2), often focusing on a single subject or image.

Here are four Cinquain poems, 1 each about Love, Nature, Beauty & Time

Cinquain on Love:

Love
Pure, divine
Embraces, enchants, endures
Heart's eternal flame
Passion

Cinquain on Nature:

Nature
Vibrant, alive
Whispers, soothes, inspires
Earth's gentle embrace
Harmony

Cinquain on Beauty:

Beauty
Graceful, serene
Captivates, enchants, delights
Soul's reflection revealed
Ethereal

Cinquain on Time:

Time
Ever-flowing
Gives, takes, transforms, endures
Life's eternal rhythm
Eternal

Here are four Cinquain poems, 1 each about Death, Dreams, Hope & Despair

Cinquain on Death:

Death
Final, silent
Ends, closes, whispers
Transition to unknown
Peace

Cinquain on Dreams:

Dreams
Whispers, hopes
Spark, inspire, beckon
Visions of possibility
Imagination

Cinquain on Hope:

Hope
Light, enduring
Guides, uplifts, sustains
Beacon in darkest nights
Renewal

Cinquain on Despair:

Despair
Heavy, dark
Weighs, consumes, suffocates
Shadows envelop the soul
Grief

Here are four Cinquain poems, 1 each about Friendship, Loneliness, Memories & Music

Cinquain on Friendship:

Friendship
Bond, connection
Laughs, shares, supports, endures
Heart's kinship, soul's refuge
Belonging

Cinquain on Loneliness:

Loneliness
Silent, isolating
Aches, echoes, isolates
Emptiness fills the void
Alone

Cinquain on Memories:

Memories
Fleeting, timeless
Echo, linger, treasure
Imprints of bygone days
Nostalgia

Cinquain on Music:

Music
Melodic, rhythmic
Soothes, inspires, transcends
Language of the heart's whispers
Harmony

Here are four Cinquain poems, 1 each about Art, Inspiration, Creativity & Courage

Cinquain on Art:

Art
Expressive, vibrant
Creates, evokes, transforms
Imagination's canvas
Creation

Cinquain on Inspiration:

Inspiration
Spark, ignite
Fuels, motivates, enlightens
Creative flame ablaze
Influence

Cinquain on Creativity:

Creativity
Innovative, boundless
Conceptualizes, crafts, explores
Endless possibilities
Ingenuity

Cinquain on Courage:

Courage
Brave, resilient
Confronts, overcomes, prevails
Strength in adversity
Fortitude

Here are four Cinquain poems, 1 each about Faith, Doubt, Solitude & Joy

Cinquain on Faith:

Faith
Steadfast, unwavering
Believes, trusts, surrenders, sustains
Soul's sacred anchor
Belief

Cinquain on Doubt:

Doubt
Uncertain, questioning
Wavers, hesitates, fears, challenges
Mind's restless turmoil
Skepticism

Cinquain on Solitude:
Solitude
Quiet, introspective
Reflects, contemplates, heals, renews
Soul's peaceful retreat
Aloneness

Cinquain on Joy:

Joy
Radiant, infectious
Smiles, dances, celebrates, uplifts
Heart's exuberant melody
Happiness

Here are four Cinquain poems, 1 each about Sorrow, Childhood, Wisdom & Innocence

Cinquain on Sorrow:

Sorrow
Heavy, burdensome
Weeps, mourns, grieves, endures
Heartache's somber song
Grief

Cinquain on Childhood:

Childhood
Carefree, innocent
Plays, laughs, learns, dreams, explores
Life's purest chapter
Wonder

Cinquain on Wisdom:

Wisdom
Ageless, profound
Teaches, guides, enlightens, inspires
Insight's sacred gift
Knowledge

Cinquain on Innocence:

Innocence
Pure, untainted
Trusts, believes, embraces, delights
Heart's gentle purity
Naivety

Here are four Cinquain poems, 1 each about Passion, Serenity, Freedom & Justice

Cinquain on Passion:

Passion
Fiery, intense
Burns, consumes, ignites, desires
Heart's fervent longing
Emotion

Cinquain on Serenity:

Serenity
Tranquil, peaceful
Calms, soothes, envelops, transcends
Mind's gentle repose
Harmony

Cinquain on Freedom:

Freedom
Liberating, boundless
Flies, soars, conquers, liberates
Soul's emancipation
Empowerment

Cinquain on Justice:

Justice
Fair, impartial
Rights, defends, restores, upholds
Equality's triumph
Righteousness

Here are four Cinquain poems, 1 each about Change, Resilience, Gratitude & Forgiveness

Cinquain on Change:

Change
Dynamic, constant
Shifts, evolves, transforms, adapts
Life's relentless cycle
Transition

Cinquain on Resilience:

Resilience
Strong, enduring
Endures, perseveres, bounces, rises
Spirit's unyielding force
Strength

Cinquain on Gratitude:

Gratitude
Thankful, humble
Appreciates, cherishes, acknowledges, blesses
Heart's abundant joy
Thankfulness

Cinquain on Forgiveness:

Forgiveness
Healing, freeing
Lets go, releases, absolves, heals
Soul's liberation
Redemption

Here are four Cinquain poems, 1 each about Longing, Belonging, Discovery & Wonder

Cinquain on Longing:

Longing
Aching, yearning
Waits, pines, craves, desires, dreams
Heart's silent plea
Yearning

Cinquain on Belonging:

Belonging
Connected, embraced
Fits, bonds, shares, nurtures, accepts
Soul's comforting refuge
Unity

Cinquain on Discovery:

Discovery
Revealing, enlightening
Unveils, explores, learns, uncovers
Mind's endless quest
Exploration

Cinquain on Wonder:

Wonder
Awe-inspiring, magical
Marvels, fascinates, amazes, delights
Soul's enchanting journey
Curiosity

Here are four Cinquain poems, 1 each about Journey, Reflection, Harmony & Imagination

Cinquain on Journey:

Journey
Adventure, exploration
Moves, travels, experiences, learns, grows
Life's unfolding path
Exploration

Cinquain on Reflection:

Reflection
Contemplative, introspective
Muses, meditates, ponders, contemplates
Mind's inner dialogue
Thoughtfulness

Cinquain on Harmony:

Harmony
Balanced, unified
Blends, synchronizes, resonates, unifies
Heart's peaceful melody
Concord

Cinquain on Imagination:

Imagination
Creative, boundless
Dreams, envisions, creates, imagines
Mind's endless canvas
Innovation

Here are four Cinquain poems, 1 each about Silence, Laughter, Tears & Strength

Cinquain on Silence:

Silence
Quiet, serene
Calms, soothes, whispers, envelops
Mind's peaceful refuge
Tranquility

Cinquain on Laughter:

Laughter
Joyful, contagious
Laughs, echoes, resonates, uplifts
Heart's delightful melody
Hilarity

Cinquain on Tears:

Tears
Sorrowful, cathartic
Fall, cleanse, heal, release
Emotion's silent language
Sorrow

Cinquain on Strength:

Strength
Resilient, unwavering
Endures, perseveres, empowers, prevails
Spirit's mighty force
Fortitude

Here are four Cinquain poems, 1 each about Vulnerability, Renewal, Acceptance & Mystery

Cinquain on Vulnerability:

Vulnerability
Open, exposed
Reveals, embraces, trusts, accepts
Heart's raw authenticity
Sensitivity

Cinquain on Renewal:

Renewal
Rebirth, transformation
Grows, flourishes, rejuvenates, evolves
Life's constant cycle
Regeneration

Cinquain on Acceptance:

Acceptance
Peaceful, embracing
Learns, forgives, embraces, transcends
Soul's serene surrender
Harmony

Cinquain on Mystery:

Mystery
Enigmatic, elusive
Intrigues, fascinates, beckons, conceals
Mind's endless wonder
Enigma

Here are four Cinquain poems, 1 each about Transformation, Eternity, Cosmos & Happiness

Cinquain on Transformation:

Transformation
Evolution, rebirth
Unfolds, empowers, enlightens
Metamorphosis complete
Renewal

Cinquain on Eternity:

Eternity
Timeless, infinite
Endures, transcends, embraces
Everlasting existence
Immortality

Cinquain on Cosmos:

Cosmos
Celestial vastness
Expands, twinkles, fascinates
Infinite cosmic dance
Mystery

Cinquain on Happiness:

Happiness
Joyful, radiant
Laughs, embraces, uplifts
Heart's purest elation
Euphoria

TERZA RIMA:

A form of poetry with interlocking tercets rhyming in the pattern ABA, BCB, CDC, etc., popularized by Dante's Divine Comedy.

Here are four Terza Rima poems, 1 each about Love, Nature, Beauty & Time

Terza Rima on Love:

In love's embrace, two souls intertwine,
Bound by passion's eternal flame,
Hearts beat as one in rhythm divine.

Through trials and storms, they stake their claim,
Love's tender whispers soothe their fears,
In each other's arms, they find their aim.

Through joy and sorrow, through laughter and tears,
Their bond grows stronger with each passing day,
In love's eternal dance, their spirits cheer.

Terza Rima on Nature:

In nature's arms, where wonders play,
Mountains soar and rivers flow,
In every breeze, life finds its way.

The forests whisper secrets low,
As sunlight dances through the trees,
In meadows green, wildflowers grow.

Beneath the sky's vast tapestry,
Nature's beauty knows no end,
In every corner, there's majesty.

Terza Rima on Beauty:

Beauty's grace, a sight to behold,
In every sunrise, every sunset's glow,
In petals unfurled, in colors bold.

In art and music, in rivers' flow,
Beauty's presence, a divine embrace,
In every story, in tales of woe.

In laughter shared, in love's warm trace,
Beauty resides in every corner,
In every heart, in every space.

Terza Rima on Time:

Time, relentless, marches on,
With each tick of the clock, it weaves,
In every moment, dusk to dawn.

In memories cherished, it retrieves,
In dreams yet to unfold, it waits,
In every heartbeat, as life breathes.

Through joys and sorrows, through love and fates,
Time's steady rhythm guides our way,
In every echo, in every gate.

Here are four Terza Rima poems, 1 each about Death, Dreams, Hope & Despair

Terza Rima on Death:

In shadows deep, where silence reigns supreme,
Death's quiet touch, a journey to the unknown,
Yet from its embrace, we cannot redeem.

Through whispered sighs, a soul's final moan,
Life's flame extinguished, its warmth withdrawn,
In death's domain, we stand alone.

But in the quiet dusk, a new dawn is drawn,
For in the cycle of life, death finds its place,
A journey's end, a spirit reborn.

Terza Rima on Dreams:

In dreams, the mind takes flight, a soaring grace,
Beyond the bounds of earthly realm's control,
In sleep's embrace, we find a sacred space.

Through starlit skies, where fantasies unroll,
Dreams weave tapestries of hopes untold,
In the realm of slumber, hearts console.

But with the dawn, dreams gently fold,
Yet in their fleeting touch, a glimpse of what could be,
In dreams, the seeds of destiny mold.

Terza Rima on Hope:

In hope's embrace, the heart finds sanctuary,
A beacon in the darkest depths of despair,
A flicker of light amidst life's tributary.

Through trials and storms, when life seems unfair,
Hope's gentle whispers soothe our fears,
In its tender touch, we find repair.

For even in the face of adversity, hope appears,
A steadfast guide, a promise in the night,
In hope's eternal flame, resilience steers.

Terza Rima on Despair:

In despair's grip, the soul quivers in fright,
Lost in the shadows of anguish and pain,
A tempest raging in the heart's darkest night.

Through tears unshed, in silent refrain,
Despair's heavy burden weighs us down,
In its suffocating embrace, we're chained.

But even in despair, a seed is sown,
For from its depths, resilience can arise,
In despair's cruel embrace, strength is honed.

Here are four Terza Rima poems, 1 each about Friendship, Loneliness, Memories & Music

Terza Rima on Friendship:

In friendship's bond, hearts intertwine with grace,
A tapestry woven with threads of trust,
Through laughter and tears, in every embrace.

In times of need, a friend is just,
A beacon of light in the darkest night,
Their presence a balm, their loyalty robust.

Through trials faced and dreams taking flight,
Friendship's warmth guides us, steadfast and true,
In the symphony of life, a cherished sight.

Terza Rima on Loneliness:

In loneliness' grasp, the soul feels the weight,
A solitary journey through the silent night,
Echoes of emptiness, an endless freight.

In crowded rooms, yet feeling out of sight,
Loneliness cloaks, a shadow in the heart,
In solitude's embrace, the mind takes flight.

Yearning for connection, for a fresh start,
Loneliness lingers, a silent foe,
In its depths, we're torn apart.

Terza Rima on Memories:

In memories' embrace, the past takes flight,
A kaleidoscope of moments, both joy and pain,
Etched in the heart, in the mind's soft light.

Through laughter shared and tears like rain,
Memories weave a tapestry of time,
In their echoes, life's beauty remains.

Through the passage of years, in every chime,
Memories endure, a treasure to hold dear,
In their embrace, we find sublime.

Terza Rima on Music:

In music's melody, the soul finds flight,
A symphony of emotion, notes dancing free,
In every chord, in every rhythm's might.

Through harmonies woven, in a melodic spree,
Music whispers secrets, tales untold,
In its embrace, we find serenity.

Through highs and lows, in melodies bold,
Music's power transcends, it soothes the soul,
In its resonance, hearts unfold.

Here are four Terza Rima poems, 1 each about Art, Inspiration, Creativity & Courage

Terza Rima on Art:

In art's canvas, colors dance and sing,
A tapestry woven with strokes of passion,
Expressions of the soul, on each painting.

Through brushstrokes bold, emotions in fashion,
Artists breathe life into the silent frame,
In galleries adorned, their visions enchain.

With every hue, they etch their name,
In art's embrace, beauty finds its voice,
In masterpieces timeless, they proclaim.

Terza Rima on Inspiration:

In inspiration's light, ideas take flight,
A spark igniting the creative flame,
In moments of wonder, in dreams of the night.

Through whispered musings, the mind lays claim,
To visions unseen, to stories untold,
In the depths of imagination, it aims.

With every thought, inspiration unfolds,
In its gentle embrace, creativity soars,
In the symphony of creation, it beholds.

Terza Rima on Creativity:

In creativity's realm, the mind explores,
A boundless landscape of ideas and dreams,
In every venture, in every course.

Through trials faced and in daring schemes,
Creativity thrives, it knows no bounds,
In its embrace, innovation gleams.

With every stroke, a masterpiece surrounds,
In the artist's hand, creation blooms,
In the dance of creativity, all resounds.

Terza Rima on Courage:

In courage's embrace, the spirit blooms,
A flame that flickers in the darkest night,
In the face of fear, it still resumes.

Through trials endured, in the toughest fight,
Courage stands tall, it does not retreat,
In its strength, the soul takes flight.

With every step forward, courage meets,
In its resolve, adversity is met,
In the heart's bravest beats.

Here are four Terza Rima poems, 1 each about Faith, Doubt, Solitude & Joy

Terza Rima on Faith:

In faith's embrace, the heart finds solace deep,
A steadfast anchor in life's stormy sea,
In trials faced, its promises we keep.

Through doubts that whisper, trying to break free,
Faith stands unwavering, a guiding light,
In its embrace, we find tranquility.

With every prayer, faith takes its flight,
In the divine, our hopes we entrust,
In faith's embrace, all wrongs make right.

Terza Rima on Doubt:

In doubt's shadows, the mind begins to rust,
Questions unanswered, uncertainties unfurl,
In the depths of doubt, we lose our trust.

Through whispers quiet, doubts slowly swirl,
Casting shadows upon the soul's bright light,
In the labyrinth of doubt, we feel the twirl.

With every query, the heart takes flight,
In doubt's grip, uncertainty does bind,
In its shadows, we lose our sight.

Terza Rima on Solitude:
In solitude's embrace, the soul can find,
A sanctuary from the world's harsh grind,
In silence deep, a gentle peace enshrined.

Through quiet moments, thoughts unwind,
In the stillness, the spirit takes its flight,
In solitude's embrace, solace we find.

With every breath, in the tranquil night,
In solitude's refuge, the soul is free,
In its embrace, we find our light.

Terza Rima on Joy:
In joy's embrace, the heart sings with glee,
A melody that echoes through the soul,
In every laugh, in every jubilee.

Through moments shared, happiness takes its toll,
In joyous rapture, we dance in delight,
In joy's embrace, we find our role.

With every smile, the world feels bright,
In joy's embrace, we find our bliss,
In its presence, everything feels right.

Here are four Terza Rima poems, 1 each about Sorrow, Childhood, Wisdom & Innocence

Terza Rima on Sorrow:

In sorrow's grip, the heart feels heavy chains,
A weight that pulls it to the depths of despair,
In tears that fall, in silent, endless rains.

Through grief that lingers, in the somber air,
Sorrow's shadow casts a pall upon the soul,
In its embrace, we feel a deep despair.

With every sigh, the pain takes its toll,
In sorrow's depths, we search for light,
In its grip, we long to be made whole.

Terza Rima on Childhood:

In childhood's realm, where dreams take flight,
Innocence reigns, in laughter's sweet refrain,
In every moment, in every delight.

Through eyes that see the world without stain,
Childhood's wonder fills each passing day,
In its embrace, we find a pure domain.

With every step, in the child's play,
In childhood's grasp, memories are made,
In its care, we forever stay.

Terza Rima on Wisdom:

In wisdom's halls, where truths are weighed,
Experience reigns, in lessons learned with age,
In every challenge, in every crusade.

Through trials faced, wisdom turns the page,
In its embrace, we find enlightenment's glow,
In its wisdom, we find solace in the sage.

With every thought, in the ebb and flow,
In wisdom's grasp, we find our guide,
In its counsel, we learn and grow.

Terza Rima on Innocence:

In innocence' embrace, the heart feels light,
A purity that shines in the soul's bright gaze,
In every smile, in every child's delight.

Through innocence' lens, the world amaze,
In untainted wonder, where all is bright,
In its embrace, we feel the gentle blaze.

With every giggle, in the day's first light,
In innocence' care, we find our way,
In its presence, everything feels right.

Here are four Terza Rima poems, 1 each about Passion, Serenity, Freedom & Justice

Terza Rima on Passion:

In passion's fire, hearts fiercely ignite,
A blaze that consumes, yet never tires,
In every touch, in each ardent fight.

Through heated whispers, desire conspires,
Passion's dance, a symphony of heat,
In its embrace, love never expires.

With every kiss, the flames repeat,
In passion's grip, souls intertwine,
In its fervor, ecstasy complete.

Terza Rima on Serenity:

In serenity's embrace, the soul finds peace,
A tranquil haven, where worries cease,
In every breath, tensions gently release.

Through whispered breezes, troubles decrease,
Serenity's touch, a balm for the heart,
In its tranquility, sorrows decrease.

With every sigh, a calm does impart,
In serenity's grasp, all feels right,
In its embrace, the soul restarts.

Terza Rima on Freedom:

In freedom's vast expanse, the spirit soars,
A boundless sky, where dreams explore,
In every step, new horizons implore.

Through open fields, freedom does restore,
Freedom's breeze, a whisper of hope,
In its embrace, limitations deplore.

With every leap, the soul learns to cope,
In freedom's grasp, courage takes flight,
In its winds, aspirations elope.

Terza Rima on Justice:

In justice's halls, equality reigns,
A beacon of light, where fairness attains,
In every verdict, truth sustains.

Through laws upheld, justice maintains,
Justice's scales, balanced and true,
In its embrace, righteousness remains.

With every ruling, justice ensues,
In justice's grasp, integrity's might,
In its decree, society ensues.

Here are four Terza Rima poems, 1 each about Change, Resilience, Gratitude & Forgiveness

Terza Rima on Change:

In change's dance, the world evolves anew,
A constant rhythm, shifting sands of time,
In every shift, old patterns bid adieu.

Through seasons' turn, in nature's prime,
Change weaves its tale, a story untold,
In its embrace, transformation's chime.

With every dawn, the future unfolds,
In change's grasp, uncertainty's reign,
In its wake, the old world molds.

Terza Rima on Resilience:

In resilience' embrace, strength is gained,
A force within, when trials assail,
In every storm, perseverance sustained.

Through hardships faced, in courage's travail,
Resilience blooms, like a sturdy oak,
In its embrace, spirits prevail.

With every setback, resilience awoke,
In resilience' grasp, adversity meets,
In its resolve, the soul bespoke.

Terza Rima on Gratitude:

In gratitude's embrace, the heart beats,
A chorus of thanks, in every breath,
In every blessing, gratitude greets.

Through moments small and in the face of death,
Gratitude shines, a beacon of light,
In its embrace, life finds its depth.

With every kindness, in day and night,
In gratitude's grasp, joy does arise,
In its embrace, hearts unite.

Terza Rima on Forgiveness:

In forgiveness' arms, wounds start to mend,
A healing balm for the soul's sore strife,
In every act, forgiveness does extend.

Through shattered dreams and the loss of life,
Forgiveness' grace, a path to peace,
In its embrace, resentment's knife.

With every step, bitterness does decrease,
In forgiveness' grasp, redemption's call,
In its release, hearts find release.

Here are four Terza Rima poems, 1 each about Longing, Belonging, Discovery & Wonder

Terza Rima on Longing:

In longing's grip, the heart yearns deep,
A restless ache that knows no end,
In every sigh, emotions sweep.

Through whispered dreams, desires tend,
Longing's embrace, a call to the unknown,
In its depths, hopes ascend.

With every moment, in silence sown,
In longing's grasp, the soul is led,
In its yearning, a journey is shown.

Terza Rima on Belonging:

In belonging's arms, the soul finds stead,
A sense of home, where hearts align,
In every bond, connections thread.

Through shared laughter and tears entwine,
Belonging's embrace, a warmth divine,
In its unity, spirits intertwine.

With every hug, love does refine,
In belonging's grasp, we find our place,
In its embrace, joy does enshrine.

Terza Rima on Discovery:

In discovery's quest, the mind defines,
A journey of knowledge, a path untrod,
In every step, new insights combine.

Through uncharted realms, where mysteries prod,
Discovery's embrace, a world unfurled,
In its depths, wonders are awed.

With every revelation, the spirit's whirl,
In discovery's grasp, curiosity fed,
In its unfolding, truth does swirl.

Terza Rima on Wonder:

In wonder's gaze, the spirit is stirred,
A sense of awe in nature's grand design,
In every vista, miracles occur.

Through starlit skies and oceans aligned,
Wonder's embrace, a magic spun,
In its beauty, the soul is inclined.

With every moment, life becomes one,
In wonder's grasp, the heart does ponder,
In its magnificence, the universe is spun.

Here are four Terza Rima poems, 1 each about Journey, Reflection, Harmony & Imagination

Terza Rima on Journey:

In journey's wake, the road unfolds ahead,
A path of twists and turns, of highs and lows,
In every step, new stories to be read.

Through valleys deep, where winds softly blow,
Journey's embrace, a traveler's delight,
In its wanderings, life's secrets to know.

With every mile, the soul takes flight,
In journey's grasp, adventure awaits,
In its unfolding, destinies unite.

Terza Rima on Reflection:

In reflection's pool, the mind takes flight,
A mirror to the soul, where thoughts entwine,
In every ponder, perspectives ignite.

Through moments stilled, where memories align,
Reflection's embrace, a journey within,
In its depths, truths intertwine.

With every insight, a new dawn to begin,
In reflection's grasp, the heart does mend,
In its introspection, wisdom does win.

Terza Rima on Harmony:

In harmony's embrace, the world does blend,
A symphony of souls, where peace resides,
In every chord, unity transcends.

Through melodies pure, where love abides,
Harmony's grace, a balm for the heart,
In its embrace, division subsides.

With every note, a new life does start,
In harmony's grasp, joy does abound,
In its rhythm, spirits impart.

Terza Rima on Imagination:

In imagination's realm, the mind confides,
A canvas vast, where dreams take shape,
In every creation, worlds collide.

Through flights of fancy, where fantasies drape,
Imagination's embrace, a realm untold,
In its wonders, possibilities escape.

With every vision, the story's unfold,
In imagination's grasp, the soul does soar,
In its embrace, realities are behold.

Here are four Terza Rima poems, 1 each about Silence, Laughter, Tears & Strength

Terza Rima on Silence:

In silence' shroud, the world finds reprieve,
A tranquil pause, where whispers cease,
In every hush, the soul finds relieve.

Through moments still, where troubles decrease,
Silence's embrace, a sanctuary serene,
In its depths, the mind finds release.

With every breath, the heart's song is seen,
In silence' grasp, clarity resides,
In its tranquility, the spirit convenes.

Terza Rima on Laughter:

In laughter's echo, joy takes flight,
A chorus of mirth, where hearts unite,
In every chuckle, spirits ignite.

Through shared humor, in the darkest night,
Laughter's embrace, a melody divine,
In its echoes, the soul finds light.

With every giggle, the world does shine,
In laughter's grasp, burdens dispel,
In its merriment, life intertwine.

Terza Rima on Tears:

In tears' cascade, emotions unbind,
A torrent of sorrow, where pain resigns,
In every drop, the soul's truth find.

Through rivers wept, where grief combines,
Tears' embrace, a catharsis complete,
In its release, the heart unwinds.

With every sob, the wounds retreat,
In tears' grasp, healing begins,
In its cleansing, the spirit greet.

Terza Rima on Strength:

In strength's fortress, resilience aligns,
A fortress of courage, where trials refine,
In every trial, resolve defines.

Through battles fought, where spirits incline,
Strength's embrace, a shield unbent,
In its fortitude, the soul's design.

With every challenge, resilience is sent,
In strength's grasp, adversity succumbs,
In its endurance, the spirit's ascent.

Here are four Terza Rima poems, 1 each about Vulnerability, Renewal, Acceptance & Mystery

Terza Rima on Vulnerability:

In vulnerability's embrace, truths unfurl,
A rawness exposed, where walls dissolve,
In every bared soul, emotions swirl.

Through moments laid bare, where hearts resolve,
Vulnerability's grip, a courage deep,
In its openness, authenticity evolves.

With every tear shed, emotions seep,
In vulnerability's grasp, connections mend,
In its honesty, souls find peace.

Terza Rima on Renewal:

In renewal's dawn, the world begins anew,
A sunrise of hope, where darkness yields,
In every bloom, life's colors accrue.

Through seasons turned, where nature wields,
Renewal's embrace, a cycle complete,
In its rebirth, destiny revealed.

With every leaf unfurled, the soul replete,
In renewal's grasp, the spirit renews,
In its transformation, the heart beats.

Terza Rima on Acceptance:

In acceptance' arms, the heart finds reprieve,
A surrender to fate, where struggles cease,
In every surrender, burdens relieve.

Through trials endured, where conflicts decrease,
Acceptance' embrace, a serenity deep,
In its release, the mind finds peace.

Every truth acknowledged, acceptance does seep,
In acceptance' grasp, harmony reigns,
In its wisdom, the soul does reap.

Terza Rima on Mystery:

In mystery's veil, the unknown weaves,
A tapestry of secrets, where whispers lie,
In every enigma, wonder perceives.

Through shadows cast, where truths belie,
Mystery's embrace, a curiosity untold,
In its allure, imagination thrives.

With every riddle solved, new mysteries unfold,
In mystery's grasp, the mind explores,
In its depths, the universe beholds.

Here are four Terza Rima poems, 1 each about Transformation, Eternity, Cosmos & Happiness

Terza Rima on Transformation:

In transformation's grasp, life finds its dance,
A journey of becoming, of growth and change,
In every shift, new opportunities enhance.

Through trials faced and obstacles rearrange,
Transformation's embrace, a metamorphosis complete,
In its evolution, destinies exchange.

With every step forward, the soul's heartbeat,
In transformation's grasp, the spirit is reborn,
In its renewal, the future does greet.

Terza Rima on Eternity:

In eternity's realm, time knows no bounds,
A timeless expanse, where moments reside,
In every breath, eternity surrounds.

Through the ages past and futures wide,
Eternity's embrace, an infinite scope,
In its vastness, destinies coincide.

With every heartbeat, the universe elope,
In eternity's grasp, souls intertwine,
In its endlessness, the cosmos cope.

Terza Rima on Cosmos:

In cosmos' vast expanse, wonders unfold,
A symphony of stars, of galaxies untold,
In every nebula, mysteries behold.

Through cosmic dance, where mysteries enfold,
Cosmos' embrace, a universe sublime,
In its majesty, the wonders behold.

With every constellation, a story's rhyme,
In cosmos' grasp, the heavens align,
In its infinity, the mysteries chime.

Terza Rima on Happiness:

In happiness' embrace, hearts alight,
A joyous symphony, where spirits soar,
In every laugh, happiness takes flight.

Through moments shared, where sorrows bore,
Happiness' embrace, a warmth divine,
In its radiance, the soul restores.

With every smile shared, the world align,
In happiness' grasp, love does bind,
In its abundance, the heart incline.

-:|:-•:*'''''*:•.-:|:-•**•-:|:-•:*'''''*:•:*'''''*:•.-:|:-•**•-:|:--:|:-•:*'''''*:•.-:|:- •**•-:|:-•:*'''''*:•:*'''''*:•.-:|:-•**•-:|:-

PANTOUM:

A poem with a specific structure of repeating lines, where the second and fourth lines of each stanza become the first and third lines of the next stanza.

Here are four Pantoum poems, 1 each about Love, Nature, Beauty & Time

Pantoum on Love:

In love's embrace, hearts intertwine,
A dance of passion under the moon's glow,
Whispers of affection like sweet wine,
In each other's arms, they feel the love flow.

A dance of passion under the moon's glow,
In every touch, emotions ignite,
In each other's arms, they feel the love flow,
Bound together, their love takes flight.

In every touch, emotions ignite,
Love's flame burns bright, fierce and true,
Bound together, their love takes flight,
In a world where only their hearts construe.

Love's flame burns bright, fierce and true,
Eternal flames that never wane,
In a world where only their hearts construe,
Their love, a melody, an everlasting refrain.

Pantoum on Nature:

In nature's embrace, serenity reigns,
Whispers of the wind through the trees,
In every sunrise, a new day gains,
Beneath the sky's vast tapestry.

Whispers of the wind through the trees,
Nature's symphony, a melody divine,
Beneath the sky's vast tapestry,
In every sunset, the day's decline.

Nature's symphony, a melody divine,
Each flower blooms in its own time,
In every sunset, the day's decline,
Stars twinkle in the evening prime.

Each flower blooms in its own time,
In every sunrise, a new day gains,
Stars twinkle in the evening prime,
In nature's embrace, serenity reigns.

Pantoum on Beauty:

Beauty, a treasure beyond measure,
In every sunrise, its splendor unfolds,
In fields of flowers, it finds its pleasure,
In cascading waterfalls, its story molds.

In every sunrise, its splendor unfolds,
A canvas painted with colors bright,
In cascading waterfalls, its story molds,
Each scene a marvel, a sheer delight.

A canvas painted with colors bright,
Beauty's essence, a sight to behold,
Each scene a marvel, a sheer delight,
In nature's wonders, its tale is told.

Beauty's essence, a sight to behold,
In fields of flowers, it finds its pleasure,
In nature's wonders, its tale is told,
Beauty, a treasure beyond measure.
Pantoum on Time:

Time, an ever-flowing stream,
In its currents, memories are spun,
With every tick, a new dream,
In the dance of seconds, life is begun.

In its currents, memories are spun,
Moments captured in its steady flow,
In the dance of seconds, life is begun,
Yet time's passage, we cannot slow.

Moments captured in its steady flow,
In each heartbeat, time whispers its song,
Yet time's passage, we cannot slow,
In its embrace, we all belong.

In each heartbeat, time whispers its song,
With every tick, a new dream,
In its embrace, we all belong,
Time, an ever-flowing stream.

Here are four Pantoum poems, 1 each about Death, Dreams, Hope & Despair

Pantoum on Death:

In death's embrace, the world stands still,
A journey to the unknown, beyond our sight,
The silence echoes, a solemn chill,
As shadows deepen into eternal night.

A journey to the unknown, beyond our sight,
The cycle of life, in its final call,
As shadows deepen into eternal night,
In death's embrace, we surrender all.

The cycle of life, in its final call,
The soul departs, to realms unseen,
In death's embrace, we surrender all,
To mysteries profound, where none have been.

The soul departs, to realms unseen,
Leaving behind memories and tears,
To mysteries profound, where none have been,
In death's embrace, all fears disappear.

Pantoum on Dreams:

Leaving behind memories and tears,
We journey forth on wings of dreams,
In the realm of sleep, free from fears,
Reality fades, and imagination gleams.

We journey forth on wings of dreams,
To lands of wonder and pure delight,
Reality fades, and imagination gleams,
In the silent hours of the night.

To lands of wonder and pure delight,
Where fantasies flourish and hopes renew,
In the silent hours of the night,
Dreams paint the sky in shades of blue.

Where fantasies flourish and hopes renew,
The dreamer wanders, unbound and free,
Dreams paint the sky in shades of blue,
In the realm of dreams, anything can be.

Pantoum on Hope:

The dreamer wanders, unbound and free,
In search of light amid darkest night,
Hope whispers softly, like a gentle plea,
Guiding the soul toward the morning light.

In search of light amid darkest night,
Through trials and tribulations, we press on,
Guiding the soul toward the morning light,
Hope's beacon shines until the dawn.

Through trials and tribulations, we press on,
Though the road is long and steep,
Hope's beacon shines until the dawn,
A promise of better days to keep.

Though the road is long and steep,
Hope whispers softly, like a gentle plea,
A promise of better days to keep,
The dreamer wanders, unbound and free.

Pantoum on Despair:

A promise of better days to keep,
Yet despair lingers in the heart's abyss,
In the depths of darkness, we silently weep,
As shadows cloak us in their cold embrace.

Yet despair lingers in the heart's abyss,
A heavy burden that weighs us down,
As shadows cloak us in their cold embrace,
We struggle to find our way around.

A heavy burden that weighs us down,
The silence echoes with our silent cries,
We struggle to find our way around,
Lost in despair's relentless ties.

The silence echoes with our silent cries,
In the depths of darkness, we silently weep,
Lost in despair's relentless ties,
A promise of better days to keep.

Here are four Pantoum poems, 1 each about Friendship, Loneliness, Memories & Music

Pantoum on Friendship:

In the garden of friendship, bonds are sown,
Each smile shared, a flower in bloom,
Through laughter and tears, we've grown,
In the warmth of camaraderie's room.

Each smile shared, a flower in bloom,
In the tapestry of life, friends weave,
In the warmth of camaraderie's room,
Together, our spirits interleave.

In the tapestry of life, friends weave,
Through thick and thin, they stand by,
Together, our spirits interleave,
Underneath the same sun and sky.

Through thick and thin, they stand by,
In the garden of friendship, bonds are sown,
Underneath the same sun and sky,
Memories cherished, eternally known.

Pantoum on Loneliness:

Underneath the same sun and sky,
Loneliness lingers like a shadow cast,
In solitude's embrace, we silently sigh,
Feeling the weight of time slipping fast.

Loneliness lingers like a shadow cast,
Echoes of emptiness, an endless chime,
Feeling the weight of time slipping fast,
Yearning for connection in the abyss of time.

Echoes of emptiness, an endless chime,
In the quiet, our voices seem small,
Yearning for connection in the abyss of time,
Longing for someone to hear our call.

In the quiet, our voices seem small,
In solitude's embrace, we silently sigh,
Longing for someone to hear our call,
Underneath the same sun and sky.

Pantoum on Memories:

In solitude's embrace, we silently sigh,
As memories flood in like a gentle stream,
Each cherished moment, a timeless tie,
In the tapestry of life, a recurring theme.

As memories flood in like a gentle stream,
We relive the laughter, the tears, the pain,
In the tapestry of life, a recurring theme,
Etched in our hearts, where they shall remain.

We relive the laughter, the tears, the pain,
Through the corridors of time, memories roam,
Etched in our hearts, where they shall remain,
A testament to the life we've known.

Through the corridors of time, memories roam,
Each cherished moment, a timeless tie,
A testament to the life we've known,
In solitude's embrace, we silently sigh.

Pantoum on Music:

Each cherished moment, a timeless tie,
Music fills the air, a melody divine,
In every note, emotions amplify,
Weaving a tale, in rhythm and rhyme.

Music fills the air, a melody divine,
Soothing the soul, stirring the heart,
Weaving a tale, in rhythm and rhyme,
In its embrace, troubles depart.

Soothing the soul, stirring the heart,
Through melodies sweet, we find release,
In its embrace, troubles depart,
And we find solace, a sense of peace.

Here are four Pantoum poems, 1 each about Art, Inspiration, Creativity & Courage

Pantoum on Art:

In strokes of color, emotions take flight,
Canvas whispers secrets, stories untold,
Each brushstroke a dance, in the artist's light,
Capturing beauty, in hues bold.

Canvas whispers secrets, stories untold,
Through the artist's eyes, the world's revealed,
Capturing beauty, in hues bold,
In every stroke, passion's zeal.

Through the artist's eyes, the world's revealed,
In every masterpiece, a soul's reflection,
In every stroke, passion's zeal,
Artistry blooms, defying perfection.

In every masterpiece, a soul's reflection,
Each brushstroke a dance, in the artist's light,
Artistry blooms, defying perfection,
In strokes of color, emotions take flight.

Pantoum on Inspiration:

In whispers of the wind, inspiration flows,
A gentle muse that sparks the creative fire,
In dreams that dance, where imagination grows,
Ideas take flight, reaching ever higher.

A gentle muse that sparks the creative fire,
In every moment, inspiration's song,
Ideas take flight, reaching ever higher,
In the depths of the soul, where dreams belong.

In every moment, inspiration's song,
In nature's beauty, in laughter's embrace,
In the depths of the soul, where dreams belong,
Inspiration blooms, leaving its trace.

In nature's beauty, in laughter's embrace,
A symphony of creativity, courage to impart,
Inspiration blooms, leaving its trace,
In whispers of the wind, stirring the heart.

Pantoum on Creativity:

In the dance of words, creativity abounds,
A symphony of thoughts, in the poet's mind,
In every verse, a universe unfounds,
Imagination's canvas, unconfined.

A symphony of thoughts, in the poet's mind,
Each line a brushstroke, on the page's expanse,
Imagination's canvas, unconfined,
In the poet's hands, worlds enhance.

Each line a brushstroke, on the page's expanse,
In the artist's studio, visions take shape,
In the poet's hands, worlds enhance,
In every creation, a piece of escape.

In the artist's studio, visions take shape,
A testament to the power of the human spirit,
In every creation, a piece of escape,
In the dance of words, creativity's merit.

Pantoum on Courage:

In the face of fear, courage takes its stand,
A quiet strength that refuses to yield,
In every step forward, a heart expands,
Bravery forged in the battlefield.

A quiet strength that refuses to yield,
In the depths of uncertainty, courage does rise,
Bravery forged in the battlefield,
In the pursuit of truth, in the quest for the wise.

In the depths of uncertainty, courage does rise,
Each obstacle faced, a test of resolve,
In the pursuit of truth, in the quest for the wise,
In the heart of adversity, courage evolves.

Each obstacle faced, a test of resolve,
In the face of fear, courage takes its stand,
In the heart of adversity, courage evolves,
A beacon of hope in a world unplanned.

Here are four Pantoum poems, 1 each about Faith, Doubt, Solitude & Joy

Pantoum on Faith:

In the darkest night, faith guides the way,
A beacon of hope, amidst the storm's roar,
Through trials and tribulations, come what may,
In faith's embrace, the soul finds its core.

A beacon of hope, amidst the storm's roar,
In the depths of despair, faith prevails,
In faith's embrace, the soul finds its core,
Through valleys low and mountaintops, it sails.

In the depths of despair, faith prevails,
An unwavering belief in the unseen,
Through valleys low and mountaintops, it sails,
In the heart's sanctuary, where dreams convene.

An unwavering belief in the unseen,
In the power of love, and the light of grace,
In the heart's sanctuary, where dreams convene,
In the darkest night, faith guides the way.

Pantoum on Doubt:

In the quiet of the night, doubts arise,
A whispering voice, questioning the path,
Through shadows cast, where truth belies,
Doubt's grip tightens, invoking its wrath.

A whispering voice, questioning the path,
In uncertainty's embrace, doubts entwine,
Doubt's grip tightens, invoking its wrath,
In the labyrinth of fear, doubts define.

In uncertainty's embrace, doubts entwine,
Each hesitation a step backward taken,
In the labyrinth of fear, doubts define,
In the depths of doubt, faith is shaken.

Each hesitation a step backward taken,
Through the fog of doubt, clarity sought,
In the depths of doubt, faith is shaken,
Yet in facing doubt, strength is wrought.

Pantoum on Solitude:

In the solitude of night, silence reigns,
A symphony of stillness, where thoughts roam,
Through the echoes of time, in quiet strains,
Solitude's embrace, a sacred home.

A symphony of stillness, where thoughts roam,
In the sanctuary of the soul's retreat,
Solitude's embrace, a sacred home,
In the gentle rhythm of the heart's beat.

In the sanctuary of the soul's retreat,
Reflections dance in the moon's soft glow,
In the gentle rhythm of the heart's beat,
In solitude's embrace, serenity's flow.

Reflections dance in the moon's soft glow,
In the solitude of night, silence reigns,
In solitude's embrace, serenity's flow,
Through the echoes of time, in quiet strains.

Pantoum on Joy:

In the laughter of children, joy abounds,
A melody of innocence, pure and bright,
Through the ups and downs, joy surrounds,
In the heart's jubilee, a radiant light.

A melody of innocence, pure and bright,
In every smile shared, happiness found,
In the heart's jubilee, a radiant light,
In joy's embrace, the soul is unbound.

In every smile shared, happiness found,
Through life's journey, in moments grand,
In joy's embrace, the soul is unbound,
In the tapestry of life, joy's strand.

Through life's journey, in moments grand,
In the laughter of children, joy abounds,
In the tapestry of life, joy's strand,
Through the ups and downs, joy surrounds.

Here are four Pantoum poems, 1 each about Sorrow, Childhood, Wisdom & Innocence

Pantoum on Sorrow:

In the depths of sorrow, shadows dwell,
A heavy burden, weighing on the soul,
Each tear shed, tolls a mournful bell,
In the heart's abyss, where sorrows roll.

A heavy burden, weighing on the soul,
Memories haunt, like ghosts in the night,
In the heart's abyss, where sorrows roll,
In the silence, grief takes its flight.

Memories haunt, like ghosts in the night,
Each ache a reminder, of loss endured,
In the silence, grief takes its flight,
In sorrow's embrace, hope obscured.

Each ache a reminder, of loss endured,
Yet in sorrow's depths, resilience found,
In sorrow's embrace, hope obscured,
From ashes of pain, strength does abound.

Yet in sorrow's depths, resilience found,
Each tear shed, tolls a mournful bell,
From ashes of pain, strength does abound,
In the depths of sorrow, shadows dwell.

Pantoum on Childhood:

In the garden of youth, dreams take flight,
Imagination blooms in the child's mind,
Each day a canvas, a world of delight,
In innocence's embrace, memories entwined.

Imagination blooms in the child's mind,
In every laughter, in every game,
In innocence's embrace, memories entwined,
In the tapestry of childhood, joys aflame.

In every laughter, in every game,
In the world of make-believe, fantasies arise,
In the tapestry of childhood, joys aflame,
In the twinkle of innocent eyes.

In the world of make-believe, fantasies arise,
Each moment cherished, in the heart's embrace,
In the twinkle of innocent eyes,
Childhood's magic, a timeless grace.

Each moment cherished, in the heart's embrace,
Each day a canvas, a world of delight,
Childhood's magic, a timeless grace,
In the garden of youth, dreams take flight.

Pantoum on Wisdom:

In the halls of wisdom, truths are spoken,
A legacy passed from age to age,
Each lesson learned, each vow unbroken,
In the scholar's quest, wisdom's stage.

A legacy passed from age to age,
In the silence of contemplation, insights arise,
In the scholar's quest, wisdom's stage,
In the depths of knowledge, the spirit flies.

In the silence of contemplation, insights arise,
Each word penned, a beacon of light,
In the depths of knowledge, the spirit flies,
In wisdom's embrace, darkness takes flight.
Each word penned, a beacon of light,
In the halls of wisdom, truths are spoken,
In wisdom's embrace, darkness takes flight,
Each lesson learned, each vow unbroken.

Pantoum on Innocence:

In the heart of innocence, purity resides,
A gentle grace, untouched by time,
Each smile shared, in innocence abides,
In the soul's sanctuary, love does chime.

A gentle grace, untouched by time,
In laughter's echo, innocence found,
In the soul's sanctuary, love does chime,
In innocence's embrace, joy does abound.

In laughter's echo, innocence found,
Each embrace a haven, each touch divine,
In innocence's embrace, joy does abound,
In the garden of innocence, love entwined.

Each embrace a haven, each touch divine,
In the heart of innocence, purity resides,
In the garden of innocence, love entwined,
Each smile shared, in innocence abides.

Here are four Pantoum poems, 1 each about Passion, Serenity, Freedom & Justice

Pantoum on Passion:

In the fire of passion, hearts collide,
A fierce intensity, burning bright,
Desires ignited, cannot be denied,
In the dance of love, emotions take flight.

A fierce intensity, burning bright,
In every touch, sparks ignite,
In the dance of love, emotions take flight,
Passion's flames, a guiding light.

In every touch, sparks ignite,
Fueling the flames, with fervent desire,
Passion's flames, a guiding light,
In the heat of passion, souls aspire.

Fueling the flames, with fervent desire,
In the fire of passion, hearts collide,
In the heat of passion, souls aspire,
Desires ignited, cannot be denied.

Pantoum on Serenity:

In the stillness of dawn, serenity reigns,
A peaceful calm, where the soul finds rest,
Through whispered breezes and gentle rains,
In nature's embrace, we are truly blessed.

A peaceful calm, where the soul finds rest,
In the quiet moments, the heart's sigh,
In nature's embrace, we are truly blessed,
Underneath the vast and endless sky.

In the quiet moments, the heart's sigh,
In serenity's embrace, worries dissolve,
Underneath the vast and endless sky,
In the tranquil depths, problems resolve.

In serenity's embrace, worries dissolve,
Through whispered breezes and gentle rains,
In the tranquil depths, problems resolve,
In the stillness of dawn, serenity reigns.

Pantoum on Freedom:

In the open sky, freedom takes flight,
A boundless expanse, where dreams soar high,
Through windswept plains and starlit night,
In the pursuit of liberty, we defy.

A boundless expanse, where dreams soar high,
In every heartbeat, the spirit yearns,
In the pursuit of liberty, we defy,
In freedom's embrace, the soul discerns.

In every heartbeat, the spirit yearns,
For the taste of freedom, sweet and pure,
In freedom's embrace, the soul discerns,
The essence of life, unchained and sure.

For the taste of freedom, sweet and pure,
Through windswept plains and starlit night,
The essence of life, unchained and sure,
In the open sky, freedom takes flight.

Pantoum on Justice:

In the halls of justice, truth prevails,
A beacon of fairness, guiding the way,
Through the echoes of voices, justice sails,
In the pursuit of equality, come what may.

A beacon of fairness, guiding the way,
In the scales of justice, balance found,
In the pursuit of equality, come what may,
Injustice challenged, its reign unbound.

In the scales of justice, balance found,
Each verdict rendered, a step toward right,
Injustice challenged, its reign unbound,
In the fight for justice, we unite.

Each verdict rendered, a step toward right,
In the halls of justice, truth prevails,
In the fight for justice, we unite,
Through the echoes of voices, justice sails.

Here are four Pantoum poems, 1 each about Change, Resilience, Gratitude & Forgiveness

Pantoum on Change:

In the dance of life, change takes its course,
A river flowing, ever shifting its path,
Through seasons of growth, with unwavering force,
In change's embrace, we find our aftermath.

A river flowing, ever shifting its path,
In every twist and turn, new horizons appear,
In change's embrace, we find our aftermath,
Embracing transformation, overcoming fear.

In every twist and turn, new horizons appear,
Adapting to the rhythms, the ebb and flow,
Embracing transformation, overcoming fear,
In change's embrace, we learn to let go.

Adapting to the rhythms, the ebb and flow,
Change brings challenges, yet also opportunities,
In change's embrace, we learn to let go,
Navigating the currents, with steadfast unity.

Change brings challenges, yet also opportunities,
Through evolution's journey, we find our way,
Navigating the currents, with steadfast unity,
In the dance of life, change takes its course.

Pantoum on Resilience:

In the face of adversity, resilience shines,
A strength forged in the fires of trial,
Through storms endured and mountains climbed,
In resilience's embrace, we find our revival.

A strength forged in the fires of trial,
In every setback, a lesson learned,
In resilience's embrace, we find our revival,
Through perseverance, our spirits yearned.

In every setback, a lesson learned,
In the depths of despair, courage found,
Through perseverance, our spirits yearned,
In resilience's fortress, hope resounds.

In the depths of despair, courage found,
A beacon of light in the darkest of days,
In resilience's fortress, hope resounds,
In the face of adversity, we find our ways.

A beacon of light in the darkest of days,
Through storms endured and mountains climbed,
In the face of adversity, we find our ways,
In the embrace of resilience, strength defined.

Pantoum on Gratitude:

In the tapestry of life, gratitude weaves,
A thread of appreciation, for blessings received,
Through moments of joy and times of reprieve,
In gratitude's embrace, hearts are relieved.

A thread of appreciation, for blessings received,
In the simplest pleasures, gratitude blooms,
In gratitude's embrace, hearts are relieved,
In the garden of thankfulness, love resumes.

In the simplest pleasures, gratitude blooms,
For every sunrise and each breath taken,
In the garden of thankfulness, love resumes,
In the beauty of life, gratitude awakens.

For every sunrise and each breath taken,
Through trials faced and victories won,
In the beauty of life, gratitude awakens,
In gratitude's embrace, we are as one.

Through trials faced and victories won,
A heart full of thanks, a soul at peace,
In gratitude's embrace, we are as one,
In the tapestry of life, gratitude weaves.

Pantoum on Forgiveness:

In the journey of healing, forgiveness begins,
A release of burdens, a letting go of pain,
Through wounds of the past, where darkness thins,
In forgiveness's embrace, hearts regain.

A release of burdens, a letting go of pain,
In the depths of forgiveness, freedom found,
In forgiveness's embrace, hearts regain,
In the light of reconciliation, love resound.

In the depths of forgiveness, freedom found,
As forgiveness flows, grace does ensue,
In the light of reconciliation, love resound,
In the act of forgiveness, redemption's cue.

As forgiveness flows, grace does ensue,
Through the power of pardon, wounds heal,
In the act of forgiveness, redemption's cue,
In forgiveness's embrace, hearts reveal.

Through the power of pardon, wounds heal,
In the journey of healing, forgiveness begins,
In forgiveness's embrace, hearts reveal,
Through wounds of the past, where darkness thins.

Here are four Pantoum poems, 1 each about Longing, Belonging, Discovery & Wonder

Pantoum on Longing:

In the quiet of night, longing takes flight,
A yearning for what's beyond our reach,
Through starlit skies, dreams ignite,
In the depths of longing, hearts beseech.

A yearning for what's beyond our reach,
Echoes of desire in the whispers of wind,
In the depths of longing, hearts beseech,
For the touch of what fate has thinned.

Echoes of desire in the whispers of wind,
In the tapestry of longing, hopes entwine,
For the touch of what fate has thinned,
In the passage of time, longing aligns.

In the tapestry of longing, hopes entwine,
Through the ache of distance, love's embrace,
In the passage of time, longing aligns,
In the quiet of night, seeking solace.

Through the ache of distance, love's embrace,
Through starlit skies, dreams ignite,
In the quiet of night, seeking solace,
In the depths of longing, hearts take flight.

Pantoum on Belonging:

In the tapestry of life, threads entwine,
A symphony of souls, in harmony's sway,
Through bonds forged, hearts align,
In the circle of belonging, we find our way.

A symphony of souls, in harmony's sway,
In the warmth of connection, spirits ignite,
In the circle of belonging, we find our way,
In the embrace of kinship, love takes flight.

In the warmth of connection, spirits ignite,
In the sanctuary of belonging, fears subside,
In the embrace of kinship, love takes flight,
In the chorus of belonging, hearts abide.

In the sanctuary of belonging, fears subside,
Through the dance of togetherness, unity's gleam,
In the chorus of belonging, hearts abide,
In the tapestry of life, a shared dream.

Through the dance of togetherness, unity's gleam,
Through bonds forged, hearts align,
In the tapestry of life, a shared dream,
A symphony of souls, in harmony's sway.

Pantoum on Discovery:

In the depths of exploration, wonders unfold,
A journey of curiosity, paths untold,
Through uncharted waters, new stories are told,
In the realm of discovery, mysteries hold.

A journey of curiosity, paths untold,
In the pursuit of knowledge, the mind's quest,
In the realm of discovery, mysteries hold,
In the quest for truth, we are blessed.

In the pursuit of knowledge, the mind's quest,
In the whispers of exploration, secrets reveal,
In the quest for truth, we are blessed,
In the heart of discovery, awe we feel.

In the whispers of exploration, secrets reveal,
In the tapestry of discovery, wonders unfold,
In the heart of discovery, awe we feel,
A journey of curiosity, paths untold.

Pantoum on Wonder:

In the silence of night, wonder prevails,
A canvas of stars, a universe untamed,
Through galaxies vast, imagination sails,
In the wonder of creation, hearts are inflamed.

A canvas of stars, a universe untamed,
In the mysteries of cosmos, magic resides,
In the wonder of creation, hearts are inflamed,
In the dance of existence, wonder abides.

In the mysteries of cosmos, magic resides,
Through the wonders of nature, beauty untold,
In the dance of existence, wonder abides,
In the song of the universe, mysteries unfold.

Through the wonders of nature, beauty untold,
In the silence of night, wonder prevails,
In the song of the universe, mysteries unfold,
A canvas of stars, a universe untamed.

Here are four Pantoum poems, 1 each about Journey, Reflection, Harmony & Imagination

Pantoum on Journey:

In the labyrinth of life, the journey begins,
A path winding through valleys and peaks,
Through trials and triumphs, losses and wins,
In the journey's embrace, destiny seeks.

A path winding through valleys and peaks,
Each step forward, a story unfolds,
In the journey's embrace, destiny seeks,
In the tapestry of time, tales retold.

Each step forward, a story unfolds,
In the dance of adventure, hearts ignite,
In the tapestry of time, tales retold,
In the pursuit of dreams, stars alight.

In the dance of adventure, hearts ignite,
Through the unknown realms, courage impels,
In the pursuit of dreams, stars alight,
In the journey's rhythm, the soul dwells.

Through the unknown realms, courage impels,
Through trials and triumphs, losses and wins,
In the journey's rhythm, the soul dwells,
In the labyrinth of life, the journey begins.

Pantoum on Reflection:

In the stillness of night, reflections arise,
A mirror to the soul, where truths are revealed,
Through echoes of memories, joys and cries,
In the depths of reflection, wisdom's sealed.

A mirror to the soul, where truths are revealed,
In the quiet moments, the mind's echo chamber,
In the depths of reflection, wisdom's sealed,
In the pool of introspection, hearts remember.

In the quiet moments, the mind's echo chamber,
Each thought a ripple, in the pond of thought,
In the pool of introspection, hearts remember,
In the labyrinth of self, truths sought.

Each thought a ripple, in the pond of thought,
Through echoes of memories, joys and cries,
In the labyrinth of self, truths sought,
In the stillness of night, reflections arise.

Pantoum on Harmony:

In the symphony of life, harmony resounds,
A melody of souls, in perfect accord,
Through chords of love, in heart's surrounds,
In the embrace of unity, voices soared.

A melody of souls, in perfect accord,
In the dance of connection, spirits entwine,
In the embrace of unity, voices soared,
In the choir of humanity, all combine.

In the dance of connection, spirits entwine,
Through the rhythm of empathy, hearts align,
In the choir of humanity, all combine,
In the symphony of life, where destinies intertwine.

Through the rhythm of empathy, hearts align,
A tapestry of diversity, colors blend,
In the symphony of life, where destinies intertwine,
In the mosaic of existence, all transcend.

A tapestry of diversity, colors blend,
Through chords of love, in heart's surrounds,
In the mosaic of existence, all transcend,
In the symphony of life, harmony resounds.

Pantoum on Imagination:

In the playground of the mind, imagination soars,
A canvas of dreams, where fantasies unfurl,
Through portals of possibility, new worlds explore,
In the realm of creativity, minds swirl.

A canvas of dreams, where fantasies unfurl,
In the tapestry of thought, ideas ignite,
In the realm of creativity, minds swirl,
In the dance of imagination, wings take flight.

In the tapestry of thought, ideas ignite,Through the kaleidoscope of vision, colors blend,
In the dance of imagination, wings take flight,
In the realm of wonder, boundaries bend.

Through the kaleidoscope of vision, colors blend,
A symphony of inspiration, in the artist's hand,
In the realm of wonder, boundaries bend,
In the playground of the mind, where dreams expand.

Here are four Pantoum poems, 1 each about Silence, Laughter, Tears & Strength

Silence:
In the quiet of the night, silence reigns,
Whispers of dreams in the silent lanes.
Thoughts like shadows, they ebb and wane,
In the quiet of the night, silence reigns.

A gentle hush blankets the land,
In solitude, hearts softly expand.
Whispers of dreams in the silent lanes,
A gentle hush blankets the land.

The stillness speaks, in subtle ways,
In silence, the soul finds its maze.
In solitude, hearts softly expand,
The stillness speaks, in subtle ways.

Amidst the noise, a tranquil sea,
In silence, the truth is set free.
In silence, the soul finds its maze,
Amidst the noise, a tranquil sea.

Laughter:
In the echo of laughter, joy unfurls,
A melody that dances, whirls and swirls.
Hearts uplifted, in laughter's twirls,
In the echo of laughter, joy unfurls.

Tears of mirth, like pearls they gleam,
In laughter's embrace, a timeless dream.
A melody that dances, whirls and swirls,
Tears of mirth, like pearls they gleam.

In shared moments, bonds are sealed,
Laughter, a language universally appealed.
In laughter's embrace, a timeless dream,
In shared moments, bonds are sealed.

Through life's trials, laughter's light,
Guiding us through the darkest night.
Laughter, a language universally appealed,
Through life's trials, laughter's light.

Tears:
In the quiet corner, tears flow free,
A river of emotions, vast as the sea.
Each drop a story, of what used to be,
In the quiet corner, tears flow free.

Sorrow's symphony, a haunting tune,
Echoes of loss in the tear-filled room.
A river of emotions, vast as the sea,
Sorrow's symphony, a haunting tune.

Yet tears cleanse the soul, they say,
Washing away pain, in their own way.
Echoes of loss in the tear-filled room,
Yet tears cleanse the soul, they say.

From tears of sorrow, strength does rise,
A phoenix from ashes, reaching the skies.
Washing away pain, in their own way,
From tears of sorrow, strength does rise.

Strength:
In the heart of adversity, strength prevails,
A beacon of hope, as the tempest hails.
Through trials and tribulations, it unveils,
In the heart of adversity, strength prevails.

Roots run deep, in the face of the storm,
Resilience blossoms, in its true form.
A beacon of hope, as the tempest hails,
Roots run deep, in the face of the storm.

With each challenge, a lesson learned,
In the forge of struggle, character earned.
Resilience blossoms, in its true form,
With each challenge, a lesson learned.

In the quiet moments, courage found,
A fortress of resolve, standing firm and sound.
In the forge of struggle, character earned,
In the quiet moments, courage found.

Here are four Pantoum poems, 1 each about Vulnerability, Renewal, Acceptance & Mystery

Vulnerability:
In moments of vulnerability, we find our strength,
Exposed to the world, we lay bare our souls,
Through cracks in the armor, we traverse great lengths,
In the openness, authenticity unrolls.

Exposed to the world, we lay bare our souls,
Embracing flaws, we discover our worth,
In the openness, authenticity unrolls,
Through vulnerability, we find rebirth.

Embracing flaws, we discover our worth,
For it's in our imperfections, beauty resides,
Through vulnerability, we find rebirth,
In the courage to be seen, the heart abides.

For it's in our imperfections, beauty resides,
In vulnerability's embrace, we learn to fly,
In the courage to be seen, the heart abides,
For it's through vulnerability, we truly thrive.

Renewal:
In the cycle of life, renewal's song resounds,
Old leaves fall, making way for the new,
Through seasons of change, life's essence astounds,
In the dance of rebirth, the spirit imbues.

Old leaves fall, making way for the new,
Nature's symphony of growth and decay,
In the dance of rebirth, the spirit imbues,
As each dawn heralds a brand-new day.

Nature's symphony of growth and decay,
Teaches us the art of letting go,
As each dawn heralds a brand-new day,
Renewal whispers, gently bestowing.

Teaches us the art of letting go,
As we shed the old, embracing the unknown,
Renewal whispers, gently bestowing,
In the cycle of life, the seeds are sown.

Acceptance:
In the embrace of acceptance, we find peace,
Letting go of resistance, we release our hold,
Surrendering to what is, our anxieties cease,
In the stillness of acceptance, truths unfold.

Letting go of resistance, we release our hold,
Flowing with the currents, rather than fight,
In the stillness of acceptance, truths unfold,
In the serenity of surrender, we find our light.

Flowing with the currents, rather than fight,
We navigate the waters with grace and ease,
In the serenity of surrender, we find our light,
In acceptance's embrace, our souls find ease.

We navigate the waters with grace and ease,
Letting life unfold as it will,
In acceptance's embrace, our souls find ease,
For in acceptance, we find peace, still.

Mystery:
In the depths of the unknown, mystery lies,
A tapestry of secrets waiting to be unfurled,
In the shadows and whispers, imagination flies,
As we explore the enigma of the world.

A tapestry of secrets waiting to be unfurled,
In the dance of the cosmos, stars shimmer bright,
As we explore the enigma of the world,
In the labyrinth of mysteries, we find our light.

In the dance of the cosmos, stars shimmer bright,
Guiding us through the darkness, towards the unknown,
In the labyrinth of mysteries, we find our light,
In the quest for answers, our curiosity is shown.

Guiding us through the darkness, towards the unknown,
Mystery beckons, calling us to explore,
In the quest for answers, our curiosity is shown,
For in the mysteries of life, there's always more.

Here are four Pantoum poems, 1 each about Transformation, Eternity, Cosmos & Happiness

Transformation:
In the cocoon, the caterpillar dreams,
Transformation whispers, unseen seams.
Metamorphosis, a silent scheme,
In the cocoon, the caterpillar dreams.

From earthbound roots, the sapling grows,
Reaching for skies, where new life flows.
Metamorphosis, a silent scheme,
From earthbound roots, the sapling grows.

The butterfly emerges, wings unfurled,
A symphony of colors, the world twirled.
Reaching for skies, where new life flows,
The butterfly emerges, wings unfurled.

From humble beginnings, beauty unfurls,
Transformation's dance, in endless swirls.
A symphony of colors, the world twirled,
From humble beginnings, beauty unfurls.

Eternity:
In the infinite expanse, stars ignite,
Eternity whispers, in the cosmic night.
Time's relentless march, in its flight,
In the infinite expanse, stars ignite.

Through the ages, galaxies spin,
In the cosmic dance, where dreams begin.
Eternity whispers, in the cosmic night,
Through the ages, galaxies spin.

Constellations shimmer, tales to tell,
Echoes of eternity, in their spell.
In the cosmic dance, where dreams begin,
Constellations shimmer, tales to tell.

In the vastness of space, the soul takes flight,
Eternity's embrace, in the cosmic light.
Echoes of eternity, in their spell,
In the vastness of space, the soul takes flight.

Cosmos:
In the depths of the cosmos, mysteries hide,
A tapestry of stars, where wonders abide.
Celestial ballet, in the universe wide,
In the depths of the cosmos, mysteries hide.

Planets dance in orbits, a cosmic waltz,
Infinite galaxies, where dreams exalt.
A tapestry of stars, where wonders abide,
Planets dance in orbits, a cosmic waltz.

Nebulas swirl, in hues of blue and gold,
A cosmic symphony, untold.
Infinite galaxies, where dreams exalt,
Nebulas swirl, in hues of blue and gold.

In the cosmic ballet, time takes flight,
A journey through space, in endless night.
A cosmic symphony, untold,
In the cosmic ballet, time takes flight.

Happiness:
In the laughter of children, joy blooms,
Happiness whispers, in every room.
Hearts aglow, dispelling gloom,
In the laughter of children, joy blooms.

Sunlight dances on fields of green,
Nature's embrace, a tranquil scene.
Happiness whispers, in every room,
Sunlight dances on fields of green.

In the embrace of loved ones, warmth found,
A symphony of love, profound.
Nature's embrace, a tranquil scene,
In the embrace of loved ones, warmth found.

With gratitude in hearts, spirits rise,
A chorus of happiness, fills the skies.
A symphony of love, profound,
With gratitude in hearts, spirits rise.

-:|:-•:*'''''*:•.-:|:-•**•-:|:-•:*'''''*:•:*'''''*:•.-:|:-•**•-:|:--:|:-•:*'''''*:•.-:|:- •**•-:|:-•:*'''''*:•:*'''''*:•.-:|:-•**•-:|:-

SESTAIN:

A six-line poem with a specific rhyme scheme, often used to explore a single theme or idea.

-:|:-•:*'''''*:•.-:|:-•**•-:|:-•:*''''''*:•:*'''''*:•.-:|:-•**•-:|:--:|:-•:*'''''*:•.-:|:- •**•-:|:-•:*'''''*:•:*'''''*:•.-:|:-•**•-:|:-

Here are four Sestain poems, 1 each about Love, Nature, Beauty & Time

Love:
In tender moments, hearts entwine,
Love's gentle touch, a sacred sign.
In every kiss, where souls align,
Love's eternal flame, divine.

Nature:
In forests deep, where secrets hide,
Nature's whispers, in every stride.
In every sunset, where colors glide,
Nature's beauty, untied.

Beauty:
In fleeting moments, grace reveals,
Beauty's essence, the heart appeals.
In every sunrise, where light conceals,
Beauty's allure, it heals.

Time:
In ticking clocks, the seconds chime,
Time's relentless march, an endless climb.
In every memory, where echoes mime,
Time's passage, sublime.

Here are four Sestain poems, 1 each about Death, Dreams, Hope & Despair

Death:
In final breaths, the spirit flies,
Death's embrace, where sorrow lies.
In every goodbye, where tears arise,
Death's mystery, it defies.

Dreams:
In slumber's realm, the mind takes flight,
Dreams' ethereal dance, in the night.
In every vision, where hopes ignite,
Dreams' promise, shining bright.

Hope:
In darkest nights, a glimmer gleams,
Hope's beacon, in the heart's extremes.
In every prayer, where faith redeems,
Hope's promise, it beams.

Despair:
In shadows deep, the soul succumbs,
Despair's grip, where darkness numbs.
In every cry, where silence hums,
Despair's void, it drums.

Here are four Sestain poems, 1 each about Friendship, Loneliness, Memories & Music

Friendship:
In laughter shared, bonds grow strong,
Friendship's embrace, where hearts belong.
In every adventure, where memories throng,
Friendship's melody, a lifelong song.

Loneliness:
In solitude's embrace, the heart retreats,
Loneliness's echo, where silence greets.
In every tear, where sadness meets,
Loneliness's burden, it depletes.

Memories:
In faded photographs, moments capture,
Memories' tapestry, where dreams enrapture.
In every smile, where hearts recapture,
Memories' treasure, ever sure.

Music:
In melodies sweet, the soul takes flight,
Music's symphony, in the heart's light.
In every note, where emotions ignite,
Music's harmony, pure delight.

Here are four Sestain poems, 1 each about Art, Inspiration, Creativity & Courage

Art:
In strokes of passion, creation's call,
Art's expression, where spirits enthrall.
In every canvas, where visions sprawl,
Art's beauty, enthralled.

Inspiration:
In whispers soft, ideas ignite,
Inspiration's spark, in darkest night.
In every muse, where thoughts take flight,
Inspiration's flame, burning bright.

Creativity:
In boundless realms, imagination soars,
Creativity's canvas, the mind explores.
In every creation, where vision pours,
Creativity's magic, it endures.

Courage:
In trembling hearts, bravery stands tall,
Courage's strength, where fears befall.
In every battle, where obstacles appall,
Courage's triumph, over all.

Here are four Sestain poems, 1 each about Faith, Doubt, Solitude & Joy

Faith:
In darkest night, a beacon shines,
Faith's guiding light, through trials and binds.
In every prayer, where hope entwines,
Faith's steadfastness, the soul aligns.

Doubt:
In shadows cast, the mind's lament,
Doubt's whispers, a constant torment.
In every question, where thoughts are spent,
Doubt's uncertainty, a turbulent descent.

Solitude:
In silent realms, the soul finds peace,
Solitude's embrace, where worries cease.
In every moment, where self-release,
Solitude's sanctuary, a gentle fleece.

Joy:
In laughter's echo, hearts unite,
Joy's melody, a symphony bright.
In every smile, where spirits take flight,
Joy's abundance, a source of light.

Here are four Sestain poems, 1 each about Sorrow, Childhood, Wisdom & Innocence

Sorrow:
In tears that fall, emotions sway,
Sorrow's burden, in shades of gray.
In every ache, where hearts betray,
Sorrow's lament, in disarray.

Childhood:
In innocent days, where dreams are spun,
Childhood's magic, beneath the sun.
In every memory, where laughter won,
Childhood's bliss, forever young.

Wisdom:
In age's embrace, the mind's ascent,
Wisdom's counsel, with years well spent.
In every lesson, where truths are meant,
Wisdom's enlightenment, heaven-sent.

Innocence:
In purity's glow, hearts entwine,
Innocence's grace, a treasure divine.
In every gaze, where virtues align,
Innocence's innocence, ever fine.

Here are four Sestain poems, 1 each about Passion, Serenity, Freedom & Justice

Passion:
In fiery hearts, desires ignite,
Passion's fervor, a beacon bright.
In every touch, where souls take flight,
Passion's intensity, pure delight.

Serenity:
In tranquil waters, the spirit calms,
Serenity's embrace, in peaceful balms.
In every breath, where tranquility alms,
Serenity's grace, the soul embalms.

Freedom:
In open skies, the soul takes flight,
Freedom's wings, in boundless height.
In every choice, where paths ignite,
Freedom's liberation, pure and right.

Justice:
In scales of truth, fairness prevails,
Justice's balance, where morality trails.
In every verdict, where justice hails,
Justice's righteousness, never fails.

Here are four Sestain poems, 1 each about Change, Resilience, Gratitude & Forgiveness

Change:
In shifting tides, the world transforms,
Change's rhythm, in constant norms.
In every shift, where fate conforms,
Change's evolution, life reforms.

Resilience:
In trials endured, the spirit prevails,
Resilience's strength, where courage sails.
In every setback, where hope avails,
Resilience's endurance, never pales.

Gratitude:
In thankful hearts, blessings flow,
Gratitude's essence, in every glow.
In every moment, where thanks bestow,
Gratitude's abundance, in life's flow.

Forgiveness:
In hearts unburdened, forgiveness thrives,
Forgiveness's grace, where healing arrives.
In every apology, where past contrives,
Forgiveness's liberation, souls revive.

Here are four Sestain poems, 1 each about Longing, Belonging, Discovery & Wonder

Longing:
In whispers soft, the heart's refrain,
Longing's ache, a constant chain.
In dreams of yore, where echoes remain,
Longing's yearning, never wane.

Belonging:
In gentle arms, a soul's embrace,
Belonging's warmth, a sacred place.
In every bond, a shared grace,
Belonging's solace, in every space.

Discovery:
In uncharted realms, the curious roam,
Discovery's thrill, a seeker's poem.
In hidden truths, yet to be known,
Discovery's journey, ever sown.

Wonder:
In starlit skies, the mind's ascent,
Wonder's awe, in vast extent.
In every marvel, where dreams are sent,
Wonder's embrace, heaven-sent.

Here are four Sestain poems, 1 each about Journey, Reflection, Harmony & Imagination

Journey:
On winding roads, the traveler strides,
Journey's path, where fate abides.
In every step, where destiny resides,
Journey's tale, forever guides.

Reflection:
In quiet moments, the soul takes flight,
Reflection's mirror, truth's insight.
In every pause, where thoughts alight,
Reflection's wisdom, ever bright.

Harmony:
In symphony's embrace, notes align,
Harmony's melody, a divine design.
In every chord, where souls entwine,
Harmony's rhythm, sublime.

Imagination:
In boundless realms, where dreams take flight,
Imagination's canvas, vast and bright.
In every thought, where worlds ignite,
Imagination's magic, infinite.

Here are four Sestain poems, 1 each about Silence, Laughter, Tears & Strength

Silence:
In hushed whispers, the world's refrain,
Silence's embrace, where peace is gained.
In tranquil moments, where minds abstain,
Silence's solace, unrestrained.

Laughter:
In joyous uproar, hearts unite,
Laughter's symphony, pure delight.
In every chuckle, where spirits alight,
Laughter's echo, ever bright.

Tears:
In silent streams, emotions flow,
Tears' release, a heart's echo.
In every drop, where sorrows grow,
Tears' catharsis, a healing glow.

Strength:
In silent resolve, the spirit stands,
Strength's fortress, against life's demands.
In every trial, where courage expands,
Strength's endurance, forever commands.

Here are four Sestain poems, 1 each about Vulnerability, Renewal, Acceptance & Mystery

Vulnerability:
In fragile moments, the heart reveals,
Vulnerability's truth, its raw appeal.
In every tear, where vulnerability seals,
Strength in fragility, it heals.

Renewal:
In dawn's first light, a new day breaks,
Renewal's promise, as morning wakes.
In every sunrise, where hope retakes,
Renewal's embrace, the soul remakes.

Acceptance:
In open arms, the heart makes room,
Acceptance's grace, dispels the gloom.
In every embrace, where judgments loom,
Acceptance's love, a sacred bloom.

Mystery:
In twilight's cloak, secrets dwell,
Mystery's allure, an ancient spell.
In every enigma, where tales foretell,
Mystery's whisper, never dispel.

Here are four Sestain poems, 1 each about Transformation, Eternity, Cosmos & Happiness

Transformation:
In dawn's soft light, a new day's birth,
Transforming shadows, renewing Earth.
From seed to bloom, life's endless mirth,
Transformation's dance, a sacred rebirth.

Eternity:
In timeless silence, stars align,
Eternal dance, where dreams entwine.
In every moment, where souls define,
Eternity's embrace, divine.

Cosmos:
In vast expanse, galaxies unfurl,
Cosmic wonders, a cosmic whirl.
In every star, where mysteries swirl,
Cosmos' majesty, the universe's pearl.

Happiness:
In laughter's echo, joy takes flight,
Hearts ablaze, in pure delight.
In every smile, where souls unite,
Happiness' embrace, ever bright.

-:|:-•:*'''''*:•.-:|:-•**•-:|:-•:*'''''*:•:*'''''*:•.-:|:-•**•-:|:--:|:-•:*'''''*:•.-:|:- •**•-:|:-•:*'''''*:•:*'''''*:•.-:|:-•**•-:|:-

VIRELAY:

A medieval French form consisting of stanzas of varying lengths with a refrain, often focusing on themes of courtly love.

-:|:-•:*'''''*:•.-:|:-•**•-:|:-•:*'''''*:•:*'''''*:•.-:|:-•**•-:|:--:|:-•:*'''''*:•.-:|:- •**•-:|:-•:*'''''*:•:*'''''*:•.-:|:-•**•-:|:-

Here are four Virelay poems, 1 each about Love, Nature, Beauty & Time

Love:
In tender whispers, love's refrain,
Heartbeats dancing, a sweet domain.
In every touch, love's gentle rain,
Forever bound, hearts entertain.

Nature:
In forest glades, nature's dance,
Leaves rustling, a wild romance.
In every breeze, nature's trance,
Earth's beauty, in every glance.

Beauty:
In sunset hues, beauty's glow,
Colors vibrant, in evening's show.
In every form, beauty's flow,
Eternal grace, in every bow.

Time:
In ticking clocks, time does pass,
Moments fleeting, like shadows cast.
In every hour, sands amassed,
Time's passage, ever steadfast.

Here are four Virelay poems, 1 each about Death, Dreams, Hope & Despair

Death:
In silent whispers, death does call,
Life's journey ends, curtains fall.
In every breath, a final thrall,
Death's embrace, encompassing all.

Dreams:
In slumber's realm, dreams unfold,
Worlds imagined, in stories told.
In every wish, dreams take hold,
Hopes and aspirations, bold.

Hope:
In darkest nights, hope's light shines,
Guiding souls, through troubled times.
In every heart, where hope aligns,
Miracles bloom, in hope's confines.

Despair:
In shadows deep, despair does lie,
Heartaches felt, beneath night sky.
In every tear, a silent cry,
Despair's grip, where dreams deny.

Here are four Virelay poems, 1 each about Friendship, Loneliness, Memories & Music

Friendship:
In bonds of friendship, hearts entwine,
Shared laughter, in sweet sunshine.
In every embrace, a friend divine,
Friendship's treasure, a cherished sign.

Loneliness:
In solitude's embrace, loneliness weeps,
Echoes silent, where sadness creeps.
In every silence, where sorrow seeps,
Loneliness' veil, where the heart sleeps.

Memories:
In whispered echoes, memories cling,
Moments cherished, in hearts they sing.
In every snapshot, memories bring,
Life's tapestry, an eternal spring.

Music:
In melodies sweet, music plays,
Notes dancing, in rhythmic sways.
In every chord, where souls amaze,
Music's symphony, in endless bays.

Here are four Virelay poems, 1 each about Art, Inspiration, Creativity & Courage

Art:
In brushstrokes bold, art takes flight,
Canvas alive, with colors bright.
In every stroke, where dreams ignite,
Art's expression, a wondrous sight.

Inspiration:
In sparks of creativity, inspiration gleams,
Ideas flowing, like winding streams.
In every muse, where vision beams,
Inspiration's fire, fuels life's dreams.

Creativity:
In boundless imagination, creativity soars,
Worlds imagined, through open doors.
In every creation, where passion pours,
Creativity's essence, forever restores.

Courage:
In the face of fear, courage stands tall,
Bravery's call, amidst the brawl.
In every act, where courage appalls,
Strength of character, where heroes fall.

Here are four Virelay poems, 1 each about Faith, Doubt, Solitude & Joy

Faith:
In steadfast belief, faith prevails,
Hope's beacon, in life's gales.
In every prayer, where faith avails,
Miracles happen, where love hails.

Doubt:
In shadows cast, doubt takes hold,
Questions unanswered, stories untold.
In every uncertainty, where fears unfold,
Doubt's grip tightens, in stories old.

Solitude:
In quiet moments, solitude's embrace,
A sanctuary found, in sacred space.
In every retreat, where souls trace,
Solitude's peace, a gentle grace.

Joy:
In laughter's echoes, joy resounds,
Hearts uplifted, in merry rounds.
In every smile, where happiness abounds,
Joy's radiance, knows no bounds.

Here are four Virelay poems, 1 each about Sorrow, Childhood, Wisdom & Innocence

Sorrow:
In tears unbidden, sorrow dwells,
Heartaches felt, in silent knells.
In every sigh, where grief swells,
Sorrow's presence, like tolling bells.

Childhood:
In innocence pure, childhood's grace,
Laughter ringing, in playful chase.
In every memory, a sacred place,
Childhood's wonder, time cannot erase.

Wisdom:
In lessons learned, wisdom gained,
Life's journey, through joy and pain.
In every trial, where knowledge attained,
Wisdom's guiding light, shall reign.

Innocence:
In purity untouched, innocence thrives,
Unwritten stories, in tender lives.
In every heart, where goodness strives,
Innocence's purity, eternally survives.

Here are four Virelay poems, 1 each about Passion, Serenity, Freedom & Justice

Passion:
In fiery hearts, passion ignites,
A burning desire, love's greatest heights.
In every kiss, love takes flight,
Passion's flame, an eternal light.

Serenity:
In tranquil moments, serenity flows,
Peaceful waters, where tranquility grows.
In quiet whispers, a gentle repose,
Serenity's embrace, a calm that bestows.

Freedom:
In open skies, freedom's call,
Boundless horizons, breaking walls.
In every choice, both big and small,
Freedom's song, within us all.

Justice:
In the court of truth, justice prevails,
Fairness and equity, balanced scales.
In every heart, where compassion hails,
Justice's voice, never fails.

Here are four Virelay poems, 1 each about Change, Resilience, Gratitude & Forgiveness

Change:
In winds of change, the world does spin,
Ever shifting, where new paths begin.
In every ending, a chance to begin,
Change's embrace, a constant kin.

Resilience:
In trials faced, resilience found,
Through storms endured, on solid ground.
In every setback, strength is crowned,
Resilience, a victor profound.

Gratitude:
In moments shared, gratitude blooms,
In thankful hearts, joy consumes.
In every blessing, a soul resumes,
Gratitude's light, forever looms.

Forgiveness:
In wounds healed, forgiveness grows,
In letting go, forgiveness shows.
In every heart, where kindness flows,
Forgiveness, a peace that glows.

Here are four Virelay poems, 1 each about Longing, Belonging, Discovery & Wonder

Longing:
In whispers carried by the wind,
Longing's melody, where dreams rescind.
In every yearning, a soul's friend,
Longing's journey, without end.

Belonging:
In bonds formed, belonging thrives,
In shared laughter, where love arrives.
In every embrace, where spirit thrives,
Belonging's warmth, forever survives.

Discovery:
In uncharted lands, discovery awaits,
Adventure's call, beyond the gates.
In every mystery, that fascinates,
Discovery's joy, illuminates.

Wonder:
In starlit skies, wonder does bloom,
In awe-inspired hearts, room to consume.
In every moment, where dreams resume,
Wonder's magic, in life's grand room.

Here are four Virelay poems, 1 each about Journey, Reflection, Harmony & Imagination

Journey:
In winding roads, the journey begins,
Through valleys low, and mountain winds.
In every step, where the soul begins,
Journey's path, where destiny rescinds.

Reflection:
In quiet moments, reflection's grace,
In mirrored waters, a soul's embrace.
In every memory, time to retrace,
Reflection's peace, in life's fast pace.

Harmony:
In symphony's chords, harmony's song,
Notes in unison, where hearts belong.
In every rhythm, both short and long,
Harmony's melody, forever strong.

Imagination:
In dreams unleashed, imagination flies,
Worlds created, beneath endless skies.
In every thought, where creativity lies,
Imagination's realm, where spirit defies.

Here are four Virelay poems, 1 each about Silence, Laughter, Tears & Strength

Silence:
In hushed whispers, silence holds sway,
In stillness found, where spirits play.
In every moment, where words decay,
Silence's peace, in night or day.

Laughter:
In joyous echoes, laughter resounds,
In shared mirth, where happiness abounds.
In every chuckle, where glee surrounds,
Laughter's melody, forever profound.

Tears:
In sorrow's veil, tears softly fall,
In heartaches felt, through life's call.
In every release, where emotions sprawl,
Tears' cleansing touch, amidst life's thrall.

Strength:
In battles fought, strength does arise,
In every struggle, where courage lies.
In every heart, where hope defies,
Strength's resilience, beneath the skies.

Here are four Virelay poems, 1 each about Vulnerability, Renewal, Acceptance & Mystery

Vulnerability:
In open hearts, vulnerability found,
In tender moments, where souls resound.
In every emotion, where truth's unbound,
Vulnerability's beauty, earthward bound.

Renewal:
In dawn's first light, renewal begins,
In every sunrise, where hope rescinds.
In every opportunity, where the soul wins,
Renewal's promise, where life begins.

Acceptance:
In arms open wide, acceptance blooms,
In every flaw, where grace resumes.
In every heart, where judgment looms,
Acceptance's embrace, dispels all glooms.

Mystery:
In shadows cast, mystery reigns,
In enigma's hold, where truth refrains.
In every question, where curiosity gains,
Mystery's allure, forever maintains.

Here are four Virelay poems, 1 each about Transformation, Eternity, Cosmos & Happiness

Transformation:
In whispers of dawn, the world takes flight,
Transformation blooms in morning light.
From cocoon's grasp, emerges might,
New beginnings, a soul's delight.

Eternity:
In timeless depths, where stars align,
Eternity's embrace, divine design.
Beyond mortal coil, spirits entwine,
Eternal dance, a love refined.

Cosmos:
In cosmic expanse, galaxies twirl,
Cosmos' vastness, a cosmic swirl.
In every constellation, a soul unfurls,
Mysteries of the universe, mysteries unfurl.

Happiness:
In laughter's echo, joy takes flight,
Happiness' song, in day or night.
In every moment, hearts ignite,
In happiness' embrace, all is bright.

EPIGRAM:

A short, witty poem often characterized by brevity and cleverness, conveying a single idea or observation.

Here are four Epigram poems, 1 each about Love, Nature, Beauty & Time

Love:
In the heart's embrace, passions intertwine,
Love's sweet symphony, a melody divine.
In every beat, a soul's valentine,
Love's eternal flame, forever shall shine.

Nature:
In the whispering breeze and babbling brook,
Nature's poetry, in every nook.
In every leaf, a soul's sacred book,
Nature's beauty, an enchanted look.

Beauty:
In the sunset's hues, painting skies aglow,
Beauty's radiance, in every shadow.
In every bloom, a soul's tale to bestow,
Beauty's wonder, a timeless show.

Time:
In the ticking of the clock's steady chime,
Time's relentless march, an endless climb.
In every moment, a soul's paradigm,
Time's fleeting passage, marking life's rhyme.

Here are four Epigram poems, 1 each about Death, Dreams, Hope & Despair

Death:
In the silent void where shadows creep,
Death's solemn embrace, where souls do sleep.
In every passing, a soul to keep,
Death's mystery, where secrets seep.

Dreams:
In the starry night where fantasies soar,
Dreams take flight, on wings that explore.
In every vision, a soul's encore,
Dreams' boundless realm, forevermore.

Hope:
In the darkest hour where shadows fall,
Hope's gentle whisper, a beacon tall.
In every dream, a soul's call,
Hope's guiding light, through every squall.

Despair:
In the depths of anguish where shadows dwell,
Despair's heavy burden, a silent knell.
In every tear, a soul's farewell,
Despair's bitter taste, a sorrowful well.

Here are four Epigram poems, 1 each about Friendship, Loneliness, Memories & Music

Friendship:
In the laughter shared and bonds that grow,
Friendship's warmth, a comforting glow.
In every smile, a soul's tableau,
Friendship's embrace, a love to show.

Loneliness:
In the silent echoes where silence cries,
Loneliness resides, where shadows lie.
In every sigh, a soul's long goodbye,
Loneliness' embrace, a muted sigh.

Memories:
In the whispered echoes of days gone by,
Memories linger, beneath the sky.
In every recollection, a soul's sigh,
Memories' tapestry, where hearts fly.

Music:
In the harmonies that dance on air,
Music's melody, beyond compare.
In every note, a soul laid bare,
Music's symphony, an answered prayer.

Here are four Epigram poems, 1 each about Art, Inspiration, Creativity & Courage

Art:
In the strokes of color that paint the scene,
Art's expression, in hues serene.
In every canvas, a soul's dream,
Art's masterpiece, a vision supreme.

Inspiration:
In the quiet moments where muses play,
Inspiration blooms, in light of day.
In every spark, a soul's essay,
Inspiration's fire, lighting the way.

Creativity:
In the blank canvas where ideas unfurl,
Creativity dances, a vibrant whirl.
In every creation, a soul's twirl,
Creativity's canvas, an endless swirl.

Courage:
In the face of fear where courage stands,
Courage's resolve, in every demand.
In every step, a soul commands,
Courage's strength, forever in command.

Here are four Epigram poems, 1 each about Faith, Doubt, Solitude & Joy

Faith:
In the unseen forces that guide the way,
Faith's unwavering light, come what may.
In every prayer, a soul's sway,
Faith's steadfast anchor, day by day.

Doubt:
In the shadows of uncertainty's call,
Doubt's whispers, where fears do sprawl.
In every hesitation, a soul's fall,
Doubt's lurking presence, a haunting pall.

Solitude:
In the quiet corners where silence reigns,
Solitude's embrace, where peace remains.
In every moment, a soul's gains,
Solitude's refuge, where solace reigns.

Joy:
In the laughter that bubbles from deep within,
Joy's effervescent dance, a joyful din.
In every smile, a soul begins,
Joy's radiant glow, a life to win.

Here are four Epigram poems, 1 each about Sorrow, Childhood, Wisdom & Innocence

Sorrow:
In the heartache that shadows every day,
Sorrow's heavy burden, in disarray.
In every tear, a soul's decay,
Sorrow's mournful cry, with nothing to say.

Childhood:
In the innocence of youth's playful lore,
Childhood's laughter, forevermore.
In every giggle, a soul's encore,
Childhood's magic, where dreams explore.

Wisdom:
In the quiet wisdom of the sage's lore,
Wisdom's counsel, forevermore.
In every lesson, a soul does soar,
Wisdom's beacon, on life's shore.

Innocence:
In the purity of heart untouched by stain,
Innocence's grace, forever reign.
In every smile, a soul's refrain,
Innocence's light, where dreams attain.

Here are four Epigram poems, 1 each about Passion, Serenity, Freedom & Justice

Passion:
In the fire of passion, hearts ignite,
Burning bright in love's eternal light.
In every touch, a soul's delight,
Passion's flame, a fervent flight.

Serenity:
In the calm embrace of tranquil seas,
Serenity whispers, a gentle breeze.
In every moment, a soul finds ease,
Serenity's peace, a silent tease.

Freedom:
In the open sky where eagles soar,
Freedom beckons, forevermore.
In every choice, a soul's encore,
Freedom's call, to explore and restore.

Justice:
In the scales of justice, truth prevails,
Balancing right against all that fails.
In every verdict, a soul exhales,
Justice's sword, where fairness sails.

Here are four Epigram poems, 1 each about Change, Resilience, Gratitude & Forgiveness

Change:
In the constant flow of life's refrain,
Change sweeps in, with its endless gain.
In every shift, a soul's terrain,
Change's rhythm, a vibrant strain.

Resilience:
In the face of storms that fiercely rage,
Resilience stands, undeterred by age.
In every trial, a soul's sage,
Resilience' strength, a steadfast stage.

Gratitude:
In the heart's song of thankfulness profound,
Gratitude echoes, in every sound.
In every blessing, a soul is crowned,
Gratitude's joy, forever unbound.

Forgiveness:
In the act of letting go and moving on,
Forgiveness heals, where wounds have drawn.
In every pardon, a soul is reborn,
Forgiveness' grace, a new dawn.

Here are four Epigram poems, 1 each about Longing, Belonging, Discovery & Wonder

Longing:
In the ache of yearning, hearts entwine,
Longing's whisper, a bittersweet sign.
In every dream, a soul's design,
Longing's path, where hopes align.

Belonging:
In the embrace of kinship's gentle fold,
Belonging blossoms, a treasure untold.
In every bond, a soul's stronghold,
Belonging's warmth, where love is extolled.

Discovery:
In the uncharted realms where wonders hide,
Discovery beckons, with secrets wide.
In every find, a soul's pride,
Discovery's quest, where dreams abide.

Wonder:
In the childlike gaze at the starlit night,
Wonder awakens, in pure delight.
In every marvel, a soul takes flight,
Wonder's magic, a celestial sight.

Here are four Epigram poems, 1 each about Journey, Reflection, Harmony & Imagination

Journey:
In the winding path where footsteps tread,
Journey unfolds, with stories unread.
In every adventure, a soul is led,
Journey's voyage, where destinies spread.

Reflection:
In the stillness of the mind's quiet space,
Reflection murmurs, with gentle grace.
In every thought, a soul's embrace,
Reflection's mirror, a sacred place.

Harmony:
In the symphony of nature's grandeur,
Harmony resonates, a timeless allure.
In every melody, a soul finds cure,
Harmony's chord, pure and sure.

Imagination:
In the boundless realm where dreams take flight,
Imagination soars, in the darkest night.
In every creation, a soul's insight,
Imagination's canvas, infinite and bright.

Here are four Epigram poems, 1 each about Silence, Laughter, Tears & Strength

Silence:
In the hush of night, where whispers cease,
Silence speaks, a melody of peace.
In every quiet, a soul's release,
Silence' calm, where worries decrease.

Laughter:
In the joyous peal that echoes clear,
Laughter rings, dispelling every fear.
In every chuckle, a soul draws near,
Laughter's chorus, forever dear.

Tears:
In the crystal drops that softly fall,
Tears cleanse the soul, answering love's call.
In every sob, a heart stands tall,
Tears' release, where healing does enthrall.

Strength:
In the iron will that refuses to yield,
Strength stands firm, on life's battlefield.
In every trial, a soul is sealed,
Strength's endurance, an unbroken shield

Here are four Epigram poems, 1 each about Vulnerability, Renewal, Acceptance & Mystery

Vulnerability:
In the rawness of exposed heart's plight,
Vulnerability reveals, in stark light.
In every admission, a soul takes flight,
Vulnerability's courage, burning bright.

Renewal:
In the dawn's embrace, where darkness wanes,
Renewal arises, breaking all chains.
In every sunrise, a soul regains,
Renewal's promise, where hope sustains.
Mystery's allure, a labyrinth to be shown.

Acceptance:
In the open arms that welcome all,
Acceptance beckons, at humanity's call.
In every embrace, a soul stands tall,
Acceptance' grace, a universal thrall.

Mystery:
In the enigma that shrouds the unknown,
Mystery whispers, in a language all its own.
In every question, a soul is thrown,

Here are four Epigram poems, 1 each about Transformation, Eternity, Cosmos & Happiness

Transformation:
In the chrysalis, a caterpillar sleeps,
Dreaming of wings as the cocoon keeps.
From earthbound crawl to skyward leap,
Transformation's secret, the soul it reaps.

Eternity:
In the cosmic dance of stars above,
Eternity whispers, endless love.
Time's illusion, a fleeting dove,
Eternity's embrace, the heavens prove.

Cosmos:
In the vast expanse where galaxies roam,
Cosmos unfolds, a celestial poem.
In every twinkle, a stellar tome,
Cosmos' mystery, our eternal home.

Happiness:
In the laughter that echoes through the night,
Happiness blooms, a radiant light.
In every smile, a heart takes flight,
Happiness' embrace, pure and bright.

-:|:-•:*'''''*:•.-:|:-•**•-:|:-•:*'''''*:•:*'''''*:•.-:|:-•**•-:|:--:|:-•:*'''''*:•.-:|:- •**•-:|:-•:*'''''*:•:*'''''*:•.-:|:-•**•-:|:-

VILLANCICO:

A Spanish poetic form often used for Christmas or other festive occasions, characterized by its lively and rhythmic nature.

-:|:-•:*'''''*:•.-:|:-•**•-:|:-•:*'''''*:•:*'''''*:•.-:|:-•**•-:|:--:|:-•:*'''''*:•.-:|:- •**•-:|:-•:*'''''*:•:*'''''*:•.-:|:-•**•-:|:-

Here are four Villancico poems, 1 each about Love, Nature, Beauty & Time

Love:
In the tender whispers of the heart's call,
Love weaves its magic, entrancing all.
In every touch, a soul's sweet thrall,
Love's embrace, never to fall.

Nature:
In the whispering breeze through the trees,
Nature sings, in melodies that tease.
In every bloom, a soul's release,
Nature's beauty, a timeless masterpiece.

Beauty:
In the rainbow's hues, a vibrant sight,
Beauty shines, in the morning light.
In every smile, a heart takes flight,
Beauty's allure, a pure delight.

Time:
In the ticking of the clock's steady beat,
Time marches on, in its relentless fleet.
In every moment, a life's complete,
Time's passage, never to defeat.

Here are four Villancico poems, 1 each about Death, Dreams, Hope & Despair

Death:
In the silent whispers of the final breath,
Death whispers softly, the end of all quest.
In every goodbye, a soul's last test,
Death's embrace, where all find rest.

Dreams:
In the realm where fantasies roam free,
Dreams take flight, in the vast blue sea.
In every hope, a soul's decree,
Dreams' journey, where hearts agree.

Hope:
In the darkest night, a flickering flame,
Hope shines bright, a guiding aim.
In every wish, a soul's acclaim,
Hope's promise, where dreams reclaim.

Despair:
In the depths of the soul's darkest plight,
Despair takes hold, with all its might.
In every tear, a heart's blight,
Despair's grip, in endless night.

Here are four Villancico poems, 1 each about Friendship, Loneliness, Memories & Music

Friendship:
In the laughter shared between dear friends,
Friendship blossoms, where love extends.
In every bond, a heart amends,
Friendship's embrace, where joy transcends.

Loneliness:
In the empty spaces where echoes dwell,
Loneliness whispers, a solitary knell.
In every sigh, a soul's farewell,
Loneliness' grip, where shadows swell.

Memories:
In the treasures stored within the mind's hall,
Memories linger, like whispers in a squall.
In every moment, a soul recalls,
Memories' embrace, where hearts enthrall.

Music:
In the melodies that dance upon the air,
Music enchants, without a care.
In every note, a soul laid bare,
Music's harmony, beyond compare.

Here are four Villancico poems, 1 each about Art, Inspiration, Creativity & Courage

Art:
In the strokes of color upon the canvas wide,
Art breathes life, where dreams reside.
In every creation, a soul's guide,
Art's beauty, a boundless tide.

Inspiration:
In the whispers of muses that softly call,
Inspiration ignites, where dreams enthrall.
In every spark, a soul stands tall,
Inspiration's fire, burning bright in all.

Creativity:
In the dance of imagination's flight,
Creativity soars, in the darkest night.
In every creation, a soul takes flight,
Creativity's magic, a wondrous sight.

Courage:
In the face of fear's relentless fight,
Courage stands strong, in the morning light.
In every step, a soul's respite,
Courage's triumph, against all plight.

Here are four Villancico poems, 1 each about Faith, Doubt, Solitude & Joy

Faith:
In the depths of darkness, a guiding light,
Faith endures, through the darkest night.
In every prayer, a soul takes flight,
Faith's embrace, a beacon bright.

Doubt:
In the shadows of uncertainty's reign,
Doubt lingers, causing hearts pain.
In every question, a mind's bane,
Doubt's whispers, driving insane.

Solitude:
In the silence of the lone heart's beat,
Solitude finds peace, in its retreat.
In every moment, a soul's sweet treat,
Solitude's calm, where thoughts greet.

Joy:
In the laughter that fills the air,
Joy dances, without a care.
In every smile, a love to share,
Joy's embrace, beyond compare.

Here are four Villancico poems, 1 each about Sorrow, Childhood, Wisdom & Innocence

Sorrow:
In the tears that fall like rain,
Sorrow weeps, a heart's refrain.
In every ache, a soul's stain,
Sorrow's weight, a constant chain.

Childhood:
In the innocence of youth's embrace,
Childhood thrives, a sacred space.
In every giggle, a pure grace,
Childhood's wonder, a cherished trace.

Wisdom:
In the lessons learned from life's toil,
Wisdom grows, from the fertile soil.
In every trial, a truth to foil,
Wisdom's insight, in its royal coil.

Innocence:
In the purity of a child's eyes,
Innocence reigns, where truth lies.
In every laugh, a soul flies,
Innocence's charm, a heart prize.

Here are four Villancico poems, 1 each about Passion, Serenity, Freedom & Justice

Passion:
In the fire that burns within the heart,
Passion ignites, a fervent start.
In every desire, a wild depart,
Passion's flames, never to depart.

Serenity:
In the calm of the tranquil sea,
Serenity finds peace, where waves flee.
In every breath, a soul's decree,
Serenity's embrace, ever free.

Freedom:
In the open skies, where birds soar high,
Freedom beckons, in the endless sky.
In every dream, a soul's reply,
Freedom's call, where dreams defy.

Justice:
In the scales that balance wrong and right,
Justice prevails, in the darkest night.
In every verdict, a truth's sight,
Justice's sword, shining bright.

Here are four Villancico poems, 1 each about Change, Resilience, Gratitude & Forgiveness

Change:
In the winds of change, a shifting tide,
Change sweeps in, where dreams abide.
In every shift, a path to guide,
Change's embrace, where fears subside.

Resilience:
In the face of adversity's blow,
Resilience stands, against the foe.
In every challenge, a strength to show,
Resilience's spirit, in its glow.

Gratitude:
In the moments of life's sweet grace,
Gratitude blooms, in every place.
In every blessing, a heart's embrace,
Gratitude's joy, in every trace.

Forgiveness:
In the act of letting go of pain,
Forgiveness heals, like gentle rain.
In every pardon, a soul's gain,
Forgiveness' peace, where love reigns.

Here are four Villancico poems, 1 each about Longing, Belonging, Discovery & Wonder

Longing:
In the depths of night, a whispered plea,
Longing echoes, across the sea.
In every sigh, a heart's decree,
Longing's ache, a symphony.

Belonging:
In the warmth of love's embrace,
Belonging thrives, in sacred space.
In every bond, a divine grace,
Belonging's song, in every place.

Discovery:
In the uncharted realms, where dreams take flight,
Discovery beckons, in the dead of night.
In every find, a guiding light,
Discovery's thrill, in boundless height.

Wonder:
In the mysteries of the universe untold,
Wonder thrives, where stars unfold.
In every marvel, a tale to behold,
Wonder's awe, where dreams enfold.

Here are four Villancico poems, 1 each about Journey, Reflection, Harmony & Imagination

Journey:
In the footsteps left upon the sand,
Journey unfolds, across the land.
In every step, a life unplanned,
Journey's path, hand in hand.

Reflection:
In the stillness of the moonlit night,
Reflection whispers, in the fading light.
In every thought, a soul's insight,
Reflection's mirror, shining bright.

Harmony:
In the symphony of nature's song,
Harmony reigns, where hearts belong.
In every chord, a melody strong,
Harmony's rhythm, forever long.

Imagination:
In the world of dreams, where fantasies roam,
Imagination soars, in the heart's home.
In every vision, a kingdom to own,
Imagination's realm, where dreams are sown.

Here are four Villancico poems, 1 each about Silence, Laughter, Tears & Strength

Silence:
In the hush of dawn, a sacred hush,
Silence reigns, in the morning's blush.
In every quiet, a soul's plush,
Silence's calm, where thoughts rush.

Laughter:
In the laughter that fills the air,
Laughter dances, beyond compare.
In every chuckle, a joy to share,
Laughter's melody, light as air.

Tears:
In the rain that falls from skies above,
Tears cascade, a symbol of love.
In every drop, a tale thereof,
Tears' release, in mourning's glove.

Strength:
In the heart that beats against the storm,
Strength rises, in its powerful form.
In every struggle, a life transformed,
Strength's resilience, to weather the norm.

Here are four Villancico poems, 1 each about Vulnerability, Renewal, Acceptance & Mystery

Vulnerability:
In the cracks of armor worn,
Vulnerability lurks, where hearts are torn.
In every fear, a soul forlorn,
Vulnerability's grip, in shadows born.

Renewal:
In the dawn of a brand new day,
Renewal blossoms, in the morning's ray.
In every sunrise, a chance to sway,
Renewal's promise, in the light's display.

Acceptance:
In the embrace of flaws and scars,
Acceptance blooms, beneath the stars.
In every flaw, a beauty that mars,
Acceptance's grace, in who we are.

Mystery:
In the depths of the unknown vast,
Mystery whispers, where shadows cast.
In every enigma, a truth amassed,
Mystery's allure, where questions last.

Here are four Villancico poems, 1 each about Transformation, Eternity, Cosmos & Happiness

Transformation:
In the quiet of the dawn's embrace,
Transformation blooms, in sacred space.
In every dawn, a new grace,
Transformation's dance, in time's embrace.

Eternity:
In the stars that dot the endless sky,
Eternity whispers, where dreams fly.
In every twinkle, a soul's sigh,
Eternity's promise, never to say goodbye.

Cosmos:
In the vast expanse of cosmic might,
Cosmos reigns, in eternal light.
In every galaxy, a story bright,
Cosmos' mystery, a celestial flight.

Happiness:
In the laughter of children's play,
Happiness reigns, in the light of day.
In every smile, a heart's bouquet,
Happiness' embrace, come what may.

-:|:-•:*''''''*:•.-:|:-•**•-:|:-•:*''''''*:•:*''''''*:•.-:|:-•**•-:|:--:|:-•:*''''''*:•.-:|:- •**•-:|:-•:*''''''*:•:*''''''*:•.-:|:-•**•-:|:-

FOUND POETRY:

Poetry created by selecting and rearranging words or phrases from existing texts, such as newspapers, magazines, or other written materials.

Here are four Found poems, 1 each about Love, Nature, Beauty & Time

Love:
In whispered promises and tender caress,
Love blooms, in hearts' soft recess.
In every glance, a love's confess,
Love's embrace, in sweet finesse.

Nature:
In the rustle of leaves and the chirp of birds,
Nature sings, in melodious words.
In every sunrise, a beauty conferred,
Nature's wonder, where peace is stirred.

Beauty:
In the hues of sunset's glow,
Beauty unfolds, in a radiant show.
In every petal, a grace to bestow,
Beauty's allure, in ebb and flow.

Time:
In the ticking of clocks, relentless and sure,
Time marches on, an enduring lure.
In every moment, a memory pure,
Time's passage, forever secure.

Here are four Found poems, 1 each about Death, Dreams, Hope & Despair

Death:
In the quiet of night's embrace,
Death whispers, leaving no trace.
In every farewell, a solemn grace,
Death's shadow, in every place.

Dreams:
In the realm of sleep and reverie,
Dreams take flight, wild and free.
In every wish, a soul's decree,
Dreams' magic, for all to see.

Hope:
In the darkest hour, a glimmer bright,
Hope shines forth, a guiding light.
In every prayer, a hope to ignite,
Hope's promise, in the darkest night.

Despair:
In the depths of sorrow's deep well,
Despair lingers, where shadows dwell.
In every tear, a silent knell,
Despair's grip, a heavy shell.

Here are four Found poems, 1 each about Friendship, Loneliness, Memories & Music

Friendship:
In the laughter shared and hands entwined,
Friendship blossoms, a bond refined.
In every hug, a love enshrined,
Friendship's warmth, forever aligned.

Loneliness:
In the silence of solitary walls,
Loneliness echoes, where darkness falls.
In every sigh, a heart's calls,
Loneliness' weight, where despair sprawls.

Memories:
In the album of time, pages unfold,
Memories linger, in tales retold.
In every snapshot, a story bold,
Memories' tapestry, in colors gold.

Music:
In the melody that dances on the air,
Music enchants, beyond compare.
In every note, a soul laid bare,
Music's rhythm, where emotions flare.

Here are four Found poems, 1 each about Art, Inspiration, Creativity & Courage

Art:
In strokes of color, on canvas laid,
Art speaks, where emotions bade.
In every masterpiece, a tale displayed,
Art's beauty, in every shade.

Inspiration:
In the muse that whispers in the ear,
Inspiration sparks, where passions sear.
In every spark, a vision clear,
Inspiration's fire, drawing near.

Creativity:
In the blank canvas and the empty page,
Creativity flows, in an endless rage.
In every creation, a new stage,
Creativity's dance, in every age.

Courage:
In the face of fear, a heart beats strong,
Courage rises, where fears belong.
In every step, a journey long,
Courage's triumph, a victorious song.

Here are four Found poems, 1 each about Faith, Doubt, Solitude & Joy

Faith:
In the silence of whispered prayers,
Faith blossoms, banishing despair.
In every step, a journey where
Faith guides, with love and care.

Doubt:
In the shadows of uncertainty's hold,
Doubt lingers, tales untold.
In every question, a truth to behold,
Doubt's grip, strong and bold.

Solitude:
In the quiet of solitary retreat,
Solitude beckons, a silent feat.
In every moment, a chance to meet,
Solitude's peace, serene and sweet.

Joy:
In the laughter of children at play,
Joy dances, in the light of day.
In every smile, a heart's display,
Joy's embrace, come what may.

Here are four Found poems, 1 each about Sorrow, Childhood, Wisdom & Innocence

Sorrow:
In the tears that silently fall,
Sorrow's weight, a heavy call.
In every ache, a soul's recall,
Sorrow's grip, encompassing all.

Childhood:
In the memories of innocence pure,
Childhood's laughter, forever endure.
In every dream, a heart secure,
Childhood's magic, ever sure.

Wisdom:
In the whispers of age-old tales,
Wisdom blooms, where knowledge hails.
In every lesson, a truth avails,
Wisdom's grace, where wisdom prevails.

Innocence:
In the purity of untouched hearts,
Innocence thrives, where innocence starts.
In every glance, in a world apart,
Innocence's light, where love imparts.

Here are four Found poems, 1 each about Passion, Serenity, Freedom & Justice

Passion:
In the fire that burns deep within,
Passion ignites, where dreams begin.
In every touch, a soul's spin,
Passion's fervor, a passionate din.

Serenity:
In the calm of twilight's hue,
Serenity whispers, dreams come true.
In every breath, a moment to renew,
Serenity's peace, ever anew.

Freedom:
In the open skies where eagles soar,
Freedom beckons, forevermore.
In every choice, a life to explore,
Freedom's call, an open door.

Justice:
In the scales that balance right and wrong,
Justice prevails, in the chorus' song.
In every verdict, a world made strong,
Justice's truth, where justice belongs.

Here are four Found poems, 1 each about Change, Resilience, Gratitude & Forgiveness

Change:
In the winds of change, a new refrain,
Change sweeps in, washing away pain.
In every shift, a chance to gain,
Change's rhythm, breaking every chain.

Resilience:
In the face of storms, resilience stands,
Resilience weathers, where hope expands.
In every trial, a strength commands,
Resilience's power, in steadfast hands.

Gratitude:
In the blessings that surround each day,
Gratitude blossoms, in every way.
In every thank you, a heart's sway,
Gratitude's joy, come what may.

Forgiveness:
In the wounds that run deep and sore,
Forgiveness heals, where hearts implore.
In every release, a soul to restore,
Forgiveness' grace, forevermore.

Here are four Found poems, 1 each about Longing, Belonging, Discovery & Wonder

Longing:
Yearning whispers in the wind,
Longing hearts, where dreams rescind.
In distant echoes, memories bind,
Longing's ache, in every kind.

Belonging:
In the warmth of family's embrace,
Belonging found, in a sacred space.
In shared laughter and tears shed,
Belonging's comfort, where hearts are led.

Discovery:
In the pages of books, worlds unfold,
Discovery's tale, in stories old.
In every journey, a truth untold,
Discovery's wonder, a treasure to behold.

Wonder:
In the dance of fireflies at night,
Wonder sparks, in nature's light.
In every star, a mystery so bright,
Wonder's enchantment, taking flight.

Here are four Found poems, 1 each about Journey, Reflection, Harmony & Imagination

Journey:
Footsteps echo, a path untold,
Journey's whispers, in tales enrolled.
In every twist, a story to behold,
Journey's adventure, both young and old.

Reflection:
In the stillness of a tranquil lake,
Reflections stir, memories awake.
In every ripple, a choice to make,
Reflection's mirror, a soul to partake.

Harmony:
In the symphony of nature's song,
Harmony weaves, where souls belong.
In every note, a peace so strong,
Harmony's melody, forever long.

Imagination:
In the boundless realms of the mind,
Imagination soars, where dreams unwind.
In every thought, a world designed,
Imagination's magic, forever entwined.

Here are four Found poems, 1 each about Silence, Laughter, Tears & Strength

Silence:
In the hush of dawn's first light,
Silence whispers, in the still of night.
In every pause, a moment's flight,
Silence's embrace, tranquil and bright.

Laughter:
In the echo of laughter's cheer,
Hearts alight, in joy sincere.
In every chuckle, a bond so dear,
Laughter's melody, ever clear.

Tears:
In the wellspring of sorrow's tide,
Tears cascade, hearts open wide.
In every drop, emotions ride,
Tears' release, in pain's stride.

Strength:
In the face of trials, courage found,
Strength emerges, unyielding, profound.
In every battle, victory crowned,
Strength's resolve, forever bound.

Here are four Found poems, 1 each about Vulnerability, Renewal, Acceptance & Mystery

Vulnerability:
In the cracks of armor, hearts laid bare,
Vulnerability's truth, a tender air.
In every tear, a soul to share,
Vulnerability's courage, beyond compare.

Renewal:
In the dawn's embrace, a new day's start,
Renewal whispers, mending the heart.
In every sunrise, a chance to depart,
Renewal's promise, a fresh start.

Acceptance:
In the embrace of flaws and scars,
Acceptance blooms, breaking bars.
In every heart, a universe of stars,
Acceptance's grace, healing scars.

Mystery:
In the shadows where secrets dwell,
Mystery weaves its enchanting spell.
In every question, a tale to tell,
Mystery's allure, where wonders swell.

Here are four Found poems, 1 each about Transformation, Eternity, Cosmos & Happiness

Transformation:
In the chrysalis cocoon,
Metamorphosis does loom.
From caterpillar to butterfly,
A transformation to the sky.

Eternity:
Time's flow, an endless stream,
In eternity, it does gleam.
From birth to death, and beyond,
Eternity's embrace, forever fond.

Cosmos:
Stars twinkling in the night,
Galaxies swirling, a cosmic sight.
Planets dance in celestial ballet,
Cosmos' mysteries, on display.

Happiness:
Laughter ringing through the air,
Joyful hearts, beyond compare.
In smiles shared, and friendships true,
Happiness blooms, in every hue.

PANTUN:

A traditional Malay verse form consisting of interlocking quatrains, with the second and fourth lines of each stanza rhyming.

-:¦:-•:*'''''*:•.-:¦:-•**•-:¦:-•:*'''''*:•:*'''''*:•.-:¦:-•**•-:¦:--:¦:-•:*'''''*:•.-:¦:- •**•-:¦:-•:*'''''*:•:*'''''*:•.-:¦:-•**•-:¦:-

Here are four Pantun poems, 1 each about Love, Nature, Beauty & Time

Love:
In love's embrace, hearts beat as one,
Underneath the moon and sun.
In every touch, a love begun,
Eternal flame, never undone.

Nature:
In nature's arms, the soul finds peace,
Where rivers flow and mountains cease.
In every breeze, a sweet release,
Nature's beauty, never to decrease.

Beauty:
In the eye of the beholder, beauty lies,
In sunsets painted across the skies.
In every flower, a beauty that belies,
Nature's art, a wondrous prize.

Time:
In the sands of time, moments slip away,
Yesterday's dreams, tomorrow's sway.
In every heartbeat, a dance to play,
Time's passage, night and day.

Here are four Pantun poems, 1 each about Death, Dreams, Hope & Despair

Death:
In death's embrace, we bid farewell,
To loved ones gone, to heaven's knell.
In every tear, a story to tell,
Death's mystery, where spirits dwell.

Dreams:
In the realm of dreams, the mind does soar,
Where fantasies fly and hopes implore.
In every wish, a dream to explore,
Dreams' magic, forevermore.

Hope:
In hope's gentle whisper, hearts arise,
In darkest night, where shadows disguise.
In every sunrise, a promise lies,
Hope's beacon, where dreams realize.

Despair:
In the depths of despair, shadows fall,
Casting darkness, a haunting pall.
In every tear, a silent call,
Despair's grip, a bitter thrall.

Here are four Pantun poems, 1 each about Friendship, Loneliness, Memories & Music

Friendship:
In friendship's bond, hearts intertwine,
Through laughter shared, through tears that shine.
In every moment, a love divine,
Friendship's embrace, forever in line.

Loneliness:
In the silence of loneliness, hearts ache,
Echoes of longing, a bitter wake.
In every sigh, a soul's mistake,
Loneliness' grasp, a heavy weight.

Memories:
In the recesses of memories past,
Moments cherished, too beautiful to last.
In every thought, a feeling amassed,
Memories' echo, where time is cast.

Music:
In the rhythm of life, music flows,
Melodies dance, where the heart glows.
In every note, a story it bestows,
Music's symphony, where passion grows.

Here are four Pantun poems, 1 each about Art, Inspiration, Creativity & Courage

Art:
In the stroke of a brush, art is born,
Colors swirling, where dreams adorn.
In every canvas, a world reborn,
Art's magic, where souls are sworn.

Inspiration:
In the whispers of inspiration's call,
Creative minds, where visions sprawl.
In every idea, a spark to enthrall,
Inspiration's touch, where dreams install.

Creativity:
In the depths of creativity's stream,
Imagination blooms, in a vibrant gleam.
In every creation, a unique scheme,
Creativity's essence, a timeless dream.

Courage:
In the face of fear, courage stands tall,
In adversity's shadow, it heeds the call.
In every step, a leap, not a crawl,
Courage's fire, where destinies enthrall.

Here are four Pantun poems, 1 each about Faith, Doubt, Solitude & Joy

Faith:
In the darkest night, stars still gleam,
Faith guides us through, like a steady beam.
In the heart's whispers, a sacred stream,
Faith blooms eternal, in life's grand scheme.

Doubt:
In the depths of doubt, shadows loom,
Casting uncertainty, like impending doom.
Yet amidst the darkness, in doubt's room,
Hope flickers faintly, dispelling gloom.

Solitude:
In the quiet of solitude, the soul finds peace,
A gentle refuge, where worries cease.
In the silence, all burdens release,
Solitude's embrace, a sweet release.

Joy:
In laughter's echo, joy takes flight,
Hearts uplifted, in sheer delight.
In every moment, where spirits ignite,
Joy's melody, a symphony of light.

Here are four Pantun poems, 1 each about Sorrow, Childhood, Wisdom & Innocence

Sorrow:
In the depths of sorrow, tears cascade,
A heavy burden, in shadows made.
Yet amidst the pain, hope does pervade,
Sorrow's touch, a path to serenade.

Childhood:
In the innocence of childhood's grace,
Dreams unfurl, in a wondrous chase.
In laughter's echo, memories embrace,
Childhood's magic, a cherished space.

Wisdom:
In the quiet whispers of wisdom's call,
Echoes of ages past, where shadows fall.
In every lesson learned, both big and small,
Wisdom guides, through life's rise and fall.

Innocence:
In the purity of innocence, hearts shine bright,
Untainted by darkness, in its sacred light.
In every smile, a glimpse of heaven's flight,
Innocence's embrace, a beacon in the night.

Here are four Pantun poems, 1 each about Passion, Serenity, Freedom & Justice

Passion:
In the fiery depths of passion's flame,
Hearts ablaze, in love's sweet game.
In every touch, a spark to claim,
Passion's embrace, forever the same.

Serenity:
In the calm embrace of serenity's song,
Tranquility reigns, where souls belong.
In nature's beauty, where dreams prolong,
Serenity whispers, a melody strong.

Freedom:
In the boundless sky, freedom's flight,
Wings unfurled, in boundless might.
In every choice, a path so bright,
Freedom's embrace, a beacon in the night.

Justice:
In the halls of justice, truth does reign,
Fairness prevails, in every domain.
In every action, where rights attain,
Justice's embrace, a society's gain.

Here are four Pantun poems, 1 each about Change, Resilience, Gratitude & Forgiveness

Change:
In the ebb and flow of life's grand dance,
Change whispers softly, in circumstance.
In every shift, a new chance,
Change's embrace, a cosmic romance.

Resilience:
In the face of adversity, resilience stands tall,
Courageous hearts, never to fall.
In every setback, a lesson to recall,
Resilience prevails, through it all.

Gratitude:
In the quiet moments of gratitude's grace,
Hearts overflow, in thankful embrace.
In every blessing, a cherished space,
Gratitude's touch, a sacred trace.

Forgiveness:
In the depths of forgiveness, hearts find peace,
Burdens lifted, in love's sweet release.
In every pardon, a chance to cease,
Forgiveness heals, where hurts decrease.

Here are four Pantun poems, 1 each about Longing, Belonging, Discovery & Wonder

Longing:
In the quiet of night, stars softly gleam,
Longing whispers in the moonlight's beam.
Heartaches echo in a silent scream,
Longing for love, lost in a dream.

Belonging:
In the circle of friends, hearts align,
Belonging found, in arms entwined.
In laughter shared, pure and kind,
Belonging blooms, in souls refined.

Discovery:
In uncharted waters, the explorer sails,
Discovery awaits, where courage prevails.
In mysteries unravelled, ancient tales,
Discovery beckons, as the wind hails.

Wonder:
In the whispers of wind, wonders unfold,
Mysteries untold, in stories old.
In the magic of nature, treasures hold,
Wonder reigns, a sight to behold.

Here are four Pantun poems, 1 each about Journey, Reflection, Harmony & Imagination

Journey:
On winding roads, the wanderer roams,
Journeying far from familiar homes.
In every step, adventure looms,
Journey's path, where dreams comb.

Reflection:
In the stillness of dusk, the mind takes flight,
Reflections dance in the fading light.
In the depths of thoughts, truth's insight,
Reflection guides, through day and night.

Harmony:
In the symphony of life, harmony thrives,
Melodies blend, where each heart strives.
In unity's embrace, where love survives,
Harmony reigns, where peace arrives.

Imagination:
In the realms of fantasy, the mind does soar,
Imagination paints worlds never seen before.
In dreams unfurled, where wonders adore,
Imagination sparks, forevermore.

Here are four Pantun poems, 1 each about Silence, Laughter, Tears & Strength

Silence:
In the hush of dawn, silence reigns supreme,
Whispers of peace in a tranquil stream.
In silence found, where hearts redeem,
Silence echoes, like a sacred theme.

Laughter:
In the echoes of laughter, joy does spring,
Hearts lightened, like birds on wing.
In shared moments, where spirits sing,
Laughter's melody, a blissful ring.

Tears:
In the quiet of night, tears softly fall,
Echoes of sorrow in the heart's call.
In the depths of pain, where shadows crawl,
Tears cleanse, like rain after a squall.

Strength:
In the crucible of life, strength does rise,
Courageous hearts, beneath stormy skies.
In every trial, where hope defies,
Strength prevails, where the soul lies.

Here are four Pantun poems, 1 each about Vulnerability, Renewal, Acceptance & Mystery

Vulnerability:
In the open heart's embrace, vulnerability blooms,
Raw and fragile, amidst life's fumes.
In honesty's tears and love's perfumes,
Vulnerability sings, where hearts resume.

Renewal:
In the quiet dawn, renewal finds its place,
A fresh start, in dawn's embrace.
In every sunrise, a brand-new space,
Renewal's grace, in life's chase.

Acceptance:
In the depths of the heart, acceptance dwells,
Letting go of burdens, breaking spells.
In every moment, where peace swells,
Acceptance blooms, where truth tells.

Mystery:
In the depths of night, mystery whispers low,
Secrets hidden, where shadows grow.
In the unknown, where dreams flow,
Mystery beckons, where hearts go.

Here are four Pantun poems, 1 each about Transformation, Eternity, Cosmos & Happiness

Transformation:
Amidst the chrysalis, the caterpillar dreams,
Transformation whispers in silent streams.
From earthbound crawl to flight's extremes,
Metamorphosis blooms in sunlit beams.

Eternity:
In the tapestry of time, eternity's song,
Echoes through galaxies, serene and strong.
In the dance of stars, where souls belong,
Eternity's embrace, where dreams prolong.

Cosmos:
In the vast expanse of the cosmic night,
Galaxies twinkle, a breathtaking sight.
In the cosmic dance, where stars take flight,
The cosmos whispers secrets, veiled from sight.

Happiness:
In laughter's echo, happiness does reign,
In hearts entwined, free from pain.
In joy's embrace, where dreams attain,
Happiness blooms, like a gentle rain.

RUBAIYAT:

A Persian form of poetry consisting of quatrains with a specific rhyme scheme (AABA).

Here are four Rubaiyat poems, 1 each about Love, Nature, Beauty & Time

Love:
In the tender whispers of love's sweet embrace,
Hearts entwine, in a passionate chase.
Through trials and triumphs, love finds its place,
A bond eternal, in time and space.

Nature:
In the quiet glades where wildflowers bloom,
Nature sings a melody, dispelling gloom.
In forests deep and mountains' loom,
Beauty thrives, dispelling any sense of doom.

Beauty:
In the gentle curve of a rose's bloom,
Beauty reigns, dispelling any sense of gloom.
From sun-kissed skies to oceans' vast expanse,
Beauty abounds in every subtle nuance.

Time:
In the sands of time, moments slip away,
A fleeting dance, in the light of day.
In time's relentless march, we find our way,
Navigating life's twists and turns, come what may.

Here are four Rubaiyat poems, 1 each about Death, Dreams, Hope & Despair

Death:
In the quiet hush of twilight's sigh,
Death casts its shadow, bidding goodbye.
Yet amidst the sorrow and the tears we cry,
In death's embrace, souls take flight, to the sky.

Dreams:
In the realm of dreams, where fantasies unfurl,
Hope takes flight, like a precious pearl.
In dreams' embrace, we transcend this world,
Exploring realms unknown, where wonders swirl.

Hope:
In the darkest hour, hope shines bright,
A beacon of light, dispelling the night.
In hope's gentle embrace, fears take flight,
As we navigate life's tumultuous plight.

Despair:
In the depths of despair, shadows loom,
Casting darkness, dispelling all bloom.
Yet amidst the sorrow and the sense of doom,
Hope's light pierces through, dispelling gloom.

Here are four Rubaiyat poems, 1 each about Friendship, Loneliness, Memories & Music

Friendship:
In the bonds of friendship, hearts entwine,
A tapestry of love, both yours and mine.
In laughter shared and tears combined,
Friendship's embrace, forever divine.

Loneliness:
In the quiet solitude of the lonely heart,
Echoes of longing, like whispers in the dark.
Yet amidst the silence, a glimmer of a spark,
In loneliness' embrace, we find our part.

Memories:
In the corridors of time, memories reside,
Echoes of laughter, in the ebb and tide.
In cherished moments, where love abides,
Memories bloom, in hearts that confide.

Music:
In the symphony of life, music does play,
A melody of emotions, night and day.
From soft whispers to thunderous fray,
Music's embrace, in every note, we sway.

Here are four Rubaiyat poems, 1 each about Art, Inspiration, Creativity & Courage

Art:
In strokes of color, on canvas spread,
Artists weave stories, from hearts that bled.
In every masterpiece, a tale is said,
Art's embrace, where souls are led.

Inspiration:
In the quiet muse of inspiration's fire,
Creativity ignites, in passion's desire.
In every spark, a dream takes flight,
Inspiration's embrace, a beacon in the night.

Creativity:
In the boundless expanse of the creative mind,
Ideas swirl, in a dance of every kind.
From the depths of imagination, dreams unwind,
Creativity's embrace, where possibilities find.

Courage:
In the face of adversity, courage stands tall,
A beacon of strength, amidst the squall.
In every challenge, big or small,
Courage's embrace, where heroes call.

Here are four Rubaiyat poems, 1 each about Faith, Doubt, Solitude & Joy

Faith:
In the heart's deepest chambers, faith does reside,
A beacon of hope, in life's tumultuous tide.
Through trials and tribulations, faith shall guide,
In the darkest hour, it's the light by our side.

Doubt:
In the labyrinth of uncertainty, doubt does weave,
Casting shadows on beliefs we once did cleave.
Yet amidst the fog, truths we may perceive,
Doubt, the crucible where clarity achieves.

Solitude:
In the silence of solitude, the soul finds its rest,
A sanctuary where thoughts can freely invest.
Away from the world's chaos, here we attest,
Solitude, a cherished companion, our quest.

Joy:
In the laughter of children, joy takes flight,
A melody of happiness, pure and bright.
In moments of bliss, our spirits alight,
Joy, the spark that makes our hearts ignite.

Here are four Rubaiyat poems, 1 each about Sorrow, Childhood, Wisdom & Innocence

Sorrow:
In the depths of despair, sorrow does dwell,
A heavy burden, a mournful knell.
Yet from sorrow's embrace, lessons swell,
In its depths, the heart finds stories to tell.

Childhood:
In the innocence of youth, childhood blooms,
A time of wonder, free from life's glooms.
Memories etched in laughter and rooms,
Childhood, a treasure chest where dreams loom.

Wisdom:
In the quiet wisdom of the aged and wise,
Lies the culmination of life's highs and tries.
Lessons learned beneath vast azure skies,
Wisdom, the beacon that forever implies.

Innocence:
In the purity of a newborn's gaze, innocence gleams,
Untouched by the world's darkness, it beams.
In innocence's embrace, life's beauty redeems,
A fleeting moment, as pure as moonbeams.

Here are four Rubaiyat poems, 1 each about Passion, Serenity, Freedom & Justice

Passion:
In the fiery depths of passion's blaze,
Hearts entwine in a mesmerizing daze.
Fueled by desire, in love's endless maze,
Passion ignites, in a fervent, radiant phase.

Serenity:
In the tranquil embrace of serenity's glow,
Calmness reigns where gentle breezes blow.
Amidst life's chaos, a peaceful undertow,
Serenity, the balm that soothes our woe.

Freedom:
In the boundless expanse of freedom's flight,
Lies the promise of dreams taking flight.
Unshackled souls, radiant and bright,
Freedom, the beacon that guides us to light.

Justice:
In the halls of justice, fairness presides,
Where truth and righteousness forever abides.
Inequality's foe, where justice divides,
Justice, the cornerstone on which society rides.

Here are four Rubaiyat poems, 1 each about Change, Resilience, Gratitude & Forgiveness

Change:
In the flux of life, change sweeps through,
A constant rhythm, ever anew.
From old to new, from false to true,
Change, the catalyst that helps us renew.

Resilience:
In the face of adversity, resilience blooms,
A steadfast strength that dispels all glooms.
Through trials and tribulations, it consumes,
Resilience, the fortress where hope resumes.

Gratitude:
In the quiet moments of reflection, gratitude grows,
A recognition of blessings, where thankfulness flows.
In gratitude's embrace, the heart overflows,
With appreciation for life's highs and lows.

Forgiveness:
In the depths of the heart, forgiveness finds its place,
A healing balm for wounds, a gesture of grace.
In forgiveness' embrace, burdens we erase,
And find peace in the sacred space.

Here are four Rubaiyat poems, 1 each about Longing, Belonging, Discovery & Wonder

Longing:
In the stillness of night, a yearning sigh,
Echoes of longing beneath the starry sky.
Lost in dreams of what could be, hopes fly,
Seeking solace in a lover's tender lullaby.

Belonging:
Amidst the crowd, a soul seeks its place,
Longing for kinship, a familiar embrace.
In bonds of friendship and love's sweet grace,
Belonging found, hearts intertwined, in space.

Discovery:
On paths uncharted, the seeker roams,
In quest of treasures, through distant zones.
Amidst hidden wonders and unknown thrones,
Discovery reigns, in whispers and in groans.

Wonder:
In the grandeur of nature, wonders lie,
Beneath azure skies, where eagles fly.
From misty valleys to mountains high,
Wonder awaits, in every breath and sigh.

Here are four Rubaiyat poems, 1 each about Journey, Reflection, Harmony & Imagination

Journey:
On winding roads, the traveler strides,
Through valleys deep and mountainsides.
With each step, new horizons he espies,
In journey's rhythm, adventure abides.

Reflection:
In the stillness of dusk, the mind does roam,
Through memories, like waves on shores foam.
Reflecting on life's journey, far from home,
Finding solace in thoughts that softly comb.

Harmony:
In nature's symphony, all voices blend,
From rustling leaves to rivers that bend.
In harmonious union, where all things tend,
The world finds peace, its brokenness to mend.

Imagination:
In the vast expanse of the mind's terrain,
Imagination soars, free from any chain.
Where dreams take flight and visions reign,
Infinite possibilities, boundless and arcane.

Here are four Rubaiyat poems, 1 each about Silence, Laughter, Tears & Strength

Silence:
In the hush of dawn, a tranquil reprieve,
Silence reigns, as morning mists weave.
In the quiet, hearts find solace and retrieve,
A sanctuary where weary souls may cleave.

Laughter:
In the heart's laughter, joy unfurls,
Echoes of mirth, like precious pearls.
In shared moments, where laughter swirls,
Life's burdens lifted, as happiness whirls.

Tears:
Beneath stormy skies, the teardrops fall,
A symphony of sorrow, a mournful call.
In each tear shed, emotions enthrall,
Washing away pain, as hearts enthrall.

Strength:
In the crucible of trial, the spirit finds its flame,
Forged in fire, resilient hearts reclaim.
Through adversity and hardship's claim,
Strength arises, undeterred by shame.

Here are four Rubaiyat poems, 1 each about Vulnerability, Renewal, Acceptance & Mystery

Vulnerability:
In the open heart's embrace, vulnerability lies,
A tender whisper, beneath starlit skies.
In the courage to expose, where truth applies,
Vulnerability blooms, where authenticity flies.

Renewal:
In the quiet dawn, the world awakes anew,
Bathed in golden light, where dreams ensue.
From darkness to light, life's cycles renew,
In each sunrise, hope's promise breaks through.

Acceptance:
In the gentle embrace of acceptance, souls find peace,
Letting go of burdens, letting anxieties cease.
In the serenity of surrender, worries release,
Acceptance blooms, like a flower's gentle crease.

Mystery:
In the depths of the night, where shadows dance,
Mystery lurks, in every hidden chance.
In the enigma of the cosmos' expanse,
The heart finds wonder in the cosmic trance.

Here are four Rubaiyat poems, 1 each about Transformation, Eternity, Cosmos & Happiness

Transformation:
From the cocoon emerges the butterfly, anew,
A metamorphosis profound, a spectacle to view.
In change's gentle hands, transformation brews,
As life unfurls its wings, vibrant and true.

Eternity:
In the vast expanse of time, eternity unfolds,
A journey without end, where tales are told.
In eternity's embrace, the universe beholds,
The secrets of existence, forever untold.

Cosmos:
In the cosmic dance of stars, the universe spins,
Galaxies whirl, and planets dance within.
In the cosmic tapestry, creation begins,
A symphony of light, where wonders begin.

Happiness:
In the warmth of a smile, happiness resides,
A beacon of light, where joy abides.
In happiness' gentle embrace, hearts confide,
In the simple pleasures, life's beauty presides

-:¦:-•:*'''''*:•.-:¦:-•**•-:¦:-•:*'''''*:•:*'''''*:•.-:¦:-•**•-:¦:--:¦:-•:*'''''*:•.-:¦:- •**•-:¦:-•:*'''''*:•:*'''''*:•.-:¦:-•**•-:¦:-

GHAZAL 2:

Apart from the previously mentioned ghazal, there are variations of this form found in different cultures,such as Urdu, Arabic, and Persian, each with its own conventions and rhyme schemes.

-:¦:-•:*'''''*:•.-:¦:-•**•-:¦:-•:*'''''*:•:*'''''*:•.-:¦:-•**•-:¦:--:¦:-•:*'''''*:•.-:¦:- •**•-:¦:-•:*'''''*:•:*'''''*:•.-:¦:-•**•-:¦:-

Here are four Ghazal 2 poems, 1 each about Love, Nature, Beauty & Time

Ghazal on Love:

In the garden of love, hearts dance with delight,
A symphony of emotions, in the moonlit night.

In the embrace of passion, souls find their flight,
Entwined in desire's fire, burning bright.

With every heartbeat, love's melody takes flight,
In the tapestry of romance, woven tight.

Oh, love's sweet torment, a beautiful plight,
In its ecstasy, souls unite.

Ghazal on Nature:

In the bosom of nature, serenity resides,
Mountains whisper secrets, rivers guide.

In the dance of leaves, the wind confides,
Underneath the open sky, freedom abides.

The sun paints the horizon with vibrant tides,
In the embrace of forests, peace presides.

Oh, nature's beauty, where all life collides,
In its vastness, harmony abides.

Ghazal on Beauty:

Beauty, a delicate flower in life's grand design,
In every petal's curve, perfection shines.

In the eyes of lovers, beauty intertwines,
In the heart's reflection, divine.

The moon's soft glow, a silver line,
In the canvas of existence, sublime.

Oh, beauty's allure, a treasure to define,
In its essence, eternity entwines.

Ghazal on Time:

Time, a relentless river flowing fast,
In its currents, memories cast.

In the dawn of youth, dreams amassed,
In the twilight years, shadows amassed.

With each passing moment, life amassed,
In the hourglass of fate, sands amassed.

Oh, time's ceaseless march, unsurpassed,
In its passage, destinies amassed.

Here are four Ghazal 2 poems, 1 each about Death, Dreams, Hope & Despair

Ghazal on Death:

In the silence of night, whispers of death's embrace,
A journey into the unknown, a solemn pace.

In the depths of darkness, souls find solace,
Eternal rest, in death's gentle grace.

With each breath's release, a farewell trace,
In the cycle of life, death takes its place.

Oh, death's quiet call, a sacred space,
In its embrace, souls find peace.

Ghazal on Dreams:

In the realm of dreams, fantasies take flight,
A world of endless possibilities, shining bright.

In the depths of slumber, imagination's might,
Visions of wonder, in the silent night.

With closed eyes, the mind's eye ignites,
In the tapestry of dreams, realities unite.

Oh, dreams' ethereal dance, a wondrous sight,
In its embrace, hopes take flight.

Ghazal on Hope:

In the heart's sanctuary, hope takes root,
A beacon in the darkness, a resolute pursuit.

In the face of adversity, resilience to refute,
Dreams of tomorrow, in the present's dispute.

With each sunrise, hope's light transmute,
In the depths of despair, a steadfast salute.

Oh, hope's unwavering flame, absolute,
In its embrace, destinies reroute.

Ghazal on Despair:

In the depths of despair, shadows loom,
A silent scream, in the heart's gloom.

In the void of emptiness, thoughts consume,
Echoes of sorrow, in the soul's tomb.

With each tear shed, a silent exhume,
In the labyrinth of despair, lost in its fume.

Oh, despair's relentless grip, a heavy plume,
In its embrace, hearts entomb.

Here are four Ghazal 2 poems, 1 each about Friendship, Loneliness, Memories & Music

Ghazal on Friendship:

In the tapestry of life, friends weave their thread,
Bound by loyalty, in moments led.

In the echoes of laughter, memories spread,
With open hearts, paths are tread.

Through the highs and lows, friendships are bred,
In the warmth of camaraderie, souls are wed.

Oh, friendship's bond, never to be shred,
In its embrace, love widespread.

Ghazal on Loneliness:

In the silent hours of night, loneliness abides,
A solitary figure, where darkness resides.

In the echoes of silence, solitude presides,
Lost in the depths, where emptiness confides.

With each passing moment, loneliness divides,
In the solitude of the soul, sorrow hides.

Oh, loneliness' silent cry, where pain collides,
In its embrace, the heart confides.

Ghazal on Memories:

In the corridors of time, memories take flight,
Echoes of laughter, in the still of night.

In the album of the mind, moments alight,
Etched in the heart, shining bright.

Through the haze of years, memories ignite,
In the tapestry of life, colors unite.

Oh, memories' sweet embrace, a guiding light,
In its reverie, past delights.

Ghazal on Music:

In the symphony of life, music's melody plays,
A harmonious blend, in its endless maze.

In the rhythm of the heart, emotions ablaze,
Notes dance freely, in the soul's ballet.

With each chord struck, the soul sways,
In the cadence of music, spirits raise.

Oh, music's enchanting grace, in its gentle gaze,
In its embrace, hearts amaze.

Here are four Ghazal 2 poems, 1 each about Art, Inspiration, Creativity & Courage

Ghazal on Art:

In strokes of color, the canvas comes alive,
A masterpiece unfolds, in every stroke we strive.

In the depths of expression, emotions contrive,
The soul's reflection, where passions thrive.

With each brushstroke, worlds derive,
In the realm of imagination, dreams arrive.

Oh, art's timeless embrace, where spirits revive,
In its creation, hearts connive.

Ghazal on Inspiration:

In the whispers of the wind, inspiration calls,
A muse's gentle touch, as the night falls.

In the depths of silence, the soul enthralls,
Ideas take flight, as creativity sprawls.

With each new dawn, the muse installs,
In the heart's sanctuary, where dreams install.

Oh, inspiration's guiding light, as darkness stalls,
In its embrace, aspirations recall

Ghazal on Creativity:

In the depths of the mind, creativity breeds,
A river of ideas, where innovation leads.

In the dance of imagination, the spirit feeds,
Limitless possibilities, in boundless speeds.

With each spark ignited, the soul heeds,
In the realm of creation, where passion bleeds.

Oh, creativity's boundless flight, where innovation exceeds, In its embrace, the soul exceeds.

Ghazal on Courage:

In the face of adversity, courage stands tall,
A beacon of strength, when fear befalls.

In the depths of uncertainty, courage calls,
Fortitude prevails, as obstacles appalls.

With each step forward, courage enthralls,
In the heart's resilience, where bravery installs.

Oh, courage's unwavering might, when darkness mauls,
In its embrace, the spirit enthralls.

Here are four Ghazal 2 poems, 1 each about Faith, Doubt, Solitude & Joy

Ghazal on Faith:

In the depths of the soul, faith takes flight,
A beacon of hope, in the darkest night.

In the whispers of prayer, spirits unite,
Trusting in the divine, with all our might.

With each trial faced, faith ignites,
In the heart's sanctuary, where faith incites.

Oh, faith's unwavering light, burning bright,
In its embrace, souls unite.

Ghazal on Doubt:

In the shadows of uncertainty, doubt resides,
A whisper of fear, where confidence hides.

In the depths of the mind, doubt collides,
Clouding the path, where clarity abides.

With each question asked, doubt presides,
In the labyrinth of thought, where certainty divides.

Oh, doubt's relentless grip, where truth confides,
In its embrace, skepticism resides.
Ghazal on Solitude:

In the quiet of solitude, the soul finds peace,
A sanctuary of serenity, where worries cease.

In the embrace of silence, worries release,
Finding solace in solitude, a gentle release.

With each breath taken, solitude's increase,
In the tranquility of solitude, the heart finds release.

Oh, solitude's gentle embrace, where worries decrease,
In its tranquility, the soul finds ease.

Ghazal on Joy:

In the laughter of children, joy takes flight,
A melody of happiness, in pure delight.

In the warmth of a smile, hearts unite,
Spreading joy and love, in the darkest night.

With each moment cherished, joy ignites,
In the tapestry of life, where happiness alights.

Oh, joy's contagious embrace, shining bright,
In its radiance, hearts ignite.

Here are four Ghazal 2 poems, 1 each about Sorrow, Childhood, Wisdom & Innocence

Ghazal on Sorrow:

In the depths of the heart, sorrow resides,
A shadow of pain, where hope subsides.

In the tears shed, emotions collide,
Seeking solace in grief, where anguish hides.

With each passing moment, sorrow abides,
In the depths of despair, where darkness presides.

Oh, sorrow's heavy burden, where sorrow resides,
In its embrace, hearts confide.

Ghazal on Childhood:

In the innocence of youth, childhood thrives,
A world of wonder, where joy arrives.

In the laughter of children, happiness survives,
Moments of pure bliss, where memories derive.

With each playful moment, childhood thrives,
In the heart's sanctuary, where dreams contrive.

Oh, childhood's precious years, where innocence thrives,
In its embrace, the soul revives.

Ghazal on Wisdom:

In the depths of knowledge, wisdom resides,
A beacon of light, where insight abides.

In the lessons learned, perspectives collide,
Seeking truth and understanding, wisdom guides.

With each experience gained, wisdom presides,
In the tapestry of life, where clarity resides.

Oh, wisdom's timeless embrace, where insight presides,
In its wisdom, the soul confides.

Ghazal on Innocence:

In the purity of heart, innocence thrives,
A gentle spirit, untouched by strife.

In the eyes of the innocent, hope revives,
A world of possibilities, where dreams come alive.

With each trusting glance, innocence survives,
In the soul's sanctuary, where goodness thrives.

Oh, innocence's tender embrace, where purity resides,
In its purity, the soul abides.

Here are four Ghazal 2 poems, 1 each about Passion, Serenity, Freedom & Justice

Ghazal on Passion:

In the fire of desire, passion ignites,
A blaze of fervor, where hearts unite.

In the heat of longing, passion incites,
A symphony of emotions, in the still of night.

With each heartbeat's rhythm, passion delights,
In the dance of love, where passion takes flight.

Oh, passion's fiery embrace, where love excites,
In its fervent grasp, souls ignite.

Ghazal on Serenity:

In the tranquil depths of silence, serenity dwells,
A calm oasis, where peace compels.

In the whispers of nature, serenity swells,
A gentle breeze, where tranquility excels.

With each breath of solitude, serenity tells,
In the heart's sanctuary, where peace dispels.

Oh, serenity's gentle embrace, where calmness dwells,
In its tranquility, the soul propels.

Ghazal on Freedom:

In the vast expanse of sky, freedom flies,
A boundless horizon, where dreams arise.

In the heart's liberation, freedom defies,
A journey of self-discovery, where courage lies.

With each step taken, freedom implies,
In the pursuit of liberty, where passion lies.

Oh, freedom's liberating embrace, where the spirit flies,
In its boundless expanse, aspirations rise.

Ghazal on Justice:

In the pursuit of righteousness, justice prevails,
A beacon of fairness, where truth unveils.

In the fight for equality, justice entails,
A chorus of voices, where justice exhales.

With each verdict rendered, justice entails,
In the scales of fairness, where justice avails.

Oh, justice's unwavering embrace, where fairness entails,
In its pursuit, righteousness sails.

Here are four Ghazal 2 poems, 1 each about Change, Resilience, Gratitude & Forgiveness

Ghazal on Change:

In the ebb and flow of life, change abounds,
A constant evolution, where destiny surrounds.

In the winds of transformation, change compounds,
A journey of growth, where new paths are found.

With each shift in the tides, change resounds,
In the tapestry of existence, where change astounds.

Oh, change's transformative embrace, where fate rebounds, It's embrace, new beginnings confound.

Ghazal on Resilience:

In the face of adversity, resilience stands tall,
A fortress of strength, where obstacles fall.

In the heart's endurance, resilience calls,
A spirit unyielding, where courage enthralls.

With each challenge overcome, resilience recalls,
In the depths of determination, where fortitude installs.

Oh, resilience's unwavering embrace, where courage enthralls, In its strength, resilience befalls.

Ghazal on Gratitude:

In the depths of the soul, gratitude resides,
A humble acknowledgment, where blessings abide.

In the heart's appreciation, gratitude confides,
A chorus of thanks, where joy presides.

With each moment cherished, gratitude guides,
In the tapestry of life, where gratitude resides.

Oh, gratitude's heartfelt embrace, where happiness subsides, In its abundance, gratitude provides.

Ghazal on Forgiveness:

In the journey of healing, forgiveness blooms,
A balm for the soul, where wounds resume.

In the act of reconciliation, forgiveness looms,
A bridge to peace, where redemption consumes.

With each step towards absolution, forgiveness fumes, In the heart's sanctuary, where forgiveness exhumes.

Oh, forgiveness's liberating embrace, where bitterness assumes, In its embrace, hearts resume.

Here are four Ghazal 2 poems, 1 each about Longing, Belonging, Discovery & Wonder

Ghazal on Longing:

In the silence of night, longing whispers soft,
A yearning deep within where dreams aloft.

In the echo of memories, longing oft,
A melody of heartache, where passions oft.

With each breath drawn, longing oft,
In the depths of desire, where hearts oft.

Oh, longing's tender embrace, where souls oft,
In its longing, desires oft.

Ghazal on Belonging:

In the embrace of kin, belonging thrives,
A sense of unity, where love survives.

In the warmth of community, belonging drives,
A bond of fellowship, where hearts contrive.

With each shared moment, belonging thrives,
In the fabric of togetherness, where souls derive.

Oh, belonging's comforting embrace, where spirits thrive, In its unity, souls revive.

Ghazal on Discovery:

In the journey of exploration, discovery unfolds,
A world of wonder, where mysteries hold.

In the pursuit of knowledge, discovery enrolls,
A path of enlightenment, where truth beholds.

With each revelation, discovery unfolds,
In the realms of curiosity, where curiosity molds.

Oh, discovery's enlightening embrace, where knowledge unfolds, In its pursuit, wisdom behold.

Ghazal on Wonder:

In the awe of creation, wonder ignites,
A marvel of existence, where beauty invites.

In the depths of imagination, wonder alights,
A realm of endless possibilities, where dreams take flight.

With each moment of wonder, inspiration excites,
In the tapestry of life, where wonder unites.

Oh, wonder's enchanting embrace, where imagination delights, In its magic, hearts unite.

Here are four Ghazal 2 poems, 1 each about Journey, Reflection, Harmony & Imagination

Ghazal on Journey:

In the winding path of life, the journey begins,
A road of adventures, where destinies spin.

In the footsteps taken, the journey wins,
A tale of discovery, where new horizons grin.

With each mile traveled, the journey thins,
In the heart's wanderlust, where passions within.

Oh, journey's endless embrace, where the spirit grins,
In its passage, the soul within.

Ghazal on Reflection:

In the stillness of the night, reflection prevails,
A moment of introspection, where truth avails.

In the echoes of the past, reflection sails,
A voyage of memories, where emotions unveil.

With each thought pondered, reflection exhales,
In the depths of the mind, where clarity entails.

Oh, reflection's profound embrace, where insight hails,
In its contemplation, the soul avails.

Ghazal on Harmony:

In the symphony of life, harmony resounds,
A chorus of unity, where peace surrounds.

In the balance of nature, harmony compounds,
A dance of rhythms, where serenity astounds.

With each chord struck, harmony rebounds,
In the melody of existence, where joy confounds.

Oh, harmony's melodic embrace, where tranquility rebounds,
In its symphony, the heart compounds.

Ghazal on Imagination:

In the canvas of the mind, imagination flies,
A realm of fantasies, where dreams arise.

In the depths of creativity, imagination defies,
A playground of ideas, where innovation lies.

With each thought conceived, imagination allies,
In the realm of possibilities, where innovation ties.

Oh, imagination's boundless embrace, where creativity allies,
In its wonder, the soul complies.

Here are four Ghazal 2 poems, 1 each about Silence, Laughter, Tears & Strength

Ghazal on Silence:

In the depths of stillness, silence prevails,
A tranquil sanctuary, where peace entails.

In the absence of words, silence unveils,
A canvas of serenity, where calmness sails.

With each breath taken, silence exhales,
In the heart's sanctuary, where solace avails.

Oh, silence's gentle embrace, where tranquility unveils,
In its serenity, the soul prevails.

Ghazal on Laughter:

In the echoes of joy, laughter rings,
A chorus of happiness, where hearts sing.

In the warmth of mirth, laughter springs,
A melody of delight, where spirits cling.

With each peal of laughter, joy brings,
In the dance of merriment, where laughter swings.

Oh, laughter's infectious embrace, where jubilance springs,
In its mirth, the heart takes wings.

Ghazal on Tears:

In the depths of sorrow, tears fall,
A river of emotions, where heartstrings call.

In the release of pain, tears enthrall,
A cleansing of the soul, where emotions sprawl.

With each drop shed, emotions enthrall,
In the tapestry of grief, where sorrows install.
Oh, tears' cathartic embrace, where emotions install,
In its release, the heart enthralls.

Ghazal on Strength:

In the face of adversity, strength prevails,
A fortress of resilience, where courage avails.

In the heart's endurance, strength unveils,
A beacon of hope, where determination exhales.

With each challenge faced, strength entails,
In the depths of fortitude, where determination entails.

Oh, strength's unwavering embrace, where resilience entails,
In its resolve, the spirit prevails.

Here are four Ghazal 2 poems, 1 each about Vulnerability, Renewal, Acceptance & Mystery

Ghazal on Vulnerability:

In the rawness of emotions, vulnerability lies,
A tender openness, where truth defies.

In the fragile heart, vulnerability cries,
A delicate balance, where courage implies.

With each bared soul, vulnerability tries,
In the depths of authenticity, where sincerity flies.

Oh, vulnerability's tender embrace, where honesty vies,
In its vulnerability, the soul tries.

Ghazal on Renewal:

In the cycle of life, renewal begins,
A rebirth of hope, where newness spins.

In the awakening of spring, renewal grins,
A rejuvenation of spirit, where light begins.

With each dawn's light, renewal wins,
In the heart's sanctuary, where growth begins.

Oh, renewal's refreshing embrace, where hope wins,
In its awakening, the soul begins.

Ghazal on Acceptance:

In the embrace of truth, acceptance thrives,
A surrender to what is, where peace derives.

In the heart's forgiveness, acceptance arrives,
A letting go of judgment, where compassion revives.

With each moment lived, acceptance contrives,
In the depths of understanding, where love survives.

Oh, acceptance's gentle embrace, where healing drives,
In its embrace, the soul arrives.

Ghazal on Mystery:

In the depths of the unknown, mystery lies,
A veil of intrigue, where curiosity implies.

In the shadows of uncertainty, mystery flies,
A sense of wonder, where imagination defies.

With each question asked, mystery supplies,
In the tapestry of existence, where curiosity relies.

Oh, mystery's enigmatic embrace, where wonder flies,
In its mystique, the soul complies.

Here are four Ghazal 2 poems, 1 each about Transformation, Eternity, Cosmos & Happiness

Ghazal on Transformation:

In the crucible of change, transformation blooms,
A metamorphosis of the soul, where new paths loom.

In the fires of adversity, transformation consumes,
A rebirth of spirit, where strength resumes.

With each challenge faced, transformation exhumes,
In the depths of evolution, where destiny fumes.

Oh, transformation's potent embrace, where growth resumes,
In its embrace, the soul assumes.

Ghazal on Eternity:

In the infinite expanse, eternity abides,
A timeless journey, where the soul glides.

In the stars' twinkling light, eternity confides,
A cosmic dance, where destiny resides.

With each passing moment, eternity guides,
In the boundless expanse, where the universe resides.

Oh, eternity's endless embrace, where time divides,
In its infinity, the soul abides.

Ghazal on Cosmos:

In the vast expanse of space, the cosmos unfolds,
A tapestry of stars, where mysteries untold.

In the dance of galaxies, the cosmos beholds,
A symphony of light, where wonders behold.

With each cosmic breath, the cosmos molds,
In the fabric of existence, where secrets enfold.

Oh, cosmos' majestic embrace, where wonders unfold,
In its magnificence, the soul extols.

Ghazal on Happiness:

In the warmth of joy, happiness resides,
A melody of laughter, where hearts confide.

In the embrace of love, happiness presides,
A symphony of emotions, where spirits collide.

With each moment cherished, happiness abides,
In the tapestry of life, where joy resides.

Oh, happiness's radiant embrace, where love resides,
In its embrace, the heart abides.

SIJO:

A traditional Korean poetic form with three lines, each with a specific syllable count and a pause in the middle, often exploring themes of nature and human emotions.

Here are four Sijo poems, 1 each about Love, Nature, Beauty & Time

Love:
In the tender embrace of love, hearts beat as one,
A symphony of passion, under the glowing sun.
In love's eternal dance, two souls find their home.

Nature:
In the embrace of nature, tranquility reigns,
A sanctuary of peace, where life's harmony remains.
In nature's boundless beauty, the soul finds sustains.

Beauty:
In the shimmering dawn's light, beauty unfolds,
A tapestry of colors, in hues of reds and golds.
In beauty's captivating embrace, the heart beholds.

Time:
In the sands of time, moments slip away,
A fleeting dance of seconds, in the course of the day.
In time's relentless march, memories find their stay.

Here are four Sijo poems, 1 each about Death, Dreams, Hope & Despair

Death:
In the stillness of night, death casts its shadow,
A solemn reminder, of life's fleeting meadow.
In death's embrace, the soul finds its final echo.

Dreams:
In the depths of slumber, dreams take flight,
A journey through realms, in the still of night.
In dreams' ethereal embrace, aspirations ignite.

Hope:
In the darkest hour, hope shines bright,
A beacon of light, in the depths of night.
In hope's unwavering embrace, futures take flight.

Despair:
In the depths of despair, shadows linger,
A suffocating weight, on hearts that wither.
In despair's cruel embrace, hope's flame flickers.

Here are four Sijo poems, 1 each about Friendship, Loneliness, Memories & Music

Friendship:
In the bonds of friendship, hearts intertwine,
A tapestry of loyalty, through the sands of time.
In friendship's enduring embrace, souls find divine.

Loneliness:
In the silence of solitude, loneliness resides,
A haunting echo, where the heart abides.
In loneliness' barren embrace, longing subsides.

Memories:
In the corridors of time, memories linger,
A treasure trove of moments, where hearts still remember.
In memories' tender embrace, love's flame burns ever brighter.

Music:
In the symphony of life, music plays on,
A melody of emotions, in every chord drawn.
In music's enchanting embrace, hearts find their song.

Here are four Sijo poems, 1 each about Art, Inspiration, Creativity & Courage

Art:
In the strokes of a brush, art comes alive,
A canvas of emotions, where passions thrive.
In art's vibrant embrace, souls find their drive.

Inspiration:
In the depths of the soul, inspiration ignites,
A spark of creativity, in the darkest of nights.
In inspiration's luminous embrace, dreams take flight.

Creativity:
In the realm of imagination, creativity soars,
A world of endless possibilities, beyond closed doors.
In creativity's boundless embrace, innovation roars.

Courage:
In the face of adversity, courage stands tall,
A beacon of strength, amidst the chaos that befalls.
In courage's unwavering embrace, fears dissolve.

Here are four Sijo poems, 1 each about Faith, Doubt, Solitude & Joy

Faith:
In the depths of despair, faith becomes the guiding light,
A beacon of hope, shining through the darkest night.
In faith's unwavering embrace, the soul finds its might.

Doubt:
In the labyrinth of uncertainty, doubt takes its toll,
A shadow that lingers, clouding the mind's stroll.
In doubt's relentless grip, fears whisper and control.

Solitude:
In the quiet of solitude, the soul finds solace,
A sanctuary of peace, away from the world's malice.
In solitude's gentle embrace, hearts find their balance.

Joy:
In the laughter of children, joy dances freely,
A melody of happiness, lifting spirits completely.
In joy's exuberant embrace, life's wonders we see.

Here are four Sijo poems, 1 each about Sorrow, Childhood, Wisdom & Innocence

Sorrow:
In the depths of sorrow, tears flow like a river,
Aching hearts heavy with burdens that they deliver.
Mmidst of darkness, hope remains, a shimmer.

Childhood:
In the playground's laughter, innocence runs free,
Imagination soaring high, like birds in the tree.
Childhood's fleeting moments, a treasure for eternity.

Wisdom:
In the quiet of reflection, wisdom slowly grows,
Lessons learned from life's journey, from highs to lows.
In the depths of understanding, true wisdom shows.

Innocence:
In the purity of a child's smile, innocence shines,
Untouched by the world's harshness, in its confines.
In innocence's embrace, the heart's purity aligns.

Here are four Sijo poems, 1 each about Passion, Serenity, Freedom & Justice

Passion:
In the fire of passion, hearts beat as one,
A symphony of desire, under the glowing sun.
In passion's fervent embrace, life's essence is spun.

Serenity:
In the tranquil embrace of nature, serenity reigns,
A calming whisper of wind, soothing life's pains.
In serenity's gentle touch, peace forever sustains.

Freedom:
In the open expanse of the sky, freedom soars,
Unbound by chains, the spirit forever explores.
In freedom's boundless embrace, the soul restores.

Justice:
In the halls of justice, truth finds its voice,
A beacon of righteousness, in which all can rejoice.
In justice's righteous embrace, fairness becomes choice.

Here are four Sijo poems, 1 each about Change, Resilience, Gratitude & Forgiveness

Change:
In the ebb and flow of life, change is constant,
Like the shifting tides, in cycles ever-distant.
In change's embrace, growth becomes resistant.

Resilience:
In the face of adversity, resilience blooms,
A strength forged in fire, dispelling all glooms.
In resilience's steadfast embrace, hope consumes.

Gratitude:
In the quiet moments of reflection, gratitude shines,
A recognition of blessings, amidst life's designs.
In gratitude's humble embrace, joy forever entwines.

Forgiveness:
In the depths of the heart, forgiveness takes root,
A healing balm for wounds, a remedy to refute.
In forgiveness' merciful embrace, burdens find mute.

Here are four Sijo poems, 1 each about Longing, Belonging, Discovery & Wonder

Longing:
In the quiet of the night, longing whispers softly,
A yearning for connection, for hearts to be lofty.
In longing's gentle embrace, dreams find clarity.

Belonging:
In the warmth of community, belonging finds a place,
A sense of kinship, in every embrace.
In belonging's comforting embrace, souls find grace.

Discovery:
In the depths of exploration, discovery unfolds,
A world of wonder, waiting to be told.
In discovery's embrace, mysteries are behold.

Wonder:
In the beauty of nature, wonder comes alive,
A symphony of colors, under skies so wide.
In wonder's awe-inspiring embrace, dreams take flight.

Here are four Sijo poems, 1 each about Journey, Reflection, Harmony & Imagination

Journey:
On winding paths we tread, each step a story told,
Valleys deep and mountains high, our spirits bold.
With each new turn we find, adventure to behold.

Reflection:
In quiet moments of the night, I ponder deep,
Choices made, the paths untrod, secrets that I keep.
In the stillness of my soul, I find the truth to reap.

Harmony:
In nature's symphony, the birdsong fills the air,
Rustling leaves, the babbling brook, a melody rare.
In perfect union with the earth, we find our solace there.

Imagination:
With eyes closed tight, beyond journey this realm,
Lands of skies, where dreams and fancies helm.
In worlds of mine, find my heart overwhelm.

Here are four Sijo poems, 1 each about Silence, Laughter, Tears & Strength

Silence:
In the hush of dawn, the world is still and calm,
No whispers heard, no echoes resound, no hint of qualm.
In the silence, I find solace, a sanctuary to balm.

Laughter:
With joyous peals, the laughter rings out loud and clear,
A chorus of mirth, a symphony of cheer.
In laughter's embrace, we find camaraderie dear.

Tears:
Beneath the moonlit sky, the tears begin to fall,
Each drop a testament to pain, a silent call.
In the tears we shed, we find release from sorrow's thrall.

Strength:
In the crucible of trial, the fire burns bright and fierce,
Yet in the midst of adversity, we find our strength to pierce.
With courage in our hearts, we rise above and persevere.

Here are four Sijo poems, 1 each about Vulnerability, Renewal, Acceptance & Mystery

Vulnerability:
In the softness of her gaze, I see a soul laid bare,
No walls, no masks, no pretense, just raw and rare.
In vulnerability, we find connection, a bond beyond compare.

Renewal:
With each dawn's light, the promise of renewal blooms,
A chance to start afresh, to leave behind the glooms.
In renewal's embrace, we find hope, like flowers in full blooms.

Acceptance:
In the quiet acceptance of life's twists and turns,
We learn to let go of what we cannot change, and yearns.
In acceptance's serenity, we find peace that forever yearns.

Mystery:
In the depths of the night, the stars twinkle and gleam,
Their secrets hidden, their mysteries unseen.
In the enigma of the cosmos, we find wonder's dream.

Here are four Sijo poems, 1 each about Transformation, Eternity, Cosmos & Happiness

Transformation:
In the cocoon's embrace, the caterpillar rests at last,
Its metamorphosis underway, a journey vast.
In transformation's dance, we find the future's die cast.

Eternity:
In the eternal dance of the cosmos, stars collide,
Galaxies swirl, and time itself is stretched wide.
In eternity's embrace, we find the universe's stride.

Cosmos:
In the vast expanse of space, the cosmos reigns supreme,
A tapestry of stars and galaxies, a cosmic dream.
In the cosmos' mysteries, we find our place, our team.

Happiness:
In the simple joys of life, happiness abounds,
The warmth of a smile, the laughter's joyful sounds.
In happiness' embrace, life's beauty truly astounds.

-:¦:-•:*'''''*:•.-:¦:-•**•-:¦:-•:*'''''*:•:*'''''*:•.-:¦:-•**•-:¦:--:¦:-•:*'''''*:•.-:¦:- •**•-:¦:-•:*'''''*:•:*'''''*:•.-:¦:-•**•-:¦:-

BLANK VERSE:

**Unrhymed poetry written in iambic pentameter,
often used in epic and dramatic poetry.**

Here are four Blank Verse poems, 1 each about Love, Nature, Beauty & Time

Love:
In the tender embrace of love, hearts entwine,
A symphony of passion that knows no bounds.
Every touch a caress of affection,
Every whisper a declaration of devotion.
In the embrace of love, we find fulfillment,
For it is in the union of souls that we find completeness,
And in the bond of love that we find purpose,
As we journey through life together, hand in hand.

Nature:
In the tranquil beauty of nature, peace reigns,
A sanctuary of serenity amidst the chaos of life.
Every tree a monument to resilience,
Every flower a testament to the beauty of creation.
In the embrace of nature, we find solace,
For it is in the embrace of Mother Earth that we find healing,
And in the wonders of the natural world that we find inspiration,
As we marvel at the majesty of the universe.

Beauty:
In the shimmering glow of beauty, magic dances,
A kaleidoscope of colors that dazzles the senses.
Every smile a reflection of inner radiance,
Every glance a glimpse of ethereal grace.
In the embrace of beauty, we find awe,
For it is in the appreciation of beauty that we find joy,
And in the recognition of our own beauty that we find confidence,
As we celebrate the splendor of the world around us.

Time:
In the relentless march of time, moments slip away,
A fleeting journey through the sands of eternity.
Every second a heartbeat in the rhythm of life,
Every hour a passage in the story of existence.
In the embrace of time, we find perspective,
For it is in the passage of time that we find wisdom,
And in the awareness of our mortality that we find urgency,
As we cherish each moment and make the most of every opportunity.

Here are four Blank Verse poems, 1 each about Death, Dreams, Hope & Despair

Death:
In the solemn shadow of death, darkness looms,
A reminder of the fragility of life.
Every breath a step closer to the inevitable,
Every heartbeat a countdown to the end.
In the embrace of death, we find acceptance,
For it is in the recognition of our mortality that we find liberation,
And in the face of death that we find clarity,
As we come to terms with the inevitable and embrace the unknown.

Dreams:
In the ethereal realm of dreams, possibilities abound,
A canvas upon which we paint the colors of our imagination.
Every vision a glimpse into the realm of possibility,
Every aspiration a beacon of hope.
In the embrace of dreams, we find inspiration,
For it is in the pursuit of our dreams that we find purpose,
And in the realization of our aspirations that we find fulfillment,
As we chase our dreams and reach for the stars.

Hope:
In the flickering flame of hope, light shines,
A beacon of optimism in the darkness of despair.
Every wish a prayer for a brighter tomorrow,
Every dream a promise of better days to come.
In the embrace of hope, we find resilience,
For it is in the belief in a better future that we find strength,
And in the anticipation of brighter days that we find courage,
As we hold onto hope and refuse to let go.

Despair:
In the depths of despair, darkness reigns,
A suffocating blanket that smothers the soul.
Every tear a testament to pain unspoken,
Every sigh a cry for help.
In the embrace of despair, we find loneliness,
For it is in the depths of our darkest moments that we feel most alone,
And in the depths of our despair that we find desperation,
As we struggle to find our way back to the light.

Here are four Blank Verse poems, 1 each about Friendship, Loneliness, Memories & Music

Friendship:
In the warm embrace of friendship, hearts unite,
A bond of camaraderie that transcends time and space.
Every laugh a symphony of shared joy,
Every conversation a treasure trove of shared secrets.
In the embrace of friendship, we find belonging,
For it is in the company of kindred spirits that we find solace,
And in the laughter of friends that we find strength,
As we journey through life together, hand in hand.

Loneliness:
In the echoing silence of loneliness, hearts ache,
A yearning for connection in a world of isolation.
Every sigh a whisper of longing,
Every tear a testament to unspoken pain.
In the embrace of loneliness, we find solitude,
For it is in the depths of our solitude that we find introspection,
And in the stillness of our loneliness that we find clarity,
As we learn to embrace our own company and find solace in the silence.

Memories:
In the tapestry of memories, stories are woven,
A patchwork of moments that shape our lives.
Every laugh a thread of joy,
Every tear a stitch of sorrow.
In the embrace of memories, we find nostalgia,
For it is in the recollection of past experiences that we find comfort,
And in the retelling of old tales that we find connection,
As we cherish the memories of days gone by and treasure the moments that define us.

Music:
In the symphony of music, emotions soar,
A melody that resonates with the soul.
Every note a chord of passion,
Every rhythm a beat of the heart.
In the embrace of music, we find harmony,
For it is in the cadence of a song that we find expression,
And in the harmony of voices that we find unity,
As we lose ourselves in the rhythm and let music guide us.

Here are four Blank Verse poems, 1 each about Art, Inspiration, Creativity & Courage

Art:
In the canvas of art, imagination takes flight,
A masterpiece of creativity that knows no bounds.
Every stroke a brush of inspiration,
Every color a splash of emotion.
In the embrace of art, we find expression,
For it is in the creation of beauty that we find purpose,
And in the exploration of creativity that we find fulfillment,
As we let our imaginations run wild and unleash our inner artist.

Inspiration:
In the spark of inspiration, creativity ignites,
A fire that burns with the intensity of a thousand suns.
Every idea a flash of brilliance,
Every insight a revelation of truth.
In the embrace of inspiration, we find motivation,
For it is in the pursuit of our passions that we find purpose,
And in the act of creation that we find fulfillment,
As we follow our muse and let inspiration guide us.

Creativity:
In the depths of creativity, ideas flow,
A river of innovation that knows no boundaries.
Every concept a seed of potential,
Every creation a testament to imagination.
In the embrace of creativity, we find liberation,
For it is in the act of creation that we find freedom,
And in the expression of our unique vision that we find fulfillment,
As we let our creativity run wild and unleash our inner artist.

Courage:
In the heart of courage, bravery shines,
A beacon of strength in the face of adversity.
Every step a leap of faith,
Every decision a stand against fear.
In the embrace of courage, we find empowerment,
For it is in the act of facing our fears that we find resilience,
And in the pursuit of our dreams that we find fulfillment,
As we bravely navigate the challenges of life and emerge stronger than before.

Here are four Blank Verse poems, 1 each about Faith, Doubt, Solitude & Joy

Faith:
In the depths of faith, hope blooms,
A garden of belief that withstands the test of time.
Every prayer a whisper of trust,
Every devotion a testament to conviction.
In the embrace of faith, we find solace,
For it is in the belief in something greater than ourselves that we find comfort,
And in the trust in the divine that we find strength,
As we navigate the uncertainties of life with faith as our guide.

Doubt:
In the shadow of doubt, uncertainty looms,
A fog of indecision that clouds the mind.
Every question a seed of confusion,
Every hesitation a whisper of insecurity.
In the embrace of doubt, we find introspection,
For it is in the questioning of our beliefs that we find clarity,
And in the examination of our doubts that we find understanding,
As we grapple with uncertainty and search for answers.

Solitude:
In the quiet of solitude, introspection beckons,
A sanctuary of stillness in a world of noise.
Every moment a chance for reflection,
Every silence a space for contemplation.
In the embrace of solitude, we find serenity,
For it is in the solitude of our own company that we find peace,
And in the moments of quietude that we find clarity,
As we embrace the solitude and allow it to nourish our souls.

Joy:
In the depths of joy, happiness abounds,
A celebration of life's blessings in abundance.
Every laugh a symphony of mirth,
Every smile a beacon of delight.
In the embrace of joy, we find contentment,
For it is in the moments of happiness that we find fulfillment,
And in the expression of our joy that we find liberation,
As we revel in the beauty of life and savor the sweetness of every moment.

Here are four Blank Verse poems, 1 each about Sorrow, Childhood, Wisdom & Innocence

Sorrow:
In the depths of sorrow, darkness looms,
A shadow that blankets the soul in despair.
Every tear a testament to pain unspoken,
Every ache a burden too heavy to bear.
In the embrace of sorrow, we find solace,
For it is in the depths of our despair that we find empathy,
And in the shared experience of grief that we find connection,
As we navigate the labyrinth of loss and emerge stronger.

Childhood:
In the innocence of childhood, magic dances,
A world of wonder where dreams take flight.
Every laugh a melody of pure delight,
Every adventure a journey into the unknown.
In the embrace of childhood, we find joy,
For it is in the simplicity of youth that we find freedom,
And in the boundless imagination of children that we find inspiration,
As we remember the innocence of our youth and cherish its fleeting moments.

Wisdom:
In the depths of wisdom, knowledge blooms,
A beacon of insight that guides us through life's trials.
Every lesson a stepping stone to enlightenment,
Every experience a thread in the tapestry of understanding.
In the embrace of wisdom, we find clarity,
For it is in the pursuit of knowledge that we find purpose,
And in the application of wisdom that we find fulfillment,
As we journey through life with open hearts and curious minds.

Innocence:
In the purity of innocence, grace abounds,
A gentle spirit untainted by the world's harsh realities.
Every smile a reflection of untarnished joy,
Every glance a glimpse of unspoiled wonder.
In the embrace of innocence, we find peace,
For it is in the purity of the heart that we find solace,
And in the innocence of the soul that we find hope,
As we strive to preserve the innocence of childhood in our hearts forever.

Here are four Blank Verse poems, 1 each about Passion, Serenity, Freedom & Justice

Passion:
In the fire of passion, desires ignite,
A blaze of intensity that consumes the soul.
Every touch a spark of electric excitement,
Every kiss a testament to the power of love.
In the embrace of passion, we find ecstasy,
For it is in the heat of passion that we find liberation,
And in the depth of our desires that we find fulfillment,
As we surrender to the flames and let passion guide us.

Serenity:
In the calm of serenity, peace reigns,
A stillness that soothes the soul and quiets the mind.
Every breath a whisper of tranquility,
Every moment a refuge from the chaos of life.
In the embrace of serenity, we find harmony,
For it is in the quietude of the heart that we find balance,
And in the serenity of the spirit that we find strength,
As we journey through life with grace and poise.

Freedom:
In the boundless expanse of freedom, possibilities abound,
A world of infinite potential where anything is possible.
Every choice a declaration of autonomy,
Every action a testament to the power of free will.
In the embrace of freedom, we find liberation,
For it is in the exercise of our freedoms that we find empowerment,
And in the pursuit of our dreams that we find fulfillment,
As we celebrate the gift of freedom and cherish its blessings.

Justice:
In the halls of justice, fairness prevails,
A beacon of equality that lights the way forward.
Every verdict a triumph of righteousness,
Every ruling a victory for the oppressed.
In the embrace of justice, we find equality,
For it is in the pursuit of justice that we find unity,
And in the fight for equality that we find strength,
As we strive to create a world where justice reigns supreme.

Here are four Blank Verse poems, 1 each about Change, Resilience, Gratitude & Forgiveness

Change:
In the whirlwind of change, transformations occur,
A constant evolution that shapes the course of life.
Every shift a chance for growth,
Every upheaval a opportunity for renewal.
In the embrace of change, we find adaptation,
For it is in the flux of change that we find resilience,
And in the uncertainty of the future that we find possibility,
As we navigate the ever-changing tides of existence.

Resilience:
In the crucible of adversity, resilience emerges,
A strength of spirit that withstands the trials of life.
Every setback a chance for perseverance,
Every challenge a opportunity for growth.
In the embrace of resilience, we find fortitude,
For it is in the face of adversity that we find courage,
And in the depths of our struggles that we find resilience,
As we rise from the ashes and persevere against all odds.

Gratitude:
In the depths of gratitude, blessings abound,
A recognition of the abundance that surrounds us.
Every smile a manifestation of thankfulness,
Every gesture a token of appreciation.
In the embrace of gratitude, we find contentment,
For it is in the practice of gratitude that we find fulfillment,
And in the acknowledgement of our blessings that we find joy,
As we cultivate an attitude of gratitude and celebrate life's abundance.

Forgiveness:
In the act of forgiveness, healing begins,
A release of resentments that frees the soul.
Every pardon a step towards liberation,
Every reconciliation a chance for renewal.
In the embrace of forgiveness, we find peace,
For it is in the forgiveness of others that we find compassion,
And in the forgiveness of ourselves that we find acceptance,
As we let go of the past and embrace the promise of the future.

Here are four Blank Verse poems, 1 each about Longing, Belonging, Discovery & Wonder

Longing:
In the depths of longing, desires stir,
A yearning for something beyond reach.
Every sigh a whisper of unfulfilled dreams,
Every ache a testament to the hunger of the heart.
In the embrace of longing, we find hope,
For it is in the depths of our desires that we find purpose,
And in the yearning of our souls that we find inspiration,
As we chase our dreams and reach for the stars.

Belonging:
In the warmth of belonging, hearts unite,
A sense of kinship that binds us together.
Every hug a confirmation of acceptance,
Every shared moment a celebration of connection.
In the embrace of belonging, we find comfort,
For it is in the embrace of loved ones that we find solace,
And in the fellowship of kindred spirits that we find strength,
As we journey through life together, hand in hand.

Discovery:
In the thrill of discovery, knowledge blooms,
A world of wonders waiting to be explored.
Every revelation a glimpse into the mysteries of existence,
Every breakthrough a triumph of curiosity.
In the embrace of discovery, we find excitement,
For it is in the pursuit of knowledge that we find purpose,
And in the exploration of new horizons that we find fulfillment,
As we uncover the secrets of the universe and marvel at its complexity.

Wonder:
In the depths of wonder, magic awaits,
A realm of enchantment where anything is possible.
Every awe-inspired gasp a testament to the marvels of creation,
Every wide-eyed gaze a tribute to the beauty of the world.
In the embrace of wonder, we find awe,
For it is in the presence of the extraordinary that we find inspiration,
And in the appreciation of life's wonders that we find joy,
As we marvel at the miracles of existence and revel in the majesty of the universe.

Here are four Blank Verse poems, 1 each about Journey, Reflection, Harmony & Imagination

Journey:
In the vast expanse of the unknown, the journey unfolds,
A winding path that stretches beyond the horizon.
Every step a testament to our resilience,
Every milestone a marker of progress made.
Along the journey, we encounter challenges and triumphs,
And in the twists and turns of the road, we discover ourselves,
For it is in the journey that we find our true purpose,
And in the act of exploration that we uncover our deepest desires.

Reflection:
In the stillness of the mind, reflection takes hold,
A moment of introspection amidst the chaos of life.
Every thought a window into the soul,
Every memory a thread in the tapestry of our existence.
Through reflection, we make sense of the world around us,
And in the quiet moments of contemplation, we find clarity,
For it is in reflection that we gain perspective,
And in the act of looking inward that we find wisdom.

Harmony:
In the symphony of life, harmony abounds,
A delicate balance that binds together the elements of existence.
Every note a contribution to the melody of the universe,
Every chord a harmony of voices singing in unison.
In the embrace of harmony, we find peace,
For it is in the unity of purpose that we find strength,
And in the alignment of energies that we find synchronicity,
As we dance to the rhythm of life's eternal song.

Imagination:
In the boundless expanse of the mind, imagination takes flight,
A canvas upon which we paint the colors of our dreams.
Every idea a spark of inspiration,
Every vision a glimpse into the realm of possibility.
Through imagination, we create worlds of wonder,
And in the depths of our imagination, we find freedom,
For it is in the realm of the imaginary that we are truly limitless,
And in the act of dreaming that we find liberation.

Here are four Blank Verse poems, 1 each about Silence, Laughter, Tears & Strength

Silence:
In the stillness of silence, peace reigns,
A quietude that envelops the soul in tranquility.
Every breath a whisper in the symphony of silence,
Every moment a pause in the cacophony of noise.
In the embrace of silence, we find solace,
For it is in the absence of sound that we hear the echoes of our own thoughts,
And in the serenity of silence that we find clarity,
As we listen to the whispers of our own hearts.

Laughter:
In the joyous peals of laughter, happiness resonates,
A melody that fills the air with warmth and light.
Every chuckle a ripple in the sea of mirth,
Every giggle a spark in the fire of delight.
In the embrace of laughter, we find joy,
For it is in the camaraderie of shared laughter that we find connection,
And in the infectiousness of laughter that we find unity,
As we revel in the simple pleasures of life's sweetest moments.

Tears:
In the silent streams of tears, emotions flow,
A torrent of sorrow and longing that cleanses the soul.
Every drop a release of pent-up emotion,
Every sob a cathartic outpouring of grief.
In the embrace of tears, we find healing,
For it is in the vulnerability of tears that we find strength,
And in the act of shedding tears that we find renewal,
As we wash away the pain of the past and embrace the promise of the future.

Strength:
In the depths of adversity, strength emerges,
A fortress of resilience that withstands the test of time.
Every challenge a crucible for character,
Every setback a chance for growth.
In the embrace of strength, we find courage,
For it is in the face of adversity that we discover our true power,
And in the act of overcoming obstacles that we find liberation,
As we rise from the ashes, stronger and more resilient than ever.

Here are four Blank Verse poems, 1 each about Vulnerability, Renewal, Acceptance & Mystery

Vulnerability:
In the open field of vulnerability, we stand exposed,
Unshielded from the arrows of judgment and fear.
Every crack in our armor a testament to our humanity,
Every tear a reminder of our shared fragility.
Yet it is in vulnerability that we find strength,
For it takes courage to embrace our weaknesses,
To lay bare our hearts in the face of uncertainty,
And to trust in the power of our own resilience.

Renewal:
In the quiet hush of dawn, renewal whispers softly,
A promise of beginnings, fresh and untainted.
Every sunrise a reminder of the cycle of life,
Every bud a symbol of potential waiting to unfurl.
In the embrace of renewal, we shed our old skins,
Letting go of what no longer serves us,
And opening ourselves to the possibility of growth,
As we step into the light of a new day.

Acceptance
In the gentle embrace of acceptance, we find peace,
A surrender to the ebb and flow of life's currents.
Every moment a lesson in letting go,
Every breath a practice in embracing what is.
Acceptance is not resignation, but liberation,
A release from the shackles of expectation,
And a recognition of the beauty in imperfection,
As we learn to love ourselves and others as we are.

Mystery:
In the depths of the unknown, mystery beckons,
A tantalizing enigma that defies explanation.
Every shadow a potential hiding place for secrets,
Every whisper a clue to a story yet untold.
In the dance of mystery, we find wonder,
For it is in the unanswered questions that magic resides,
And in the unexplored territories that adventure awaits,
As we journey into the heart of the unknown.

Here are four Blank Verse poems, 1 each about Transformation, Eternity, Cosmos & Happiness

Transformation:
In the crucible of change, transformation unfolds,
A metamorphosis of the soul, wrought by fire and trial.
Every trial a crucible for growth,
Every hardship a chisel shaping our destiny.
Transformation is not easy, nor is it painless,
But it is in the process of becoming that we find our true selves,
And in the act of transformation that we discover our inner strength,
As we emerge from the fire, reborn and renewed.

Eternity:
In the vast expanse of time, eternity stretches out before us,
A never-ending journey through the cosmos.
Every star a marker in the tapestry of existence,
Every galaxy a testament to the infinite.
Eternity is not bound by mortal constraints,
But transcends the boundaries of space and time,
And in its boundless expanse, we find solace,
As we contemplate our place in the grand scheme of things.

Cosmos:
In the depths of the cosmos, mystery reigns,
A vast and wondrous expanse, stretching beyond the horizon.
Every planet a world unto itself,
Every nebula a canvas painted with the colors of the universe.
In the embrace of the cosmos, we find humility,
For it is in the face of such enormity that we realize our own insignificance,
And yet, in that realization, we find a sense of wonder,
As we gaze upon the stars and ponder the mysteries of creation.

Happiness:
In the fleeting moments of joy, happiness dances,
A melody that echoes through the chambers of our hearts.
Every laugh a note in the symphony of life,
Every smile a ray of sunshine on a cloudy day.
Happiness is not a destination, but a journey,
A state of being that transcends circumstance,
And in the pursuit of happiness, we find fulfillment,
As we savor the sweetness of life's simple pleasures.

RONDEAU:

A French form of poetry consisting of 15 lines with a specific rhyme scheme and a repeating refrain.

Here are four Rondeau poems, 1 each about Love, Nature, Beauty & Time

Love:
In love's sweet dance, hearts intertwine,
A melody of passion, divine.
With every kiss, the world's a blur,
In love's embrace, we find our cure,
For in each other, we shine.

Nature:
In nature's arms, we find our peace,
A symphony of colors, a masterpiece.
The rustle of leaves, the song of the stream,
In nature's embrace, we dare to dream,
For in her beauty, all worries cease.

Beauty:
In beauty's gaze, we find our grace,
A reflection of our inner space.
In every sunset, in every rose,
Beauty's presence, forever glows,
For in her embrace, we find our place.

Time:
With every tick, with every chime,
Time marches on, an eternal climb.
In every moment, past and present blend,
In time's embrace, our stories mend,
For in its flow, we find our prime.

Here are four Rondeau poems, 1 each about Death, Dreams, Hope & Despair

Death:
In death's cold grip, we must submit,
A final journey, where shadows flit.
Though fear may reign, and tears may fall,
In death's embrace, we find our call,
For in its mystery, lies our transit.

Dreams:
In dreams' vast sea, we take our flight,
A world of wonder, in the dead of night.
Through realms unknown, we roam and soar,
In dreams' embrace, we seek for more,
For in our slumber, we glimpse the light.

Hope:
In hope's gentle whisper, we find our way,
A guiding star, in the darkest day.
With every step, with every stride,
In hope's embrace, we choose our side,
For in its promise, we choose to stay.

Despair:
In despair's heavy burden, we must tread,
A weight that crushes, that fills with dread.
Though darkness looms, and shadows creep,
In despair's embrace, we dare to weep,
For in its depths, we find our thread.

Here are four Rondeau poems, 1 each about Friendship, Loneliness, Memories & Music

Friendship:
In friendship's bond, we find our cheer,
A loyal companion, always near.
Through thick and thin, through storm and strife,
In friendship's embrace, we build our life,
For in each other, we find our mirror.

Loneliness:
In loneliness' silence, we feel the ache,
A hollow void, we cannot shake.
Though solitude may reign, and hearts may yearn,
In loneliness' embrace, we begin to learn,
For in its depths, we find what's at stake.

Memories:
In memories' embrace, we hold the past,
A treasure trove, too fleeting to last.
Through laughter and tears, through joy and pain,
In memories' embrace, we dance again,
For in their embrace, our stories are cast.

Music:
In music's melody, we find our soul,
A symphony of emotions, beyond control.
With every note, with every chord,
In music's embrace, our spirits soared,
For in its rhythm, we find our role.

Here are four Rondeau poems, 1 each about Art, Inspiration, Creativity & Courage

Art:
In art's creation, we find our voice,
A canvas of expression, our hearts rejoice.
With every stroke, with every hue,
In art's embrace, we find what's true,
For in its beauty, we make our choice.

Inspiration:
In inspiration's whisper, we find our muse,
A spark of genius, we cannot refuse.
With every thought, with every spark,
In inspiration's embrace, we leave our mark,
For in its flame, we refuse to lose.

Creativity:
In creativity's flow, we find our flow,
A river of ideas, we cannot stow.
With every creation, with every design,
In creativity's embrace, we define,
For in its depths, our passions grow.

Courage:
In courage's call, we rise to the fight,
A warrior's spirit, burning bright.
With every step, with every stand,
In courage's embrace, we make our stand,
For in its power, we claim our right.

Here are four Rondeau poems, 1 each about Faith, Doubt, Solitude & Joy

Faith:
In faith's embrace, we find our strength,
A steadfast belief, we carry the length.
Through trials and tribulations, we hold on tight,
In faith's embrace, we find our light,
For in its guidance, we go to any length.

Doubt:
In doubt's shadow, we find our fears,
A nagging voice, that lingers near.
Though uncertainties may cloud our sight,
In doubt's embrace, we seek for light,
For in its questions, the truth appears.

Solitude:
In solitude's silence, we find our peace,
A moment of stillness, a sweet release.
Though loneliness may seem our fate,
In solitude's embrace, we contemplate,
For in its quiet, our souls increase.

Joy:
In joy's embrace, we find our song,
A symphony of laughter, loud and long.
With every smile, with every cheer,
In joy's embrace, we have no fear,
For in its presence, we all belong.

Here are four Rondeau poems, 1 each about Sorrow, Childhood, Wisdom & Innocence

Sorrow:
In sorrow's depths, we find our pain,
A well of tears, we cannot feign.
With every sob, with every sigh,
In sorrow's embrace, we learn to fly,
For in its depths, we rise again.

Childhood:
In childhood's innocence, we find our glee,
A world of wonder, pure and free.
With every laugh, with every game,
In childhood's embrace, we find our aim,
For in its magic, we learn to see.

Wisdom:
In wisdom's silence, we find our peace,
A treasure trove, that never shall cease.
With every lesson, with every thought,
In wisdom's embrace, we find what's sought,
For in its counsel, our souls release.

Innocence:
In innocence's purity, we find our grace,
A gentle spirit, in every face.
With every smile, with every gleam,
In innocence's embrace, we find our dream,
For in its light, we find our place.

Here are four Rondeau poems, 1 each about Passion, Serenity, Freedom & Justice

Passion:
In passion's fire, we find our flame,
A burning desire, we cannot tame.
With every touch, with every kiss,
In passion's embrace, we find our bliss,
For in its heat, we stake our claim.

Serenity:
In serenity's calm, we find our rest,
A tranquil haven, we love the best.
With every breath, with every sigh,
In serenity's embrace, we learn to fly,
For in its peace, we are truly blessed.

Freedom:
In freedom's call, we find our wings,
A boundless sky, where the heart sings.
With every step, with every leap,
In freedom's embrace, we find our keep,
For in its flight, we find our things.

Justice:
In justice's call, we find our voice,
A righteous stand, we cannot rejoice.
With every plea, with every fight,
In justice's embrace, we seek what's right,
For in its fairness, we find our choice.

Here are four Rondeau poems, 1 each about Change, Resilience, Gratitude & Forgiveness

Change:
In change's dance, we find our way,
A shifting path, from night to day.
With every shift, with every turn,
In change's embrace, we feel the burn,
For in its motion, we find our sway.

Resilience:
In resilience's heart, we find our fight,
A warrior's spirit, in the darkest night.
With every blow, with every fall,
In resilience's embrace, we stand tall,
For in its strength, we find our might.

Gratitude:
In gratitude's heart, we find our peace,
A thankful heart, that will not cease.
With every blessing, with every gift,
In gratitude's embrace, our spirits lift,
For in its grace, our worries decrease.

Forgiveness:
In forgiveness's grace, we find our peace,
A release of burdens, that will not cease.
With every pardon, with every grace,
In forgiveness's embrace, we find our space,
For in its healing, our sorrows decrease.

Here are four Rondeau poems, 1 each about Longing, Belonging, Discovery & Wonder

Longing:
In longing's ache, we find our need,
A yearning heart, that will not cede.
With every sigh, with every tear,
In longing's embrace, we hold what's dear,
For in its depths, our desires feed.

Belonging:
In belonging's arms, we find our place,
A welcoming embrace, in every face.
With every smile, with every tear,
In belonging's embrace, we feel near,
For in its warmth, we find our grace.

Discovery:
In discovery's quest, we find our way,
An explorer's spirit, in every fray.
With every step, with every find,
In discovery's embrace, we expand our mind,
For in its journey, we learn to play.

Wonder:
In wonder's gaze, we find our awe,
A sense of magic, without a flaw.
With every sight, with every sound,
In wonder's embrace, our spirits are bound,
For in its mystery, we find our draw.

Here are four Rondeau poems, 1 each about Journey, Reflection, Harmony & Imagination

Journey:
In journey's path, we find our road,
A winding trail, with burdens to unload.
With every step, with every mile,
In journey's embrace, we find our smile,
For in its adventure, we find our abode.

Reflection:
In reflection's gaze, we find our truth,
A mirror of memories, from days of youth.
With every thought, with every tear,
In reflection's embrace, we face our fear,
For in its clarity, we find our sleuth.

Harmony:
In harmony's melody, we find our chord,
A symphony of souls, in one accord.
With every note, with every key,
In harmony's embrace, we are set free,
For in its unity, we find our reward.

Imagination:
In imagination's realm, we find our flight,
A canvas of dreams, in the dead of night.
With every thought, with every scheme,
In imagination's embrace, we find our dream,
For in its vision, we find our might.

Here are four Rondeau poems, 1 each about Silence, Laughter, Tears & Strength

Silence:
In silence's depth, we find our peace,
A moment of calm, where worries cease.
With every breath, with every sigh,
In silence's embrace, we hear the sky,
For in its stillness, we find release.

Laughter:
In laughter's echo, we find our joy,
A chorus of mirth, without alloy.
With every chuckle, with every grin,
In laughter's embrace, we begin again,
For in its humor, we find our ploy.

Tears:
In tears' release, we find our pain,
A river of sorrow, we cannot feign.
With every sob, with every sigh,
In tears' embrace, we question why,
For in its cleansing, we find our gain.

Strength:
In strength's embrace, we find our might,
A warrior's heart, ready to fight.
With every trial, with every test,
In strength's embrace, we rise abreast,
For in its power, we stand upright.

Here are four Rondeau poems, 1 each about Vulnerability, Renewal, Acceptance & Mystery

Vulnerability:
In vulnerability's grasp, we find our truth,
A raw honesty, uncensored and uncouth.
With every fear, with every tear,
In vulnerability's embrace, we confront our jeer,
For in its openness, we find our proof.

Renewal:
In renewal's dawn, we find our rebirth,
A fresh start, upon the earth.
With every sunrise, with every bloom,
In renewal's embrace, we leave our gloom,
For in its promise, we find our worth.

Acceptance:
In acceptance' arms, we find our peace,
A letting go, of struggles that won't cease.
With every flaw, with every scar,
In acceptance' embrace, we embrace who we are,
For in its grace, we find release.

Mystery:
In mystery's allure, we find our quest,
A riddle of life, we cannot rest.
With every clue, with every sign,
In mystery's embrace, we seek to define,
For in its enigma, we find our zest.

Here are four Rondeau poems, 1 each about Transformation, Eternity, Cosmos & Happiness

Transformation:
In transformation's fire, we find our bloom,
A metamorphosis, from darkness to room.
With every change, with every shift,
In transformation's embrace, we make our gift,
For in its process, we find our room.

Eternity:
In eternity's grasp, we find our span,
A never-ending journey, since time began.
With every cycle, with every turn,
In eternity's embrace, we forever yearn,
For in its infinity, we find our plan.

Cosmos:
In the vast expanse of the cosmos, we find our place,
A speck of dust in the endless space.
With every star, with every galaxy,
In the cosmos' embrace, we find our legacy,
For in its wonder, we seek our grace.

Happiness:
In happiness' embrace, we find our smile,
A beacon of joy, that lasts for miles.
With every laugh, with every cheer,
In happiness' embrace, we hold what's dear,
For in its warmth, we find our style.

-:|:-•:*'''''*:•.-:|:-•**•-:|:-•:*'''''*:•:*'''''*:•.-:|:-•**•-:|:--:|:-•:*'''''*:•.-:|:- •**•-:|:-•:*'''''*:•:*'''''*:•.-:|:-•**•-:|:-

TRIOLET:

A short poetic form with eight lines, often humorous or light-hearted, with a specific rhyme scheme and repeated lines.

-:|:-•:*''''*:•.-:|:-•**•-:|:-•:*''''*:•:*''''*:•.-:|:-•**•-:|:--:|:-•:*''''*:•.-:|:- •**•-:|:-•:*''''*:•:*''''*:•.-:|:-•**•-:|:-

Here are four Triolet poems, 1 each about Love, Nature, Beauty & Time

Love:
In the tender embrace, love's flame burns bright,
A beacon of warmth, in the darkest night.
In the tender embrace, love's flame burns bright,
Hearts entwine, in passion's flight,
In love's embrace, souls unite.

Nature:
In the wild expanse, nature's wonders unfold,
A tapestry of beauty, in hues untold.
In the wild expanse, nature's wonders unfold,
Mountains rise, rivers meander bold,
In nature's embrace, serenity takes hold.

Beauty:
In the eye of the beholder, beauty lies,
A symphony of grace, beneath azure skies.
In the eye of the beholder, beauty lies,
Petals unfurl, like butterflies,
In beauty's embrace, the soul sighs.

Time:
In the ticking of the clock, time slips away,
A fleeting moment, with every passing day.
In the ticking of the clock, time slips away,
Memories fade, like colors of a bouquet,
In time's embrace, life finds its way.

Here are four Triolet poems, 1 each about Death, Dreams, Hope & Despair

Death:
In the shadows of night, death whispers low,
A silent passage, where all must go.
In the shadows of night, death whispers low,
Life's final breath, a bittersweet blow,
In death's embrace, souls learn to grow.

Dreams:
In the realm of sleep, dreams take flight,
A canvas of possibilities, shining bright.
In the realm of sleep, dreams take flight,
Visions dance, in the moon's soft light,
In dreams' embrace, imagination's might.

Hope:
In the heart's chamber, hope takes hold,
A flame that flickers, through trials untold.
In the heart's chamber, hope takes hold,
Through darkest nights, its warmth unfolds,
In hope's embrace, dreams enfold.

Despair:
In the depths of despair, darkness prevails,
A shroud of sadness, where light pales.
In the depths of despair, darkness prevails,
Echoes of sorrow, like mournful wails,
In despair's embrace, resilience scales.

Here are four Triolet poems, 1 each about Friendship, Loneliness, Memories & Music

Friendship:
In the warmth of a friend, hearts intertwine,
A bond so strong, enduring and fine.
In the warmth of a friend, hearts intertwine,
Through laughter and tears, the ties refine,
In friendship's embrace, love's design.

Loneliness:
In the silence of night, loneliness sighs,
A solitary soul beneath starlit skies.
In the silence of night, loneliness sighs,
Echoes of longing, like mournful cries,
In loneliness' grip, the heart denies.

Memories:
In the recesses of the mind, memories reside,
A tapestry of moments, woven side by side.
In the recesses of the mind, memories reside,
Each cherished scene, a treasure to confide,
In memories' embrace, the past is guide.

Music:
In the melody's dance, music takes flight,
A symphony of notes, pure and bright.
In the melody's dance, music takes flight,
With every chord, emotions ignite,
In music's embrace, hearts unite.

Here are four Triolet poems, 1 each about Art, Inspiration, Creativity & Courage

Art:
In strokes of color, art comes alive,
A canvas of dreams, where imaginations thrive.
In strokes of color, art comes alive,
Each creation, a story to contrive,
In art's embrace, beauty will survive.

Inspiration:
In the whisper of wind, inspiration flows,
A muse that dances, where creativity grows.
In the whisper of wind, inspiration flows,
Ideas bloom, like a fragrant rose,
In inspiration's embrace, creativity glows.

Creativity:
In the depths of the mind, creativity soars,
A symphony of ideas, like waves on distant shores.
In the depths of the mind, creativity soars,
Imagination roams, through endless doors,
In creativity's embrace, innovation explores.

Courage:
In the face of fear, courage stands tall,
A beacon of strength, breaking through the wall.
In the face of fear, courage stands tall,
Heart beats strong, answering the call,
In courage's embrace, barriers fall.

Here are four Triolet poems, 1 each about Faith, Doubt, Solitude & Joy

Faith:
In the depths of the soul, faith takes flight,
A steadfast belief, guiding through the night.
In the depths of the soul, faith takes flight,
Through trials and tests, it burns bright,
In faith's embrace, hope alights.

Doubt:
In the shadows of doubt, uncertainty looms,
A whispering voice that clouds and consumes.
In the shadows of doubt, uncertainty looms,
Questions unanswered, fears that zoom,
In doubt's grip, confusion fumes.

Solitude:
In the quiet of solitude, peace is found,
A sanctuary of silence, tranquil and profound.
In the quiet of solitude, peace is found,
Thoughts wander, dreams unbound,
In solitude's embrace, serenity surrounds.

Joy:
In the heart's expanse, joy takes flight,
A burst of laughter, a beacon of light.
In the heart's expanse, joy takes flight,
Smiles blossom, hearts unite,
In joy's embrace, life feels right.

Here are four Triolet poems, 1 each about Sorrow, Childhood, Wisdom & Innocence

Sorrow:
In the depths of despair, sorrow takes hold,
A heavy weight upon the soul, cold.
In the depths of despair, sorrow takes hold,
Tears cascade, stories untold,
In sorrow's grasp, hearts unfold.

Childhood:
In the innocence of youth, childhood's glow,
A world of wonder, where dreams grow.
In the innocence of youth, childhood's glow,
Laughter rings, hearts aglow,
In childhood's embrace, memories flow.

Wisdom:
In the quiet of age, wisdom resides,
A wellspring of knowledge, time's guide.
In the quiet of age, wisdom resides,
Lessons learned, truths implied,
In wisdom's shadow, understanding abides.

Innocence:
In the purity of heart, innocence thrives,
A gentle spirit, untouched by lies.
In the purity of heart, innocence thrives,
Smiles brighten, souls revive,
In innocence's embrace, love arrives.

Here are four Triolet poems, 1 each about Passion, Serenity, Freedom & Justice

Passion:
In the fiery depths of the heart, passion ignites,
A blaze of desire that burns through the night.
In the fiery depths of the heart, passion ignites,
Fueling the soul with its fervent delights,
In its embrace, love's flame shines bright.

Serenity:
In the calm of the dawn, serenity reigns,
A gentle peace that soothes all pains.
In the calm of the dawn, serenity reigns,
With each breath, tranquility regains,
In serenity's embrace, the spirit maintains.

Freedom:
In the wide-open sky, freedom takes flight,
A boundless expanse, devoid of fright.
In the wide-open sky, freedom takes flight,
Breaking chains, embracing the light,
In freedom's embrace, dreams ignite.

Justice:
In the halls of the just, fairness presides,
A beacon of truth that never hides.
In the halls of the just, fairness presides,
With impartiality, injustice derides,
In the pursuit of justice, righteousness abides.

Here are four Triolet poems, 1 each about Change, Resilience, Gratitude & Forgiveness

Change:
In the ebb and flow of life, change is near,
A constant dance, shifting without fear.
In the ebb and flow of life, change is near,
Embrace the transformation, let go of the leer,
Through change, new beginnings appear.

Resilience:
In the face of adversity, resilience stands tall,
A beacon of strength, refusing to fall.
In the face of adversity, resilience stands tall,
Through storms and trials, it answers the call,
With unwavering courage, it conquers all.

Gratitude:
In the heart's embrace, gratitude blooms,
A chorus of thanks, in life's many rooms.
In the heart's embrace, gratitude blooms,
Each moment cherished, dispelling gloom,
With gratitude, joy and abundance looms.

Forgiveness:
In the depths of the soul, forgiveness takes flight,
A release of burdens, in the still of the night.
In the depths of the soul, forgiveness takes flight,
Letting go of resentment, embracing the light,
With forgiveness, wounds heal, wrongs set right.

Here are four Triolet poems, 1 each about Longing, Belonging, Discovery & Wonder

Longing:
In the quiet of night, a whisper of yearning,
Longing's embrace, the heart's silent burning.
In the quiet of night, a whisper of yearning,
Echoes of desire, in the soul's deep turning,
In the depths of longing, dreams keep churning.

Belonging:
In the circle of kin, belonging is found,
A bond of love, forever unbound.
In the circle of kin, belonging is found,
With open arms, hearts tightly wound,
In the embrace of family, roots are crowned.

Discovery:
In the vast expanse, discovery awaits,
A journey of wonder, beyond the gates.
In the vast expanse, discovery awaits,
Through unknown lands, and mysterious states,
In the pursuit of knowledge, the spirit elevates.

Wonder:
In the awe of creation, wonder shines bright,
A tapestry of magic, in the soft moonlight.
In the awe of creation, wonder shines bright,
Each star a story, each sight a delight,
In the beauty of existence, our spirits take flight.

Here are four Triolet poems, 1 each about Journey, Reflection, Harmony & Imagination

Journey:
On the winding road, our journey unfolds,
With each step, new stories are told.
On the winding road, our journey unfolds,
Through valleys deep and mountains bold,
In the adventure of life, our spirits behold.

Reflection:
In the stillness of thought, reflection begins,
Mirroring the soul's deepest sins.
In the stillness of thought, reflection begins,
Through introspection, the truth rescinds,
In the pool of self-awareness, growth wins.

Harmony:
In the symphony of life, harmony plays,
A melody that brightens our days.
In the symphony of life, harmony plays,
Each note resonates, each chord sways,
In unity and peace, our spirits raise.

Imagination:
In the boundless realm of thought, imagination soars,
Unlocking the secrets of worlds and more.
In the boundless realm of thought, imagination soars,
Through dreams and visions, new worlds implore,
In the infinite expanse, creativity pours.

Here are four Triolet poems, 1 each about Silence, Laughter, Tears & Strength

Silence:
In the quiet of night, silence descends,
A peaceful embrace, where the soul mends.
In the quiet of night, silence descends,
Whispers of stars, where the universe blends,
In the depths of silence, clarity transcends.

Laughter:
In the joyous cacophony, laughter resounds,
Echoes of mirth in every sound.
In the joyous cacophony, laughter resounds,
In its embrace, happiness abounds,
With laughter, life's true beauty is found.

Tears:
In the gentle cascade, tears softly fall,
A testament to emotions that enthrall.
In the gentle cascade, tears softly fall,
Each drop a story, each sorrow, a call,
Through tears, hearts find solace in the squall.

Strength:
In the crucible of life, strength is honed,
A force that carries us through the unknown.
In the crucible of life, strength is honed,
In resilience and courage, it's shown,
With each trial faced, its power is known.

Here are four Triolet poems, 1 each about Vulnerability, Renewal, Acceptance & Mystery

Vulnerability:
In the open heart, vulnerability resides,
A tender space where fears confide.
In the open heart, vulnerability resides,
Embrace the truth it bravely guides,
For strength lies in the tears we've cried.
In the open heart, vulnerability resides.

Renewal:
In the dawn's soft glow, renewal is found,
Each sunrise whispers of hope unbound.
In the dawn's soft glow, renewal is found,
From ashes, new beginnings abound,
With each breath, the earth's heart beats sound.
In the dawn's soft glow, renewal is found.

Acceptance:
In the stillness of self, acceptance begins,
Letting go of judgment, embracing our skins.
In the stillness of self, acceptance begins,
Embrace the flaws, the cracks, the sins,
For in acceptance, true healing begins.
In the stillness of self, acceptance begins.

Mystery:
In the shadows of night, mysteries abound,
Secrets whispered in the wind's soft sound.
In the shadows of night, mysteries abound,
Unraveling riddles, truth profound,
In the dance of shadows, magic is found.
In the shadows of night, mysteries abound.

Here are four Triolet poems, 1 each about Transformation, Eternity, Cosmos & Happiness

Transformation:
In the cocoon of time, change is near,
Metamorphosis whispers its tune.
In the cocoon of time, change is near,
Embrace the shift, release the fear.
From darkness, emerge the butterfly's bloom.
In the cocoon of time, change is near.

Eternity:
Eternal dance of stars, timeless and bright,
Infinite cosmos, stretching beyond measure.
Eternal dance of stars, timeless and bright,
In the vast expanse, dreams take flight,
Each twinkle a promise of endless treasure.
Eternal dance of stars, timeless and bright.

Cosmos:
In the cosmic ballet, galaxies twirl,
Infinite wonders unfurl in the night.
In the cosmic ballet, galaxies twirl,
Planets dance in a celestial whirl,
A tapestry of beauty, a breathtaking sight.
In the cosmic ballet, galaxies twirl.

Happiness:
In the heart's embrace, joy takes flight,
Laughter echoes, filling the air.
In the heart's embrace, joy takes flight,
Banish the shadows, let in the light,
Embrace the moment, without a care.
In the heart's embrace, joy takes flight.

-:¦:-•:*'''''*:•.-:¦:-•**•-:¦:-•:*'''''*:•:*'''''*:•.-:¦:-•**•-:¦:--:¦:-•:*'''''*:•.-:¦:- •**•-:¦:-•:*'''''*:•:*'''''*:•.-:¦:-•**•-:¦:-

HAIBUN:

A combination of prose and haiku, often used to describe a journey or experience with elements of both narrative and poetic reflection.

-:|:-•:*'''''*:•.-:|:-•**•-:|:-•:*'''''*:•:*'''''*:•.-:|:-•**•-:|:--:|:-•:*'''''*:•.-:|:- •**•-:|:-•:*'''''*:•:*'''''*:•.-:|:-•**•-:|:-

Here are four Haibun poems, 1 each about Love, Nature, Beauty & Time

Love:
In the tender embrace of love, I find solace in the warmth of another's touch. It is a bond that transcends words, a connection that reaches deep into the soul. Love is not merely an emotion, but a force that binds us together in an eternal dance of affection and devotion. And as I lose myself in the depths of love's embrace, I am filled with a sense of belonging and fulfillment, knowing that in the arms of my beloved, I have found my home.
soft whispers of love
hearts beat as one in the night
forever entwined

Nature:
In the heart of the wilderness, I find solace in the embrace of nature. It is a sanctuary of the soul, a refuge from the chaos and noise of the modern world. Nature is not merely a place, but a living, breathing tapestry of life – a symphony of sights, sounds, and sensations that fills me with wonder and awe. And as I lose myself in the beauty and tranquility of the natural world, I am reminded of the interconnectedness of all things, and the importance of living in harmony with the earth.
rustle of leaves
nature's symphony plays on
peace fills the air

Beauty:
In the delicate petals of a flower, I find solace in the embrace of beauty. It is a treasure that lies hidden in plain sight, waiting to be discovered in the most unexpected of places. Beauty is not merely a superficial quality, but a reflection of the divine that shines forth from within. And as I lose myself in the splendor of a sunset or the majesty of a mountain peak, I am filled with a sense of awe and reverence for the beauty that surrounds me, and the miracle of existence itself.
blossoms in bloom
beauty unfolds in the light
heart sings with delight

Time:
In the passage of time, I find solace in the rhythm of life's ebb and flow. It is a constant companion, marching ever onward with relentless determination. Time is not merely a measurement, but a precious commodity that we must cherish and make the most of while we can. And as I watch the seconds tick by, I am filled with a sense of urgency and purpose, knowing that each moment is a gift, and that the time we have is fleeting.
clock ticks away
time slips through fingers like sand
cherish each moment

Here are four Haibun poems, 1 each about Death, Dreams, Hope & Despair

Death:
In the silence of the night, I am confronted by the inevitability of death. It is a specter that lurks in the shadows, casting a long shadow over the land of the living. Death is not merely an end, but a transition - a passage from one state of being to another. And yet, even in the face of death, there is beauty to be found. For it is in embracing the impermanence of life that we come to appreciate the preciousness of each moment, and the importance of living with intention and purpose.
moonlight on the grave
death whispers in the darkness
life blooms from the earth

Dreams:
In the quiet of the night, I find solace in the embrace of dreams. They are like stars that light up the darkness, guiding us towards our deepest desires and aspirations. Dreams are not merely flights of fancy, but a roadmap to the future - a vision of what could be if only we dare to reach for the stars. And as I lose myself in the world of dreams that unfolds before me, I am filled with a sense of hope and possibility, knowing that anything is possible if only we believe.
stars twinkle above
dreams take flight in the night sky
hope shines bright within

Hope:
In the depths of despair, I find solace in the flickering flame of hope. It is a beacon that lights up the darkness, guiding us through even the darkest of nights. Hope is not merely a wish, but a belief in the possibility of a better tomorrow - a conviction that no matter how bleak things may seem, there is always a glimmer of light on the horizon. And as I hold onto hope with all my heart, I am filled with a sense of courage and determination, knowing that as long as hope burns within me, I can overcome any obstacle that stands in my way.
candle in the dark
hope flickers bright and steady
lighting up the night

Despair:
In the depths of despair, I am engulfed by the darkness that surrounds me. It is a heavy weight that presses down upon my soul, suffocating me with its suffocating embrace. Despair is not merely a feeling, but a state of being - a sense of hopelessness and futility that threatens to consume me whole. And yet, even in the depths of despair, there is a glimmer of light. For it is in embracing our darkest moments that we find the strength to rise above them, and the courage to face whatever challenges lie ahead.
shadows close around
despair whispers in the night
light still burns within

Here are four Haibun poems, 1 each about Friendship, Loneliness, Memories & Music

Friendship:
In the warmth of companionship, I find solace in the embrace of friendship. It is a bond that transcends time and space, connecting us heart to heart in a tapestry of love and support. Friendship is not merely a relationship, but a lifeline - a source of strength and encouragement that carries us through the trials and tribulations of life. And as I share laughter and tears with those closest to me, I am reminded of the power of friendship to uplift, to inspire, and to enrich the journey of life.
laughter fills the air
friendship's bond unbreakable
hearts beat as one

Loneliness:
In the silence of solitude, I am haunted by the shadows of loneliness. It is a weight that presses down upon my soul, casting a pall over even the brightest of days. Loneliness is not merely a lack of company, but a profound sense of isolation - a feeling of being adrift in a sea of emptiness and despair. And yet, even in the depths of loneliness, there is solace to be found. For it is in embracing our solitude that we come to understand ourselves more fully and appreciate the beauty of our own company.
echoes in the night
loneliness whispers softly
healing begins here

Memories:
In the recesses of my mind, I find solace in the embrace of memories. They are like treasures tucked away in the corners of my heart, each one a snapshot of a moment in time - a smile, a laugh, a tear. Memories are not merely relics of the past, but a living tapestry that weaves together the fabric of our lives, connecting us to the people and places that have shaped us into who we are today. And as I close my eyes and lose myself in the memories that dance across my mind, I am filled with a sense of gratitude for the richness and depth of my experiences.
flicker of candlelight
memories dance in shadows
heart sings with each one

Music:
In the melody of a song, I find solace in the embrace of music. It is a language that speaks to the soul, transcending barriers of time and space to touch us in the deepest parts of ourselves. Music is not merely a sound, but a symphony of emotion - a chorus of joy, sorrow, and everything in between. And as I lose myself in the rhythm and flow of the music that surrounds me, I am filled with a sense of wonder and awe at the power of sound to uplift, to inspire, and to connect us to the beauty and wonder of existence.
notes on the breeze
music fills the air with song
hearts beat in time

Here are four Haibun poems, 1 each about Art, Inspiration, Creativity & Courage

Art:
In the quiet of the gallery, I am mesmerized by the beauty and complexity of art. Each brushstroke tells a story, each sculpture a testament to the artist's vision and skill. Art is not merely a creation, but a reflection of the human spirit - a mirror that reflects our deepest hopes, fears, and desires. And as I lose myself in the colors and shapes that dance across the canvas, I am reminded of the power of art to inspire, to uplift, and to transcend the boundaries of time and space.
canvas comes to life
art whispers in the silence
beauty surrounds us

Inspiration:
In the depths of my soul, I find inspiration in the most unexpected places. It is a spark that ignites my creativity and fuels my passion for life. Inspiration is not merely a muse, but a force that drives me forward, propelling me towards my dreams with unwavering determination. And as I open myself up to the possibilities that lie within, I am filled with a sense of excitement and anticipation, knowing that the world is full of endless opportunities waiting to be discovered.
fire in the heart
inspiration lights the way
dreams take flight

Creativity:
In the stillness of the studio, I am surrounded by the magic of creation. It is a dance of imagination and intuition, a symphony of colors and shapes that come together to form something new and beautiful. Creativity is not merely a skill, but a way of being – a mindset that embraces experimentation and embraces failure as essential steps on the path to innovation. And as I lose myself in the process of creation, I am filled with a sense of joy and fulfillment, knowing that I am tapping into the boundless well of creativity that lies within.
blank page comes to life
creativity flows free
possibilities abound

Courage:
In the face of uncertainty, I find courage in the depths of my soul. It is a fire that burns bright, a strength that sustains me through even the darkest of days. Courage is not merely a lack of fear, but a willingness to confront our fears head-on and move forward with conviction and determination. And as I stand on the precipice of the unknown, I am filled with a sense of purpose and resolve, knowing that with courage by my side, I can overcome any obstacle that stands in my way.
fear fades away
courage lights the path ahead
heart beats strong and true

Here are four Haibun poems, 1 each about Faith, Doubt, Solitude & Joy

Faith:
In the quiet of the chapel, I find solace in the embrace of faith. It is a sanctuary of the soul, a refuge from the storms of life where I can turn to find comfort and strength. Faith is not merely a belief in something greater than ourselves, but a deep-seated trust in the goodness of the universe and the interconnectedness of all things. And as I bow my head in prayer, I am filled with a sense of peace and serenity, knowing that I am never alone.
candles flicker bright
faith illuminates the dark
hope guides the way

Doubt:
In the depths of uncertainty, I am haunted by the shadows of doubt. It creeps in like a thief in the night, casting doubt upon even the firmest of convictions. Doubt is a relentless adversary, a nagging voice that whispers in the ear and clouds the mind with uncertainty. And yet, even in the face of doubt, there is strength. For it is in questioning our beliefs that we find the courage to seek out the truth and grow in wisdom and understanding.
storm clouds gather near
doubt casts a shadow over
lightning strikes the soul

Solitude:
In the silence of solitude, I find solace in the company of my own thoughts. It is a sacred space, a refuge from the noise and distractions of the world where I can turn inward and reconnect with the deepest parts of myself. Solitude is not merely a state of isolation, but a choice – a conscious decision to disconnect from the outside world and journey inward. And as I lose myself in the stillness of the moment, I am filled with a sense of peace and tranquility, knowing that I am exactly where I need to be.
whispers of the wind
solitude soothes the weary soul
peace blooms in the heart

Joy:
In the laughter of loved ones, I find joy in the simple pleasures of life. It is a feeling of warmth that spreads through my heart like wildfire, filling me with happiness and contentment. Joy is not merely a fleeting emotion, but a state of being – a choice to embrace the beauty and wonder of the world around us, even in the midst of adversity. And as I bask in the glow of laughter and love, I am reminded of the power of joy to uplift, to inspire, and to transform even the darkest of days.
sunshine on my face
joy dances in the breeze
laughter fills the air

Here are four Haibun poems, 1 each about Sorrow, Childhood, Wisdom & Innocence

Sorrow:
In the depths of despair, I am enveloped by the heavy shroud of sorrow. It weighs upon my heart like a stone, casting a shadow over even the brightest of days. Sorrow is a companion that walks beside me, a reminder of the fragility of life and the pain of loss. And yet, even in the darkest of moments, there is a glimmer of hope – a flicker of light that pierces the darkness and reminds me that I am not alone.
tears fall softly
sorrow's silent lament
healing begins

Childhood:
In the innocence of youth, I find joy in the simple pleasures of childhood. It is a time of wonder and exploration, of wide-eyed curiosity and boundless imagination. Childhood is a treasure chest filled with memories of laughter and play, of scraped knees and secret hideaways. And as I look back on those carefree days, I am filled with a sense of nostalgia for the innocence of youth – a time when the world seemed full of endless possibilities and anything was possible.
laughter echoes bright
childhood memories dance
in fields of dreams

Wisdom:
In the quiet of reflection, I am humbled by the wisdom of age. It is a gift earned through years of experience and introspection, a treasure trove of knowledge that guides me through life's twists and turns. Wisdom is not merely a matter of intellect, but a deep-seated understanding of the human condition and the complexities of existence. And as I listen to the whispers of wisdom that echo through the ages, I am filled with a sense of reverence for the journey that has brought me to this moment.
ancient oak stands tall
wisdom etched in gnarled bark
roots run deep and strong

Innocence:
In the purity of innocence, I find solace in the untainted beauty of the world. It is a gentle reminder of the innocence that resides within each of us – a purity of heart and spirit that remains untouched by the trials and tribulations of life. Innocence is not merely a state of naivety, but a source of strength and resilience that allows us to see the world through eyes unclouded by judgment or fear. And as I embrace the innocence within me, I am filled with a sense of wonder and awe at the beauty and wonder of existence.
butterfly alights
innocence takes flight
freedom in its wings

Here are four Haibun poems, 1 each about Passion, Serenity, Freedom & Justice

Passion:
In the heat of the moment, I am consumed by the fiery flames of passion. It is a force that ignites my soul, driving me forward with an intensity that cannot be contained. Passion is not merely a feeling, but a fire that burns deep within, urging me to pursue my dreams with unwavering determination. And as I lose myself in the pursuit of my passions, I am filled with a sense of purpose and fulfillment, knowing that I am living life to the fullest.
embers glow bright
passion ignites the night sky
dreams take flight

Serenity:
In the stillness of the dawn, I find solace in the embrace of serenity. It is a quiet calm that washes over me, soothing my soul and quieting the noise of the world around me. Serenity is not merely the absence of chaos, but a state of inner peace that transcends the trials and tribulations of everyday life. And as I bask in the tranquility of the morning light, I am reminded of the beauty and wonder of existence, and the importance of finding moments of peace amidst the chaos.
morning mist descends
serenity fills the air
peace blooms within

Freedom:
In the wide open spaces of the world, I find freedom in the wind that blows through my hair and the sun that warms my face. It is a liberation born of exploration and adventure, a sense of boundlessness that fills me with exhilaration and joy. Freedom is not merely the absence of constraints, but the ability to live life on my own terms, to pursue my dreams and passions with abandon. And as I roam the open road, I am filled with a sense of freedom and possibility, knowing that the world is mine to explore and conquer.
wings spread wide
freedom soars on the breeze
sky knows no bounds

Justice:
In the pursuit of righteousness, I stand firm in the face of injustice. It is a commitment to fairness and equality, a belief in the inherent dignity and worth of every human being. Justice is not merely a legal concept, but a moral imperative that calls upon us to fight for what is right, to speak out against oppression and discrimination. And as I raise my voice in defense of the marginalized and oppressed, I am filled with a sense of purpose and conviction, knowing that in the struggle for justice lies the key to a better world for all.
voices rise strong
justice marches on
equality prevails

Here are four Haibun poems, 1 each about Change, Resilience, Gratitude & Forgiveness

Change:
In the quiet of the morning, I am confronted by the inevitability of change. The world around me is in a constant state of flux, evolving and shifting with each passing moment. Change can be both frightening and exhilarating, a force that pushes us out of our comfort zones and into the unknown. And yet, it is in embracing change that we find growth and transformation. Like the seasons, we too must change and adapt to the ever-changing rhythms of life. And as I stand on the threshold of a new day, I am filled with a sense of excitement and anticipation, knowing that change is the catalyst for new beginnings and endless possibilities.
leaves fall to the ground
change whispers in the wind
a new chapter begins

Resilience:
In the face of adversity, I discover the strength of the human spirit. It is a resilience born of hardship and struggle, a determination to persevere in the face of life's challenges. Resilience is not merely about bouncing back from setbacks, but finding the courage to rise above them, stronger and more resilient than before. And as I weather life's storms with grace and dignity, I am reminded of the power of resilience to heal, to transform, and to inspire.
storm clouds gather near
resilience stands firm and strong
hope shines bright within

Gratitude:
In the quiet moments of reflection, I am filled with a sense of gratitude for the blessings in my life. It is a feeling of thankfulness for the simple pleasures, the moments of joy and beauty that surround me each and every day. Gratitude is not merely a fleeting emotion, but a deep-seated appreciation for the abundance of love and abundance in my life. And as I count my blessings and give thanks for all that I have, I am filled with a sense of peace and contentment, knowing that I am truly blessed beyond measure.
sunshine kisses cheeks
gratitude blooms in the heart
love fills the soul

Forgiveness:
In the quiet of the evening, I come face to face with the power of forgiveness. It is a journey of letting go, of releasing the burdens of anger and resentment that weigh heavy on the heart. Forgiveness is not merely about absolving others of their wrongs, but freeing ourselves from the shackles of bitterness and pain. And as I extend forgiveness to others and to myself, I am filled with a sense of liberation and healing, knowing that in forgiveness lies the key to true peace and freedom.
moonlight bathes the soul
forgiveness whispers soft
healing begins anew

Here are four Haibun poems, 1 each about Longing, Belonging, Discovery & Wonder

Longing:
In the stillness of the night, I am consumed by a deep sense of longing. It is a yearning that gnaws at my soul, pulling me towards the unknown with an irresistible force. I long for connection, for understanding, for a sense of purpose that eludes me. And yet, even in the depths of my longing, there is beauty. For it is in the longing that we find the courage to reach for the stars, to pursue our dreams with unwavering determination. And as I gaze up at the night sky, I am filled with a sense of hope and wonder, knowing that even in the darkest of nights, there is always the promise of a new dawn.
moonlight whispers soft
longing echoes in the night
dreams take flight

Belonging:
In the embrace of loved ones, I find a sense of belonging that fills my heart with warmth. It is a feeling of connection, of being part of something greater than myself, that grounds me and gives me strength. Belonging is not merely a matter of proximity, but a deep-seated sense of acceptance and love that transcends time and space. And as I share laughter and tears with those closest to me, I am reminded of the power of community to uplift, to support, and to nourish the soul.
hearts beat as one
belonging in each other's arms
love knows no bounds

Discovery:
In the pursuit of knowledge, I embark on a journey of discovery that fills me with wonder and awe. Each new revelation is a gift, a treasure waiting to be uncovered in the vast expanse of the universe. Discovery is not merely about finding answers, but asking questions, exploring the unknown, and embracing the mysteries that lie beyond. And as I delve deeper into the realms of science and exploration, I am filled with a sense of excitement and anticipation, knowing that there is always something new to learn, to explore, and to discover.
footsteps on the path
discovery awaits ahead
adventure beckons

Wonder:
In the presence of nature's beauty, I am filled with a sense of wonder that takes my breath away. The world is a vast and wondrous place, filled with marvels both great and small. From the majesty of towering mountains to the delicate beauty of a flower in bloom, there is wonder to be found in every corner of the earth. And as I gaze out at the awe-inspiring landscapes before me, I am reminded of the power of nature to inspire, to uplift, and to fill the heart with joy.
sunrise paints the sky
wonder fills the morning air
beauty surrounds us

Here are four Haibun poems, 1 each about Journey, Reflection, Harmony & Imagination

Journey:
On the winding path of life, I embark on a journey of self-discovery. Each step forward is a new adventure, a chance to explore the depths of my soul and uncover the hidden truths that lie within. Along the way, I encounter obstacles and challenges, but I press on with determination and courage. The journey is not always easy, but it is in the struggle that I find growth and transformation. And as I continue on my way, I am filled with a sense of wonder and excitement, eager to see where the road will lead me next.
footsteps on the path
journeying towards the light
adventure awaits

Reflection:
In the quiet of the evening, I sit by the water's edge and reflect on the day's events. The gentle lapping of the waves against the shore soothes my soul, as I contemplate the highs and lows of life. Reflection is a mirror that reveals the truth of who we are, a chance to pause and ponder the mysteries of existence. In these moments of introspection, I am filled with gratitude for the beauty and wonder of the world around me. And as I gaze out at the shimmering waters, I am reminded of the interconnectedness of all things, and the importance of living with intention and purpose.
ripples on the lake
reflecting the changing sky
peace fills the heart

Harmony:
In the heart of the forest, I am surrounded by the symphony of nature. The birds sing their songs, the trees sway in the breeze, and all around me, there is a sense of harmony and balance. It is a reminder of the interconnectedness of all things, and the beauty that arises when we are in sync with the rhythms of the natural world. In this moment of harmony, I feel at peace, as if I am a part of something greater than myself. And as I breathe in the fresh air and soak in the beauty of my surroundings, I am filled with a sense of gratitude for the gift of life and the beauty of the world around me.
forest whispers soft
in harmony with the earth
nature's song unfolds

Imagination:
In the realm of imagination, anything is possible. It is a world of endless possibilities, where dreams take flight and creativity knows no bounds. In my mind's eye, I conjure up fantastical landscapes, mythical creatures, and epic adventures. Imagination is the fuel that drives innovation and fuels the fires of creativity. It is in the realm of imagination that I find solace and escape from the rigors of everyday life. And as I lose myself in the depths of my imagination, I am reminded of the power of creativity to inspire, to uplift, and to transform the world around us.
in dreams we wander
beyond the bounds of reason
imagination soars

Here are four Haibun poems, 1 each about Silence, Laughter, Tears & Strength

Silence:
In the heart of the forest, I find solace in the embrace of silence. The trees stand tall and still, their leaves rustling softly in the breeze. It is a sacred moment, a pause in the chaos of life, where I can simply be, without the need for words or distractions. In the silence, I hear the gentle rhythm of my own breath, the steady beat of my heart. It is a reminder of the power of silence to heal, to rejuvenate, to connect us to the deepest parts of ourselves and the natural world around us.
deep forest silence
whispers of ancient wisdom
peace fills the soul

Laughter:
In the company of friends, I am swept away by the infectious sound of laughter. It is a symphony of joy, a melody that lifts my spirits and fills my heart with warmth. We share stories and jokes, our laughter ringing out like bells in the night. In these moments, I feel alive, connected, and free from the burdens of everyday life. Laughter is a gift, a reminder of the simple pleasures that bring us together and remind us of the beauty and humor in the world.
laughter echoes bright
hearts entwined in joyful song
lightness fills the air

Tears:
In the quiet of my room, I am overcome by a flood of tears. They flow freely, unchecked, as I release the pent-up emotions that have been building inside me. Each tear is a testament to the depth of my feelings, a reflection of the pain and sorrow that weighs heavy on my heart. And yet, even in my darkest moments, there is beauty in the tears. For they are a cleansing rain, washing away the hurt and sadness, and leaving behind a sense of clarity and peace. In the tears, I find release, healing, and the strength to carry on.
tears fall softly down
washing away pain and sorrow
healing begins anew

Strength:

In the face of adversity, I discover the untapped reservoirs of strength within me. It is a quiet strength, born of resilience and determination, that allows me to weather life's storms with grace and courage. I stand tall, my feet planted firmly on the ground, as I face whatever challenges come my way. It is in these moments of trial that I find my true strength, my inner warrior rising to meet the challenges head-on. And though the road may be long and difficult, I know that I am not alone. For in the strength of my spirit, I find the power to overcome, to persevere, and to emerge stronger than before.
roots run deep and strong
weathering life's storms with grace
strength blooms within

Here are four Haibun poems, 1 each about Vulnerability, Renewal, Acceptance & Mystery

Vulnerability:
In the stillness of the evening, I confront my vulnerability. Like a delicate flower swaying in the breeze, I feel exposed, raw, and open to the world. It is a frightening sensation, to stand on the precipice of vulnerability, to expose the tender parts of myself to the harsh realities of life. And yet, in this vulnerability, I find strength. For it is only by embracing our vulnerability that we can truly connect with others, share our struggles and fears, and forge deep and meaningful connections. As I embrace my vulnerability, I realize that it is not a weakness, but a source of courage and resilience.
fragile petals bend
in the wind of vulnerability
strength blooms within

Renewal:
In the heart of the forest, I witness the miracle of renewal. Spring has arrived, and with it, new life bursts forth in a riot of color and sound. The trees stretch their branches towards the sky, unfurling their leaves in a dance of renewal and rebirth. It is a reminder that even in the darkest of times, there is always the promise of renewal, of new beginnings and fresh starts. As I walk among the blossoming flowers and budding trees, I feel a sense of hope and optimism wash over me. For in the cycle of renewal, I find solace, knowing that no matter what challenges may come my way, I have the power to begin again.
blossoms bloom bright
renewal dances in the air
hope springs eternal

Acceptance:
In the quiet of the evening, I come face to face with acceptance. It is a bittersweet moment, to let go of the past and embrace the present, to accept things as they are, rather than as we wish them to be. And yet, in this acceptance, I find peace. For it is only by accepting the truth of our circumstances that we can truly move forward, finding strength and resilience in the face of adversity. As I surrender to acceptance, I feel a weight lifted from my shoulders, a sense of freedom and liberation washing over me. For in the embrace of acceptance, I find the courage to let go and the grace to embrace what lies ahead.
waves crash against shore
acceptance washes over
peace fills the soul

Mystery:
In the darkness of the night, I am drawn to the mystery that surrounds me. The stars twinkle overhead, their secrets hidden behind a veil of darkness. It is a reminder that there is so much we do not know, so much left to explore and discover. And yet, in the mystery, there is beauty. For it is the unknown that sparks our curiosity, ignites our imagination, and inspires us to seek out answers to life's greatest questions. As I gaze up at the night sky, I am filled with a sense of wonder and awe, humbled by the vastness and complexity of the universe. For in the mystery, I find magic, possibility, and the infinite potential of the human spirit.
stars shimmer bright
mystery whispers in the night
a universe unfolds

Here are four Haibun poems, 1 each about Transformation, Eternity, Cosmos & Happiness

Transformation:
In the quiet of the forest, I witness the dance of transformation. The trees shed their leaves, releasing what no longer serves them, embracing the cycle of renewal. I too feel the pull of change, the urge to shed old habits and beliefs, to make way for new growth. As I walk among the fallen leaves, I am reminded that transformation is not always easy, but it is necessary for growth and renewal. Like the trees, I too am shedding the old to make way for the new, embracing the beauty of transformation in all its forms.
autumn leaves fall
whispering secrets of change
a new beginning

Eternity:
Beneath the vast expanse of the night sky, I am reminded of the eternity that surrounds us. The stars twinkle overhead, timeless guardians of the cosmos, reminding me of the infinite nature of the universe. In this moment, I feel small and insignificant, a mere speck in the grand tapestry of existence. And yet, I also feel connected to something greater than myself, a part of the eternal dance of life and death that spans the ages. As I gaze up at the stars, I am filled with a sense of wonder and awe, humbled by the beauty and mystery of eternity.
stars shimmer bright
a timeless dance unfolds
infinite beauty

Cosmos:
In the silence of the night, I lose myself in the vastness of the cosmos. The galaxies swirl and spin, countless stars twinkling in the darkness, each one a world unto itself. I am filled with a sense of wonder and awe as I contemplate the sheer magnitude of the universe. It is a humbling reminder of our place in the cosmos, of the interconnectedness of all things. In this moment, I feel a sense of peace and harmony, knowing that we are all part of something greater than ourselves, a cosmic symphony that echoes through the ages.
cosmic dance
stars shimmer in the night sky
a song of creation

Happiness:
In the quiet moments of reflection, I find happiness in the simple joys of life. The warmth of the sun on my face, the laughter of loved ones, the beauty of nature all around me – these are the things that fill my heart with joy. Happiness is not a destination, but a state of being, a choice we make each and every day. As I breathe in the fresh air and soak in the beauty of the world around me, I am filled with gratitude for the gift of life and the moments of happiness that make it all worthwhile.
sunshine kisses cheeks
laughter echoes in the breeze
happiness blooms bright

-:¦:-•:*''''*:•.-:¦:-•**•-:¦:-•:*''''*:•:*''''*:•.-:¦:-•**•-:¦:--:¦:-•:*''''*:•.-:¦:- •**•-:¦:-•:*''''*:•:*''''*:•.-:¦:-•**•-:¦:-

PROSE POETRY:

Poetry written in prose form, blurring the lines between prose and poetry with its lyrical and evocative language.

-:¦:-•:*'''''*:•.-:¦:-•**•-:¦:-•:*'''''*:•:*'''''*:•.-:¦:-•**•-:¦:--:¦:-•:*'''''*:•.-:¦:- •**•-:¦:-•:*'''''*:•:*'''''*:•.-:¦:-•**•-:¦:-

Here are four Prose poems, 1 each about Love, Nature, Beauty & Time

Love:
Love is the gentle whisper of the heart, the silent symphony that plays in the depths of our souls. It is the unspoken bond that connects us to one another, the force that binds us together in a web of compassion and understanding. Love is not merely a feeling, but a choice, a commitment to nurture and cherish the ones we hold dear. It is the warmth of a mother's embrace, the laughter shared between friends, the passion that ignites between lovers. Love is the greatest gift we can give and receive, a treasure beyond measure that fills our lives with meaning, purpose, and joy.

Nature:
Nature is the canvas upon which the universe paints its masterpiece, a symphony of colors, textures, and sounds that captivate the senses and nourish the soul. It is the rustle of leaves in the wind, the song of birds at dawn, the scent of flowers in bloom. Nature is not merely a backdrop to our lives, but a source of inspiration, healing, and renewal. It is in the embrace of nature that we find solace, serenity, and a deep sense of connection to the world around us. And yet, nature can also be fierce, untamed, unpredictable. It is in respecting and honoring nature that we find balance, harmony, and a profound reverence for the beauty and majesty of the natural world.

Beauty:
Beauty is the light that shines from within, the radiance that emanates from the soul. It is the sparkle in a child's eyes, the laughter that dances on the wind, the kindness that warms the heart. Beauty is not merely a superficial trait, but a reflection of our innermost selves, a manifestation of our character, our values, our essence. It is in the beauty of a smile, the grace of a gesture, the elegance of a thought that we find the true essence of beauty – a force that transcends time and space, touching us on a primal level and reminding us of the inherent goodness and wonder of existence.

Time:
Time is the river that flows inexorably onward, carrying us along in its relentless current. It is the great equalizer, the one thing that binds us all together in the tapestry of life. Time is not merely a measurement of seconds, minutes, and hours, but a precious commodity that must be savored and cherished. It is in the passing of time that we find growth, change, and the opportunity to create lasting memories and experiences. And yet, time can also be fleeting, slipping through our fingers like grains of sand. It is in embracing the present moment, in living fully and authentically, that we find the true richness and beauty of time – a gift that should never be taken for granted.

Here are four Prose poems, 1 each about Death, Dreams, Hope & Despair

Death:
Death is the great equalizer, the inevitable end that awaits us all. It is the final chapter in the book of life, the closing of the curtain on the stage of existence. Death is not the end, but a transition, a passage from one state of being to another. It is the natural order of things, the cycle of life and death that has shaped the universe since time immemorial. And yet, death is also a mystery, a journey into the unknown, a realm shrouded in darkness and uncertainty. It is in facing the inevitability of death that we find the courage to live fully, to cherish each moment, and to embrace the beauty and fragility of life.

Dreams:
Dreams are the whispers of the soul, the visions that dance in the darkness of the night. They are the seeds of possibility, the sparks of inspiration that ignite our imaginations and fuel our aspirations. Dreams are not merely figments of the imagination, but glimpses of our deepest desires, our highest aspirations, our truest selves. They are the driving force behind our greatest achievements, the guiding light that leads us on our journey through life. And yet, dreams can also be elusive, fleeting, like wisps of smoke that vanish upon waking. It is in pursuing our dreams that we find purpose, fulfillment, and the courage to reach for the stars.

Hope:
Hope is the beacon that shines in the darkness, the light that guides us through the storms of life. It is the belief in better days ahead, the conviction that no matter how dire the circumstances, there is always a glimmer of light at the end of the tunnel. Hope is not blind optimism, but a steadfast faith in the resilience of the human spirit, the power of love, and the possibility of redemption. It is in the darkest moments, when all seems lost, that hope shines brightest, illuminating the path forward and inspiring us to persevere against all odds. And yet, hope can also be fragile, easily shattered by the harsh realities of life. It is in nurturing hope, in cultivating it like a delicate flower, that we find strength, resilience, and the courage to face whatever challenges may come our way.

Despair:
Despair is the abyss that threatens to swallow us whole, the darkness that engulfs us when all hope seems lost. It is the heavy weight that presses down upon the soul, suffocating us with its suffocating embrace. Despair is not merely sadness, but a deep-seated feeling of hopelessness, of powerlessness, of being trapped in a never-ending cycle of suffering. It is in the depths of despair that we feel most alone, most vulnerable, most afraid. And yet, even in the darkest moments, there is a glimmer of light, a flicker of hope that refuses to be extinguished. It is in confronting despair, in acknowledging its presence and its power, that we find the strength to rise above it, to reclaim our lives, and to embrace the possibility of a brighter tomorrow.

Here are four Prose poems, 1 each about Friendship, Loneliness, Memories & Music

Friendship:
Friendship is the gentle embrace of kindred spirits, the bond that weaves hearts together in a tapestry of love and laughter. It is the hand that reaches out in times of need, the shoulder to lean on when the world feels heavy. Friendship is not merely a connection, but a lifeline, a source of strength and solace in a world of uncertainty. It is in the laughter shared, the tears shed, the memories made, that we find the true essence of friendship – a treasure beyond measure, a gift that enriches our lives in countless ways.

Loneliness:
Loneliness is the silent companion that walks beside us in the dark, a shadow that follows wherever we go. It is the ache of an empty heart, the longing for connection that echoes in the depths of the soul. Loneliness is not merely the absence of company, but a deep-seated feeling of disconnection, of isolation, of being adrift in a sea of faces. It is in the quiet moments of solitude, the empty spaces left unfilled, that we feel the weight of loneliness pressing down upon us – a heavy burden that weighs upon the spirit, dimming the light of hope and casting a pall over the world.

Memories:
Memories are the threads that bind us to the past, the tapestry of moments woven together in the fabric of time. They are the snapshots of joy and sorrow, love and loss, that shape our lives and define who we are. Memories are not merely reflections of the past, but living, breathing entities that dance across the canvas of our minds, evoking emotions both sweet and bitter. It is in the memories we hold dear, the stories we cherish, the experiences we treasure, that we find solace, comfort, and a sense of continuity in a world that is ever-changing.

Music:
Music is the universal language of the soul, the melody that resonates deep within our hearts and stirs our emotions. It is the rhythm of life, the harmony that connects us to one another and to the world around us. Music is not merely a collection of notes and chords, but a symphony of sound that speaks to our very essence, transcending language and culture to touch us on a primal level. It is in the melodies that uplift us, the lyrics that move us, the beats that compel us to dance, that we find the true power of music – a force that brings us together, heals our wounds, and uplifts our spirits in times of joy and sorrow alike.

Here are four Prose poems, 1 each about Art, Inspiration, Creativity & Courage

Art:
Art is the canvas upon which humanity paints its dreams, its fears, its deepest desires. It is the expression of the human spirit, a reflection of the beauty and complexity of life. Art transcends boundaries, connecting us to one another and to the world around us. It is the language of the soul, speaking to us in whispers and shouts, in colors and shapes, in melodies and words. Art is not merely something to be admired, but a powerful force that can transform hearts and minds, sparking change and inspiring greatness. It is in the creation and appreciation of art that we find meaning, connection, and the boundless possibilities of the human imagination.

Inspiration:
Inspiration is the spark that ignites the flames of creativity, the gentle whisper that stirs the soul to action. It is the lightbulb moment that illuminates the mind, the sudden rush of insight that propels us forward on our journey. Inspiration is not something that can be forced or controlled, but rather a gift that comes when we least expect it, when we open ourselves up to the possibilities of the universe. It is in the moments of inspiration that we find clarity, purpose, and the courage to follow our dreams. And yet, inspiration can also be elusive, fleeting, like a butterfly that flits just out of reach. It is in embracing inspiration that we find the courage to listen to our inner voice, to trust in our instincts, and to pursue our passions with unwavering determination.

Creativity:
Creativity is the lifeblood of the human spirit, the wellspring from which innovation and imagination flow. It is the ability to see the world in new and unexpected ways, to connect seemingly disparate ideas and concepts, to transform the ordinary into the extraordinary. Creativity is not limited to artists and inventors, but is a fundamental aspect of being human, a gift that each of us possesses in our own unique way. It is in the act of creation that we find joy, fulfillment, and the freedom to express ourselves fully. And yet, creativity can also be daunting, a blank canvas waiting to be filled, a blank page waiting to be written. It is in embracing creativity that we find the courage to embrace uncertainty, to take risks, and to boldly explore the vast and infinite possibilities of the human imagination.

Courage:
Courage is the quiet strength that resides within each of us, the inner fire that burns bright in the face of adversity. It is the willingness to face our fears, to step out of our comfort zones, to embrace the unknown with open arms. Courage is not the absence of fear, but rather the determination to move forward in spite of it, to rise above our doubts and insecurities, and to pursue our dreams with unwavering conviction. It is in acts of courage that we find resilience, fortitude, and the power to overcome life's greatest challenges. And yet, courage can also be daunting, a leap of faith into the unknown, a journey into the depths of the soul. It is in embracing courage that we find the strength to persevere, to grow, and to become the best versions of ourselves.

Here are four Prose poems, 1 each about Faith, Doubt, Solitude & Joy

Faith:
Faith is the unwavering belief that guides us through the darkest nights and the brightest days. It is the light that shines within us, illuminating the path ahead with hope and courage. Faith is not blind, but rather a steadfast trust in the unseen, a conviction that there is meaning and purpose beyond what our eyes can perceive. It is the anchor that steadies us in the storms of life, the rock upon which we build our dreams and aspirations. With faith as our compass, we navigate the uncertain waters of existence, knowing that even in the face of adversity, we are never truly alone.

Doubt:
Doubt is the shadow that looms over us, casting doubt on our beliefs, our choices, our very sense of self. It is the nagging voice of uncertainty that whispers in our ear, sowing seeds of fear and confusion. Doubt is not the enemy, but rather a natural part of the human experience, a reflection of our innate desire to seek truth and understanding. It is through doubt that we question, that we challenge, that we grow. And yet, doubt can also paralyze us, holding us back from embracing life's opportunities and fulfilling our potential. It is in overcoming doubt that we find strength, resilience, and the courage to trust in ourselves and our abilities.

Solitude:
Solitude is the sanctuary of the soul, a quiet refuge from the noise and chaos of the world. It is the space where we can retreat, to reflect, to recharge, to reconnect with ourselves and the world around us. Solitude is not loneliness, but rather a precious gift that allows us to tune into our innermost thoughts and feelings, to listen to the whispers of our heart. It is in solitude that we find clarity, peace, and the freedom to be truly ourselves. And yet, solitude can also be daunting, a vast expanse of emptiness that stretches out before us. It is in embracing solitude that we find strength, resilience, and the courage to embrace the beauty of our own company.

Joy:
Joy is the melody that dances in our hearts, the symphony of laughter that echoes through the air. It is the warm embrace of loved ones, the simple pleasures of everyday life, the exhilarating rush of experiencing something new. Joy is not a fleeting emotion, but rather a state of being, a deep sense of contentment and fulfillment that radiates from within. It is in the moments of joy that we feel truly alive, truly connected to ourselves and the world around us. And yet, joy can also be elusive, fleeting, like a butterfly flitting just out of reach. It is in embracing joy that we find gratitude, appreciation, and the courage to savor each precious moment of life.

Here are four Prose poems, 1 each about Sorrow, Childhood, Wisdom & Innocence

Sorrow:
Sorrow is the shadow that lingers in the depths of the soul, the heavy burden that weighs upon the heart. It is the ache of loss, the sting of betrayal, the emptiness of longing unfulfilled. Sorrow is the silent tears that fall in the darkness of night, the quiet sobs that echo in the stillness of solitude. It is the reminder of our humanity, our vulnerability, our capacity to feel deeply. And yet, in the embrace of sorrow, we find empathy, compassion, and the courage to endure, knowing that even in our darkest moments, there is light.

Childhood:
Childhood is the magic of innocence, the wonder of discovery, the joy of boundless imagination. It is the laughter that bubbles up from deep within, the endless games played under the sun's warm embrace. Childhood is the time of firsts – first steps, first words, first dreams dreamed. It is a time of innocence, of trust, of unbridled curiosity. And yet, childhood is fleeting, a precious moment in time that slips through our fingers like grains of sand. And yet, in the memories of childhood, we find nostalgia, sweetness, and the enduring spirit of youth.

Wisdom:
Wisdom is the quiet voice of experience, the guiding light that illuminates the path ahead. It is the culmination of years lived, lessons learned, and truths discovered. Wisdom is not merely knowledge but understanding, a deep insight into the complexities of life and the human condition. It is the ability to see beyond the surface, to discern the deeper meaning behind the veil of appearances. And yet, wisdom is humble, knowing that there is always more to learn, more to discover, more to explore. And yet, in the wisdom of age, we find clarity, perspective, and the timeless wisdom of the ages.

Innocence:
Innocence is the purity of the heart, the untarnished beauty of the soul. It is the laughter of children, the wide-eyed wonder of discovery, the boundless joy of being alive. Innocence is the belief in the goodness of the world, the trust in the kindness of strangers, the faith in the power of love. It is a fragile flower, easily bruised by the harsh realities of life. And yet, in the innocence of youth, we find hope, optimism, and the promise of a better tomorrow. And yet, in the innocence of the heart, we find the capacity for forgiveness, for compassion, for unconditional love.

Here are four Prose poems, 1 each about Passion, Serenity, Freedom & Justice

Passion:
Passion is the wildfire that ignites the soul, the flame that burns bright in the darkest of nights. It is the driving force behind our dreams, our desires, our deepest yearnings. Passion fuels our creativity, our ambition, our pursuit of excellence. It is the spark that lights the path to greatness, the fuel that propels us forward against all odds. With passion as our guide, we dare to dream, to create, to love with all our hearts, knowing that with each passionate embrace, we come alive.

Serenity:
Serenity is the calm at the center of life's storms, the quiet refuge where peace resides. It is the gentle breeze that soothes the soul, the stillness that envelops us in tranquility. Serenity is not the absence of chaos but the presence of inner harmony, a deep sense of calm that remains unshaken by life's ups and downs. It is in the embrace of serenity that we find solace, clarity, and the strength to weather life's challenges with grace and resilience.

Freedom:
Freedom is the wind beneath our wings, the open road stretching out before us. It is the liberation from constraints, from limitations, from the chains that bind us. Freedom is the birthright of every soul, the inalienable right to choose our own path, to speak our own truth, to live our lives according to our own values and beliefs. It is in the embrace of freedom that we find empowerment, self-expression, and the opportunity to live our lives to the fullest.

Justice:
Justice is the moral compass that guides our actions, the beacon of fairness that lights the way. It is the pursuit of truth, of equality, of accountability in the face of injustice. Justice is not merely a concept but a fundamental principle of society, a cornerstone of democracy and human rights. It is in the pursuit of justice that we find integrity, compassion, and the courage to stand up for what is right, knowing that with each act of justice, we bring hope, healing, and the promise of a better world.

Here are four Prose poems, 1 each about Change, Resilience, Gratitude & Forgiveness

Change:
Change is the constant companion on life's journey, the ever-shifting landscape that shapes our experiences and defines our paths. It is the gentle breeze that whispers of new beginnings, the raging storm that tests our resolve, and the steady current that carries us forward into the unknown. Change is the catalyst for growth, the force that challenges us to adapt, evolve, and embrace the possibilities that lie ahead. It is in the embrace of change that we find the courage to let go of the past and embrace the future with open arms.

Resilience:
Resilience is the silent strength that resides within us all, the unwavering spirit that rises in the face of adversity. It is the inner fire that burns bright in times of darkness, the steadfast resolve that refuses to be broken by life's challenges. Resilience is the power to bounce back from setbacks, to rise from the ashes of defeat, and to emerge stronger, wiser, and more determined than ever before. It is in the depths of resilience that we find the courage to persevere, to overcome, and to thrive in the face of life's greatest trials.

Gratitude:
Gratitude is the gentle reminder to pause and appreciate the blessings that surround us each day. It is the heartfelt thank you that acknowledges the kindness of others, the simple joys that bring light to our lives, and the countless gifts that we often take for granted. Gratitude is the antidote to despair, the balm that soothes the wounds of the soul, and the key to unlocking the door to happiness and fulfillment. It is in the practice of gratitude that we find contentment, peace, and a deep sense of connection to the world around us.

Forgiveness:
Forgiveness is the ultimate act of compassion, the gift that we give ourselves and others to heal the wounds of the past and move forward with grace and dignity. It is the release of resentment, anger, and bitterness that weigh heavy on the heart, the choice to let go of the need for vengeance and embrace the power of love and understanding. Forgiveness is the pathway to freedom, the liberation from the shackles of the past, and the opportunity to create a future filled with peace, joy, and reconciliation. It is in the act of forgiveness that we find closure, healing, and the courage to start anew.

Here are four Prose poems, 1 each about Longing, Belonging, Discovery & Wonder

Longing:
Longing is the ache of the heart, the yearning for something just out of reach. It is the whisper of desire that stirs the soul and ignites the imagination. Longing is the bittersweet melody that plays in the depths of the night, calling us to venture into the unknown in search of what we crave. It is the pull of distant shores, the longing for connection, for purpose, for meaning. Longing is the reminder that we are alive, that we are capable of feeling deeply, of yearning for something greater than ourselves.

Belonging:
Belonging is the warmth of a shared embrace, the comfort of knowing that we are not alone in this vast and wondrous world. It is the sense of kinship that binds us together, the feeling of being seen, understood, and accepted for who we truly are. Belonging is the thread that weaves through the fabric of our lives, connecting us to our families, our friends, our communities. It is the foundation upon which we build our identities, our relationships, our sense of self. Belonging is the reminder that we are part of something greater than ourselves, that we are all connected in this beautiful tapestry of existence.

Discovery:
Discovery is the thrill of exploration, the joy of uncovering new worlds and possibilities. It is the curiosity that drives us to seek out the unknown, to push the boundaries of what we thought possible. Discovery is the spark of inspiration that ignites our imaginations, fueling our desire to learn, to grow, to evolve. It is the exhilaration of stumbling upon hidden treasures, of unraveling mysteries, of making unexpected connections. Discovery is the reminder that there is always more to learn, more to explore, more to discover in this vast and infinite universe.

Wonder:
Wonder is the awe-inspiring beauty of the world, the magic that surrounds us in every moment. It is the sense of wonderment that fills our hearts when we gaze up at the stars, when we witness a breathtaking sunset, when we marvel at the intricacies of nature. Wonder is the childlike curiosity that keeps us curious, that sparks our imagination, that reminds us of the infinite possibilities of existence. Wonder is the reminder that life is a wondrous adventure, filled with endless opportunities for exploration, discovery, and joy.

Here are four Prose poems, 1 each about Journey, Reflection, Harmony & Imagination

Journey:
Life is a journey, winding and unpredictable. Each step forward is a venture into the unknown, a path laid out before us with twists and turns, highs and lows. Along the way, we encounter obstacles and opportunities, triumphs and tribulations. It is in the journey that we discover who we are, where we've been, and where we're headed. With each new destination, we find growth, wisdom, and the courage to continue on, embracing the adventure that lies ahead.

Reflection:
In moments of quiet reflection, the mind wanders and the heart speaks. It is a time to pause, to look inward and contemplate the experiences that have shaped us. Reflection is not merely a recollection of memories but a deeper exploration of our thoughts, emotions, and beliefs. It is in the stillness of reflection that we find clarity, insight, and the wisdom to navigate life's complexities with grace and understanding.

Harmony:
In the symphony of life, harmony abounds. It is the delicate balance of opposing forces, the dance of light and shadow, yin and yang. Harmony is not merely a state of being but a conscious effort to find unity and balance in a world of chaos and discord. It is in the harmonious relationships between individuals, the rhythm of nature, and the alignment of mind, body, and spirit that we find peace, serenity, and the beauty of existence.

Imagination:
In the boundless realm of imagination, anything is possible. It is a place where dreams take flight, where creativity knows no bounds. Imagination is not merely a flight of fancy but a powerful force that shapes our reality, inspiring innovation, invention, and exploration. It is in the depths of imagination that we find wonder, curiosity, and the endless possibilities of what could be.

Here are fourProse poems, 1 each about Silence, Laughter, Tears & Strength

Silence:
In the embrace of silence, the world pauses. It is a moment of stillness amidst the chaos, a sanctuary for the weary soul. Silence is not merely the absence of sound but a profound presence, a space where thoughts can settle and hearts can listen. In the quiet of silence, we find clarity, connection, and the gentle rhythm of our own breath, reminding us to slow down and savor the beauty of the present moment.

Laughter:
In the symphony of laughter, joy resounds. It is the melody of happiness, the spontaneous eruption of mirth that fills the air with warmth and light. Laughter is not merely a sound but a celebration, a release of tension and a connection between souls. It is in the shared laughter of friends, the contagious giggle of children, and the belly-deep chuckle that we find solace, camaraderie, and the simple pleasure of being alive.

Tears:
In the gentle cascade of tears, emotions flow. It is the language of the heart, the silent expression of grief, joy, or longing. Tears are not a sign of weakness but a testament to the depth of human experience, a release of pent-up emotions and a cleansing of the soul. It is in the tears shed in sorrow, the tears shed in gratitude, and the tears shed in love that we find healing, catharsis, and the strength to carry on.

Strength:
In the quiet resolve of strength, resilience thrives. It is the unyielding spirit that rises in the face of adversity, the steadfast determination to persevere against all odds. Strength is not measured by physical might but by inner fortitude, a deep well of courage and resilience that lies within each of us. It is in the quiet acts of bravery, the unwavering commitment to one's values, and the steadfast support of others that we find true strength, empowering us to overcome obstacles and embrace life's challenges with grace.

Here are four Prose poems, 1 each about Vulnerability, Renewal, Acceptance & Mystery

Vulnerability:
In the quiet depths of vulnerability lies a raw and tender beauty. It is the unguarded moments when masks slip away and true selves are revealed. Vulnerability is not weakness but a courageous act of openness, a willingness to expose the tender parts of our hearts to the world. It is in these moments of vulnerability that connections are forged, empathy is born, and the human experience is shared in its most authentic form.

Renewal:
In the cycle of renewal, nature whispers secrets of transformation. Each season brings its own magic – the promise of new beginnings in spring's blossoms, the abundant growth of summer's fields, the vibrant hues of autumn's foliage, and the quiet introspection of winter's snowfall. Renewal is not merely a change of seasons but a metaphor for the endless possibilities of rebirth and growth that exist within each of us, waiting to be embraced.

Acceptance:
In the gentle embrace of acceptance, there is freedom. It is the surrender to what is, releasing the need to control or change circumstances beyond our power. Acceptance is not resignation but a profound acknowledgment of reality, a letting go of resistance and a welcoming of what life presents. It is in acceptance that we find peace, serenity, and the wisdom to navigate life's twists and turns with grace.

Mystery:
In the enigmatic depths of mystery, the universe reveals its secrets. It is the unanswered questions that beckon us to explore, the hidden truths that elude comprehension, and the awe-inspiring wonders that defy explanation. Mystery is not a puzzle to be solved but a journey of discovery, a constant reminder of the vastness and complexity of existence. It is in embracing the mystery that we open ourselves to wonder, curiosity, and the endless possibilities of the unknown.

Here are four Prose poems, 1 each about Transformation, Eternity, Cosmos & Happiness

Transformation:
In the heart of a chrysalis, a caterpillar undergoes a miraculous metamorphosis. Bound within silk threads, it surrenders to the transformative powers of nature. Cell by cell, it sheds its former self, embracing the unknown with courage. Emerging as a resplendent butterfly, it takes flight, symbolizing the beauty and resilience of transformation.

Eternity:
In the vast expanse of time, eternity unfolds like an endless tapestry. It stretches beyond the reaches of human comprehension, weaving together the moments of existence into an infinite continuum. From the birth of stars to the whispers of the cosmos, eternity whispers secrets that transcend mortal understanding, reminding us of our place in the grand scheme of existence.

Cosmos:
In the depths of space, the cosmos dances with celestial splendor. Galaxies swirl in a cosmic ballet, stars twinkle like jewels, and nebulas blaze with vibrant hues. Across the vastness of the universe, planets orbit their suns, each one a testament to the wonders of creation. In the cosmos, we find both mystery and majesty, inviting us to contemplate the infinite.

Happiness:
In the embrace of happiness, the heart sings with joyous abandon. It is the laughter of children echoing through sunlit meadows, the warmth of a loved one's smile, and the contentment found in simple moments of peace. Happiness is not merely an emotion but a state of being, a radiant light that illuminates even the darkest corners of the soul, reminding us that life is a gift to be cherished.

-:|:-•:*'''''*:•.-:|:-•**•-:|:-•:*'''''*:•:*'''''*:•.-:|:-•**•-:|:--:|:-•:*'''''*:•.-:|:- •**•-:|:-•:*'''''*:•:*'''''*:•.-:|:-•**•-:|:-

VILLANELLA:

Similar to a villanelle but with a different rhyme scheme and stanza structure, originating from Italian poetry.

-:|:-•:*'''''*:•.-:|:-•**•-:|:-•:*'''''*:•:*'''''*:•.-:|:-•**•-:|:--:|:-•:*'''''*:•.-:|:- •**•-:|:-•:*'''''*:•:*'''''*:•.-:|:-•**•-:|:-

Here are four Villanella poems, 1 each about Love, Nature, Beauty & Time

Love:
In hearts entwined where passions play,
Love's flame burns bright in the light of day,
Each touch a promise, come what may,
In love's embrace, forever we'll stay.

Through trials endured, where doubts may sway,
In love's tender care, we find our way,
A bond unbroken, come what may,
In the dance of love, our souls will sway.

Through time's relentless march, shadows may lay,
In love's eternal flame, we find our way,
A beacon of hope in life's array,
In love's embrace, forever we'll stay.

Nature:
In forests deep where whispers play,
Nature's symphony sings in the light of day,
Each tree a guardian, come what may,
In Mother Earth's embrace, we find our way.

Through meadows green where wildflowers sway,
In nature's beauty, we find our way,
A tapestry of life in bright array,
In harmony with Earth, forever we'll stay.

Through seasons' cycle where changes may lay,
In nature's rhythm, we find our way,
A dance of renewal in life's display,
In reverence for creation, forever we'll stay.

Beauty:
In sunsets' hues where dreams may lay,
Beauty shines forth in the light of day,
Each color a stroke in nature's play,
In the canvas of life, forever we'll stay.

Through starlit skies where wishes may sway,
In beauty's radiance, we find our way,
A sparkle of magic in night's ballet,
In the poetry of aesthetics, forever we'll stay.

Through eyes that see beyond the gray,
In beauty's essence, we find our way,
A glimpse of divinity in life's array,
In the pursuit of grace, forever we'll stay.

Time:
In sands that slip where moments may lay,
Time marches on in the light of day,
Each tick a reminder, come what may,
In the passage of time, forever we'll sway.

Through memories cherished where shadows may play,
In time's relentless flow, we find our way,
A journey through life's maze, day by day,
In the rhythm of existence, forever we'll stay.

Through dreams pursued where destinies may sway,
In time's embrace, we find our way,
A journey of growth, come what may,
In the dance of eternity, forever we'll stay.

Here are four Villanella poems, 1 each about Death, Dreams, Hope & Despair

Death:
In shadows deep where silence may lay,
Death's somber song sings in the light of day,
Each breath a reminder, come what may,
In the cycle of life, forever we'll sway.

Through tears shed where memories may stray,
In death's embrace, we find our way,
A passage to the unknown, come what may,
In the journey's end, forever we'll stay.

Through grief's embrace where sorrows may play,
In death's quietude, we find our way,
A solemn farewell to life's ballet,
In the stillness of eternity, forever we'll stay.

Dreams:
In slumber's embrace where fantasies may lay,
Dreams take flight in the light of day,
Each vision a journey, come what may,
In the realm of imagination, forever we'll sway.

Through aspirations lofty where hopes may stray,
In dreams' embrace, we find our way,
A path to the stars, in night's array,
In the pursuit of passion, forever we'll stay.

Through waking hours where realities may weigh,
In dreams' reverie, we find our way,
A glimpse of the possible, in life's fray,
In the pursuit of purpose, forever we'll stay.

Hope:
In darkest nights where fears may lay,
Hope's beacon shines in the light of day,
Each glimmer a promise, come what may,
In the resilience of the human spirit, forever we'll sway.

Through trials endured where doubts may stray,
In hope's embrace, we find our way,
A guiding light in life's disarray,
In the heart's resilience, forever we'll stay.

Through storms of life where shadows may play,
In hope's enduring grace, we find our way,
A promise of brighter days, come what may,
In the depths of despair, forever we'll stay.

Despair:
In depths of sorrow where shadows may lay,
Despair's grip tightens in the light of day,
Each sigh a burden, come what may,
In the abyss of anguish, forever we'll sway.

Through tears shed where dreams may decay,
In despair's clutches, we find our way,
A journey through the darkness, come what may,
In the depths of despair, forever we'll stay.

Through trials endured where doubts may weigh,
In despair's grip, we find our way,
A struggle to find the light, in life's fray,
In the battle for redemption, forever we'll stay.

Here are four Villanella poems, 1 each about Friendship, Loneliness, Memories & Music

Friendship:
In bonds of trust where hearts align,
Friendship blossoms, pure and fine,
Each shared moment a cherished sign,
In laughter's echo, souls entwine.

Through trials faced, where shadows dine,
In friendship's warmth, we find our shrine,
A haven true in life's design,
In loyalty, our hearts incline.

Through distance vast, our souls combine,
In friendship's glow, we find our line,
A constellation in life's confine,
In friendship's embrace, forever mine.

Loneliness:
In silent hours where echoes cling,
Loneliness whispers, a silent sting,
Each empty moment a tethered wing,
In solitude's embrace, a sorrowing.

Through crowded streets where voices ring,
In loneliness's grip, we find our king,
A kingdom cold where shadows sing,
In isolation's sorrowing.

Through nights so long, where shadows fling,
In loneliness's grasp, we find our thing,
A melody of absence, a muted string,
In longing's song, we find our sting.

Memories:
In hallowed halls where echoes play,
Memories linger, come what may,
Each moment etched in light's array,
In nostalgia's embrace, we find our way.

Through years gone by, where shadows stray,
In memories' dance, we find our sway,
A tapestry of colors in disarray,
In recollection's grace, we come to stay.

Through joys and tears, where hearts convey,
In memories' embrace, we find our play,
A treasure trove of yesterday,
In reminiscing, come what may.

Music:
In melodies that softly sway,
Music dances in the light of day,
Each note a story, a journey's bay,
In harmony's embrace, we find our way.

Through rhythms wild, where passions lay,
In music's symphony, we find our way,
A chorus of emotions in bright array,
In the cadence's sway, we come to play.

Through silence broken, where echoes may,
In music's reverie, we find our way,
A sonnet sung, a ballad's sway,
In music's embrace, forever may.

Here are four Villanella poems, 1 each about Art, Inspiration, Creativity & Courage

Art:
In strokes of color where visions play,
Art unfolds in the light of day,
Each canvas a tale, a world's display,
In creativity's embrace, we find our way.

Through mediums vast, where passions sway,
In art's expression, we find our way,
A symphony of emotions in bright array,
In the artist's soul, forever may.

Through sculpted forms, where shapes betray,
In art's creation, we find our way,
A masterpiece in clay, in stone's array,
In the artist's hands, forever may.

Inspiration:
In whispers soft where dreams may stray,
Inspiration sparks in the light of day,
Each idea a spark, a pathway,
In creativity's embrace, we find our way.

Through muses' call, where passions sway,
In inspiration's grace, we find our way,
A fountainhead of thoughts, in bright array,
In the artist's mind, forever may.

Through moments still, where thoughts convey,
In inspiration's whisper, we find our way,
A symphony of ideas, in grand array,
In the poet's pen, forever may.

Creativity:
In realms of imagination, where wonders may play,
Creativity blooms in the light of day,
Each creation a journey, a pathway,
In innovation's embrace, we find our way.

Through blank pages, where words betray,
In creativity's flow, we find our way,
A tapestry of ideas, in bright array,
In the artist's mind, forever may.

Through brushes dipped in colors, where dreams sway,
In creativity's dance, we find our way,
A masterpiece unveiled, in vivid array,
In the artist's hands, forever may.

Courage:
In moments of fear where shadows may lay,
Courage rises in the light of day,
Each step forward a battle's foray,
In bravery's embrace, we find our way.

Through trials endured, where doubts may sway,
In courage's strength, we find our way,
A beacon of hope in life's disarray,
In determination, come what may.

Through doubts and fears, where shadows may play,
In courage's flame, we find our way,
A warrior's heart, in bright array,
In facing challenges, come what may.

Here are four Villanella poems, 1 each about Faith, Doubt, Solitude & Joy

Faith:
In moments of doubt where shadows may cling,
Faith arises in the light of day,
Each belief a song that hearts may sing,
In trust's embrace, we find our way.

Through trials endured, where doubts may fling,
In faith's strength, we find our way,
A beacon of hope in life's disarray,
In perseverance, come what may.

Through storms of doubt where fears may sting,
In faith's serenity, we find our way,
A guiding light in the darkness' sway,
In unwavering belief, come what may.

Doubt:
In shadows deep where fears may spring,
Doubt whispers softly, a silent thing,
Each question a doubt, a fragile wing,
In uncertainty's embrace, a troubling.

Through mazes of uncertainty where thoughts may cling,
In doubt's grip, we find our questioning,
A labyrinth of queries in a tangled string,
In skepticism's fog, we find our sting.

Through introspection's lens where doubts may bring,
In doubt's scrutiny, we find our reckoning,
A search for truth in every fling,
In skepticism's grip, we find our thing.

Solitude:
In silent hours where echoes play,
Solitude whispers in the light of day,
Each moment alone, a peaceful bay,
In introspection's embrace, we find our way.

Through crowded spaces where minds may fray,
In solitude's sanctuary, we find our stay,
A refuge from life's disarray,
In quiet contemplation, come what may.

Through inner landscapes where thoughts may sway,
In solitude's serenity, we find our way,
A communion with the soul, in bright array,
In self-discovery, come what may.

Joy:
In laughter's echo where hearts may sing,
Joy dances freely in the light of day,
Each smile a note, a melody's fling,
In happiness's embrace, we find our way.

Through moments of bliss where dreams may spring,
In joy's exuberance, we find our way,
A celebration of life's offering,
In jubilation's dance, we come to play.

Through tears of gladness where emotions may wing,
In joy's elation, we find our way,
A symphony of delight, in bright array,
In gratitude, forever may.

Here are four Villanella poems, 1 each about Sorrow, Childhood, Wisdom & Innocence

Sorrow:
In shadows deep, where heartstrings fray,
Sorrow weaves its somber lay,
Each tear a testament to betray,
In darkness deep, where dreams decay.

Through trials faced, where shadows play,
In sorrow's grip, we find our way,
A symphony of night and day,
In grief's embrace, we come to stay.

Through mourning's veil, we learn to sway,
In sorrow's dance, we find our way,
A path of thorns, where hearts convey,
The pain we bear, day by day.

Childhood:
In fields of green where memories sway,
Childhood's laughter holds the day,
Each moment a treasure in its array,
In innocence, where dreams hold sway.

Through games we played in sun's bright ray,
In childhood's innocence, we find our way,
A world of wonder, come what may,
In carefree days of endless play.

Through years gone by, where shadows lay,
In childhood's embrace, we find our way,
A journey back to yesterday,
In nostalgia's bittersweet display.

Wisdom:
In ancient tomes where secrets lay,
Wisdom whispers in the light of day,
Each lesson learned, a price to pay,
In knowledge gained along the way.

Through trials faced, where doubts betray,
In wisdom's counsel, we find our way,
A beacon bright in life's array,
In seeking truth, come what may.

Through ages past, where sages play,
In wisdom's grace, we find our way,
A path of light in shades of gray,
In enlightenment, we find our way.

Innocence:
In purest hearts where dreams hold sway,
Innocence dances in the light of day,
Each smile a promise to convey,
In untainted souls, where hopes may lay.

Through trials faced, where shadows play,
In innocence's embrace, we find our way,
A sanctuary from life's array,
In purity, we come to stay.

Through fleeting years, where memories stray,
In innocence's glow, we find our way,
A reminder of a simpler day,
In cherishing the child at play.

Here are four Villanella poems, 1 each about Passion, Serenity, Freedom & Justice

Passion:
In flames that burn where hearts hold sway,
Passion ignites in the heat of day,
Each touch a spark, a fervent display,
In the dance of desire, come what may.

Through storms of love, where doubts betray,
In passion's embrace, we find our way,
A symphony of hearts in wild array,
In the fire's glow, we come to play.

Through trials endured, where passions fray,
In passion's fervor, we find our way,
A blaze that lights the darkest day,
In love's embrace, we find our way.

Serenity:
In tranquil depths where waters sway,
Serenity whispers in the light of day,
Each moment a calm, a peaceful bay,
In the stillness of mind, where troubles may lay.

Through storms of life, where chaos may play,
In serenity's embrace, we find our way,
A sanctuary from life's disarray,
In inner peace, we come to stay.

Through trials faced, where fears betray,
In serenity's tranquility, we find our way,
A gentle breeze on a summer's day,
In quiet grace, we find our way.

Freedom:
In open skies where dreams may sway,
Freedom beckons in the light of day,
Each breath a choice, a path to stray,
In liberation's call, come what may.

Through chains of doubt, where shadows lay,
In freedom's embrace, we find our way,
A flight of soul in bold array,
In breaking bonds, we come to play.

Through struggles fought, where courage may sway,
In freedom's triumph, we find our way,
A victory song in bright array,
In liberation's light, we find our way.

Justice:
In scales of truth where fairness lay,
Justice prevails in the light of day,
Each verdict a verdict, a price to pay,
In equality's realm, where rights hold sway.

Through trials faced, where doubts betray,
In justice's embrace, we find our way,
A beacon bright in life's array,
In upholding rights, come what may.

Through systems flawed, where shadows play,
In justice's pursuit, we find our way,
A quest for truth, in shades of gray,
In fairness and equity, we find our way.

Here are four Villanella poems, 1 each about Change, Resilience, Gratitude & Forgiveness

Change:
In winds of time where seasons sway,
Change whispers in the light of day,
Each shift a shift, a new display,
In the ebb and flow, come what may.

Through cycles spun where destinies play,
In change's embrace, we find our way,
A journey forward, come what may,
In transformation, night and day.

Through trials faced, where doubts betray,
In change's rhythm, we find our way,
A metamorphosis in bright array,
In evolution's dance, we come to stay.

Resilience:
In storms of life where tempests may sway,
Resilience rises in the light of day,
Each challenge met, a price to pay,
In strength of spirit, come what may.

Through trials endured, where doubts betray,
In resilience's embrace, we find our way,
A fortress built in life's array,
In overcoming obstacles, we come to play.

Through battles fought, where fears may lay,
In resilience's triumph, we find our way,
A testament to the human fray,
In resilience, we find our way.

Gratitude:
In moments still where blessings sway,
Gratitude blooms in the light of day,
Each breath a gift, a debt to repay,
In thankfulness, where hearts may lay.

Through trials faced, where doubts betray,
In gratitude's embrace, we find our way,
A recognition of gifts in life's array,
In counting blessings, come what may.

Through hardships borne, where shadows play,
In gratitude's warmth, we find our way,
A beacon bright in darkest day,
In appreciation, we come to stay.

Forgiveness:
In hearts once wounded where scars may lay,
Forgiveness heals in the light of day,
Each pardon a choice, a debt to repay,
In letting go, where burdens may sway.

Through trials endured, where grudges may stay,
In forgiveness's embrace, we find our way,
A release from bitterness's decay,
In reconciliation, come what may.

Through conflicts resolved, where peace may weigh,
In forgiveness's grace, we find our way,
A bridge rebuilt in disarray,
In forgiveness, we find our way.

Here are four Villanella poems, 1 each about Longing, Belonging, Discovery & Wonder

Longing:
In whispered dreams where desires sway,
Longing lingers in the light of day,
Each sigh a plea, a wish to convey,
In yearning hearts where passions may lay.

Through distance vast, where dreams betray,
In longing's grip, we find our way,
A journey back to yesterday,
In searching for what went astray.

Through fleeting moments, where hopes may fray,
In longing's embrace, we find our way,
A yearning for a brighter day,
In longing's song, we come to play.

Belonging:
In bonds of love where souls may sway,
Belonging blooms in the light of day,
Each connection a thread in life's array,
In unity, where spirits may lay.

Through trials endured, where doubts betray,
In belonging's embrace, we find our way,
A sense of home in hearts astray,
In acceptance, we come to stay.

Through paths untrod, where fears may sway,
In belonging's warmth, we find our way,
A family forged along life's way,
In togetherness, we find our way.

Discovery:
In uncharted realms where mysteries sway,
Discovery beckons in the light of day,
Each step a revelation, a path to assay,
In exploration's call, where wonders may lay.

Through journeys taken, where maps betray,
In discovery's embrace, we find our way,
A quest for knowledge, come what may,
In uncovering truths, day by day.

Through trials faced, where doubts may weigh,
In discovery's wonder, we find our way,
A universe of secrets in disarray,
In curiosity, we come to play.

Wonder:
In starlit skies where dreams may sway,
Wonder sparkles in the light of day,
Each moment a marvel, a world at play,
In awe of creation, where marvels may lay.

Through eyes opened wide, where minds betray,
In wonder's embrace, we find our way,
A journey into the unknown, come what may,
In seeking magic, day by day.

Through life's mysteries, where fears may sway,
In wonder's gaze, we find our way,
A celebration of life's grand display,
In marveling at the universe's array.

Here are four Villanella poems, 1 each about Journey, Reflection, Harmony & Imagination

Journey:
Along the winding road we stray,
Through valleys deep and mountains gray,
Each step a tale of yesterday,
In every dawn, a brand-new day.

With courage as our guiding ray,
We venture forth, come what may,
Through trials dark and skies of May,
In search of truths that lead the way.

Through twists and turns, we find our sway,
In every choice, a price to pay,
Yet in the journey, come what may,
We find ourselves along the way.

Reflection:
In mirrored pools where shadows play,
Reflections dance at close of day,
Each ripple whispers what we may,
In silent depths where dreams hold sway.

Through memories old, we find our way,
In echoes of the past's array,
A journey inward, come what may,
In quiet moments, thoughts astray.

Through introspection, we convey,
The truths we seek in disarray,
In mirrored pools, where thoughts array,
Reflection guides us, night or day.

Harmony:
In melodies that gently sway,
Harmony's embrace holds sway,
Each note a promise to convey,
In symphonies that never stray.

Through chords that bind, hearts in array,
In rhythm's dance, we find our way,
In harmonies that never fray,
In unity, we come to stay.

Through dissonance that fades away,
In music's grace, we find our play,
A symphony of night and day,
In harmony, we find our way.
In imagination, we find our way.

Imagination:
In realms where dreams and fantasies play,
Imagination leads the way,
Each thought a universe in sway,
In worlds of wonder, come what may.

Through stories spun in shades of gray,
In flights of fancy, we portray,
A canvas vast where minds convey,
In endless dreams, we find our way.

Through boundless realms where thoughts astray,
In creativity's bright array,
A tapestry of night and day,

Here are four Villanella poems, 1 each about Silence, Laughter, Tears & Strength

Silence:
In hush of night, where whispers stray,
Silence reigns in quiet array,
Each moment held in still display,
In depths of peace, where shadows play.

Through noiseless realms where echoes may,
In silence, secrets gently sway,
A symphony of night and day,
In quiet grace, we find our way.

Through tranquil calm, our fears allay,
In silent echoes, thoughts convey,
In silence, hearts begin to weigh,
The truths we seek, come what may.

Laughter:
In echoes bright, where joy holds sway,
Laughter dances in the light of day,
Each chuckle, a melody to play,
In symphony of life's ballet.

Through merry moments, cares betray,
In laughter's dance, our troubles stray,
A chorus of hearts in full array,
In laughter's embrace, we find our way.

Through bonds of humor, fears decay,
In laughter's echo, spirits gay,
A celebration, come what may,
In laughter's bliss, we find our way.

Tears:
In salty streams where sorrows lay,
Tears flow freely, come what may,
Each drop a tale of disarray,
In ocean depths, where emotions sway.

Through anguish deep, where shadows play,
In tears, we find release, they say,
A cleansing rain to wash away,
The pain we bear from day to day.

Through rivers of grief, we find our way,
In tears shed for what we betray,
Yet in their waters, hope holds sway,
In tears, we find the light of day.

Strength:
In battles fought, where warriors lay,
Strength arises, come what may,
Each trial faced, a price to pay,
In courage's embrace, we find our way.

Through trials dire, where shadows sway,
In strength, we rise to face the fray,
A beacon bright in night's dismay,
In fortitude, we find our way.

Through hardships faced, we don't dismay,
In strength, we stand, come what may,
A testament to life's affray,
In resilience, we find our way.

Here are four Villanella poems, 1 each about Vulnerability, Renewal, Acceptance & Mystery

Vulnerability:
In tender hearts where fears betray,
Vulnerability holds sway,
Each crack a testament to fray,
In fragile moments, come what may.

Through walls we build, in disarray,
In vulnerability, we find our way,
A strength in showing where we lay,
Our hopes and fears in stark display.

Through open wounds, emotions play,
In vulnerability, we find our way,
A bridge to understanding, they say,
In embracing truth, come what may.

Renewal:
In morning's light, where shadows stray,
Renewal blooms in the light of day,
Each dawn a promise to convey,
In every sunrise, a chance to sway.

Through cycles old, where seasons play,
In renewal, life finds its way,
A constant rhythm, night and day,
In every breath, a fresh bouquet.

Through endings grim, beginnings may,
In renewal's embrace, we find our way,
A phoenix rising from the fray,
In every ending, a new display.

Acceptance:
In moments still, where thoughts betray,
Acceptance dawns in quiet sway,
Each breath a lesson to convey,
In letting go, we find our way.

Through struggles faced, where shadows lay,
In acceptance, we find our way,
A peace in knowing, come what may,
In surrendering to life's ballet.

Through paths unknown, where fears decay,
In acceptance's grace, we find our way,
A gentle breeze on stormy day,
In embracing truth, we find our way.

Mystery:
In whispers soft, where secrets play,
Mystery dances in shadows' sway,
Each question a puzzle to relay,
In enigma's grasp, come what may.

Through veils of mist, where moonbeams stray,
In mystery's cloak, we find our way,
A journey deep, where minds betray,
In seeking answers, night and day.

Through unknown lands, where doubts hold sway,
In mystery's embrace, we find our way,
A labyrinth of mind's ballet,
In embracing the unknown, we find our way.

Here are four Villanella poems, 1 each about Transformation, Eternity, Cosmos & Happiness

Transformation:
In whispers soft, the winds declare,
A dance of leaves in autumn's air,
Transforming green to gold so rare,
As seasons weave their tapestry fair.

Through shadows deep, the moon's bright flare,
Reveals the night's enchanted lair,
Where dreams take flight without a care,
In realms where magic fills the air.

But change is constant, ever there,
In every heartbeat, everywhere,
A symphony of life's affair,
In endless cycles, beyond compare.

Eternity:
In timeless depths where stars ignite,
Eternity unfolds its might,
Through galaxies that gleam so bright,
In cosmic ballet of endless flight.

In silent realms of darkest night,
Where time dissolves, out of sight,
Infinity's embrace burns bright,
In cosmic whispers, pure and white.

Through ages past and futures bright,
Eternal echoes, infinite,
A symphony of boundless height,
In realms where time takes flight.

Cosmos:
In cosmic dance, the galaxies spin,
A grand celestial mandolin,
With nebulae that swirl and grin,
In cosmic tapestry, woven thin.

Among the stars, where dreams begin,
In realms where light and darkness kin,
A universe of might and sin,
In cosmic chaos, we are akin.

From distant realms, where suns grow dim,
To black holes where light cannot swim,
The cosmos hums its ancient hymn,
In cosmic silence, ever prim.

Happiness:
In laughter's echo, joy's refrain,
A melody that soothes all pain,
In hearts where love will ever reign,
Happiness is found again.

Through every trial, every strain,
In sunshine after storm and rain,
In friendships forged and bonds that chain,
Happiness forever will sustain.

In moments fleeting, yet remain,
In memories where we regain,
The simple joys that keep us sane,
In happiness, we find our bane.

LAI:

A medieval French poetic form with a specific stanza structure and rhyme scheme, often used for narrative or lyrical poetry.

Here are four Lai poems, 1 each about Love, Nature, Beauty & Time

Love:
In tender whispers, love takes flight,
Hearts entwined in passion's light.
With every touch, the soul ignites,
Love, the bond that feels just right.

Nature:
In forests deep, nature's song resounds,
Whispers of wind, in leaves that abound.
With every breath, serenity surrounds,
Nature, the canvas where beauty astounds.

Beauty:
In sunset's glow, beauty does shine,
A palette of colors, in hues divine.
With every sight, the soul aligns,
Beauty, the essence of the sublime.

Time:
In steady rhythm, time marches on,
Moments fleeting, then they're gone.
With every tick, a new dawn,
Time, the river where life's drawn.

Here are four Lai poems, 1 each about Death, Dreams, Hope & Despair

Death:
In shadows deep, death's whispers call,
A silent journey, where shadows fall.
With every breath, the spirit enthralls,
Death, the passage where darkness sprawls.

Dreams:
In whispered wishes, dreams take flight,
A world of possibilities, in the night.
With every slumber, the soul takes light,
Dreams, the realm where fantasies ignite.

Hope:
In darkest nights, hope's light does gleam,
A beacon of promise, in the unseen.
With every prayer, the heart does deem,
Hope, the anchor where dreams redeem.

Despair:
In heart's abyss, despair does dwell,
A shadowed burden, a painful spell.
With every tear, the soul's farewell,
Despair, the void where anguish quells.

Here are four Lai poems, 1 each about Friendship, Loneliness, Memories & Music

Friendship:
In bonds of trust, friendship weaves,
Through joyous days and stormy eves.
With every laugh, the heart believes,
Friendship, the tie that never leaves.

Loneliness:
In silent halls, loneliness prevails,
Echoes of emptiness, where silence trails.
With every sigh, the heart unveils,
Loneliness, where solitude pales.

Memories:
In faded photographs, memories bloom,
Capturing moments in life's vast room.
With every glance, the heart resumes,
Memories, the tapestry where stories loom.

Music:
In melodies sweet, music takes flight,
Notes dancing freely, in the silent night.
With every chord, the soul takes delight,
Music, the language where emotions ignite.

Here are four Lai poems, 1 each about Art, Inspiration, Creativity & Courage

Art:
Brush strokes dance on canvas bare,
Colors swirl with utmost care.
With every stroke, emotions flare,
Art, the soul's vivid affair.

Inspiration:
In whispered winds, inspiration flows,
A muse's kiss, where creativity glows.
With every idea, the mind bestows,
Inspiration, the spark that grows.

Creativity:
In boundless realms, creativity flies,
Imagination soars, where dreams arise.
With every creation, the spirit tries,
Creativity, the force that defies.

Courage:
In silent resolve, courage takes flight,
Facing fears, with all its might.
With every step, the heart shines bright,
Courage, the flame that guides through the night.

Here are four Lai poems, 1 each about Faith, Doubt, Solitude & Joy

Faith:
In faith's embrace, the heart takes flight,
Beyond the veil, where hope ignites.
With every prayer, the soul alights,
Faith, the beacon in the darkest nights.

Doubt:
In shadows cast, doubt lingers near,
Questioning truths, whispering fear.
With every query, uncertainty steers,
Doubt, the shadow that veils what's clear.

Solitude:
In quiet retreat, solitude dwells,
Embracing silence, where the heart swells.
With every moment, the soul tells,
Solitude, the sanctuary where peace excels.

Joy:
In laughter's echo, joy resounds,
Hearts uplifted, in happiness' bounds.
With every smile, life astounds,
Joy, the melody where love rebounds.

Here are four Lai poems, 1 each about Sorrow, Childhood, Wisdom & Innocence

Sorrow:
In silent tears, sorrow finds voice,
A heavy heart, in pain's cruel choice.
With every ache, the soul's rejoice,
Sorrow, the echo where sadness hoists.

Childhood:
In fields of green, childhood does roam,
Carefree days, in laughter's home.
With every game, the heart does comb,
Childhood, the haven where dreams dome.

Wisdom:
In quietude, wisdom does speak,
A sage's words, in knowledge's creek.
With every lesson, the mind does seek,
Wisdom, the guide where insights peek.

Innocence:
In purest hearts, innocence blooms,
Untainted souls, where light consumes.
With every smile, the world resumes,
Innocence, the grace where love looms.

Here are four Lai poems, 1 each about Passion, Serenity, Freedom & Justice

Passion:
In fiery hearts, passion ignites,
A blaze of desire, in passionate flights.
With every kiss, the soul takes flight,
Passion, the flame that burns bright.

Serenity:
In tranquil waters, serenity flows,
Whispers of calm, where peace bestows.
With every breath, the spirit glows,
Serenity, where tranquility shows.

Freedom:
In open skies, freedom takes flight,
Wings unfurling, in boundless height.
With every breeze, the soul alights,
Freedom, the essence of life's delight.

Justice:
In balanced scales, justice prevails,
Fairness and truth, where righteousness hails.
With every verdict, integrity sails,
Justice, the beacon where fairness prevails.

Here are four Lai poems, 1 each about Change, Resilience, Gratitude & Forgiveness

Change:
In shifting winds, the world transforms,
Through seasons' dance, and shifting norms.
With every shift, new patterns forms,
Change, the constant that informs.

Resilience:
In storms of life, the spirit stands,
Battered but unbroken, it expands.
With every trial, it commands,
Resilience, where strength demands.

Gratitude:
In whispered thanks, the heart reveals,
Appreciating life's many veils.
With every blessing, it feels,
Gratitude, where the soul heals.

Forgiveness:
In tender hearts, forgiveness flows,
Releasing burdens, letting go.
With every act, redemption grows,
Forgiveness, where healing shows.

Here are four Lai poems, 1 each about Longing, Belonging, Discovery & Wonder

Longing:
In whispers soft, the heart does yearn,
For distant shores, where dreams return.
With every sigh, the flames burn,
Longing, the tide where passions churn.

Belonging:
In circles wide, the hearts unite,
Bound by love, in purest light.
With every bond, the spirits take flight,
Belonging, where souls ignite.

Discovery:
In uncharted lands, the explorer roams,
Through valleys deep, and mountain domes.
With every step, new tales compose,
Discovery, where adventure looms.

Wonder:
In wide-eyed gaze, the world unfolds,
In nature's beauty, and stories untold.
With every sight, the heart beholds,
Wonder, where magic enrolls.

Here are four Lai poems, 1 each about Journey, Reflection, Harmony & Imagination

Journey:
In footsteps traced, the journey begins,
Through valleys deep, and mountains' chins.
With every step, the soul wins,
Journey, where adventure spins.

Reflection:
In mirrored waters, reflections sway,
Echoes of thoughts, in gentle play.
With every ponder, the mind may,
Reflection, where insights may stay.

Harmony:
In melody's embrace, harmony sings,
Notes intertwine, on delicate wings.
With every chord, the soul springs,
Harmony, where peace brings.

Imagination:
In boundless realms, imagination soars,
Dreams take flight, through open doors.
With every idea, the spirit explores,
Imagination, where creativity pours.

Here are four Lai poems, 1 each about Silence, Laughter, Tears & Strength

Silence:
In hushed embrace, the silence speaks,
Whispering secrets, in quiet streaks.
With every pause, the soul seeks,
Silence, where tranquility peaks.

Laughter:
In merry dance, the laughter rings,
Echoes of joy, in joyful springs.
With every chuckle, the heart sings,
Laughter, the melody that happiness brings.

Tears:
In gentle streams, the tears do flow,
Expressing sorrows, in ebb and low.
With every drop, emotions grow,
Tears, the language where feelings show.

Strength:
In quiet resolve, the strength does rise,
Through trials endured, beneath the skies.
With every test, the spirit flies,
Strength, the fortress where courage lies.

Here are four Lai poems, 1 each about Vulnerability, Renewal, Acceptance & Mystery

Vulnerability:
In whispered fears, the heart reveals,
Exposed to wounds that time conceals.
With open soul, the spirit kneels,
Vulnerability, where healing steals.

Renewal:
In morning's light, the world awakes,
A new beginning, as dawn breaks.
With every sunrise, the earth remakes,
Renewal, where hope partakes.

Acceptance:
In quiet surrender, peace is found,
Embracing truths, both lost and found.
With every breath, serenity crowned,
Acceptance, where grace surrounds.

Mystery:
In shadows deep, the secrets hide,
Beyond the veil, where darkness bides.
With every step, curiosity guides,
Mystery, where the unknown resides.

Here are four Lai poems, 1 each about Transformation, Eternity, Cosmos & Happiness

Transformation:
In quiet dawn, the seed awakes,
From slumber deep, its form it shakes.
With gentle push, the earth it breaks,
Transformation, as life partakes.

Eternity:
In endless stretch of sky above,
Where stars dance in eternal love.
With cosmic grace, they soar and shove,
Eternity, the realm thereof.

Cosmos:
In cosmic dance, the galaxies whirl,
Where planets spin, and comets twirl.
With every breath, the cosmos unfurl,
A wondrous tapestry, in cosmic swirl.

Happiness:
In laughter's song, the heart does sing,
Through joyous days, and moments spring.
With every smile, the world takes wing,
Happiness, the bliss it brings.

SKELTONIC VERSE:

Named after English poet John Skelton, this verse form is characterized by short lines with irregular meter and rhyme, often used for comic effect.

-:¦:-•:*'''''*:•.-:¦:-•**•-:¦:-•:*'''''*:•:*'''''*:•.-:¦:-•**•-:¦:--:¦:-•:*'''''*:•.-:¦:- •**•-:¦:-•:*'''''*:•:*'''''*:•.-:¦:-•**•-:¦:-

Here are four Skeltonic Verse poems, 1 each about Love, Nature, Beauty & Time

Love:
In tender hearts, love finds its place,
A gentle touch, a warm embrace.
With every beat, love leaves its trace,
Love, the bond that cannot efface.

Nature:
In forests deep, nature's voice resounds,
Whispering winds, in leaves that abound.
With every breath, its beauty surrounds,
Nature, the canvas where life abounds.

Beauty:
In sunset's glow, beauty does shine,
A palette of colors, in hues divine.
With every sight, our souls entwine,
Beauty, the essence of the sublime.

Time:
In steady march, time's rhythm flows,
A fleeting moment, then it goes.
With every tick, its story shows,
Time, the river where life bestows.

Here are four Skeltonic Verse poems, 1 each about Death, Dreams, Hope & Despair

Death:
In shadows deep, death's whispers sigh,
The final breath, the last goodbye.
With every loss, we question why,
Death, the end where souls may lie.

Dreams:
In slumber's embrace, dreams unfold,
A world of wonders, stories untold.
With every vision, our hearts behold,
Dreams, the realm where fantasies mold.

Hope:
In darkest nights, hope's light does gleam,
A beacon bright, in the darkest stream.
With every wish, we dare to dream,
Hope, the spark in life's grand scheme.

Despair:
In heart's deep well, despair does drown,
A heavy burden, a thorny crown.
With every tear, the soul does frown,
Despair, the shadow that weighs us down.

Here are four Skeltonic Verse poems, 1 each about Friendship, Loneliness, Memories & Music

Friendship:
In bonds of trust, friendship takes flight,
Shared laughter and secrets, a guiding light.
With every moment, hearts unite,
Friendship, the bond that feels just right.

Loneliness:
In silent echoes, loneliness prevails,
Empty spaces, where sadness trails.
With every sigh, the heart exhales,
Loneliness, the void where hope sails.

Memories:
In faded photographs, memories bloom,
Echoes of laughter, in every room.
With every glance, the heart resumes,
Memories, the treasure that forever looms.

Music:
In melodies sweet, music takes hold,
Notes dancing freely, in stories untold.
With every chord, emotions unfold,
Music, the language that never grows old.

Here are four Skeltonic Verse poems, 1 each about Art, Inspiration, Creativity & Courage

Faith:
In whispered prayers, faith takes flight,
Guiding hearts through darkest night.
With every hope, it burns bright,
Faith, the beacon in the night's height.

Doubt:
In shadowed minds, doubt does dwell,
Casting shadows, where fears swell.
With every question, its grip does tell,
Doubt, the skeptic's silent knell.

Solitude:
In silent chambers, solitude holds sway,
Embracing quietude, where thoughts may stray.
With every moment, peace finds its way,
Solitude, the stillness where souls may play.

Joy:
In hearts uplifted, joy does sing,
Dancing freely, on laughter's wing.
With every smile, life's treasures spring,
Joy, the melody that makes hearts ring.

Here are four Skeltonic Verse poems, 1 each about Faith, Doubt, Solitude & Joy

Faith:
In hearts aglow, faith takes flight,
Guiding souls through darkest night.
With every prayer, the spirit's light,
Faith, the beacon burning bright.

Doubt:
In shadows deep, doubt takes hold,
Casting doubts, where fears unfold.
With every question, truth untold,
Doubt, the skeptic's stronghold.

Solitude:
In silent spaces, solitude reigns,
Echoes of quiet, where peace sustains.
With every breath, the soul reclaims,
Solitude, where serenity trains.

Joy:
In hearts uplifted, joy does dance,
Laughing freely, in blissful trance.
With every smile, life's sweet expanse,
Joy, the melody of life's romance.

Here are four Skeltonic Verse poems, 1 each about Sorrow, Childhood, Wisdom & Innocence

Sorrow:
In shadowed depths, sorrow resides,
Echoes of pain, where sadness bides.
With every tear, the heart abides,
Sorrow, the tide where grief collides.

Childhood:
In playful realms, childhood sings,
Laughter and joy, where innocence springs.
With every game, the heart takes wings,
Childhood, the time where wonder brings.

Wisdom:
Wisdom whispers in the sage's word,
Knowledge unfurled, where truth is heard.
With every lesson, the mind is stirred,
Wisdom, the light where insight's stirred.

Innocence:
In purest hearts, innocence blooms,
Untainted souls, where dreams resume.
With every smile, the world resumes,
Innocence, the grace where love entombs.

Here are four Skeltonic Verse poems, 1 each about Passion, Serenity, Freedom & Justice

Passion:
In fiery hearts, passion ignites,
Flames of desire, in fervent heights.
With every touch, the soul alights,
Passion, the spark that ignites.

Serenity:
In tranquil spaces, serenity dwells,
Whispers of peace, where silence swells.
With every breath, the spirit tells,
Serenity, where calmness quells.

Freedom:
Freedom soars in boundless skies,
Wings outstretched, where eagles rise.
With every flight, the soul defies,
Freedom, where limits demise.

Justice:
In balanced scales, justice prevails,
Fairness guides, where truth unveils.
With every verdict, the gavel hails,
Justice, where righteousness sails.

Here are four Skeltonic Verse poems, 1 each about Change, Resilience, Gratitude & Forgiveness

Change:
Change whispers softly, a shifting breeze,
Transforming landscapes, rustling trees.
With every turn, it aims to please,
Change, the dance that never freeze.

Resilience:
Resilience stands tall amidst the storm,
Through trials faced, its heart stays warm.
With every challenge, it transforms,
Resilience, the fire that reforms.

Gratitude:
In quiet moments, gratitude blooms,
In whispered thanks and sunlit rooms.
With every blessing, the heart resumes,
Gratitude, the light that consumes.

Forgiveness:
Forgiveness whispers, a gentle breeze,
Easing burdens, granting ease.
With every act, it aims to appease,
Forgiveness, the peace that frees.

Here are four Skeltonic Verse poems, 1 each about Longing, Belonging, Discovery & Wonder

Longing:
In whispered sighs, the longing weaves,
Through starlit nights and moonlit eves.
With every hope, the heart believes,
Longing, the yearning that never leaves.

Belonging:
In circles wide, the belonging finds,
In shared laughter and gentle minds.
With every bond, the spirit binds,
Belonging, the solace that reminds.

Discovery:
In uncharted seas, the discovery sings,
Through unexplored lands and hidden springs.
With every quest, the adventurer brings,
Discovery, the joy that exploration brings.

Wonder:
In wide-eyed gaze, the wonder thrives,
Through cosmic vistas and secret hives.
With every mystery, the spirit strives,
Wonder, the spark that makes us alive.

Here are four Skeltonic Verse poems, 1 each about Journey, Reflection, Harmony & Imagination

Journey:
In winding paths, the journey unfolds,
Through valleys deep and mountains cold.
With every step, new tales are told,
Journey, the adventure, bold and old.

Reflection:
In mirrored waters, reflections gleam,
Echoes of memories, a silent stream.
With every ponder, the mind does dream,
Reflection, the mirror of life's scheme.

Harmony:
In symphony's embrace, the notes entwine,
Melodies dancing in perfect line.
With every chord, hearts align,
Harmony, the song divine.

Imagination:
In boundless realms, the mind takes flight,
Dreams and visions, a vivid light.
With every thought, a new height,
Imagination, the realm of might.

Here are four Skeltonic Verse poems, 1 each about Silence, Laughter, Tears & Strength

Silence:
In stillness deep, the silence reigns,
Echoes of quiet in nature's domains.
In whispered breaths, the soul maintains,
Silence, the canvas where peace sustains.

Laughter:
In bubbling streams, the laughter flows,
A symphony of joy that endlessly grows.
With every chuckle, the spirit glows,
Laughter, the melody that life bestows.

Tears:
In salty streams, the tears do fall,
Echoes of sorrow, a universal call.
With every drop, emotions enthrall,
Tears, the language when words stall.

Strength:
In iron will, the strength abides,
Through trials endured, it silently guides.
With every challenge, the spirit confides,
Strength, the fortress where resilience resides.

Here are four Skeltonic Verse poems, 1 each about Vulnerability, Renewal, Acceptance & Mystery

Vulnerability:
In naked truth, we find our strength,
Vulnerability, at arm's length.
With open hearts, we go to great lengths,
Vulnerability, the inner strength.

Renewal:
In dawn's first light, a fresh start,
Renewal whispers in every heart.
With every sunrise, we play our part,
Renewal's dance, a brand new start!

Acceptance:
In quiet surrender, we find peace,
Acceptance, where all struggles cease.
With open arms, our fears release,
Acceptance's grace, our hearts increase.

Mystery:
In shadows' dance, secrets weave,
Mystery's cloak, we dare to believe.
With every question, our minds perceive,
Mystery's allure, we dare to achieve.

Here are four Skeltonic Verse poems, 1 each about Transformation, Eternity, Cosmos & Happiness

Transformation:
In caterpillar's crawl, a change unfolds,
Metamorphosis, a tale retold.
From earthbound creature to wings of gold,
Transformation, the story bold!

Eternity:
In timeless dance, the stars align,
Eternity's embrace, divine.
Through endless nights, the cosmos shines,
Eternity, the grand design!

Cosmos:
In galaxies vast, the planets soar,
Cosmic symphony, forevermore.
Through nebulae's mist, the heavens explore,
Cosmos's wonder, we adore!

Happiness:
In laughter's echo, joy does bloom,
Happiness, like a sweet perfume.
In hearts entwined, there is no gloom,
Happiness, life's sweetest plume!

HAIGA:

A combination of haiku and visual art, often featuring a painting, photograph, or drawing alongside a haiku poem.

-:¦:-•:*'''''*:•.-:¦:-•**•-:¦:-•:*''''''*:•:*'''''*:•.-:¦:-•**•-:¦:--:¦:-•:*'''''*:•.-:¦:- •**•-:¦:-•:*''''''*:•:*'''''*:•.-:¦:-•**•-:¦:-

Here are four Haiga poems, 1 each about Love, Nature, Beauty & Time

Love:
Image: Two swans gracefully gliding on a tranquil pond, their necks forming a heart shape
Swans in graceful dance,
Love's embrace upon the waves,
Hearts entwined as one.

Nature:
Image: A majestic waterfall cascading down moss-covered rocks in a lush forest
Waterfall's descent,
Nature's symphony of life,
Echoes in the woods.

Beauty:
Image: A delicate rose in full bloom, its petals kissed by morning dew
Rose in morning light,
Beauty's essence in each fold,
Nature's perfect art.

Time:
Image: A sundial casting a shadow on the ground, surrounded by fallen leaves
Shadow marks the hour,
Time's eternal dance unfolds,
Leaves whisper secrets.

Here are four Haiga poems, 1 each about Death, Dreams, Hope & Despair

Death:
Image: A solitary gravestone standing in a field of wildflowers
Silent stone sentinel,
Whispers of those gone before,
Memory's embrace.

Dreams:
Image: A person sleeping peacefully under a blanket of stars, surrounded by fantastical creatures in their dreams
In dreams' realm we soar,
Stars weave tales in midnight sky,
Fantasy takes flight.

Hope:
Image: A single sunflower reaching towards the sun, bathed in golden light
Petals open wide,
Hope blooms in the morning light,
Promise in each ray.

Despair:
Image: A lone figure sitting in darkness, head bowed, surrounded by shadows
Shadows close around,
Despair's grip tightens its hold,
Silent tears unseen.

Here are four Haiga poems, 1 each about Friendship, Loneliness, Memories & Music

Friendship:
Image: Two trees standing close together, their branches intertwining
Roots entwined as one,
Friendship's bond in nature's hands,
Strength in unity.

Loneliness:
Image: A single boat adrift on a vast ocean, surrounded by fog
Lost in endless sea,
Loneliness whispers softly,
Echoes in the mist.

Memories:
Image: A vintage photograph album with sepia-toned pictures spilling out
Pages filled with time,
Memories etched in shadows,
Echoes of the past.

Music:
Image: A violin resting on a wooden chair, bathed in soft lamplight
Strings whisper secrets,
Melodies dance in moonlight,
Music's gentle embrace.

Here are four Haiga poems, 1 each about Art, Inspiration, Creativity & Courage

Art:
Image: A paintbrush dipped in vibrant colors, poised above a blank canvas
Brush strokes tell the tale,
Colors dance on empty space,
Art breathes life anew.

Inspiration:
Image: A solitary figure standing at the edge of a cliff, gazing at a breathtaking sunset
Sunset's golden hue,
Inspiration fills the air,
Dreams take flight at dusk.

Creativity:
Image: A blank notebook surrounded by scattered art supplies, waiting to be filled
Empty page awaits,
Creativity's playground,
Ink spills dreams to life.

Courage:
Image: A lone wolf standing on a cliff, howling at the full moon amidst a starry sky
Howl in the moon's light,
Courage roars in wilderness,
Strength in solitude.

Here are four Haiga poems, 1 each about Faith, Doubt, Solitude & Joy

Faith:
Image: A lone figure walking along a misty forest path, guided by a distant light
Through the mist I walk,
Faith's lantern guides my footsteps,
Hope's gentle embrace.

Doubt:
Image: Ripples spreading across the surface of a still pond, distorting reflections
Uncertain whispers,
Doubt's ripples distort the truth,
Shadows in the soul.

Solitude:
Image: A solitary figure sitting on a rocky cliff, overlooking a vast expanse of ocean
Silent solitude,
Echoes of the soul's whispers,
Ocean's endless song.

Joy:
Image: A field of sunflowers basking in golden sunlight, with bees buzzing around them
Sunflowers sway tall,
Joy's laughter in every petal,
Nature's symphony.

Here are four Haiga poems, 1 each about Sorrow, Childhood, Wisdom & Innocence

Sorrow:
Image: Raindrops falling on a wilted flower in a darkened garden
Petals wet with tears,
Sorrow's weight upon the heart,
Grief blooms in the rain.

Childhood:
Image: Children playing in a sunlit meadow, surrounded by wildflowers
Laughter fills the air,
Innocent hearts dance and sing,
Childhood's joyful light.

Wisdom:
Image: An old tree with gnarled branches stretching towards the sky, bathed in golden sunlight
Roots deep in the earth,
Branches reaching for the stars,
Wisdom's silent strength.

Innocence:
Image: A newborn baby sleeping peacefully in a crib, surrounded by soft blankets
Dreams in newborn eyes,
Innocence pure and untouched,
Guardian angels near.

Create 4 unique Haiga poems, 1 each about Passion, Serenity, Freedom & Justice

Passion:
Image: Flames dancing in a fireplace, casting flickering shadows
Embers burn bright red,
Passion's fire ignites the soul,
Flames dance in the dark.

Serenity:
Image: A tranquil lake reflecting a clear blue sky and surrounding trees
Still waters reflect,
Serenity's gentle grace,
Peace in every ripple.

Freedom:
Image: A bird soaring high in a cloudless sky, wings outstretched
Wings spread wide in flight,
Freedom's breath beneath feathers,
Sky's endless embrace.

Justice:
Image: Scales balanced perfectly against a blue sky, held by a strong hand
Balance in the light,
Justice wields impartial truth,
Scales tip with fairness.

Here are four Haiga poems, 1 each about Change, Resilience, Gratitude & Forgiveness

Change:
Image: Leaves changing colors on trees during autumn
Seasons turn and twist,
Leaves dance in vibrant hues,
Change whispers its song.

Resilience:
Image: A lone flower growing amidst cracked pavement
Petals unfurl strong,
Blossoming through adversity,
Resilience blooms bright.

Gratitude:
Image: Hands holding a cup of steaming tea, with mist rising into the air
Steam swirls in the air,
Sipping gratitude's warm brew,
Heart brims with thankfulness.

Forgiveness:
Image: A broken chain lying on the ground, with light shining through the gaps
Chains of bitterness,
Shattered by forgiveness' light,
Freedom's sweet release.

Here are four Haiga poems, 1 each about Longing, Belonging, Discovery & Wonder

Longing:
Image: A lone figure standing on a cliff, gazing at the distant horizon
Heart seeks the unknown,
Yearning in the depths of soul,
Longing for the stars.

Belonging:
Image: A group of friends gathered around a campfire, sharing stories and laughter
Circle of friendship,
Warmth of souls intertwined,
Belonging's embrace.

Discovery:
Image: A person's silhouette exploring a cave with a torch, illuminating hidden treasures
Light pierces the dark,
Revealing secrets unseen,
Discovery's delight.

Wonder:
Image: A child with wide eyes staring up at the night sky, mesmerized by the stars
Eyes wide with wonder,
Lost in the cosmic expanse,
Universe's embrace.

Here are four Haiga poems, 1 each about Journey, Reflection, Harmony & Imagination

Journey:
Image: Footprints in the sand leading into the horizon
Footprints in the sand,
Path unfolds beneath the sun,
Journey to the unknown.

Reflection:
Image: Still waters reflecting a cloudy sky
Mirror of the soul,
Clouds dance upon tranquil depths,
Reflection whispers.

Harmony:
Image: A symphony orchestra performing in perfect synchronization. Notes in harmony,
Melody weaves through the air,
Unity in sound.

Imagination:
Image: A child drawing with colorful crayons, surrounded by fantastical creatures
In a world of dreams,
Crayons sketch the impossible,
Imagination soars.

Here are four Haiga poems, 1 each about Silence, Laughter, Tears & Strength

Silence:
Image: A tranquil lake with mist rising from its surface
Silent lake at dawn,
Mist whispers in quiet hush,
Stillness speaks volumes.

Laughter:
Image: Friends gathered around a bonfire, laughing under the stars
Flames dance in the night,
Echoes of laughter ring loud,
Warmth in friendship's glow.

Tears:
Image: Raindrops falling gently on a windowpane
Tears from heavens weep,
Soothing sorrows with soft rain,
Cleansing the spirit.

Strength:
Image: A lone tree standing tall against a stormy sky
Against raging storms,
Unyielding tree stands steadfast,
Strength in resilience.

Here are four Haiga poems, 1 each about Vulnerability, Renewal, Acceptance & Mystery

Vulnerability:
Image: A fragile butterfly perched on a delicate flower
Wings of vulnerability,
Fluttering in the gentle breeze,
Embrace the fragility.

Renewal:
Image: A seedling breaking through the soil
In the soil's embrace,
New life bursts forth with each dawn,
Renewal's tender kiss.

Acceptance:
Image: Ripples on a calm lake reflecting the sky
Acceptance like water,
Reflecting life's twists and turns,
Serene in its depths.

Mystery:
Image: Mist enveloping a forest, with hidden creatures lurking within
Veil of mystery,
Enshrouding the unknown depths,
Whispers in the mist.

Here are four Haiga poems, 1 each about Transformation, Eternity, Cosmos & Happiness

Transformation:
Image: A caterpillar crawling on a leaf
Transformation's dance,
Cocoon cradles hidden dreams,
Butterfly emerges.

Eternity:
Image: Infinity symbol drawn in the sand with waves washing over it
Endless waves of time,
Infinity's gentle kiss,
Eternity's embrace.

Cosmos:
Image: A galaxy swirling in space
Cosmic dance of stars,
Infinite galaxies whirl,
Cosmos's grand waltz.

Happiness:
Image: A sunflower basking in sunlight
Sunlight's warm embrace,
Petals stretch towards the sky,
Happiness blooms bright.

-:¦:-•:*'''''*:•.-:¦:-•**•-:¦:-•:*'''''*:•:*'''''*:•.-:¦:-•**•-:¦:--:¦:-•:*'''''*:•.-:¦:- •**•-:¦:-•:*'''''*:•:*'''''*:•.-:¦:-•**•-:¦:-

NONSENSE VERSE:

Playful and humorous poetry that often uses invented words, nonsense language, and whimsical themes.

-:¦:-•:*'''''*:•.-:¦:-•**•-:¦:-•:*'''''*:•:*'''''*:•.-:¦:-•**•-:¦:--:¦:-•:*'''''*:•.-:¦:- •**•-:¦:-•:*'''''*:•:*'''''*:•.-:¦:-•**•-:¦:-

Here are four Nonsense Verse poems, 1 each about Love, Nature, Beauty & Time

Love:
In whispered vows, the love does bloom,
Through moonlit nights and sunlit gloom.
With every kiss, the heart's perfume,
Love, the dance in life's grand room.

The tender touch, the gentle gaze,
In love's embrace, we find our blaze.
Through every moment, every phase,
Love, the symphony that amazes.

Nature:
In whispers soft, the nature sings,
Through rustling leaves and fluttering wings.
With every breath, the spirit springs,
Nature, the melody where life clings.

The babbling brook, the towering tree,
In nature's embrace, we find our glee.
Through every wonder, every spree,
Nature, the canvas that's so free.

Beauty:
In colors bright, the beauty gleams,
Through radiant smiles and sunlit beams.
With every glance, the heart it deems,
Beauty, the spark that forever streams.

The rose in bloom, the sunset's glow,
In beauty's embrace, we start to grow.
Through every grace, every show,
Beauty, the magic that we bestow.

Time:
In whispers low, the time does flow,
Through ticking clocks and shadows' glow.
With every moment, the currents grow,
Time, the river where life's ripples show.

The fleeting hour, the passing day,
In time's embrace, we find our way.
Through every journey, every sway,
Time, the melody we can't delay.

Here are four Nonsense Verse poems, 1 each about Death, Dreams, Hope & Despair

Death:
In shadows deep, the darkness creeps,
Through silent halls where sorrow weeps.
With whispered sighs, the spirit sleeps,
Death, the silence where memory keeps.

The final breath, the closing door,
In death's embrace, we seek no more.
Through every sorrow that we bore,
Death, the peace forevermore.

Dreams:
In moonlit skies, the dreams take flight,
Through starry paths and endless night.
With every wish, the heart alight,
Dreams, the canvas of our might.

The whispered hope, the silent prayer,
In dreams' embrace, we dare to care.
Through every vision that we bear,
Dreams, the magic we declare.

Hope:
In shadows' grasp, the hope does glow,
Through darkest nights and coldest snow.
With steadfast heart, the spirit knows,
Hope, the beacon where courage flows.

The candle's flame, the morning's light,
In hope's embrace, we stand upright.
Through every trial, every fight,
Hope, the dawn after the night.

Despair:
In echoes cold, the despair resounds,
Through shattered dreams and silent grounds.
With heavy heart, the spirit drowns,
Despair, the darkness where hope confounds.

The silent scream, the tear-stained face,
In despair's embrace, we find no grace.
Through every shadow that we chase,
Despair, the void we must embrace.

Here are four Nonsense Verse poems, 1 each about Friendship, Loneliness, Memories & Music

Friendship:
In laughter's dance, the friendship gleams,
Through shared jokes and shared dreams.
With every hug, the bond it beams,
Friendship, the treasure that redeems.

The secret handshake, the knowing smile,
In friendship's embrace, we walk the mile.
Through every storm, every trial,
Friendship, the light that's versatile.

Loneliness:
In shadows deep, the loneliness broods,
Through silent nights and solitude's moods.
With heavy heart, the spirit eludes,
Loneliness, the void that intrudes.

The empty room, the silent phone,
In loneliness's embrace, we feel alone.
Through every ache, every groan,
Loneliness, the echo of the unknown.

Memories:
In whispers soft, the memories sing,
Through faded photographs and olden fling.
With every scent, the past it brings,
Memories, the treasure in life's ring.

The childhood laugh, the summer's breeze,
In memories' embrace, we find our ease.
Through every tale, every tease,
Memories, the anchor in life's seas.

Music:
In melodies sweet, the music flows,
Through harmonies high and rhythms that grow.
With every note, the spirit knows,
Music, the language that the soul sows.

The symphony's swell, the ballad's cry,
In music's embrace, we reach the sky.
Through every chord, every sigh,
Music, the heartbeat that can't lie.

Here are four Nonsense Verse poems, 1 each about Art, Inspiration, Creativity & Courage

Art:
In strokes of color, the canvas speaks,
Through swirling hues and hidden peaks.
With every stroke, the story leaks,
Art, the language that the soul seeks.

The sculptor's chisel, the poet's pen,
In art's embrace, we find our ken.
Through every masterpiece, every yen,
Art, the symphony that transcends.

Inspiration:
In whispers soft, the muse does call,
Through dreams that rise and shadows fall.
With open heart, we heed the thrall,
Inspiration, the muse that enthralls.

The spark that ignites, the flame that burns,
In inspiration's embrace, our spirit learns.
Through every whisper, every turn,
Inspiration, the fire that yearns.
Courage, the armor of circumstance.

Creativity:
In boundless realms, the creativity soars,
Through uncharted lands and open doors.
With every idea, the spirit roars,
Creativity, the river that explores.

The inventor's mind, the artist's eye,
In creativity's embrace, we reach the sky.
Through every venture, every try,
Creativity, the wings that let us fly.

Courage:
In quiet hearts, the courage beats,
Through trials faced and foes it meets.
With every step, the courage greets,
Courage, the warrior that defeats.

The lion's roar, the soldier's stance,
In courage's embrace, we take our chance.
Through every battle, every lance,

Here are four Nonsense Verse poems, 1 each about Faith, Doubt, Solitude & Joy

Faith:
In whispers soft, the faith does rise,
Through darkest nights and clouded skies.
With steadfast heart, the soul defies,
Faith, the beacon that never dies.

The candle's flame, the guiding light,
In faith's embrace, we take our flight.
Through every trial, every plight,
Faith, the star that shines so bright.

Doubt:
In shadows deep, the doubt does creep,
Through whispered fears and troubled sleep.
With questioning mind, the thoughts they sweep,
Doubt, the canyon that's so steep.

The skeptic's eye, the skeptic's tongue,
In doubt's embrace, we feel undone.
Through every battle that's begun,
Doubt, the shadow beneath the sun.

Solitude:
In quiet corners, solitude waits,
Through whispered thoughts and open gates.
With introspective gaze, it orchestrates,
Solitude, the canvas where life creates.

The silent forest, the empty room,
In solitude's embrace, we find our bloom.
Through every silence, every gloom,
Solitude, the stillness that consumes.

Joy:
In laughter's chorus, joy does sing,
Through sunny days and blossoming spring.
With every heart, the bells do ring,
Joy, the melody that makes us wing.

The child's giggle, the lover's kiss,
In joy's embrace, we find our bliss.
Through every moment, every miss,
Joy, the spark that we cannot dismiss.

Here are four Nonsense Verse poems, 1 each about Sorrow, Childhood, Wisdom & Innocence

Sorrow:
In shadows deep, the sorrow sighs,
Through tear-stained cheeks and mournful eyes.
With heavy hearts, the spirit cries,
Sorrow, the echo that never dies.

The raindrop's fall, the stormy night,
In sorrow's embrace, we seek the light.
Through darkest hour, we hold tight,
Sorrow, the veil that masks our sight.

Childhood:
In laughter's ring, the childhood gleams,
Through endless days and fanciful dreams.
With every leap, the spirit deems,
Childhood, the realm of flowing streams.

The playground's joy, the skipping rope,
In childhood's embrace, we dare to hope.
Through every bound, every scope,
Childhood, the memory we elope.
Innocence, the lullaby that cannot lie.

Wisdom:
In whispers wise, the wisdom flows,
Through ancient scrolls and tales of woes.
With every lesson, the knowledge grows,
Wisdom, the river where insight shows.

The sage's gaze, the scholar's book,
In wisdom's embrace, we come to look.
Through every turn, every nook,
Wisdom, the beacon in life's brook.

Innocence:
In purity's light, the innocence gleams,
Through rose-tinted glass and untainted dreams.
With every smile, the heart redeems,
Innocence, the echo of heavenly themes.

The child's laughter, the newborn's cry,
In innocence's embrace, we wonder why.
Through every sigh, every goodbye,

Here are four Nonsense Verse poems, 1 each about Passion, Serenity, Freedom & Justice

Passion:
In flames that dance, the passion gleams,
Through whispered vows and moonlit dreams.
With every touch, the fire beams,
Passion, the song of flowing streams.

The artist's stroke, the poet's rhyme,
In passion's embrace, we mark the time.
Through every peak, every climb,
Passion, the rhythm in our prime.

Serenity:
In whispers soft, the serenity sings,
Through tranquil woods and angel wings.
With every breath, the peace it brings,
Serenity, the melody that clings.

The gentle breeze, the silent lake,
In serenity's embrace, we partake.
Through every dawn, every wake,
Serenity, the calm in the quake.

Freedom:
In open skies, the freedom soars,
Through boundless fields and open doors.
With every leap, the spirit roars,
Freedom, the wind that never bores.

The eagle's flight, the wild wind's blow,
In freedom's embrace, we come to know.
Through every trial, every foe,
Freedom, the fire that we stow.

Justice:
In scales that tip, the justice weighs,
Through righteous deeds and honest bays.
With every plea, the truth conveys,
Justice, the beacon in life's maze.

The gavel's fall, the courtroom's call,
In justice's embrace, we stand tall.
Through every verdict, every thrall,
Justice, the voice that speaks for all.

Here are four Nonsense Verse poems, 1 each about Change, Resilience, Gratitude & Forgiveness

Change:
In whispers soft, the winds decree,
Through tangled woods and endless sea.
With every turn, the world's decree,
Change, the dance of destiny.

The caterpillar's crawl, the butterfly's flight,
In change's embrace, we find our light.
Through day and night, through wrong and right,
Change, the constant in our sight.

Resilience:
In rocky shores, the waves do roar,
Through storms that rage, and tempests bore.
With every crash upon the shore,
Resilience, the tide that does restore.

The phoenix's rise, the ember's spark,
In resilience's embrace, we find our mark.
Through trials dark, through shadows stark,
Resilience, the beacon in the dark.

Gratitude:
In whispers soft, the heart does sing,
Through every joy, through every sting.
With every breath, the echoes ring,
Gratitude, the melody of spring.

The sun's warm kiss, the rain's embrace,
In gratitude's dance, we find our grace.
Through every moment, every space,
Gratitude, the smile upon our face.

Forgiveness:
In shadows deep, the heart does weigh,
Through wounds that bleed, and debts to pay.
With every step upon the way,
Forgiveness, the dawn of a new day.

The olive branch, the outstretched hand,
In forgiveness's embrace, we understand.
Through every rift, through every strand,
Forgiveness, the bond that we command.

Here are four Nonsense Verse poems, 1 each about Longing, Belonging, Discovery & Wonder

Longing:
In whispers soft, the longing calls,
Through misty dreams and ancient halls.
With yearning hearts, the curtain falls,
Longing, the echo that enthralls.

The distant star, the unreachable shore,
In longing's embrace, we search for more.
Through endless nights, we dare to explore,
Longing, the fire we can't ignore.

Belonging:
In circles wide, we find our kin,
Through laughter's dance and tears within.
With open arms, we start to spin,
Belonging, the warmth beneath our skin.

The puzzle's piece, the missing part,
In belonging's melody, we find our start.
Through every beat, in every heart,
Belonging, the home where we impart.

Discovery:
In shadows deep, the secrets sleep,
Through whispered winds and oceans' sweep.
With curious minds, the journey's steep,
Discovery, the treasure we keep.

The hidden door, the unknown quest,
In discovery's embrace, we are blessed.
Through every trial, every test,
Discovery, the adventure we manifest.

Wonder:
In starlit skies, the wonder gleams,
Through galaxies and cosmic streams.
With wide-eyed gaze, the world it seems,
Wonder, the magic of our dreams.

The butterfly's dance, the flower's bloom,
In wonder's embrace, we find our room.
Through nature's hymn, through every plume,
Wonder, the universe's infinite loom.

Here are four Nonsense Verse poems, 1 each about Journey, Reflection, Harmony & Imagination

Journey:
In shoes of stars, we start to tread,
Along the path where dreams are spread.
With maps of clouds, our hearts are led,
Journey, the tale where hopes are fed.

Through valleys deep, and mountains high,
In journey's dance, we touch the sky.
With every step, we question why,
Journey, the adventure, we can't deny.

Reflection:
In mirrors' gaze, the echoes sing,
Reflections of our everything.
With pondered thoughts, we take to wing,
Reflection, the song that life does bring.

The pond's still surface, the moon's soft gleam,
In reflection's pool, we start to dream.
Through memories' dance, we find our seam,
Reflection, the mirror of our esteem.

Harmony:
In chords of rainbows, the harmony hums,
In symphony's embrace, the melody strums.
With notes that dance, like bees with drums,
Harmony, the song where everything becomes.

The wind's soft whisper, the river's flow,
In harmony's embrace, we start to glow.
With every beat, the rhythm does show,
Harmony, the dance where hearts do grow.

Imagination:
In dreamscape's realm, we start to play,
In colors wild, we find our way.
With whispered tales, we seize the day,
Imagination, the world where we hold sway.

The paper's blank, the canvas white,
In imagination's flight, we take our flight.
With every stroke, we paint the night,
Imagination, the spark that sets alight.

Here are four Nonsense Verse poems, 1 each about Silence, Laughter, Tears & Strength

Silence:
In hushed whispers, the silence sings,
Of secret realms and unseen things.
With quiet steps, it softly springs,
Silence, the song that silence brings.

The empty page, the blank expanse,
In silence, we find our chance.
To hear the world in silent trance,
Silence, the dance of circumstance.

Laughter:
In bubbles bright, laughter does soar,
From bellies deep, to ceilings' floor.
With giggles wild, it does implore,
Laughter, the key to open every door.

The snicker's snort, the chuckle's cheer,
In laughter's symphony, we draw near.
To joy's embrace, without a fear,
Laughter, the melody we hold dear.

Tears:
In salty streams, the teardrops flow,
From eyes that weep, in ebb and low.
With sorrow's weight, they gently grow,
Tears, the rivers of emotions aglow.

The raindrop's fall, the ocean's cry,
In tears, we find the reasons why.
Through pain and loss, we reach the sky,
Tears, the healing balm, we can't deny.

Strength:
In silent resolve, strength does stand,
With sturdy feet on solid land.
Against the tempest's wild demand,
Strength, the fortress, forever grand.

The mighty oak, the mountain's peak,
In strength, we find what we do seek.
Through trials fierce, though we feel weak,
Strength, the beacon, it does speak.

Here are four Nonsense Verse poems, 1 each about Vulnerability, Renewal, Acceptance & Mystery

Vulnerability:
In socks with holes, a mouse does hide,
In corners dark, it seeks to bide.
With timid squeaks, it scurries wide,
Vulnerability, it cannot hide.

A heart laid bare, like open sky,
In vulnerability, we can't deny.
With courage, though we may be shy,
We spread our wings and learn to fly.

Renewal:
In springtime's kiss, the buds unfurl,
From winter's grasp, they start to swirl.
With dewdrop tears, the petals twirl,
Renewal's dance, the world does whirl.

The sun's embrace, the rain's soft touch,
Renewal blooms, it's not too much.
In nature's cycle, we find as such,
Renewal's promise, a gentle clutch.

Acceptance:
In mismatched socks, we find our stride,
Acceptance walks by our side.
With quirks and flaws, we cannot hide,
Acceptance, in ourselves, we confide.

Like puzzle pieces, odd and strange,
Acceptance, we don't rearrange.
In every corner, every range,
Acceptance, a melody of change.

Mystery:
In shadows deep, the whispers hush,
Mystery's cloak, a silent rush.
With secrets kept, in twilight's blush,
Mystery's enigma, a gentle crush.

The moon's soft glow, the stars that gleam,
Mystery's allure, a timeless dream.
In every puzzle, every scheme,
Mystery's dance, a cosmic stream.

Here are four Nonsense Verse poems, 1 each about Transformation, Eternity, Cosmos & Happiness

Transformation:
In the meadow's dance, a froggy leap,
With lily pads, it does a sweep.
Croak and ribbit, then quite profound,
Turns into a prince, all around!

From warty skin to silk and gold,
Transformation, a tale retold.
The pond's magic, a mystic sound,
A frog no more, but princely bound!

Eternity:
In timeless fields where stars do play,
Eternity holds night and day.
The clock's hands still, they never sway,
Forever night, forever day.

In endless loops, the moon does soar,
And rivers flow forevermore.
Eternal dance, in endless sway,
Where time itself has lost its way.

Cosmos:
In cosmic storms, the planets whirl,
Through galaxies, they twist and twirl.
The stars, like gems, in darkness hurled,
In cosmic tapestry, they unfurl.

Black holes sing their cosmic song,
Where time and space doth both belong.
In cosmic dance, we all belong,
To the grandeur of the cosmic throng.

Happiness:
In laughter's echoes, joy does ring,
In hearts that dance, and souls take wing.
The sun shines bright, the birds do sing,
In happiness, life's joys we bring.

A hug, a smile, a friendly face,
In happiness, we find our grace.
In every corner, every place,
Happiness, a warm embrace.

-:¦:-•:*'''''*:•.-:¦:-•**•-:¦:-•:*'''''*:•:*'''''*:•.-:¦:-•**•-:¦:--:¦:-•:*'''''*:•.-:¦:- •**•-:¦:-•:*'''''*:•:*'''''*:•.-:¦:-•**•-:¦:-

TONGUE-TWISTER:

Poetry involves creating verses that are intentionally difficult to articulate due to their complex or repetitive phonetic patterns.

Here are four tongue-twister poems, each about Love, Nature, Beauty, and Time:

Lively lovers laugh in the lilting light,
Whispering wishes in the wondrous night.
Hearts entwined in the heavenly height,
Embracing, enchanting, in the endless flight.

Nimble nymphs nestle in the noisy nest,
Fluttering feathers in the forest's fest.
Rustling leaves in the rhythmic rest,
Dancing, darting, in the delicate quest.

Beautiful blossoms bloom in the blooming bower,
Petals perfumed in the peaceful power.
Radiant rainbows in the radiant hour,
Gleaming, glowing, in the glorious glower.

Ticking timepieces tock in the tumultuous tide,
Counting centuries in the cunning collide.
Whispering winds in the wise worldwide,
Passing, pausing, in the panoramic pride.

Here are four unique tongue-twister poems, each about Death, Dreams, Hope, and Despair:

Dreadful darkness descends in the dismal night,
Grim reapers roam in the ghostly flight.
Haunting echoes in the harrowing height,
Lurking, looming, in the lifeless light.

Dreamy desires dance in the dreamy dale,
Floating fantasies in the fanciful tale.
Whimsical wishes in the wistful whale,
Drifting, daring, in the delightful sail.

Hopeful hearts hum in the hopeful hue,
Glimmering glows in the gentle view.
Radiant rays in the resolute brew,
Shining, soaring, in the steadfast stew.

Desperate cries crack in the desolate den,
Grieving ghosts in the gloomy glen.
Tearful torrents in the tempest's ten,
Sinking, struggling, in the sorrowful pen.

Here are four unique tongue-twister poems, each about Friendship, Loneliness, Memories, and Music:

Friendly faces frolic in the festive fray,
Bonding buddies in the bright bouquet.
Loyal laughter in the loving lay,
Embracing, enduring, in the endless array.

Lonely laments linger in the lonely lane,
Echoing emptiness in the eerie domain.
Isolated illusions in the icy rain,
Lingering, longing, in the languid chain.

Memorable moments meld in the misty maze,
Recalling recollections in the radiant blaze.
Nostalgic narratives in the noble daze,
Reminiscing, reflecting, in the rhythmic craze.

Melodic melodies meander in the musical mead,
Harmonizing harmonies in the heavenly heed.
Rhythmic rhythms in the radiant reed,
Enchanting, entertaining, in the echoing creed.

Here are four unique tongue-twister poems, each about Art, Inspiration, Creativity, and Courage:

Artistic strokes sweep in the scenic sprawl,
Painting portraits in the peaceful pall.
Masterful murals in the magical mall,
Creating, crafting, in the colorful call.

Inspirational insights ignite in the infinite sky,
Sparking thoughts in the silent sigh.
Radiant revelations in the resplendent rye,
Motivating, moving, in the mindful fly.

Creative currents churn in the creative cache,
Generating genius in the gentle gash.
Inspired inventions in the imaginative lash,
Innovating, imagining, in the intuitive hash.

Courageous hearts hammer in the heartfelt hearth,
Braving battles in the boundless berth.
Fearless fighters in the fiery firth,
Conquering, confronting, in the courageous mirth.

Here are four unique tongue-twister poems, each about Faith, Doubt, Solitude, and Joy:

Faithful flames flicker in the faithful fold,
Burning bright in the brave and bold.
Steadfast stars in the silent sky behold,
Trusting, believing, in the tale untold.

Doubtful shadows dance in the doubtful gloom,
Whispering worries in the weary room.
Lingering doubts in the dimly-lit tomb,
Questioning, wondering, in the quiet zoom.

Solitary souls seek in the silent shade,
Embracing emptiness in the echoing arcade.
Quietude quells in the quaint cascade,
Reflecting, retreating, in the remote raid.

Joyful jingles jangle in the joyful jive,
Sparkling smiles in the sunny survive.
Blissful beams in the blessed beehive,
Laughing, leaping, in the lively dive.

Here are four unique tongue-twister poems, each about Sorrow, Childhood, Wisdom, and Innocence:

Sorrowful sighs sweep through the silent night,
Mourning melodies in the moon's muted light.
Tearful tempests in the tumultuous flight,
Weeping, wailing, in the woeful wight.

Childhood chortles chase in the cheerful chase,
Giggling games in the golden grace.
Innocent imaginations in the intimate embrace,
Playing, prancing, in the playful place.

Wise whispers wander in the winding way,
Pearls of wisdom in the poetic play.
Sage sayings in the silent sway,
Guiding, growing, in the grand array.

Innocent eyes illuminate in the innocent gaze,
Pure hearts in the peaceful praise.
Untainted tales in the tender phase,
Blossoming, blooming, in the bright blaze.

Here are four unique tongue-twister poems, each about Passion, Serenity, Freedom, and Justice:

Passionate flames flicker in the fiery fold,
Burning bright in the bold and brave bold.
Intense infernos in the intimate mold,
Igniting, inciting, in the infinite cold.

Serene streams meander in the silent shade,
Calming currents in the cool cascade.
Tranquil waters in the tender tirade,
Soothing, settling, in the sunlit serenade.

Freedom's flag flies in the fearless sky,
Fluttering freely as the clouds pass by.
Liberated lives in the lofty lullaby,
Soaring, singing, in the celestial sigh.

Just judgments justify in the justified gale,
Fair verdicts in the faithful tale.
Equitable ethics in the earnest entail,
Balancing, believing, in the bountiful bail.

Here are four unique tongue-twister poems, each about Change, Resilience, Gratitude, and Forgiveness:

Change cascades in the capricious current's chase,
Transforming tides in the tumultuous space.
Shifting shapes in the shadows' embrace,
Altering, adapting, in the airy ace.

Resilient roots rise in the rugged ravine,
Standing strong in the storm's serene.
Unyielding oaks in the open evergreen,
Weathering, withstanding, in the wondrous scene.

Grateful gestures grace in the gentle glow,
Thankful thoughts in the tranquil flow.
Radiant rays in the radiant rainbow,
Appreciating, acknowledging, in the aglow aglow.

Forgiving hearts flourish in the forgiving fold,
Releasing regrets in the resolute mold.
Tender touches in the tender threshold,
Letting go, letting love, in the legend's hold.

Here are four unique tongue-twister poems, each about Longing, Belonging, Discovery, and Wonder:

Longing lingers in the lonely, languid lane,
Aching echoes in the eerie evening's reign.
Wistful wishes whisper in the wind's refrain,
Yearning yearns in the yonder's yawn again.

Belonging blossoms in the boundless blue,
Uniting under the umbrella's hue.
Cozy comrades congregate in the crew,
Embracing, enduring, in the endless ewe.

Discoveries delve in the deep, daring dive,
Unveiling unknowns in the vibrant vive.
Bold explorers explore in the endeavor's drive,
Unraveling, unearthing, in the alive alive.

Wondrous wonders whirl in the whimsical way,
Enchanting eyes in the enchanting sway.
Magical mysteries meander in the mystical may,
Mesmerizing, mystifying, in the marvelous ray.

Here are four unique tongue-twister poems, each about Journey, Reflection, Harmony, and Imagination:

Journeying jesters jaunt in the jungle's jive,
Trekking through tangled trails, twists they survive.
Adventurous aspirations in the air arrive,
Roaming, romping, racing in the river's rive.

Reflective ripples ripple in the radiant lake,
Mirroring memories in the mirror's make.
Contemplative currents cascade in the quake,
Glistening, glimmering, glowing in the gleaming wake.

Harmonious hymns hum in the hallowed hall,
Melodies melding in the music's maul.
Serene serenades soar in the sky's sprawl,
Resonating, reverberating, rejoicing in the call.

Imaginative ideas ignite in the infinite night,
Dancing in dreams, daring to take flight.
Whimsical wonders wander in the wondrous sight,
Sparkling, shimmering, soaring in the starry light.

Here are four unique tongue-twister poems, each about Silence, Laughter, Tears, and Strength:

Silent whispers in the stillness of the night,
Hushed echoes in the hidden hollows.
Serene silence, softly shimmering bright,
Peaceful pauses in the peaceful bellows.

Laughing lads leap in the lively lane,
Giggling girls gather in the garden.
Joyful jesters join in the jubilant refrain,
Chuckling chums charm in the charming pardon.

Tumultuous tears trickle in the twilight,
Sorrowful streams in the solemn symphony.
Weeping willows wail in the waning moonlight,
Tearful torrents in the tender tapestry.

Steadfast soldiers stand in the storm's strong surge,
Resilient resolve in the raging riot.
Mighty mountains mount in the majestic merge,
Indomitable determination in the dauntless diet.

Here are four unique tongue-twister poems, each about Vulnerability, Renewal, Acceptance, and Mystery:

Vulnerable violets, timid and trembling,
Whispering worries in the wind's wild wail.
Fragile feelings, fluttering and fumbling,
Tender tendrils of trust in a tempest's tale.

Renewal rises in the rising sun,
Reviving roots in the rain's soft rhythm.
Fresh foliage, flourishing and fun,
A vibrant vision in nature's prism.

Acceptance arrives in a quiet sigh,
Embracing endings with an open heart.
Serene surrender, soaring and spry,
Finding freedom in life's depart.

Mysterious moonlight, murmuring in the night,
Shrouded shadows in the shimmering shade.
Enigmatic enigmas, elusive and light,
Veiled visions in the vast cascade.

Here are four unique tongue-twister poems, about Transformation, Eternity, Cosmos, and Happiness:

Transforming through tumultuous trials,
Timid tadpoles turning to triumphant toads.
Twisting tendrils, tangled and tried,
Transitioning tumultuously, tales to be told.

Eternity echoes in endless expanse,
Everlasting echoes in ethereal embrace.
Enigmatic eternity, ever entrancing,
Enveloping existence with eternal grace.

Celestial cosmos, swirling and spinning,
Sparkling stars in the sky, silently singing.
Cosmic chaos, colliding in colors,
Captivating comets, careening and curling.

Happiness hums in hearts aglow,
Radiant rays of joy in a resplendent show.
Gleeful giggles, gathering and growing,
Blissful beams, boundless and overflowing.

-:|:-•:*''''''*:•.-:|:-•**•-:|:-•:*''''''*:•:*''''''*:•.-:|:-•**•-:|:--:|:-•:*''''''*:•.-:|:- •**•-:|:-•:*''''''*:•:*''''''*:•.-:|:-•**•-:|:-

By now, you've learned how to create your own amazing list of creative poetic prompts. Continue testing your favorite poetic prompts with different models and styles.

HERE ARE SOME SILLY PHRASES YOU MAY ALSO WANT TO TEST

You've Got A Hungry Friend	**For The Maid**	**Grooming Our Dog**
Happy Birthday	**Hello From England**	**Opening A New Business**
Graduated From High School	**Accepted Into Medical School**	**You Look Great**
Sorry You Lost	**You've Learned To Drive**	**First Day Of Winter**
You Remembered	**Fixing My Flat Tire**	**Sorry I Missed Your Birthday**
Thinking Of You	**I Like You**	**For My Work Out Partner**
You've Learned To Swim	**It Was A Lot Of Fun**	**Our New Apartment**
Thank You	**The Season Is Over**	**For My Rabbi**
Sorry I Missed Our Date	**I Quit Smoking**	**Get Over That Cold Soon**
Please Forgive	**Happy Hanukkah**	**I Lost Ten Pounds**
Happy Anniversary	**For A Stocking Stuffer**	**I Quit Drinking**
I'm Really Sorry	**Thanks For A Back Rub**	**1st Day In Kindergarten**
First Day Of Summer	**For My Babysitter**	**I Want You To Like Me**
For The Paper Boy	**You've Having A Baby**	**We're Getting Divorced**
Welcome Back	**Thanks For Doing The Dishes**	**For No Reason At All**
To Help Your Forget	**My Personal Trainer**	**Sorry The Market Dropped**
To Your New Job	**Farwell Dear Friend**	**Don't Retire Refocus**
For Your Hair Stylist	**Thanks For A Great Dinner**	**Shoveling The Walkway**
Graduation From College	**Your 1st Day In High School**	**Get Well Soon**
Happy Mother's Day	**I Love You**	**You Played Great**
Great Show	**You've Learned To Dance**	**You Got A New Pet**
For The Gardener	**Accepted Into College**	**Accepted Into Law School**
First Grade Graduation	**Remember Me**	**Please Write**
For My Minister	**For The Car Porter**	**You're Joining The Military**
Offering A Sweet Bribe	**New Love**	**Please Write**
Job Promotion	**Housewarming Party**	**Can I Use Your Car**
Washing My Car	**Mowing The Lawn**	**Welcome Home**
Happy Father's Day	**Our New House**	**Happy New Year**
For My Pets	**Your 1st Day In College**	**It's A Great Party**
Happy Valentine's Day	**Merry Christmas**	**Thenks For The Haircut**
New Hair Colors	**Don't Marry A Millionaire**	**Please Call Me**
Plastic Surgery Success	**You Married A Millionaire**	**First Day Of Fall**
Pick A Hot Stock	**First Day Of Sprint**	
Thanks For Being You	**Here's Candy & Flowers**	

Congratulations, by now you've learned how to have fun while creating unique and exciting prompt images!

LYNN & RICHARD VOIGT

Artists, Authors, Educators, Inventors & Publishers

Paint Dreams - Sell Ideas - Market Messages

Look For More RIVO Book Titles Available On Amazon

GLUTEN FREE RECIPE JOURNAL
A Journal For All My Favorite Recipes

SNACKS & APETIZER RECIPE JOURNAL
A Journal For All My Favorite Recipes

BREAD RECIPE JOURNAL
A Journal For All My Favorite Recipes

SOUP & SALAD RECIPE JOURNAL
A Journal For All My Favorite Recipes

MAIN DISH RECIPE JOURNAL
A Journal For All My Favorite Recipes

DESSERT RECIPE JOURNAL
A Journal For All My Favorite Recipes

MY FAVORITE ALL-TIME RECIPE JOURNAL
A Journal For All My Favorite Recipes

KID'S FAVORITE RECIPE JOURNALS
A Journal For All My Favorite Recipes

WHY RETIRE - REFOCUS
Pursue Your Passion Now

ONCE UPON A TIME...
Creating Short Stories From Your LIfe

THE ART OF JOURNALING
Finding Your Voice

MY GARDEN JOURNAL
For a Year Of Amazing Discoveries

FROM PEN TO PAPER
by Marvin Louis Beauchamp
A Lifetime Of Sentences Waiting To Be Heard

FROM PEN TO PAPER
by Marvin Louis Beauchamp
My Second Collection Of
Tangible Thoughts - Concrete Feelings

Jim & Rachel Andrae's
WWII LOVE LETTERS
Found In A Shoebox
With Family Photos
& Other Wartime Letters

13,000 AI PROMPTS
Turning Words Into Visions

5555 Fun & Funny Prompts
Turn Words Into Images

5000 Simple Word Prompts
Creating Images With Phrases

8,400 CLICHÉ PROMPTS
A Golden Opportunity

POETIC PROMPTS
Turn Poems Into Images

---- COMING SOON ----

A STRANGE & LOVELY MAN
Richard's Biography - Forever 12

POETIC PROMPTS
TURN POEMS INTO IMAGES
RICHARD MARVIN VOIGT

Thank you so very much for your interest and support in purchasing one of my latest publications. I always love hearing from my readers from around the world as to how this book may have helped you create more imaginative artwork.

While this educational publication is meant solely as a guide, you will constantly need to tweak your prompts as needed to accomplish the perfect image or idea you're after. These prompts are a great way to get started on your creative journey, whether you're an artist, author or simply seeking some great ideas. Enjoy your journey as you continue to refine, develop and releasing your unlimited imaginative powers.

Now it's up to you to begin or expand your AI Art adventures by refining and creating prompts that clearly illustrate the idea you have roaming inside your head. Finding appropriate words to build your AI prompts will become even more satisfying as you continue to create masterpieces, whether for personal enjoyment or business opportunities. Enjoy your journey!

I would deeply appreciate if you would take the time to leave an honest and candid review of this book at Amazon books. Simply, log into your Amazon account and enter the title:

"POETIC PROMPTS – Turn Poems Into Images"

I recommend creating a written review in a word document first, making spell-check easier. Then simply copy, paste and insert. Remember to click the submit review button to complete the review. Once the book title appears you will see a blue link that says, 'Customer Reviews,' Click it, and you'll be led to a new page and a button where you 'Create Your Own Review.'

Again, I sincerely want to thank you in advance for taking time to leave your review of this book on Amazon. It's because of you sharing your review that the word gets out to the rest of the world. "Keep The Love Growing."

Don't have an Amazon account? Feel free to email me **support@ART262.com.** I look forward to hearing from you and your prompt questions, as well as, your prompt successes.

Richard Marvin Voigt – RIVO

Made in the USA
Monee, IL
05 November 2026

67858063R00188